JOSEPH ANDREWS

❧ ❧ ❧

SHAMELA

RIVERSIDE EDITIONS

RIVERSIDE EDITIONS

UNDER THE GENERAL EDITORSHIP OF

Gordon N. Ray

Henry Fielding

JOSEPH ANDREWS

❧ ❧ ❧ AND ❧ ❧ ❧

SHAMELA

EDITED WITH AN INTRODUCTION AND NOTES BY

MARTIN C. BATTESTIN

UNIVERSITY OF VIRGINIA

HOUGHTON MIFFLIN COMPANY · BOSTON

Henry Fielding: 1707–1754

JOSEPH ANDREWS was first published in 1742
SHAMELA was first published in 1741

PRINTED IN THE U.S.A.
ISBN: 0-395-05150-9

INTRODUCTION

Martin C. Battestin

A NOVEL, like any of its characters, has its own story — its own origins, its own shape and spirit, its own meaning. The story of *Joseph Andrews* is one of the most curious and significant in the history of English letters. In the early 1740's, after years of gestation which led it through the realistic allegories of Bunyan, the satiric fantasies of Swift, and the fictional biographies of Defoe, the English novel came all at once into being as an art form, its two main directions — inward, toward the individual personality, and outward, toward the panorama of society — arising from the conflicting temperaments and literary motives of two very different men, Samuel Richardson and Henry Fielding. It could hardly be called a marriage, but from the rude and often hilarious conjunction of Richardson's feminine sensibilities and Fielding's robust masculinity, the modern novel was born. Richardson's *Pamela* began it all. Reaching the bookstalls in November 1740, it enjoyed almost immediately a popularity so vast and vociferous that Fielding, who despised the book, could describe the commotion only as an "epidemical phrenzy" that needed to be checked and cured. In his brilliant parody, *Shamela* (April 1741), he set about the destructive task of exposing, uproariously, the absurdities of Richardson's work. In *Joseph Andrews* (February 1742) he offered his own alternative conception of the art and purpose of the novel.

In his fifties when he wrote *Pamela*, Fielding's rival was another sort of man, another sort of writer, entirely. Whereas Fielding was tall and hale, with a lusty, open-hearted zest for life and a sharpness of vision that could penetrate its masks and gaudy surfaces, Richardson was short and round in stature, shy and fastidious and a little inclined to a quiet pomposity. He preferred the salon and the society of the ladies, whose hearts he understood (or so they liked to think) better than they did themselves. He was a man who lived so much in a world of pose and posture that, in *Pamela* at least (*Clarissa* is another and a better story), he could mistake for truth the artifice and pretense of his own creation. By profession he was a master-printer, not an author, but from his childhood he had developed his hand at the art of letter writing — and a noble art it was, esteemed by his contemporaries but nowadays unhappily lost! Always a little self-righteous, at the tender age of ten he had written an anonymous letter to an elderly widow castigating her for being a malicious gossip; and at thirteen he had taken to "ghost-writing" the love notes of the older girls of the neighborhood. As a writer of letters, he achieved such skill and local fame that in 1739 he was approached by booksellers who persuaded him to compose a practical little volume known as the *Familiar Letters,* a kind of correspondent's guide and conduct book for all occasions, intended not only to furnish the illiterate with model letters, but also to teach them, by examples, "how to think and act justly and prudently in the common concerns of human life."

It was while he was engaged in writing this work that Richardson hit upon the idea of expanding one of the illustrative situations it contained (in Letters 138 and 139, "A father to a daughter in service, on hearing of her master's attempting her virtue" and the reply) into that celebrated first novel, which he called, in the expansive and explicit manner of his day, *Pamela: or, Virtue Rewarded. In a Series of Familiar Letters from a Beautiful Young Damsel, to her Parents. Now first Published in order to cultivate the Principles of Virtue and Religion in the Minds of the Youth of Both Sexes.* Briefly, his story tells of the conspicuous chastity of a pretty young servant girl who — ubiquitously, in summer-house, closet, or bed — preserves her "virtue" from the hot assaults and clumsy intrigues of her ardent master, bringing him at last to his knees in capitulation and marriage. The plot is certainly simple enough and timeless, a variation, as one critic has remarked, on the old tale of the Beauty and the Beast, transformed by an eleventh-hour metamorphosis into the charming Prince. And to Richardson's age, an age in which a cash- and property-conscious middle class was beginning more and more to assert itself, an age that tended to equate a young woman's virtue and her virginity and to view the latter as a kind of saleable commodity to be exchanged as dearly as possible for the social advancement of both daughter and family, the theme struck a sympathetic chord. Although it was not original with him, Richardson's method of narration also helps to explain the book's extraordinary appeal. To tell his story, he used the epistolary form most natural to him, having his heroine describe the events and confess her sentiments in candid letters to her parents. In this way, Richardson achieved a curious and fascinating effect: the reader becomes a kind of *voyeur* and eavesdropper, over-hearing Pamela's private thoughts, as it were, and seeing into her life with an intimacy made possible by the detail and expansive-ness of Richardson's manner. At times, indeed, as in Pamela's accounts of Mr. B.'s fruitless attempts to ravish her in her bed, the narrative becomes almost too vivid for comfort: it was all doubtless done, as Richardson impatiently insisted, in the cause of morality, but he had managed to evoke his scenes so graphically that he had teased and titillated his readers as much as he had chastened them.

It is no wonder, then, that *Pamela* became, almost overnight, the sensation of London, running through five editions in less than a year. By January 1741 *The Gentleman's Magazine* could observe that it was already "in town as great a sign of want of curiosity not to have read *Pamela*, as not to have seen the French and Italian dancers." The simple, as well as the sophisticated, took Richardson's heroine to heart, trembling over her trials and exulting in her triumph. In the country the villagers of Slough gathered at the smithy to hear her story read aloud, and they communally celebrated her marriage by ringing the church bells. "Like the snow, that lay last week, upon the earth and all her products," Richardson's friend, Aaron Hill, wrote to the author not two months after the novel had appeared, "[Pamela] covers every other image, with her own unbounded whiteness." It was this claim — the "whiteness," the moral purity, of Richardson's shrewdly chaste young servant maid — that especially irked Henry Fielding. Even the clergy, the custodians of the public morality, were broadcasting their approval: there was, for ex-ample, the exasperating case of Dr. Benjamin Slocock, who sounded Pamela's praises from the pulpit of St. Saviour's, South-wark, as if, it must have seemed to Fielding, Richardson had written not a mere romance after all, but another book of Scrip-ture. And Alexander Pope, England's greatest living poet and a man from whom he might have expected better sense, had also been taken in by Pamela's "virtue": the novel, he was reported about town as saying, "will do more good than many volumes of sermons." In the midst of this uproar, it would have been hard indeed for Fielding to hold his peace about a book he deplored.

Richardson had thus unintentionally set the spark that kindled Fielding's real genius as a writer, driving him in a spirit half amused, half indignant, to discover for himself the rich possibilities of the art of fiction. But in other ways, as well, the time was right for him to try his hand at something new. To see his situation in 1741 more sharply, let us briefly turn to certain salient and significant features in the background. Born on 22 April 1707 into the younger line of an old and distinguished family, Fielding had grown up in the green fields and fresh country air of Dorsetshire, storing memories that he later contrasted in his writings, nostalgically, with the dirty streets and noxious vapors of the town. After learning his accidence from a kindly neighborhood curate named Parson Oliver, whom he seems to have remembered in the good clergyman of *Shamela*, he received his formal education first at Eton and then, after a brief interlude in London, at the University of Leyden, across the Channel in Holland. At these schools he developed a respect for useful learning (as distinguished from empty pedantry) and a love of classical Greek and Latin literature that is evident in nearly everything he wrote: Parson Adams' impromptu critique of the *Iliad* delivered in Mr. Wilson's parlor is, for example, only one of many instances in *Joseph Andrews* where Fielding's impressive knowledge of the classical authors and their critics serves to enliven the characterization and the comedy.

Fielding's family connections and his education notwithstanding, there was little money available to him, and the young man had to make his own way. His choice of a career lay, as he liked to say, between being a hackney writer or a hackney coachman. At the age of twenty-three he returned from Leyden with a play in his pocket and the ambition to make his mark in the London theater as a dramatist vaguely in the comic tradition of William Congreve, the genius of the Restoration stage. As a playwright, however, the disciple was no match for the master: in general, Fielding's comedies lack the brilliant repartee and the sense of situation and structure that distinguish Congreve's best work; today most of them seem rather dry and lifeless. But in the lesser modes of farce and burlesque he excelled, creating, for example, in *The Tragedy of Tragedies: or The Life and Death of Tom Thumb the Great* (1731) one of the true masterpieces of dramatic burlesque, a travesty so skillful and amusing that it enjoys the distinction of having made Jonathan Swift laugh for the second time in his life! (or so the Dean himself supposedly declared, doubtless with a touch of hyperbole). One clear reason why Fielding's plays succeeded on the London stage is that they sparkled with timely and spirited satire, much of it at the expense of contemporary "pollitricks," as he used to say, and of Sir Robert Walpole, the prime minister, in particular. For at the height of his theatrical career in 1736, Fielding, in search of a patron for his purse and of an honest government for England, had enlisted on the side of Chesterfield, Lyttelton, Pulteney, and the rest of the self-styled Patriots who led the noisy and vigorous Opposition to Walpole's administration. He became, in fact, his party's principal satirist, his pen one of its sharpest weapons against the minister. His "squibs and crackers," delivered to the delighted audiences that packed The Little Theatre in the Haymarket, were "let off in the country and sometimes at Court," exploding everywhere to Walpole's embarrassment. Unfortunately for Fielding, however, his heavy-handed ridicule of the ministry in *Pasquin* (1736) and *The Historical Register* (1737) proved too successful, since it stirred the government, irate and uneasy over the immense popularity of these farces, to put an end to such abuse and, incidentally, to the career of the man mainly responsible. The result was the passing in June 1737 of the Theatrical Licensing Act, which placed the playhouses under the Lord Chamberlain's strict control and shut the doors of Fielding's theater against him. "Like another Erostratus," sneered Colley Cibber with metaphors typically mixed, Fielding had "set fire to his stage, by writing up to an Act of Parliament to demolish it."

This was indeed a dark time for Fielding. In 1734, during his more prosperous days, he had married Charlotte Cradock, a remarkably pretty young woman whom he had loved and courted for four years; she was, he later said, the "one from whom I draw all the solid comfort of my life," and his deep affection for her is embodied in the good and charming women of his novels — Mrs. Wilson, Sophia, Amelia — for whom she was the model. By 1737, when the Licensing Act had cut him off from his livelihood, Fielding had two infant daughters as well as a wife to support. In near desperation he began to search for other means of providing comfortably for himself and his family. In November he entered the Middle Temple, but, though eleven years later he was to become one of London's most effective and prominent magistrates, the law was at first an inadequate solution. To supplement a meager income, Fielding was forced to turn hackney author in earnest and to resume his labors—now as Captain Hercules Vinegar, editor of *The Champion* — on behalf of the Opposition. The number of miscellaneous and fugitive productions —translations, poems, essays of every description—that came from his pen during the little more than two years preceding the appearance of *Joseph Andrews* suggests that his need was urgent. In Mr. Wilson's doleful acount of his brief and unprofitable career in London, we may see something of his author's own plight.

In the midst of these gloomy, arid days, the storm over *Pamela* broke. Clearly, there were ample reasons, more practical than moral and artistic indignation, that prompted Fielding's response. A "spoof" of Richardson's immensely popular book was sure to be financially rewarding, and Fielding desperately needed the money. But it would be a serious and rather cynical distortion to underestimate the importance of those other, less mercenary motives, which, after all, are the ones that chiefly matter to us as expressions of Fieldings' art and his thought. To Fielding, London had gone wild over an egregiously bad and pretentious book — a book morally contemptible and technically incompetent. To sense the full force of these sentiments in the genesis of *Shamela* and *Joseph Andrews,* we must first understand how Fielding, together with the best of his contemporaries, looked upon the job of the writer, especially the writer of satire. It is a mode and an attitude somewhat strange to our own times. Fielding wrote when the English Augustan Age — the Age of Satire, as it has been called — was not long past and when the greatest of its wits, Swift and Pope, were still living. To these men the satirist's craft was a responsible one: he wrote with the Horatian design to instruct, as well as to delight, his readers; he acted, in a real sense, as the arbiter and custodian of the good manners, morals, and taste of his society. Though laughter is his mode, the satirist is, then, fundamentally a moralist; though he makes us wince as he wields the knife of ridicule, he is, Fielding declared, "to be regarded as our physician, not our enemy." Solidly in this tradition, Fielding chose, as he variously put it, to speak truth with a smiling countenance, to laugh mankind out of their favorite follies and vices, to tickle them into good manners. Richardson's fatuous performance — as the noise of applause, even from those who should have known better, convinced him — needed to be exposed and corrected. Later, in 1748, Fielding would write his rival a warm and generous letter praising *Clarissa*, but *Pamela* was another matter entirely. It was bad morality and bad art. In *The Champion* Fielding had set himself up as Captain Hercules Vinegar, "great champion and censor of Great Britain," arraigning an old antagonist, the laureate-comedian Colley Cibber, before the bench of the Court of Censorial Inquiry on the charge of murdering the English language; now, as parodist, he would bring Richardson to justice.

Thus, early in 1741, Fielding interrupted his work as journalist for the Patriots to write the first, and by far the best, of the anti-*Pamela*'s — as the spate of "spoofs" and satires and criticisms spawned in reaction to Richardson's novel has come to be called. Published pseudonymously on April 4th,[1] the full title of this brilliant and bawdy parody suggests the line of attack that he hilariously pursues:

> *An Apology for the Life of Mrs. Shamela Andrews. In which, the many notorious Falsehoods and Misrepresentations of a Book called* Pamela, *Are exposed and refuted; and all the matchless Arts of that young Politician, set in a true and just Light. Together with a full Account of all that passed between her and Parson Arthur Williams; whose Character is represented in a manner something different from what he bears in* Pamela. *The whole being exact Copies of authentic Papers delivered to the Editor. Necessary to be had in all Families. By Mr. Conny Keyber.*

By the time the burlesque has run its course, the absurdities and pretensions of *Pamela* have been exposed once and for all. Fielding's skill at this delightful bathetic art had been developed and sharpened on several previous occasions and in several different genres: in the drama, for example, there were *The Covent-Garden Tragedy* and *The Tragedy of Tragedies;* in poetry there were the mock-epic *Vernoniad* and *Juvenal's Sixth Satire Modernised in Burlesque Verse;* and in *The Champion,* more crudely, there were amusing imitations of the "ultra sublime" style of Colley Cibber's *Apology.* With *Shamela* Fielding brought the art of parody near to perfection. What he provides, in some seventy pages, is a comic abridgement, down to the smallest details, of the very form and substance of *Pamela.* Richardson, for example, maintained the ruse of posing as an editor of Pamela's letters; so Fielding has his Parson Oliver purvey the "authentic" correspondence of Shamela, of which Richardson's version is said to be the grossest misrepresentation. Richardson had indulged his vanity

---

[1] It was not until well into this century that Fielding's authorship of *Shamela* was established beyond any reasonable doubt. The story of the accumulation of evidence that has led to the general acceptance of the work as Fielding's is interesting in itself, but too long to rehearse here. The best single discussion of the subject is Charles B. Woods' article, "Fielding and the Authorship of *Shamela,*" *Philological Quarterly,* XXV (1946), 256–72.

by prefixing to the second edition of his novel some twenty-four pages of commendatory letters and a poem; so Fielding includes his own "puffs," one, appropriately enough, from the editor to himself. Richardson, at times somewhat clumsily and at the expense of probability, had his heroic servant maid relate her adventures in long, detailed, and quite literate letters, often employing the present tense for greater immediacy of effect; so Shamela — her pen, even in bed, never out of hand — tells her story in the same epistolary fashion, but eschewing (with a vengeance!) her rival's delicacy of phrase. Richardson's best scenes are all here, but they are impudently imaged in the parodist's fun-house mirror. Pamela's mock drowning to cover her attempted escape from Mrs. Jewkes now becomes Shamela's device to divert attention from an amorous tryst with Parson Williams. In the novel Mr. B., out for a drive with his bride-to-be and her father, comes upon Williams taking a solitary walk and reading in a book, and thereupon, in a magnanimous gesture of reconciliation with the man who has interfered with the progress of his libertinism, he invites him to enter the carriage and sit beside Pamela; in the parody Williams is caught poaching hares in the squire's meadow, but Booby, choking down his ire in fear of a display of tears from his wife, relinquishes his place in the coach to her lover and takes to his horse. Best of all, of course, is the rough and uproarious handling of the bedroom scenes. Indeed, at every turn Fielding has taken his cue from his original: already in the novel, for instance, there is Mr. B.'s suspicion that Parson Williams' interest in Pamela is not entirely dutiful; there is Pamela's happy knack of fainting away whenever the emergency requires; there is, despite her prodigious virtue, Pamela's own embarrassment at her secret admiration for the handsome rake who has been trying to ravish her; and she ends, after all, by consenting to marry the villain on her own terms.

Fielding's mimicry is complete and it is devastating. By changing the perspective of vision — by taking a hostile and sardonic view of Richardson's triumphant virgin, seeing her chastity (so wonderfully profitable to her!) as artful rather than innocent — he has inverted, and subverted, Richardson's whole design. Take, for instance, the bedroom scenes, two episodes that point to the real cause of Fielding's quarrel with his rival. Fielding has caught the contradiction implicit in the presence of such "inflaming descriptions" in a book professedly intended to inculcate "the principles of virtue and religion." In these scenes, to use the phrase of the appreciative Parson Tickletext, he saw *Pamela,* girl and novel both, "with all the pride of ornament cast off": what is revealed is the sham of Richardson's whole pose and performance, and the Sham, as the theory of the Ridiculous set forth in the Preface to *Joseph Andrews* attests, was Fielding's special province as a satirist. Delighted to catch the prude staging a peep show, Fielding has turned Richardson's drama into a bawdy game of cat and mouse — exchanging only the identity of the predator! Worst of all, of course, was the naïve moral assumption that underlies the novel and glares forth garishly from the subtitle: the notion that virtue is rewarded, not in the Christian hereafter, but in the here and now, and with pounds and social position — a comfortable doctrine, Fielding observed in *Tom Jones,* "to which we have but one objection, namely, that it is not true." A morality based on such mercenary motives was a kind of prostitution masquerading as virtuousness. As Shamela wryly declares to her mother: "I thought once of making a little fortune by my person. I now intend to make a great one by my vartue." With such absurdities already latent in the novel, the distorted image mirrored in the parodist's glass is somehow closer to the truth than the original.

But Richardson and *Pamela* are not the only game that come under fire in *Shamela,* and most of these targets are fixed again in *Joseph Andrews.* There are hits, for example, at Fielding's old adversary, Colley Cibber, whose autobiography, *An Apology for the Life of Mr. Colley Cibber, Comedian* (1740), not only offended Fielding's taste by the violence it committed upon the English language, but also revived their old quarrel by calling him names. The title of *Shamela* humorously mimics that of Cibber's book, and the pseudonym, Conny Keyber, was sure to call him to mind.[2] Conny was also meant to evoke Conyers Middleton, whose *Life of Cicero* (published in February, little more than a month before *Shamela*) had disparaged the work of Fielding's friend, George Lyttelton. In his own Dedication, Fielding mocks Middleton's, which was fulsomely addressed to the effeminate Lord Hervey, a political ally of Walpole and a man known to his enemies, since Pope's famous gibe, as "Lord Fanny." In John Puff's letter, Walpole (or *"his Honour"*) himself comes in for some rather indelicate abuse in reference to the

---

[2] Conny, a colloquialism for dupe, looks and sounds like Colley; and in the *Apology* Cibber had alluded to himself as "Minheer Keiber," a name given him in *Mist's Weekly Journal*

prime minister's inability to keep his wife at home. All these cuts add to the fun and variety of Fielding's satire.

More pervasive and significant, however, is the irreverent treatment accorded the clergy, whose critical social function in preserving the public morality made them the special objects of Fielding's concern, defending them when they were unjustly contemned, rebuking them when they failed in their office. The importance of this theme in *Shamela* explains why Fielding chose to frame his story in an exchange of letters between two clergymen, one the naïve Parson Tickletext, the other the wise Parson Oliver, who corrects his friend's misapprehensions about *Pamela* and supplies him with the "genuine" papers; and it further accounts for the prominence of Parson Williams, to whom Richardson had assigned a relatively minor role. More than anything else, what seems to have set Fielding to work in this vein was the crass enthusiasm of clergymen like Dr. Slocock who encouraged that "epidemical phrenzy" raging in town over a silly and immoral book by making it, in Tickletext's words, their "common business here, not only to cry it up, but to preach it up likewise." By so doing, they were, however unwittingly, betraying their public trust and giving cause to that regrettable contempt of their order which was "the fashionable vice of the times." In the spring of 1740, Fielding had published in *The Champion* a series of leaders which he called an "Apology for the Clergy," four essays designed to correct the general contempt of the priesthood and to define the qualities of the true and the false clergyman. The same motives are evident in *Shamela* and, as we shall see, in *Joseph Andrews*.

The substance of Fielding's satire of the clergy in *Shamela* is embodied in Parson Williams, who is the very type of the false divine: As Oliver admonishes his brethren, "if a clergyman would ask me by what pattern he should form himself, I would say, Be the reverse of Williams." A consummate hedonist and hypocrite, Williams has every vice imaginable, but Fielding has given his portrait special point by making this scoundrel an admirer of the fiery evangelist, George Whitefield, who, along with John Wesley, was just then founding a new sect, Methodism. Fielding, himself an Anglican of the latitudinarian school that made religion a matter rather of the performance of good works than of belief or ceremony, distrusted Methodism from the start and continued to attack it throughout his career. He saw in its Antinomian emphasis upon salvation through grace and faith and the imputed righteousness of Christ a doctrine potentially pernicious to social morality. In general, he was among those who were appalled by what seemed to be the import of Whitefield's message: "So you say you believe in the Lord Jesus Christ, you may live the life of devils." Thus, with the aid of Whitefield's works and Williams' counsel, Shamela rationalizes her frequent fornication — the pleasures of which, "tho' not strictly innocent, are . . . to be purged away by frequent and sincere repentance" — and her paramour is made to preach upon the text, *"Be not righteous over-much,"* the subject of a sustained and heated controversy between Whitefield and Dr. Joseph Trapp. Into Williams, Fielding poured all the faults of which the Methodists were popularly accused — in particular, their alleged claims of a special dispensation of grace, exempting them from good works and excusing sinful self-indulgence since salvation was a matter of confidence, not performance. Thus Shamela relates the gist of Williams' casuistry:

> Well, on Sunday Parson Williams came, according to his promise, and an excellent sermon he preached; his text was, *Be not righteous over-much;* and, indeed, he handled it in a very fine way: he showed us that the Bible doth not require too much goodness of us, and that people very often call things goodness that are not so. That to go to church, and to pray, and to sing psalms, and to honour the clergy, and to repent, is true religion; and 'tis not doing good to one another, for that is one of the greatest sins we can commit, when we don't do it for the sake of religion. That those people who talk of vartue and morality, are the wickedest of all persons. That 'tis not what we do, but what we believe, that must save us, and a great many other good things; I wish I could remember them all.

Later, as they ride together in the coach, the learned parson subtly expatiates to Shamela on the matrimonial implications of the separateness of the Spirit and the Flesh, demonstrating with a supple logic the moral justification of adultery. An extension of the campaign begun in *The Champion,* Williams stands as the embodiment of the corrupt priest, not as an indictment of his whole order, as some readers, mistaking Fielding's motives, suppose — Parson Oliver, we recall, has in effect the last word and laugh — but as an object lesson of abuses to be avoided and corrected.

Shamela is superbly the inspiration of Fielding's antic muse: the jester's spirit, and something of his very mode, prevails in the droll mimicry of this brilliant burlesque. But if Fielding preferred the cap and bells to the preacher's somber gown, he wore them wisely — like Shakespeare's clowns — and in the service of truth. There is bite and purpose in his laughter. One after another, Richardson, Cibber, Middleton, Walpole, Whitefield, the corrupt or incompetent among the clergy — all feel the sting of the satirist's lash. To speak of such a coarse and bawdy book as serving the cause of morality and good taste may seem a contradiction to the fastidious, but Fielding's sexual comedy is free and open and hearty, unlike the pornographic melodrama of Richardson's bedroom scenes, for example, in which a sensual leer hides beneath the mask of gravity. Of all the remedies against a hyperactive libido, there is none better than laughter. Though one can scarcely imagine its being recommended from the pulpit, there is something essentially healthier in *Shamela's* lusty good humor than in the prurient sobriety of *Pamela*. In its own right and of its kind, *Shamela* is a remarkable performance — perhaps even, as Sheridan Baker would have it, "the best parody in English literature." It enjoys, furthermore, the distinction of being, so far as we know, the first prose fiction that Fielding wrote, the work that began his transformation from a second-rate playwright and hackney scribbler to one of the greatest of novelists. It stands as a kind of fulcrum between *Pamela* and *Joseph Andrews*, the two works that gave direction and shape to the English novel.

But *Shamela*, despite its virtues, could have done little to ease the straitened financial circumstances in which Fielding found himself during 1741. Indeed, by the late fall and winter, when he was hard at work on his first novel, his own private gray skies seem to have darkened with the season. In March, just before *Shamela* appeared, Fielding's poverty had driven him into debt; and in June the death of his father, a distinguished soldier but rather improvident with his money, only added to his misfortunes without augmenting his income. Before the year was out, his troubles were made more acute by the sickness that ravaged his family and eventually, in March 1742, took the life of his favorite daughter, Charlotte.

In June, furthermore, Fielding had made a puzzling decision when he severed his long-standing connection with *The Champion* and also, it seems, with the Opposition, whose cause that journal was supporting. This was a crucial election year in England, and the Patriots were marshalling all their forces in an effort — successful, as it proved in February of 1742 — to depose

Walpole, prime minister for the past two decades. The reasons for Fielding's break with his former friends at a time when he desperately needed money and when his services would have been most useful to them are difficult to determine, but one inference seems inevitable. As the signs of their eventual victory became clear, the Patriots were fast forgetting their grand professions and entering instead upon a furious race for power and place in government; what is more, they were not adequately rewarding him for his labors on their behalf. They had proved themselves hypocrites and ingrates, and Fielding could no longer afford to sacrifice the interests of himself and his family in a bad cause. If we read carefully, his disaffection from the Opposition is implicit in an obscure, but interesting, episode in *Joseph Andrews* (II, 7–9), a kind of political parable in which Parson Adams encounters a blustering fellow who speaks out vehemently against the Standing Army and the ineffectual pursuit of the war with Spain; the gentlemans' loud protestations of valor and self-sacrifice for one's country soon prove empty, however, as he flees in fear of his life at the first hint of real danger. Fielding's readers would have been sure to penetrate the thin veil of this allegory and to associate this man of false courage with those Patriots (with a capital *P*) whose principles he shares and whose treacherous conduct he emulates. Appropriately delivered to this same gentleman, Adams' "notable dissertation" on his political adventures reveals that the parson, as well as his author, has experienced the hypocrisy and thanklessness of those members of the Country Party whom he helped to elect. The situation is even clearer in the curious six-penny pamphlet, *The Opposition: A Vision*, which Fielding interrupted work on *Joseph Andrews* to publish in December, just as the new Parliament was meeting to decide Walpole's fate: in this satire Fielding acidly rebuked his former allies for double-dealing and ingratitude, and, stranger still, he warmly praised his old enemy, the prime minister, for his generosity and good intentions. Had Fielding, then, changed his politics altogether and accepted Walpole's patronage in an effort to provide for his family? There is considerable evidence, too involved for summary here, to suggest that he had.[3] In the midst of these distressing circumstances — in debt and neglected by his former friends among the Patriots, his wife ill and his daughter dying — Fielding late in 1741 labored, with incredible detach-

[3] For a full discussion of the' subject, see Battestin, "Fielding's Changing Politics and *Joseph Andrews*," *Philological Quarterly*, XXXIX (1960), 39–55.

ment, to write the first masterful comic novel in English: namely, *Joseph Andrews*. In what proved to be the beginning of a long and friendly relationship, Andrew Millar published the book on 22 February 1742, paying the author £183 11s. for the copyright; it was quite a generous sum for those days, and one that Fielding urgently needed.

In describing Lady Booby's vain attempts to seduce her virtuous footman — brother, it appears, to the celebrated Pamela — the opening chapters of *Joseph Andrews* cleverly invert the central situation of Richardson's book. This amusing parallel has given rise to a perplexing and (as it has proved) inhibiting assumption about the genesis of the novel: specifically, that Fielding at first meant *Joseph Andrews* as yet another parody of *Pamela,* but that somehow, by some marvelous stroke of luck, the novel got gloriously out of hand. When Fielding stumbled upon the irrepressible Parson Adams, so the argument goes, he found his true subject and, like Cervantes leading his hero at random from one roadside adventure to another, gave us a very different book from the one he intended. Before we can understand what Fielding was about in this novel and what he achieved, this notion must be abandoned for good and all. Despite the clear warning in his Preface, the trouble begins in a failure to distinguish between the modes of parody and satire, or, to use his own terms, the *burlesque* and the *comic,* than which "no two species of writing can differ more widely." *Joseph Andrews* was the first example in English of a new genre, what Fielding called "the comic prose epic." In this kind of writing, he asserted, occasional "parodies or burlesque imitations" may be admitted in the *diction* — those passages, for instance, in which characteristic epic rhetoric is, by inversion, ludicrously imitated, as in the comparison of the predatory Mrs. Slipslop to "a hungry tigress" or the extended, mock-heroic description of the battle with the dogs — but they must be excluded from the "sentiments and characters." But even without this caveat, the most casual comparison of *Shamela* and the opening chapters of *Joseph Andrews,* where the recollection of *Pamela* is most vivid, should be proof enough that in the novel Fielding intended something much different — more ambitious, more his own — from what he had attempted in his parody. With one or two deliberate exceptions, such as Joseph's two letters to his sister, there is no attempt to mimic the manner and style of Richardson's book. Throughout the novel, Fielding speaks in his own voice.

Another source of difficulty has been the tendency to confuse the very different *motives* that separate the travesty from the towering achievement of the epic. In writing *Shamela*, Fielding wished primarily to expose the inherent foolishness of Richardson's novel, an objective that could best be accomplished by the undermining process of parody, the destructive mimicry of the very substance and texture of *Pamela*. *Shamela* superbly achieves this goal: after reading it through, we can never again read Richardson's novel as once we did, never again take it quite so seriously. As one anonymous versifier in *The London Magazine* put it, *Shamela*, once and for all, had revealed Richardson's heroine in her true colors — mostly, it would seem, a rather fleshy pink. There was no need to resume the attack with the same weapons. Furthermore, the value of travesty is limited: it is essentially a negative mode, a kind of parasite deriving its life from its prey. *Joseph Andrews*, on the other hand, has from the start a spirit and design all its own. There are of course facetious resemblances to Richardson's novel — Lady Booby's attempts on her footman's virtue, Joseph's letters to his sister, the eventual introduction of Pamela and her squire — but, unlike the method of *Shamela*, they are satirically *allusive* rather than *imitative;* they are meant primarily to recall the technical and intellectual inadequacies of *Pamela*, while the main narrative of *Joseph Andrews* offers instead a mature and antithetic alternative — the sweeping social comedy of the epic of the road. With reference to the art of fiction as Fielding conceived it, Richardson's book was above all an example of "the true Ridiculous," as absurd in its own way as the affected and hypocritical justices, clergymen, innkeepers, and fops of society who are the targets of Fielding's satire. Someone, the painter Picasso I believe, has remarked that the best criticism of a work of art is another work of art. The observation is especially appropriate here. Fielding recalls his rival not to mimic him as before, but rather to establish a sorry alternative, a kind of foil to the philosophic and esthetic intuitions that inform his own book from the first sentence to the last. What he offered in return was his own — and, for its time, a highly sophisticated — view of the art of the novel.

The salient features of that view he delineated in the novel itself, both in the introductory chapters where the author, to use George Eliot's metaphor, draws his armchair to the proscenium to address his audience in person, and especially in the Preface, itself one of the very interesting and valuable documents in the history of criticism. The Preface to *Joseph Andrews* stands as a kind of manifesto of Fielding's conception of his art, of the aims and nature of that "new species of writing" he was introducing to England. At this time, prose fiction was held in low esteem, generally regarded as light, escapist literature at best (such were the immense French romances of Mlle. de Scudéry or La Calprenède) or as petty sensationalism at worst (witness the scandalous *romans à clefs* of Mrs. Mary Manley). As Plato scorned the poets of his day, expelling them from his Republic for dealing in lies and emotionalism, so Fielding's contemporaries looked upon the novelists. Fielding himself rejected the title, preferring to be called a "biographer" or a "historian" of his times, for he held the artist's glass up to nature, recording a truth even more profound and universal than what was to be found in the work of the professional historians or "topographers," to use his own term for them, who described cities and countries more accurately than they did the characters of men. In his Preface, however, he makes the most ambitious claim of all for his book: by the use of Aristotelian criteria he defines it as nothing less than "a comic epic-poem in prose" and therefore a variety of the highest of literary kinds. "The EPIC, as well as the DRAMA," he observes, "is divided into tragedy and comedy." Just as Homer, the father of the serious epic, is thought to have written another, the *Margites*, in the comic mode, so Fielding will follow his example in *Joseph Andrews*, writing, as befits his humbler subject, in prose instead of verse.

He is at pains, as well, to define the nature and province of comedy, which is not mere burlesque, since burlesque, like caricature, distorts its subject in grotesque fashion, whereas the comic artist strives for "the exactest copying of nature." In making this distinction, Fielding was in effect asserting his membership in the great comic tradition that embraces both his friend, the painter William Hogarth, and the dramatist Ben Jonson. It is a kind of art, implying a kind of vision, unfortunately alien to our own times. Although Fielding disparages caricature — the exaggeration for effect of certain prominent aspects of one's subject and the subordination of other, less distinctive features — this mode, as it is presently understood, provides a useful analogue to the technique of all three men; for in their characterizations they were less interested in a close and scrupulously detailed verisimilitude than in the typical or universal aspects, in an Aristotelian sense, of their subjects. In Dr. Johnson's *Rasselas*, Imlac, speak-

ing from similar principles, insists that the poet's business is "to
remark general properties and large appearances," not to "number the streaks of the tulip." Thus Ben Jonson in his "humors"
comedies will make a Volpone the very incarnation of avarice,
and Hogarth's rake will sum up his own kind. With the exception
of the supreme achievement of Parson Adams, who is too much
himself to stand for anyone else, all the characters in *Joseph
Andrews* illustrate Fielding's declaration: "I describe not men,
but manners; not an individual, but a species." The lustful Lady
Booby, the miserly Peter Pounce, the cowardly man of courage,
the impotent fop Beau Didapper, the bovine Mrs. Slipslop, the
swinish Parson Trulliber, all are typical portraits taken from
the rogue's gallery of human nature; Fanny and Joseph, on the
other hand, are the very image of a healthy innocence and virtue.
This method of universalizing his people, of paring away the
fullness of their individuality and reducing them to essentially
symbolic figures of two dimensions, marvelously colorful and
vivid but a little static and flat, is one of the conventional
resources of the comic writer, who, as Maynard Mack has
pointed out, wishes us to look at the spectacle of life with
detachment enough to laugh at it.[4] Looking at these characters,
we may take solace in the fact that they bear no resemblance to
us. But in so doing we only deceive ourselves, for what we face
in them is a kind of essential symbolic truth, stripped of the
distracting camouflage that normally conceals it comfortably
from our eyes, a truth that is more real, basically, than what daily
passes by the name of reality. The apprehension and communication of this truth is one of the special functions of the artist.
It is perhaps among the things that Fielding had in mind when he
insisted that he was copying nature exactly.

"The Ridiculous only . . . falls within my province in the
present work." In the effort to define the nature of the comic,
the first term in his new genre, Fielding strikes, heroically, into
a tangled ground that has fascinated, and defeated, more astute
philosophers from Hobbes to Bergson. What is laughter? The
question Fielding sets himself is one of those timeless riddles —
like, What is truth, or man? — that have no final solution. His
own answer is too simple, even to explain his practice in *Joseph
Andrews:* "The only source of the true Ridiculous (as it appears
to me) is affectation," which "proceeds from one of these two

[4] See the Introduction to the Rinehart edition of *Joseph Andrews* (New
York, 1948).

causes, vanity or hypocrisy." This theory, not unlike that of
Hobbes, who believed that all laughter is an expression of
contempt, is an account of derisive, *satiric* laughter only; it fails
to explain, for example, the warm-hearted *comedy* of Parson
Adams. The distinction perhaps lies in the difference between
Hobbes' "sudden glory," elation at the proud sense of our own
superiority over the object of our derision, and that spontaneous,
empathic joy we feel at Adams' childlike innocence. In his
Essay on Comedy George Meredith has caught this distinction
between the modes of Satire and Irony and what he calls Humor:
"You may estimate your capacity for comic perception by being
able to detect the ridicule of them you love without loving them
less. . . . If you laugh all round [the ridiculous person], tumble
him, roll him about, deal him a smack, and drop a tear on him,
own his likeness to you, and yours to your neighbor, spare him
as little as you shun, pity him as much as you expose, it is a spirit
of Humor that is moving you." "Parson Adams," he continues,
"is a creation of humor."[5] We must be careful, then, to distinguish between the simply comic or humorous aspects of Fielding's
good men and the Ridiculous, which is the target for exposure
and correction. "I defy the wisest man in the world," says Joseph
Andrews, "to turn a true good action into ridicule." Adams' innocence and fond idealism or Joseph's militant chastity may excite our laughter, but never the moral castigation and contempt
implicit in Fielding's definition of the Ridiculous. Fielding the
satirist is particularly concerned with the incongruities of life, the
discrepancy between illusion and truth, between what we profess
to be and what we are; he would reveal all our shamming, tear
off the pleasant masks we wear. Like our physician or priest, he
would "hold the glass to thousands in their closets, that they may
contemplate their deformity, and endeavour to reduce it, and
thus by suffering private mortification may avoid public shame."
The lustful Lady Booby, who affects respectability yet burns for
amorous sport with her footman; the prudish lady in the coach
who ogles Joseph's nakedness between the sticks of her fan; the
swaggering patriot who loudly protests his valor and flees in
fright at the first sign of danger; the ignorant parson who pretends to a knowledge of Greek; the generous gentleman who
promises Adams a prosperous new cure but intends nothing: all

[5] Meredith's essay, together with Henri Bergson on "Laughter," may be
found in *Comedy,* a useful paperback volume edited by Wylie Sypher
(Doubleday Anchor Books: New York, 1956).

these and many more corroborate the theory set forth in the Preface, and all come under the corrective lash of ridicule. But ultimately for Fielding the chief vice, subsuming all others, was simply vanity, understood in a darker sense than its use in the Preface would imply; this is the real object of his savage indignation. Synonymous with self-love and selfishness, "Vanity," Mr. Wilson asserts, "is the worst of passions, and more apt to contaminate the mind than any other." The full significance of this term to Fielding's satiric rationale is perhaps best revealed in a long, burlesque apostrophe in *Joseph Andrews* (I, 15), where Vanity is seen as busy everywhere and in everyone, deceiving mankind under the false faces of pity or generosity or heroism, lurking behind the passions of avarice or lust or fear, prompting us selfishly "to withdraw from others what we do not want, or to withhold from them what they do." In this sense, vanity is the ultimate source of the Ridiculous and the ultimate target of Fielding's ridicule.

Clearly, then, satire is not a frivolous mode; nor is it, as the havoc laughingly wreaked by its practitioners might suggest, an entirely destructive one. The satirist's laughter is purposeful. He levels the whited jakes and brothels of society in order to construct something better in their stead. To grasp the moral implications of this kind of writing, we must hold in mind two distinct thematic layers that function concomitantly: a thesis attacking vice and folly, and an antithesis comprising a positive ethical alternative, the standard against which the satirized are measured and judged. To be properly read, therefore, *Joseph Andrews* must be placed, first of all, against the intellectual backgrounds that conditioned Fielding's thought. In the latter half of the preceding century, a controversy had arisen in England over a question of crucial significance to moral and religious philosophy: namely, What is man, both in himself and in relation to his God? In effect, the debate resumed the old quarrel between St. Augustine and Pelagius, the one maintaining that man, fallen with Adam, could be redeemed only by the grace of God and faith in Christ, the other asserting the innate goodness of man and his ability, by the right exercise of his will leading to deeds of righteousness, to earn his salvation. Within the Established Church, Augustinian theology was virtually the orthodox position, supported by the Calvinistic tenor of the Thirty-Nine Articles. Working within this tradition, for example, Dean Swift in *Gulliver's Travels* could depict the essential depravity of

human kind in the figure of the noisome Yahoo. And this pessi-
mistic view was endorsed by the cynical secular philosophy of
Hobbes, Mandeville, and La Rochefoucauld, who saw man as an
ignoble creature whose every act was prompted by self-love.
Against this gloom, the so-called latitudinarian divines — such
rationalist theologians as Isaac Barrow, John Tillotson, Samuel
Clarke, and Benjamin Hoadly — proposed a cheerful Pelagianism,
confidently affirming the inherent health of the human spirit and
turning Christianity into a kind of moral system, the foundation
of which was charity rather than Christ, goodness rather than
grace. Even a Turk could be saved, they declared, if he lived a
virtuous life. And, since they stressed the importance of the
benevolent social affections that lead men to sympathize with
their neighbors and to relieve their distresses with charitable
acts, these divines spurned, too, a popular neo-Stoicism that, like
Swift's Houyhnhnms, contemned *all* passion as effeminate or
dangerous. The basic tenets of the latitudinarian position, which
already, perhaps, made too much of man, too little of God, were
carried to a logical extreme by the Deists and especially by
Anthony Ashley Cooper, the Third Earl of Shaftesbury, who,
rejecting the "rod and sweetmeat" incentives of a "superstitious"
religion, declared that the natural beauty of virtue was the only
necessary imperative to moral action. But here, even for the
liberal churchmen whose lead he followed, Shaftesbury had gone
too far. Together, the latitudinarians and the school of Shaftesbury were the primary sources of the strain of sentimentalism and
benevolism that runs through so much of the literature of the
eighteenth century, appearing, for example, in such different
writers as Thomson, Richardson, Sterne, MacKenzie, and, of
course, Fielding.

What is especially interesting here is a development of this
position that emerged at this time, inspired largely by the writings
of the homilists: it was the notion of a new kind of hero — the
Good Man or, as Richard Steele called him, the Christian Hero.
Opposed to the "great" and bloody conquerors of history and
literature — Achilles, Hector, Alexander, Caesar, Charles XII
of Sweden — whose triumphs were gained at the cost of humanity, the good man was heroic for virtue's sake, imitating the
examples of Christ and the patriarchs of the Old Testament by
bravely resisting temptation and affirming the true faith in the
midst of the godless. Typically, the homilists defined their
hero's goodness as consisting in the comprehensive virtues of

chastity (symbolic of the rational control of the passions) with respect to himself, and *charity* with respect to society. A good heart took the place of prowess with the sword. The vogue of the Christian hero is attested to in many ways — he even became the subject of a poetry contest conducted by *The Gentleman's Magazine* in 1736 — but in none more useful than his place in the theories set forth by poets and critics alike in defense of the biblical epic. Although Homer and Virgil were unmatched as craftsmen, their subjects were no longer suitable for a Christian writer; instead, the Bible offered themes and characters that far surpassed those of paganism. On the Continent the stories of Joseph and Abraham furnished a rich mine of material for the epic. In England Abraham Cowley began the discussion when, in the Preface to his unfinished epic, the *Davideis* (1656), he recommended the Scriptures as a repository of "bright and magnificent subjects." To Milton in *Paradise Lost*, the Fall of Man was an argument "not less but more heroic" than the wrath of Achilles. And the examples of these two giants evoked a host of undistinguished imitators. The Christian hero, the man of moral courage and a generous heart, carried the day.

As champion and censor of his age, Fielding, too, was concerned with the good man, his own views of human nature and morality closely reflecting the Pelagian doctrine of the latitudinarian divines whose works he read with care and admiration. Central to his definition of the moral man is his own version of a familiar benevolist concept: that of "good nature." This, indeed, is the vital principle behind all the heroes of his fiction, imparting life and humanity to Heartfree, Tom Jones, Squire Allworthy, Captain Booth, Doctor Harrison, and, pre-eminently, to Parson Adams. Basically, in contradiction of Hobbes and the Calvinists, good nature is an innate predisposition to virtue — a full, innocent, open heart that responds empathically to the joys and griefs of mankind, and this so strongly that it impels us to translate sentiment into action, love into charity. In an early poem Fielding describes this quality as "the glorious lust of doing good"

> The heart that finds its happiness to please
> Can feel another's pain, and taste his ease;
> The cheek that with another's joy can glow,
> Turn pale and sicken with another's woe;
> Free from contempt and envy, he who deems
> Justly of life's two opposite extremes,
> Who to make all and each man truly bless'd
> Doth all he can and wishes all the rest.

Or, as he elsewhere expresses it: "Good-nature is that benevolent and amiable temper of mind, which disposes us to feel the misfortunes, and enjoy the happiness of others; and consequently, pushes us on to promote the latter, and prevent the former; and that without any abstract contemplation on the beauty of virtue, and without the allurements or terrors of religion." The compassion of the postilion and Betty the chambermaid for the suffering of Joseph, beaten and stripped naked by thieves; the tender pity of Fanny for the hare worried and torn by the dogs; the rapture of Parson Adams at the reunion of Joseph and Fanny, flinging his cherished Æschylus into the flames in an impulsive gesture of self-forgetful joy: these are random instances from the novel of good nature operative. Indeed, Parson Adams — forever capering in delight at the happiness of men, or groaning in grief at their misfortunes and follies — is the very incarnation of this principle, despite his fifty years one of the heroic, sainted children of this world, whose love, spontaneous and inexhaustible, conquers all.

But, as the legion of vain and hypocritical innkeepers, justices, clergymen, squires, fops, and coquettes that parade through his novels vividly attests, Fielding was not so naïve as to suppose that good nature is characteristic of the generality of men. It is a rare flower "that only grows in soils almost divine"; the saints of this world never abound. Like Alexander Pope, Fielding subscribed to the theory of a predominant passion to account for inherent differences among men: the avarice of Peter Pounce, for example, or the lust of Lady Booby or the cowardice of the false patriot. Only if the passion of love or benevolence prevailed could the truly good-natured man develop. Disputing with Adams the relative merits of private or public schools, Joseph Andrews observes that if a man, like a horse, is vicious by nature, no amount of correction will improve him. And from the later novels we recall the examples of Tom Jones and Blifil, or Amelia and her sister Betty; each pair is raised in the same environment and given a similar education, but the characters that emerge from this background are as diametrically different as good and evil. The theory of the passions is one reason why Fielding, opposing the Deism of Shaftesbury, staunchly argued the indispensable social utility of religion, whose inducements to morality appealed to two of the strongest passions in man, hope and fear. At the same time, however, unlike his own Captain Booth before his conversion, he was no fatalist, a position to which the theory of the passions is logically conducive. Much of the folly and vice of the world, he felt, was the result of the corrupt or incompetent institutions of society — its government, its schools, its church. Man was essentially a rational creature, born with an intuitive moral sense that needed cultivation to encourage its growth. In *Joseph Andrews*, Mr. Wilson attributes his disastrous career in London to his "early introduction into life, without a guide," and Lady Booby with her "town-education" and the "roasting" squire with his too indulgent tutor reinforce the point. Each of us, Fielding imagined, is perpetually engaged in a kind of psychomachy, a pitched battle in the mind between reason and a mutinous army of passions; the first prerequisite to moral action is thus the conquest of oneself, what Fielding called "that glorious precept *vince teipsum*," the necessity for the individual, by reason and will, to direct and order the passions. The case is most clearly put in *Joseph Andrews* as the desperate Lady Booby, spurned in her overtures to Joseph, abandons herself to lust and hate and pride, sacrificing reputation, character, and rank to "the mean indulgence of a vile appetite." Indeed, even the good-natured man stands in need of reason, since his impetuous, open heart and unsuspecting innocence may lead him — as they lead Heartfree into the toils of Jonathan Wild, or Parson Adams into the tub of the "roasting" squire — into actions harmful to himself or to society. There is a difference, in other words, between the sentimental fool and the truly good-natured man, a difference residing in a Lockean strain in Fielding's concept: that is, good judgment. As satirist and reformer, Fielding strove to root out those weeds — bad education, bad custom, bad example — that were inhibiting the moral development of society, and to further the growth of the individual, who is by nature capable of much goodness, in reason and love.

Good nature, furthermore, is closely related to a second important feature of Fielding's Pelagianism: namely, his continuing insistence upon an energetic and universal charity as "the most Christian Virtue," necessary both for the salvation of the private soul and for the health of society. Without its manifestation in action, the mere inclination to benevolence is not enough. "A generous disposition to relieve the distressed" is Parson Adams' partial definition of charity. (To allow the miser Peter Pounce to betray himself, Adams' version omits the further requirement that, in Isaac Barrow's words, "we should really express that disposition in our practice.") Even the wily Pounce, tight-fisted hypocrite that he is, will accept these terms: " 'There is something in that definition,' answered Peter, 'which I like well enough; it is, as you say, a disposition — and does not so much consist in the act as in the disposition to do it.' " But earlier Adams had revealed his own conviction to the itinerant Catholic priest: " 'Sir . . . if I had the greatest sum in the world — ay, if I had ten pounds about me — I would bestow it all to rescue any Christian in distress.' " Good nature, then, though it is the essential characteristic of Fielding's heroes, is finally subsumed within a larger, more exalted concept. It is the natural predisposition to charity, which is the end of morality — and to Fielding a distinctively Christian virtue, having been more clearly and expressly "enjoined by the divine dispensation." Only in the teachings of Christ may one find that highest maxim of morality, "Forgive the acts of your enemies," that transcendent pitch of charity beyond the scope of "the religion of nature." Despite his good heart, for example, Joseph is unable to pardon the thieves who had attacked him and in vain asks the punch-drinking Parson Barnabas to make that duty clear. Like that of the latitudinarians, Fielding's Christianity is practical and social in temper and aim. Good works an active benevolence, is the sum of his religion. This is the criterion of Adams' condemnation of the niggardly Parson Trulliber, a modern-day Pharisee who knows the letter of the Scriptures but neglects to translate that knowledge into charitable deeds. And here, too, is the source of Adams' quarrel with George Whitefield, who "set up the detestable doctrine of faith against good works." Adams' impassioned diatribe against Whitefield, who stands as the personification of everything Fielding feared and deplored in religion, is the crucial exposition in the novel of his author's own views: Whitefield's was a licentious doctrine, a convenient rationale for hypocrisy, and, above all, a doctrine pernicious to society, making salvation a matter of credulity and confidence rather than the practical exercise of virtue and charity. Again like many of the divines, Fielding believed that salvation was offered to all men, infidels as well as believers, upon the conditions of sincerity and good works.

Fielding's Pelagian ethic is neither very profound nor very systematic. He had little use, as he confessed in *The Champion,* for "the metaphysics," for the sophistries of philosophers like the Deist Square in *Tom Jones,* whose chop-logic speculations were inadequate to the business of life. But behind his antic pose, beneath all the hearty common sense of his comedy, there were two things at least that he thought about long and seriously: they were, to use his own analogy, the complex arts of fiction and life. The two, he felt, were intimately related. By the practice of his craft, the novelist aimed not only to entertain his reader, but also to instruct him in the shaping of that greater artifact, the good man. These motives underlie his first novel; and, indeed, they help to determine its very form and pattern.

Joseph Andrews was not the lucky child of fortune that many readers have supposed. From the start the novel was meant, not as another parody of Richardson, another *Shamela*, but as the embodiment of Fielding's own conception of the art of fiction. As the title-page announces, there was, of course, an original to follow: Cervantes' comic masterpiece, *Don Quixote*. And there is clearly a resemblance between the innocent quixotism of Cervantes' hero and that of Parson Adams, Fielding's errant Christian knight, who in the confrontation of the vanities of this world tilts against less substantial, but no less formidable, windmills of his own. Other models exist as well, among them Homer's *Odyssey* and Fénelon's *Télémaque*, the latter a prose epic recounting the journey of Telemachus and his spiritual guide, Mentor, in search of the young man's father. But this is a theme that has occupied authors from Homer to James Joyce. Whatever hints Fielding may have received from previous literature, he made *Joseph Andrews* distinctively his own. To begin with, we must dismiss the notion that, like the conventional picaresque fiction that preceded it, *Joseph Andrews* is aimlessly constructed, a mere beadstring of random adventures strung along the highway. Fielding was too much aware of the important principle of unity, "that epic regularity" as he called it, to compose in any such haphazard fashion. Though he admired *Don Quixote*, as a critic he disapproved its looseness of structure. But it is Parson Adams himself who, in his enthusiastic analysis of the *Iliad*, calls Mr. Wilson's attention to one of its chief perfections, its adherence to the principle of artistic unity which Adams terms *Harmotton*, the correlation of structure and meaning.

Though it is the warm breath of laughter that animates *Joseph Andrews* — that cheerful, sunshiny, breezy spirit that Coleridge remarked — it is Fielding's moral vision that gives the book both meaning and a coherent pattern. Against "the true Ridiculous," the vain and hypocritical of all ranks and regions of society, Fielding in his first chapter promises to oppose the examples of two good men. To determine the precise nature of the roles his heroes were to play as "valuable patterns" of virtue in this mock-epic odyssey of the road, Fielding turned to the theory of the good man, the Christian hero, whose twin virtues of chastity and charity summed up morality. In the writings of the homilists, further-more, two of the great Old Testament figures were commonly invoked as *exempla* of the good man's essential qualities: namely, Joseph, whose rejection of the seductive blandishments of Poti-phar's wife made him the proverbial type of chastity; and the patriarch Abraham, who was the epitome of human faith ex-pressed in works, selflessly leaving his native country to wander as a pilgrim, affirming the true faith in strange and idolatrous lands. What is more, an adaptation of the stories of Joseph and Abraham — already on the Continent the subjects of several epic poems — would be in accord with the theories of the biblical epic then prevalent in England, and Fielding, as he announced in his Preface, was working in the epic mode. So, much as Pope in *The Rape of the Lock* ludicrously mimicked the machinery of *Paradise Lost* and the *Iliad*, Fielding in his own mock-epic turned the careers of Joseph and Abraham into the high comedy of low life — his Joseph becoming a virtuous footman nervously withstand-ing the temptations of a Mayfair lady, his Abraham appearing as a good-natured country curate, brandishing his crabstick like a pilgrim's staff as he journeys homeward through a country alien to him and to his ideals. Though Fielding clearly intended his opening chapters as another ironic slap at *Pamela*, the situation is most carefully designed to point up the comic analogy between Joseph Andrews and his "namesake," thus sounding at the start one of the twin themes of the novel; it has, in other words, a positive function of its own within the thematic context and design of the novel. The ambivalence of the mock-heroic ana-logue, the device that Fielding here employs, works admirably for him, adding a further, richer dimension to both the comic and serious sides of the book: it amuses us by exploiting the contrast between the magnificent, heroic figure of the past and his minia-ture modern-day counterpart; but at the same time, paradoxically, it serves to ennoble and elevate the little man by attaching to him something of the stature and timeless significance of his greater double. So it is, for example, with that later Ulysses, the wanderer Leopold Bloom; and so it is with Fielding's Joseph and Abraham, who make us smile at their petty misadventures and their perhaps too earnest pursuit of virtue, yet who, despite our condescending laughter, emerge in their innocence and simple humanity as heroes indeed. The victims and butts of this world, they triumphantly put it to shame.

It would, of course, be scarcely conceivable that the author of *Tom Jones* should undertake his first novel as a straight-faced defense of male chastity, in any narrow sense of the term. This was the age of the "double standard" when, as Sarah Fielding's Miss Baden says in *The History of Ophelia*, chastity "was even made the subject of ridicule in such men as were possessed of it," and Fielding himself, the apologies of some of his biographers notwithstanding, seems to have been more than a little given in his youth to amorous conversation with the ladies. Joseph Andrews' forcible expulsion of the warm-blooded Betty from his room at the Dragon Inn is certainly continence carried to a ludicrous extreme. Despite her promiscuity in these matters, Betty has our sympathy because her heart is open to everyone as well as her arms. At the same time, however, it would be a mistake to underestimate the importance of chastity — even male chastity — in Fielding's morality. Adultery, he observes in *Joseph Andrews,* is a catastrophe that has its tragic, as well as its comic consequences, and in *The Covent-Garden Journal* his spokesman, the good-natured Axylus, urged the enactment of a law against it. Betty's slip with Mr. Tow-wouse is a subject more for mirth than tears, but one of the rare dark moments in the novel is Mr. Wilson's account of the gradual degradation of the young girl he debauched, who ends her life miserably, a common prostitute, in Newgate Prison. Elsewhere, the nearly tragic complications of Captain Booth's inconstancy pose a grave problem in *Amelia,* and even Tom Jones must repent and learn to discipline his passions before he is accepted by Sophia. Upon occasion Fielding might excuse weakness in sexual matters, but he never justifies it. The chastity of Joseph Andrews, however, has wider implications than merely the preservation of his virginity. As it is in the homilies that defined the good man and made the biblical Joseph exemplar of his duty to himself, chastity here is *symbolic,* a sign of the fulfillment of "that glorious precept *vince teipsum*": it is the physical condition that signifies the individual's ability to control and discipline his appetites. This, too, is the sense of another traditional symbol that Fielding amusingly employs — namely, the expert horsemanship of his hero, who could ride "the most spirited and vicious horses to water, with an intrepidity which surprised everyone." One consequence of the lack of this self-discipline is Mr. Wilson's frequent visits to his surgeon.

Another is implied in the burlesque apostrophe to "Love" (the variety known to Lady Booby), which, like the enchantress Circe — or, to use Fielding's own analogues, like the pantomimist John Rich or the improbable grammarian Colley Cibber — turns "the heart of man inside out," distorting the human senses of its victim in a grotesque metamorphosis. As the vigor of his love-making to Fanny attests, Joseph Andrews is no very cold-blooded young man; but with good sense, reinforced by the good advice and good example of Parson Adams, he keeps his love chaste and clean for Fanny's sake, and for his own, just as he treasures Fanny's gold coin, which means only cash profits to Mrs. Tow-wouse, but which signifies a different order of values to Joseph. At times, admittedly, his virtue is a little hard to bear; but it nevertheless serves as a wholesome alternative to the predatory and self-destructive appetites of Lady Booby, Mrs. Slipslop, Beau Didapper, the "roasting" squire, and even Mr. Wilson in his days as a rake. Together with the charity of Parson Adams, the innocent, healthy love of Fanny and Joseph redeems the world of the novel, a world sick and fallen despite its comic aspects. They offer, as it were, a strain of the pure pastoral in the rank and ruined garden of England.

But Parson Adams is the supreme achievement of the novel, the best character that Fielding ever created and among the most memorable in any literature. He is one of the triumphs of art, endowed with so full a measure of life and humanity that he strides forth on those incredibly long legs of his out of the flat and narrow terrain of the printed page into an ample world of his own, like ours in its color and depth, but somehow better. In this respect, one thinks to compare him only with Shakespeare's fat knight, Jack Falstaff, a character whom he resembles in no other way. In his tattered cassock or his nakedness, he is one of the blessed perennial innocents of this world, as his name implies, a latter-day Adam who has not meddled with the tree of knowledge. Like the completely good-natured man that he is, when he is most himself he acts generously on intuition and impulse, spontaneous in joy and sorrow — snapping his fingers, fetching a groan, dancing about the room in a rapture, brandishing his crabstick. Founded upon the literature of better times than his own, the classics and the Scriptures, his idealism is invincible. So little a part of this world, so ignorant of its ways: We hear him interrupting Mr. Wilson's narrative of his licentious London days with a cry of "Good Lord! what wicked times these are!" Or we see him, abstracted, wading up to his middle through a flooded road-way, oblivious of the dry passage on the other side of the hedge. So little a part of this world, yet in the goodness of his heart so much involved in it, and assailed by it: his quixotic sallies or charitable embassies find him drenched in hog's puddings, soaked with the contents of a chamber pot, fouled in the mire of a pigsty. He has his faults, of course. For one, he is too much given to impractical theorizing, conscientiously brow-beating the grief-stricken Joseph with the empty doctrine of a Christian Stoicism that his own sympathetic heart contradicts. And if his idealism is indomitable, so, to his frequent embarrassment, is his simplicity, which leaves him prey to the malicious and hypocritical whom he never suspects. He even has his cherished vanities — his pride in his sermons or in his ability as a schoolmaster — though these are in a good cause and not at all comparable to the selfishness of those whom Fielding ridicules. But even the good parson's faults make for his humanity. Unlike Squire Allworthy of *Tom Jones* or Doctor Harrison of *Amelia*, Adams is a man and not a staid and lifeless paragon. He has our sympathy all the more.

Adams, furthermore, is the perfect vehicle for Fielding's satire. As the embodiment of good nature, the quality that his author placed at the heart of morality, he stands in bright contrast to the tarnished souls that people the world through which he moves. It is scarcely by accident that he performs in the novel a function similar to that of the *persona* of formal satire, operating both separately and simultaneously in the three characters that May-nard Mack attributes to the satirist: (1) the *vir bonus* or moral man; (2) the *naïf*, simple and unsophisticated, passing implicit judgment upon the immorality that bewilders him; and (3) the *hero*, indignant and courageous, defending virtue and the public good.[6] But in his role as comic exemplar of the good man, the essential analogy is to Abraham, type of the individual's duty to God and to society, the exercise of faith and charity. Close or specific parallels between the parson's career and that of the patriarch are rare, the most amusing being the incident of the "drowning" of Adams' son, which is a comic adaptation of Abra-ham's sacrifice of Isaac: "Had Abraham so loved his son Isaac as to refuse the sacrifice required, is there any of us," Adams asks Joseph, "who would not condemn him?" — at which moment a messenger brings the false report of his son's death and Adams dissolves in a paroxysm of grief. The good parson's paternal tenderness has overwhelmed his Stoic principles and even the admired example of his namesake. But, in general, Fielding was too much engaged with his own creation to trouble himself with any detailed parallelism. To his readers, familiar with the theory of the good man, Adams' name and character and the general pattern of his journey through strange and idolatrous lands (so uncharitable that "he almost began to suspect that he was sojourning in a country inhabited only by Jews and Turks'") would have been enough to establish the analogy and to suggest the nature of his role in this Christian epic of the road. Pilgrim, patriarch, and priest, he moves through society speaking out for charity and the true religion, praising Bishop Hoadly's latitudinarianism, condemning Whitefield's Methodism, and exposing in his helpless innocence the uncharitableness of those whom he encounters. In this respect, Adams is indispensable to the very method of Fielding's satire, which is to oppose, in a given situation, the selfish and the social passions, and to direct our critical laughter against those whose avarice or lust or ambition or vanity subdues the requirements of compassion. A lack of charity is, in fact, the source of the Ridiculous, which consists principally, as Fielding declared in *The Covent-Garden Journal,* in the deviation from "the most golden of all rules, no less than that *of doing unto all men as you would they should do unto you.*" The sentiments of the satirized in *Joseph Andrews* may be finally reduced to Mrs. Tow-wouse's exclamation: "'Common charity, a f—t!'" The good Abraham Adams, by his words and his example, makes all this clear, serving as a foil to the selfishness and depravity that surround him.

But we must not leave Parson Adams without noticing his part in an important secondary theme of the novel, Fielding's further pursuit of the campaign, begun in *The Champion* and continued in *Shamela,* to reform the clergy and to correct that popular contempt of their order that was undermining the cause of religion. In his Preface, Fielding declares that he has made his hero a clergyman for a good reason: "no other office could have given him so many opportunities of displaying his worthy inclinations." The true priest, whose function is ultimately social as well as religious, is pre-eminently in a position to direct and amend public morality. But, as we have already seen in the ale-guzzling hypocrite Arthur Williams and the simple-minded Tickletext of *Shamela,* the office was being abused and required the satirist's attention. Besides Parson Adams, there are no fewer than six clergymen in *Joseph Andrews*, of whom the pleasure-loving Barnabas and the pharisaical Trulliber are most notable: all six are corrupt or incompetent — ignorant, vain, ambitious, worldly — and all feel the bite of Fielding's lash. Again Adams is the foil, advocating the example of primitive Christianity (the only doctrine of Whitefield's worth preserving, he feels) and imitating that example in his own practice. Learned in the Scriptures to the point of emending the King James' translation, refusing to truckle to the rich or powerful when conscience or duty is at stake, exhorting his parishioners (or "his children," as he prefers to call them) to the exercise of charity and temperance, and reinforcing that counsel with the general conformity of his life, Adams is indeed a "valuable pattern" of the Christian hero, wayfaring in a godless country badly in need of him. Indicative of that contempt of his order that was characteristic of "the present taste and times," Lady Booby restricts him to her kitchen when he calls, and the "roasting" squire sets his dogs, some of a human species, on him. It is not Adams, however, but those who contemn or torment him that are the objects of Fielding's ridicule.

Fielding's moral vision, given focus by the theory of the good man, thus helped to determine the characters and mock-heroic identities of Joseph Andrews and Abraham Adams. What is more, it influenced the structure and pattern of the novel, which was not nearly so fortuitously evolved as it would seem at first glance. Theme imparts both meaning and cohesiveness to the loosely strung adventures and episodes of *Joseph Andrews*. In adopting this technique — one that comprehends the devices of parable and allegory — Fielding was only following a commonplace of neoclassical epic theory. To Le Bossu, for example, his favorite critic among the moderns, the action of an epic was designed to embody and exemplify its moral, which is primary; and this is only another way of putting what Parson Adams understood by the term *Harmotton*, the agreement of action to subject.

Familiar to any reader of John Bunyan's *Pilgrim's Progress*, a further conventional element in the discussions of the Christian hero was the comparison of his life to an arduous pilgrimage from the Babylon of this world through a land of vanity and vexation to his true home in a better country. In *Joseph Andrews*, Fielding skillfully imposed this coherent pattern upon the traditional form of the picaresque novel; the journey of his hero from

London toward reunion in the country with Fanny and Parson Adams thus assumes a broadly allegorical dimension, symbolic of the movement from vanity and vice to virtue and true contentment. For Fielding, following a venerable tradition that reaches back to Juvenal and Virgil, town and country were always morally antithetical, types, respectively, of vice and virtue. In the novel he most clearly defines and objectifies this polarity of values in the contrasting lives of Mr. Wilson, but it informs the main narrative as well. Joseph Andrews withstands the solicitations of his Mrs. Potiphar and preserves his chastity even in the hostile environment of Mayfair; but exposure to the vanities of the town immediately begins to corrupt his manners: he dresses his hair after the latest fashion, leads the rioting of the footmen at the playhouses, and — most dangerous sign of all — is lax in his attendance and behavior at church. In all this, much to her delight, Lady Booby "plainly saw the effects which the town-air hath on the soberest constitutions." Fortified by Adams' good counsel and good example, however, Joseph resists temptation and recognizes the thorough degeneracy of the Great City, where the highest precept of morality goes unobserved: "London is a bad place," he writes to Pamela, "and there is so little good fellowship, that the next-door neighbours don't know one another." The antidote, of course, is depicted in the account of Mr. Wilson's solution: a rural life of retirement, simplicity, industry, and mutual love — Fielding's adaptation of a familiar classical ideal. As the host of selfish and hypocritical country squires, innkeepers, justices, and parsons that crowd his novels plainly attests, Fielding's preference for the country was not the product of any foolish idealism about the absence of vice in a rural setting. But, though human nature is essentially the same everywhere, he did feel that in the country it is found in a "more plain and simple manner," without "all the high French and Italian seasoning of affectation and vice which courts and cities afford." In the country, at least, a man could breathe the natural air and attend to the basic values of life, free from the toxic pressures of the town. Joseph's flight from the city to Parson Adams' country parish becomes, in effect, a quest to regain a rural paradise lost after the arrival in London. This symbolic movement traces, too, the development of a related theme that Fielding seems to have intended: namely, the gradual progress of Joseph, "now in the one and twentieth year of his age," from adolescence to adulthood, from the virtuous, but precarious, innocence of his London days to a moral maturity based

on a surer knowledge of the world.[7] We find him losing his
dependence upon Parson Adams, his spiritual father and guide —
from experience, cautioning Adams against the false promiser,
debating with him a question of the relative merits of private and
public schools, asserting his own views on charity, and, in a
reversal of their former roles, guiding the clergyman, embarrassed
and bewildered, out of Fanny's bedchamber and toward his own.
With his practical common sense, Joseph comes, as it were, to
play a more dignified Sancho to the parson's Don Quixote. Upon
his arrival in the country and the discovery of his true relationship
with Mr. Wilson, Joseph's moral pilgrimage ends, consummated
in his marriage to the chaste and loving Fanny Goodwill and
fulfilled in their adoption of the mode of country living approved
by the Wilsons.

The thread of Joseph's maturation is rather clumsily — and,
with our thanks, unobtrusively — drawn through the rich and
various fabric of the novel. As an artist, Fielding was beyond
Richardson's reach, but his talents were less suited than his rival's
to the psychological exploration of character. Our attention
centers not upon the education of the book's titular hero, but
upon the lively figure of Parson Adams and upon the colorful
panorama of the world through which he moves. While the opening chapters sound the theme of chastity and virtuous love in the
mock-heroic redaction of the story of Joseph and Potiphar's wife,
the main thematic motif, the doctrine of charity, principally informs Part II of the novel (Book I, Chapter 11, through Book III),
containing the adventures along the road and dominated, appropriately enough, by the good patriarch and priest, Abraham
Adams. At the start of Joseph's journey, Fielding again employs a
favorite device, the analogue, to introduce his major theme: here,
ingeniously, it is the dramatic recasting of the Good Samaritan
parable. Prompted by the lawyer's questions, "What shall I do
to inherit eternal life?" and "Who is my neighbor?" the parable
was frequently cited by such divines as Benajmin Hoadly as
inculcating "the great duty of universal charity, and a most comprehensive compassion." This also is the message of *Joseph
Andrews*. Robbed by thieves, beaten, stripped, and left for dead
by the roadside, Joseph is grudgingly rescued by the self-inter-
ested passengers of the stage and given lodgings in the Dragon

---

[7] For a discussion of the theme of Joseph's coming of age, see Dick
Taylor, Jr., "Joseph as Hero of *Joseph Andrews*," *Tulane Studies in English*,
VII (1957), 91–109.

Inn. His only real comfort comes from the Samaritan offices of two social outcasts, a postilion "since transported for robbing a hen-roost" and a chambermaid, who clothe his nakedness in a traditional gesture of charity. With this as overture, the road adventures to follow sound their variations on the common theme: to Mrs. Tow-wouse, charity begins and ends at home; Whitefield prefers faith to it; Trulliber, his ale and his hogs; to the false promiser, it is an empty word easily spoken; to Peter Pounce, it is a disposition (which he never feels), not a deed. And Adams, too, helps to unite the scattered fragments of the book's central narrative. In his double role as both champion, espousing the cause of charity, and victim, exposing its absence in others, the good parson is the perfect instrument for the statement and development of the theme. Indeed, he is its incarnation.

A final word needs saying about that aspect of the book's architecture apparently most offensive to modern readers whose taste has been formed upon the post-Coleridgean shibboleth of "organic unity": I refer, of course, to the "digressions" of the novel, and especially to the episode of Mr. Wilson. Fielding himself would have insisted upon the novelist's right to digress, citing the precedents of authors from Homer and Apuleius to Cervantes and Le Sage, and invoking an esthetic principle of his own — "the art of contrast," he called it in *Tom Jones*. But the Wilson episode can be defended on grounds more congenial to our own times. Admittedly, though they do lend the spice of variety to the narrative and though their themes of vanity and false love and marriage are relevant to the novel as a whole, it is questionable whether the stories of Leonora and Leonard and Paul are worth the telling. Located at the heart of *Joseph Andrews*, the Wilson episode, however, is essential: it is, in a sense, the philosophic, as well as the structural, center of the book. For vanity is Fielding's satiric subject and "vanity of vanities" is Mr. Wilson's theme as he moves, like Hogarth's rake, through every stage of affectation and vice that London affords. It is through Wilson's account of the Great City, the very type and habitation of vanity, that Fielding completes the sweep of his satiric panorama of English society; in this way Abraham Adams, whose wayfaring is restricted to the open road, is exposed to and permitted to comment upon the folly and iniquity of a present-day Sodom. The episode thus serves, economically, as a narrative version of what is dramatically, and therefore more effectively, represented in the final third of *Tom Jones*. Mr. Wilson's story, furthermore, has its own significance; it is a sort of novel within a novel. Like that of Captain Booth in *Amelia*, it is essentially a tale of moral education and regeneration. At the start of his London career, Mr. Wilson assumes the foppish ways of vanity and plunges deeper into spiritual degradation, repudiating religion in his flirtation with the atheistical "Rule of Right" club and finally, in the symbolic purchase of the lottery ticket, abandoning Providence altogether to place his trust in Fortune. But, sunk in debtor's prison in a nadir of despair, he is rescued, providentially, by the love and charity of his future wife and with her flees the realm of vanity to adopt a way of life according to the classical ideal, which, if not edenic (the brutal incursion of the squire attests to this), is as close to it as possible in this fallen world. Fielding, moreover, has given this "digression" a meaning and a pattern that make it relevant to the novel as a whole. *Joseph Andrews* represents the moral pilgrimage of its hero, accompanied by his spiritual father and guide, from the vanity of London toward marriage in the country with the virtuous Fanny Goodwill. The career of Mr. Wilson, Joseph's real father, focuses and moralizes this movement by tracing his own progress — nearly disastrous because "without a guide" — through the corrupting vanities of the town to a life of wisdom, love, charity, and contentment in a setting reminiscent of the Golden Age. The episode thus provides, in little, a sharp definition of the symbolic polarity (city-country, vanity-virtue) that governs the action and meaning of the novel. It is the lesson of Mr. Wilson, painfully learned, that Joseph and Fanny follow.

The English novel, ever a vigorous and unpredictable child, thus appropriately began in the collision of Richardson and Fielding, so completely opposite in temperament and in the practice of their craft. But, though Richardson roused Fielding to his true vocation, *Joseph Andrews* was much more than the "lewd and ungenerous engraftment" upon *Pamela* that Fielding's flustered rival pronounced it. Valuable in itself and for what it led to — *Tom Jones* and the tradition of Dickens and Thackeray — it makes its own brilliant contribution to the art of fiction, introducing to English letters the panoramic novel of social satire "in imitation of the manner of Cervantes." Like most good books, this one may be read for many reasons — for the sheer delight of its comedy and the truth of its characters, for the wisdom (disarmingly simple) of its interpretation of the human scene and condition, for the sense of history it conveys. To William Hazlitt, for instance, it was unsurpassed as a full and faithful portrait of its age: "I should be at a loss where to find in any authentic documents of the same period so satisfactory an account of the general state of society, and of moral, political and religious feeling in the reign of George II as we meet with in the *Adventures of Joseph Andrews and his Friend Mr. Abraham Adams.*" But, ultimately, even Hazlitt's generous tribute misses the mark. Although *Joseph Andrews* mirrors its age, it does much more: it achieves that highest pitch of great art — the creation of its *own* world, alive with its own people, illuminated by its own cheerful spirit, shaped and ordered by its own moral vision. It is a world abundant and for all time.

A CHRONOLOGICAL TABLE

❧ ❧ ❧

The following is a table of some of the principal dates and events in Fielding's life, with special emphasis given to the period before the publication of *Joseph Andrews*.

1707 (Apr. 22)   Fielding born, probably at Sharpham Park, Somersetshire.

1709–1719   His boyhood spent on the farm in East Stour, Dorsetshire.

1719–1724   Education at Eton.

1728 (Jan. 29)   His first work published: a satiric poem entitled *The Masquerade*.

    (Feb. 16)   His first play produced at Drury Lane: *Love in Several Masques*.

    (Mar. 16)   Registers as a student of letters at the University of Leyden.

1729 (Aug.)   Discontinues studies at Leyden.

    (autumn)   Takes up residence in London.

1730–1737   His career as a dramatist. During this period Fielding produced more than a score of plays, all of them comedies (including two translations of Molière), farces, and burlesques. Some of the more notable are: *The Author's Farce* (1730), *Rape upon Rape* (1730), *The Tragedy of Tragedies* (1731), *The Grub-Street Opera* (1731), *The Modern Husband* (1732), *The Miser* (1733), *Don Quixote in England* (1734), *Pasquin* (1736), *The Historical Register* (1737).

1734 (Nov. 28)   Fielding's elopement and marriage with Charlotte Craddock.

1736 (Apr. 27)   Their first child, Charlotte, born.

    As the year advances, Fielding begins more actively to take sides with the Opposition against Sir Robert Walpole.

1737 (June 21)   Passage of the Theatrical Licensing Act, which ends Fielding's career as a playwright.

    (Nov. 1)   Undertakes the study of the law at the Middle Temple.

    Second daughter, Harriot, born (exact date unknown).

1739 (Nov. 15)–   Fielding edits *The Champion*, an Opposition journal.
1741 (June)

1740 (June 20)   Fielding called to the Bar at the Middle Temple.

    (Nov. 6)   Richardson's *Pamela* published.

1741   An important year for our purposes, as *Pamela* sets Fielding to writing fiction. Fielding, in debt, continues his fugitive writing, much of it political, and maintains his association with *The Champion* until June. He subsequently breaks with the Opposition and, late in the year, apparently takes up Walpole's faltering cause. In the autumn and winter, with himself and his family ill, he writes *Joseph Andrews*

(Apr. 4)   *Shamela* published.

(June)   Severs connections with *The Champion*.
Death of his father, Lieutenant-General Edmund Fielding.

(Dec. 15)   *The Opposition* published.

1742 (Feb. 2)   Fall of Walpole.

(Feb. 22)   *Joseph Andrews* published.

(Mar.)   Death of Fielding's eldest daughter, buried Mar. 9.

1743 (Apr. 12)   *Miscellanies* published, including *Jonathan Wild* and *A Journey from This World to the Next*, together with poems, essays, and two plays.

1744 (Nov.)   Death of Fielding's wife, Charlotte, buried Nov. 14.

1745 (Nov. 5)–   Fielding edits *The True Patriot*, supporting the Hanover-
1746 (June 17)   ian cause against the Pretender, Prince Charles Edward.

1747 (Nov. 27)   Fielding marries Mary Daniel, who later bore him five children.

1747 (Dec. 5)–   He edits *The Jacobite's Journal*, again supporting the
1748 (Nov. 5)   Hanoverian government.

1748 (Oct. 15)   He writes to his old rival, Richardson, praising *Clarissa*.

(Oct. 25)   Fielding commissioned as justice of the peace for the district of Westminster in London, and subsequently made magistrate of all Middlesex.

1749 (Feb. 28)   *Tom Jones* published.

1751 (Dec. 19)   *Amelia* published.

1752 (Jan. 4–   Fielding edits *The Covent-Garden Journal*.
Nov. 25)

1753 (autumn–   He successfully executes a plan for the suppression of
winter)   gangsterism and crime in London.

1754 (Apr.)   Fielding, seriously ill, resigns his office as magistrate.

(June 26–   His voyage to Lisbon, the *Journal* of which was posthu-
Aug. 7)   mously published in 1755.

(Oct. 8)   Fielding's death in Junqueira near Lisbon.

SELECT BIBLIOGRAPHY

❧ ❧ ❧

Over the next several years the Wesleyan University Press, Middletown, Connecticut, will publish the first textual and annotated edition of Fielding's complete works. At present, no satisfactory edition of the works exists; that of William E. Henley (London, 1903, 16 vols.) is the best of those available, but, among other deficiencies, it omits *Shamela*. The J. Paul de Castro edition of *Joseph Andrews* (London, 1929) is useful for its notes. The best biography of Fielding is still Wilbur L. Cross, *The History of Henry Fielding* (New Haven, 1918, 3 vols.); F. Homes Dudden, *Henry Fielding: His Life, Works, and Times* (Oxford, 1952, 2 vols.) covers much of the same ground and contains lengthy discussions of the novels and of relevant matters of background. Both of these works, however, are rather long and detailed; perhaps the best brief introduction is John Butt, *Fielding*, "Writers and Their Work," No. 57 (London, 1954). Two important essays on Fielding's social, moral, and religious thought are James A. Work, "Henry Fielding, Christian Censor," in *The Age of Johnson* (New Haven, 1949), pp. 139–48, and George Sherburn, "Fielding's Social Outlook," *Philological Quarterly*, XXXV (1956), 1–23. Frederic T. Blanchard, *Fielding the Novelist: A Study in Historical Criticism* (New Haven, 1926), provides an exhaustive study of the reception of the novels.

The following books and articles discuss *Joseph Andrews* or *Shamela* from a variety of viewpoints:

Baker, Ernest A., *The History of the English Novel*, Vol. IV, London, 1930, ch. 4.

Baker, Sheridan W., Jr., ed., *An Apology for the Life of Mrs. Shamela Andrews* by Henry Fielding, Berkeley and Los Angeles, 1953, Introduction.

Battestin, Martin C., *The Moral Basis of Fielding's Art: A Study of "Joseph Andrews,"* Middletown, Conn., 1959.

———, "Fielding's Changing Politics and *Joseph Andrews*," *Philological Quarterly*, XXXIX (1960), 39–55.

Cauthen, I. B., Jr., "Fielding's Digressions in *Joseph Andrews*," *College English*, XVII (April 1956), 379–82.

Digeon, Aurélien, *Les Romans de Fielding*, Paris, 1923; trans. *The Novels of Fielding*, London, 1925.

Kettle, Arnold, *An Introduction to the English Novel*, Vol. I, London, 1951, Pt. II, sec. iv.

Mack, Maynard, ed., *The History of the Adventures of Joseph Andrews,* by Henry Fielding, Rinehart Editions: New York, 1948, Introduction.

McKillop, Alan D., *The Early Masters of English Fiction,* Lawrence, Kansas, 1956, ch. 3.

Spilka, Mark, "Comic Resolution in Fielding's *Joseph Andrews,*" *College English,* XV (October 1953), 11–19.

Taylor, Dick, Jr., "Joseph as Hero of *Joseph Andrews,*" *Tulane Studies in English,* VII (1957), 91–109.

Woods, Charles B., "Fielding and the Authorship of *Shamela,*" *Philological Quarterly,* XXV (1946), 248–72.

THE
HISTORY
OF THE
ADVENTURES
OF
JOSEPH ANDREWS,
And of his FRIEND

Mr. *ABRAHAM ADAMS.*

Written in Imitation of

The *Manner* of CERVANTES,
Author of *Don Quixote.*

IN TWO VOLUMES.

VOL. I.

LONDON:
Printed for A. MILLAR, over-againſt
St. Clement's Church, in the *Strand.*
M.DCC.XLII.

[Title page of the first edition, 1742]

CONTENTS

❧ ❧ ❧

BOOK I.

BOOK III.

AUTHOR'S PREFACE

As it is possible the mere English reader may have a different idea of romance with the author of these little volumes, and may consequently expect a kind of entertainment not to be found, nor which was even intended, in the following pages, it may not be improper to premise a few words concerning this kind of writing, which I do not remember to have seen hitherto attempted in our language.

The EPIC, as well as the DRAMA, is divided into tragedy and comedy. HOMER, who was the father of this species of poetry, gave us a pattern of both these, though that of the latter kind is entirely lost; which Aristotle tells us, bore the same relation to comedy which his *Iliad* bears to tragedy. And perhaps, that we have no more instances of it among the writers of antiquity, is owing to the loss of this great pattern, which, had it survived, would have found its imitators equally with the other poems of this great original.

And farther, as this poetry may be tragic or comic, I will not scruple to say it may be likewise either in verse or prose: for though it wants one particular, which the critic enumerates in the constituent parts of an epic poem, namely metre; yet, when any kind of writing contains all its other parts, such as fable, action, characters, sentiments, and diction, and is deficient in metre only, it seems, I think, reasonable to refer it to the epic; at least, as no critic hath thought proper to range it under any other head, or to assign it a particular name to itself.

Thus the *Telemachus* of the Archbishop of Cambray appears to me of the epic kind, as well as the *Odyssey* of Homer; indeed, it is much fairer and more reasonable to give it a name common with that species from which it differs only in a single instance, than to confound it with those which it resembles in no other. Such are those voluminous works commonly called Romances, namely, *Clelia, Cleopatra, Astræa, Cassandra,* the *Grand Cyrus,* and innumerable others, which contain, as I apprehend, very little instruction or entertainment.

Now, a comic romance is a comic epic-poem in prose; differing from comedy, as the serious epic from tragedy: its action being more extended and comprehensive; containing a much larger circle of incidents, and introducing a greater variety of characters.

7

It differs from the serious romance in its fable and action, in this; that as in the one these are grave and solemn, so in the other they are light and ridiculous: it differs in its characters by introducing persons of inferior rank, and consequently, of inferior manners, whereas the grave romance sets the highest before us: lastly, in its sentiments and diction, by preserving the ludicrous instead of the sublime. In the diction, I think, burlesque itself may be sometimes admitted; of which many instances will occur in this work, as in the description of the battles, and some other places, not necessary to be pointed out to the classical reader, for whose entertainment those parodies or burlesque imitations are chiefly calculated.

But though we have sometimes admitted this in our diction, we have carefully excluded it from our sentiments and characters; for there it is never properly introduced, unless in writings of the burlesque kind, which this is not intended to be. Indeed, no two species of writing can differ more widely than the comic and the burlesque; for as the latter is ever the exhibition of what is monstrous and unnatural, and where our delight, if we examine it, arises from the surprising absurdity, as in appropriating the manners of the highest to the lowest, or *è converso*; so in the former, we should ever confine ourselves strictly to nature, from the just imitation of which will flow all the pleasure we can this way convey to a sensible reader. And perhaps there is one reason why a comic writer should of all others be the least excused for deviating from nature, since it may not be always so easy for a serious poet to meet with the great and admirable; but life everywhere furnishes an accurate observer with the ridiculous.

I have hinted this little concerning burlesque, because I have often heard that name given to performances which have been truly of the comic kind, from the author's having sometimes admitted it in his diction only; which, as it is the dress of poetry, doth, like the dress of men, establish characters (the one of the whole poem, and the other of the whole man), in vulgar opinion, beyond any of their greater excellencies: but surely, a certain drollery in style, where the characters and sentiments are perfectly natural, no more constitutes the burlesque, than an empty pomp and dignity of words, where everything else is mean and low, can entitle any performance to the appellation of the true sublime.

And I apprehend my Lord Shàftesbury's opinion of mere burlesque agrees with mine, when he asserts, "There is no such thing to be found in the writings of the ancients." But perhaps I have less abhorrence than he professes for it; and that, not because I have had some little success on the stage this way, but rather as it contributes more to exquisite mirth and laughter than any other; and these are probably more wholesome physic for the mind, and conduce better to purge away spleen, melancholy, and ill affections, than is generally imagined. Nay, I will appeal to common observation, whether the same companies are not found more full of good-humour and benevolence, after they have been sweetened for two or three hours with entertainments of this kind, than when soured by a tragedy or a grave lecture.

But to illustrate all this by another science, in which, perhaps, we shall see the distinction more clearly and plainly, let us examine the works of a comic history-painter, with those performances which the Italians call *Caricatura*, where we shall find the true excellence of the former to consist in the exactest copying of nature; insomuch that a judicious eye instantly rejects anything *outré*, any liberty which the painter hath taken with the features of that *alma mater*. Whereas in the *Caricatura* we allow all licence. Its aim is to exhibit monsters, not men; and all distortions and exaggerations whatever are within its proper province.

Now, what *Caricatura* is in painting, Burlesque is in writing; and in the same manner the comic writer and painter correlate to each other. And here I shall observe, that, as in the former the painter seems to have the advantage; so it is in the latter infinitely on the side of the writer; for the *Monstrous* is much easier to paint than describe, and the *Ridiculous* to describe than paint.

And though perhaps this latter species doth not in either science so strongly affect and agitate the muscles as the other; yet it will be owned, I believe, that a more rational and useful pleasure arises to us from it. He who should call the ingenious Hogarth a burlesque painter, would in my opinion do him very little honour; for sure it is much easier, much less the subject of admiration, to paint a man with a nose, or any other feature, of a preposterous size, or to expose him in some absurd or monstrous attitude, than to express the affections of men on canvas. It hath been thought a vast commendation of a painter, to say his figures *seem to breathe*; but surely it is a much greater and nobler applause, *that they appear to think.*

But to return. — The Ridiculous only, as I have before said, falls within my province in the present work. — Nor will some explanation of this word be thought impertinent by the reader, if he considers how wonderfully it hath been mistaken, even by writers who have professed it: for to what but such a mistake can we attribute the many attempts to ridicule the blackest villainies, and, what is yet worse, the most dreadful calamities? What could exceed the absurdity of an author, who should write *the Comedy of Nero, with the merry Incident of ripping up his Mother's Belly?* or what would give a greater shock to humanity, than an attempt to expose the miseries of poverty and distress to ridicule? And yet, the reader will not want much learning to suggest such instances to himself.

Besides, it may seem remarkable, that Aristotle, who is so fond and free of definitions, hath not thought proper to define the Ridiculous. Indeed, where he tells us it is proper to comedy, he hath remarked that villainy is not its object: but he hath not, as I remember, positively asserted what is. Nor doth the Abbé Bellegarde, who hath writ a treatise on this subject, though he shows us many species of it, once trace it to its fountain.

The only source of the true Ridiculous (as it appears to me) is affectation. But though it arises from one spring only, when we consider the infinite streams into which this one branches, we shall presently cease to admire at the copious field it affords to an observer. Now, affectation proceeds from one of these two causes, vanity or hypocrisy: for as vanity puts us on affecting false characters, in order to purchase applause; so hypocrisy sets us on an endeavour to avoid censure, by concealing our vices under an appearance of their opposite virtues. And though these two causes are often confounded (for there is some difficulty in distinguishing them), yet, as they proceed from very different motives, so they are as clearly distinct in their operations: for indeed, the affectation which arises from vanity is nearer to truth than the other, as it hath not that violent repugnancy of nature to struggle with, which that of the hypocrite hath. It may be likewise noted, that affectation doth not imply an absolute negation of those qualities which are affected; and, therefore, though, when it proceeds from hypocrisy, it be nearly allied to deceit; yet when it comes from vanity only, it partakes of the nature of ostentation: for instance, the affectation of liberality in a vain man differs visibly from the same affectation in the avaricious; for though the vain man is not what he would appear, or hath not the virtue he affects, to the degree he would be thought to have it; yet it sits less awkwardly on him than on the avaricious man, who *is* the very reverse of what he would *seem* to be.

From the discovery of this affectation arises the Ridiculous — which always strikes the reader with surprise and pleasure; and that in a higher and stronger degree when the affectation arises from hypocrisy, than when from vanity: for to discover anyone to be the exact reverse of what he affects, is more surprising, and consequently more ridiculous, than to find him a little deficient in the quality he desires the reputation of. I might observe that our Ben Jonson, who of all men understood the Ridiculous the best, hath chiefly used the hypocritical affectation.

Now, from affectation only, the misfortunes and calamities of life, or the imperfections of nature, may become the objects of ridicule. Surely he hath a very ill-framed mind who can look on ugliness, infirmity, or poverty, as ridiculous in themselves: nor do I believe any man living, who meets a dirty fellow riding through the streets in a cart, is struck with an idea of the Ridiculous from it; but if he should see the same figure descend from his coach and six, or bolt from his chair with his hat under his arm, he would then begin to laugh, and with justice. In the same manner, were we to enter a poor house and behold a wretched family shivering with cold and languishing with hunger, it would not incline us to laughter (at least we must have very diabolical natures if it would); but should we discover there a grate, instead of coals, adorned with flowers, empty plate or china dishes on the sideboard, or any other affectation of riches and finery either on their persons or in their furniture, we might then indeed be excused for ridiculing so fantastical an appearance. Much less are natural imperfections the object of derision; but when ugliness aims at the applause of beauty, or lameness endeavours to display agility, it is then that these unfortunate circumstances, which at first moved our compassion, tend only to raise our mirth.

The poet carries this very far:

> None are for being what they are in fault,
> But for not being what they would be thought.

Where if the metre would suffer the word *Ridiculous* to close the first line, the thought would be rather more proper. Great vices are the proper objects of our detestation, smaller faults, of our pity; but affectation appears to me the only true source of the Ridiculous.

But perhaps it may be objected to me, that I have against my own rules introduced vices, and of a very black kind, into this work. To which I shall answer: first, that it is very difficult to pursue a series of human actions and keep clear from them. Secondly, that the vices to be found here are rather the accidental consequences of some human frailty or foible, than causes habitually existing in the mind. Thirdly, that they are never set forth as the objects of ridicule, but detestation. Fourthly, that they are never the principal figure at that time on the scene; and, lastly, they never produce the intended evil.

Having thus distinguished *Joseph Andrews* from the productions of romance writers on the one hand, and burlesque writers on the other, and given some few very short hints (for I intended no more) of this species of writing, which I have affirmed to be hitherto unattempted in our language; I shall leave to my good-natured reader to apply my piece to my observations, and will detain him no longer than with a word concerning the characters in this work.

And here I solemnly protest, I have no intention to vilify or asperse anyone; for though everything is copied from the book of nature, and scarce a character or action produced which I have not taken from my own observations and experience; yet I have used the utmost care to obscure the persons by such different circumstances, degrees, and colours, that it will be impossible to guess at them with any degree of certainty; and if it ever happens otherwise, it is only where the failure characterized is so minute, that it is a foible only, which the party himself may laugh at as well as any other.

As to the character of Adams, as it is the most glaring in the whole, so I conceive it is not to be found in any book now extant. It is designed a character of perfect simplicity; and as the goodness of his heart will recommend him to the good-natured, so I hope it will excuse me to the gentlemen of his cloth; for whom, while they are worthy of their sacred order, no man can possibly have a greater respect. They will therefore excuse me, notwithstanding the low adventures in which he is engaged, that I have made him a clergyman; since no other office could have given him so many opportunities of displaying his worthy inclinations.

BOOK I.

CHAPTER I.

Of writing lives in general, and particularly of Pamela; *with a word by the bye of Colley Cibber and others.*

IT is a trite but true observation, that examples work more forcibly on the mind than precepts: and if this be just in what is odious and blameable, it is more strongly so in what is amiable and praiseworthy. Here emulation most effectually operates upon us, and inspires our imitation in an irresistible manner. A good man therefore is a standing lesson to all his acquaintance, and of far greater use in that narrow circle than a good book.

But as it often happens that the best men are but little known, and consequently cannot extend the usefulness of their examples a great way; the writer may be called in aid to spread their history farther, and to present the amiable pictures to those who have not the happiness of knowing the originals; and so, by communicating such valuable patterns to the world, he may perhaps do a more extensive service to mankind than the person whose life originally afforded the pattern.

In this light I have always regarded those biographers who have recorded the actions of great and worthy persons of both sexes. Not to mention those ancient writers which of late days are little read, being written in obsolete, and as they are generally thought, unintelligible languages, such as Plutarch, Nepos, and others which I heard of in my youth; our own language affords many of excellent use and instruction, finely calculated to sow the seeds of virtue in youth, and very easy to be comprehended by persons of moderate capacity. Such are the history of John the Great, who, by his brave and heroic actions against men of large and athletic bodies, obtained the glorious appellation of the Giant-killer; that of an Earl of Warwick, whose Christian name was Guy; the lives of Argalus and Parthenia; and above all, the history of those seven worthy personages, the Champions of Christendom. In all these, delight is mixed with instruction, and the reader is almost as much improved as entertained.

But I pass by these and many others, to mention two books lately published, which represent an admirable pattern of the amiable in either sex. The former of these, which deals in male virtue, was written by the great person himself, who lived the life he hath recorded, and is by many thought to have lived such a life only in order to write it. The other is communicated to us by an historian who borrows his lights, as the common method is, from authentic papers and records. The reader, I believe, already conjectures, I mean the lives of Mr. Colley Cibber and of Mrs. Pamela Andrews. How artfully doth the former, by insinuating that he *escaped* being promoted to the highest stations in Church and State, teach us a contempt of worldly grandeur! how strongly doth he inculcate an absolute submission to our superiors! Lastly, how completely doth he arm us against so uneasy, so wretched a passion as the fear of shame! how clearly doth he expose the emptiness and vanity of that phantom, reputation!

What the female readers are taught by the memoirs of Mrs. Andrews is so well set forth in the excellent essays or letters prefixed to the second and subsequent editions of that work, that it would be here a needless repetition. The authentic history with which I now present the public is an instance of the great good that book is likely to do, and of the prevalence of example which I have just observed: since it will appear that it was by keeping the excellent pattern of his sister's virtues before his eyes, that Mr. Joseph Andrews was chiefly enabled to preserve his purity in the midst of such great temptations. I shall only add that this character of male chastity, though doubtless as desirable and becoming in one part of the human species as in the other, is almost the only virtue which the great Apologist hath not given himself for the sake of giving the example to his readers.

CHAPTER II.

Of Mr. Joseph Andrews, his birth, parentage, education, and
great endowments; with a word or two concerning ancestors.

MR. JOSEPH ANDREWS, the hero of our ensuing history, was esteemed to be the only son of Gaffar and Gammar Andrews, and brother to the illustrious Pamela, whose virtue is at present

so famous. As to his ancestors, we have searched with great
diligence, but little success; being unable to trace them farther
than his great-grandfather, who, as an elderly person in the
parish remembers to have heard his father say, was an excellent
cudgel-player. Whether he had any ancestors before this, we
must leave to the opinion of our curious reader, finding nothing
of sufficient certainty to rely on. However, we cannot omit inserting an epitaph which an ingenious friend of ours hath communicated:

> Stay, traveller, for underneath this pew
> Lies fast asleep that merry man Andrew;
> When the last day's great sun shall gild the skies,
> Then he shall from his tomb get up and rise.
> Be merry while thou canst: for surely thou
> Shalt shortly be as sad as he is now.

The words are almost out of the stone with antiquity. But it
is needless to observe that Andrew here is writ without an *s*,
and is besides a Christian name. My friend, moreover, conjectures
this to have been the founder of that sect of laughing philosophers, since called Merry Andrews.

To waive, therefore, a circumstance which, though mentioned
in conformity to the exact rules of biography, is not greatly
material, I proceed to things of more consequence. Indeed, it
is sufficiently certain that he had as many ancestors as the best
man living, and perhaps if we look five or six hundred years
backwards, might be related to some persons of very great figure
at present, whose ancestors within half the last century are buried
in as great obscurity. But suppose for argument's sake we should
admit that he had no ancestors at all, but had sprung up, according to the modern phrase, out of a dunghill, as the Athenians
pretended they themselves did from the earth, would not this
autokopros° have been justly entitled to all the praise arising
from his own virtues? Would it not be hard that a man who hath
no ancestors should therefore be rendered incapable of acquiring
honour; when we see so many who have no virtues enjoying the
honour of their forefathers? At ten years old (by which time his
education was advanced to writing and reading) he was bound
an apprentice, according to the statute, to Sir Thomas Booby, an
uncle of Mr. Booby's by the father's side. Sir Thomas having
then an estate in his own hands, the young Andrews was at first
employed in what in the country they call "keeping birds." His

° In English, sprung from a dunghill. — F.

office was to perform the part the ancients assigned to the god Priapus, which deity the moderns call by the name of Jack o' Lent; but his voice being so extremely musical, that it rather allured the birds than terrified them, he was soon transplanted from the fields into the dog-kennel, where he was placed under the huntsman, and made what sportsmen term a "whipper-in." For this place likewise the sweetness of his voice disqualified him; the dogs preferring the melody of his chiding to all the alluring notes of the huntsman, who soon became so incensed at it, that he desired Sir Thomas to provide otherwise for him, and constantly laid every fault the dogs were at to the account of the poor boy, who was now transplanted to the stable. Here he soon gave proofs of strength and agility beyond his years, and constantly rode the most spirited and vicious horses to water, with an intrepidity which surprised everyone. While he was in this station, he rode several races for Sir Thomas, and this with such expertness and success, that the neighbouring gentlemen frequently solicited the knight to permit little Joey (for so he was called) to ride their matches. The best gamesters, before they laid their money, always inquired which horse little Joey was to ride; and the bets were rather proportioned by the rider than by the horse himself; especially after he had scornfully refused a considerable bribe to play booty on such an occasion. This extremely raised his character, and so pleased the Lady Booby, that she desired to have him (being now seventeen years of age) for her own footboy.

Joey was now preferred from the stable to attend on his lady, to go on her errands, stand behind her chair, wait at her tea-table, and carry her prayer-book to church; at which place, his voice gave him an opportunity of distinguishing himself by singing psalms: he behaved likewise in every other respect so well at divine service, that it recommended him to the notice of Mr. Abraham Adams, the curate, who took an opportunity one day, as he was drinking a cup of ale in Sir Thomas's kitchen, to ask the young man several questions concerning religion; with his answers to which he was wonderfully pleased.

CHAPTER III.

*Of Mr. Abraham Adams the curate, Mrs. Slipslop the chamber-
maid, and others.*

MR. ABRAHAM ADAMS was an excellent scholar. He was a
perfect master of the Greek and Latin languages; to which he
added a great share of knowledge in the Oriental tongues, and
could read and translate French, Italian, and Spanish. He had
applied many years to the most severe study, and had treasured
up a fund of learning rarely to be met with in a university. He
was besides a man of good sense, good parts, and good nature;
but was at the same time as entirely ignorant of the ways of this
world as an infant just entered into it could possibly be. As he
had never any intention to deceive, so he never suspected such
a design in others. He was generous, friendly, and brave to an
excess; but simplicity was his characteristic: he did, no more
than Mr. Colley Cibber, apprehend any such passions as malice
and envy to exist in mankind; which was indeed less remarkable
in a country parson than in a gentleman who hath passed his
life behind the scenes, — a place which hath been seldom thought
the school of innocence, and where a very little observation would
have convinced the great Apologist that those passions have a real
existence in the human mind.

His virtue and his other qualifications, as they rendered him
equal to his office, so they made him an agreeable and valuable
companion, and had so much endeared and well recommended
him to a bishop, that at the age of fifty, he was provided with
a handsome income of twenty-three pounds a year; which, however, he could not make any great figure with, because he lived
in a dear country, and was a little encumbered with a wife and
six children.

It was this gentleman, who having, as I have said, observed
the singular devotion of young Andrews, had found means to
question him concerning several particulars; as, how many books
there were in the New Testament? which were they? how many
chapters they contained? and such like; to all which, Mr. Adams
privately said, he answered much better than Sir Thomas, or
two other neighbouring justices of the peace could probably have
done.

Mr. Adams was wonderfully solicitous to know at what time,

and by what opportunity, the youth became acquainted with these matters: Joey told him that he had very early learnt to read and write by the goodness of his father, who, though he had not interest enough to get him into a charity school, because a cousin of his father's landlord did not vote on the right side for a churchwarden in a borough-town, yet had been himself at the expense of sixpence a week for his learning. He told him likewise, that ever since he was in Sir Thomas's family, he had employed all his hours of leisure in reading good books; that he had read the Bible, the *Whole Duty of Man*, and Thomas à Kempis; and that as often as he could, without being perceived, he had studied a great good book which lay open in the hall window, where he had read, "as how the devil carried away half a church in sermon-time, without hurting one of the congregation"; and "as how a field of corn ran away down a hill with all the trees upon it, and covered another man's meadow." This sufficiently assured Mr. Adams that the good book meant could be no other than Baker's *Chronicle*.

The curate, surprised to find such instances of industry and application in a young man who had never met with the least encouragement, asked him, If he did not 'extremely regret the want of a liberal education, and the not having been born of parents who might have indulged his talents and desire of knowledge? To which he answered, "He hoped he had profited somewhat better from the books he had read than to lament his condition in this world. That for his part, he was perfectly content with the state to which he was called; that he should endeavour to improve his talent, which was all required of him, but not repine at his own lot, nor envy those of his betters." "Well said, my lad," replied the curate, "and I wish some who have read many more good books, nay, and some who have written good books themselves, had profited so much by them."

Adams had no nearer access to Sir Thomas or my lady than through the waiting-gentlewoman; for Sir Thomas was too apt to estimate men merely by their dress or fortune; and my lady was a woman of gaiety, who had been blest with a town-education, and never spoke of any of her country neighbours by any other appellation than that of "The Brutes." They both regarded the curate as a kind of domestic only, belonging to the parson of the parish, who was at this time at variance with the knight; for the parson had for many years lived in a constant state of civil war, or, which is perhaps as bad, of civil law, with

Sir Thomas himself and the tenants of his manor. The foundation of this quarrel was a modus, by setting which aside, an advantage of several shillings *per annum* would have accrued to the rector; but he had not yet been able to accomplish his purpose, and had reaped hitherto nothing better from the suits than the pleasure (which he used indeed frequently to say was no small one) of reflecting that he had utterly undone many of the poor tenants, though he had at the same time greatly impoverished himself.

Mrs. Slipslop, the waiting-gentlewoman, being herself the daughter of a curate, preserved some respect for Adams: she professed great regard for his learning, and would frequently dispute with him on points of theology; but always insisted on a deference to be paid to her understanding, as she had been frequently at London, and knew more of the world than a country parson could pretend to.

She had in these disputes a particular advantage over Adams: for she was a mighty affecter of hard words, which she used in such a manner that the parson, who durst not offend her by calling her words in question, was frequently at some loss to guess her meaning, and would have been much less puzzled by an Arabian manuscript.

Adams therefore took an opportunity one day, after a pretty long discourse with her on the *essence* (or, as she pleased to term it, the *incence*) of matter, to mention the case of young Andrews; desiring her to recommend him to her lady as a youth very susceptible of learning, and one whose instruction in Latin he would himself undertake; by which means he might be qualified for a higher station than that of a footman; and added, she knew it was in his master's power easily to provide for him in a better manner. He therefore desired that the boy might be left behind under his care.

"La! Mr. Adams," said Mrs. Slipslop, "do you think my lady will suffer any *preambles* about any such matter? She is going to London very *concisely,* and I am *confidous* would not leave Joey behind her on any account; for he is one of the genteelest young fellows you may see in a summer's day, and I am *confidous* she would as soon think of parting with a pair of her grey mares, for she values herself as much on one as the other." Adams would have interrupted, but she proceeded: "And why is Latin more *necessitous* for a footman than a gentleman? It is very proper that you clargymen must learn it, because you can't preach without it: but I have heard gentlemen say in London, that it is fit for nobody else. I am *confidous* my lady would be angry with me for mentioning it; and I shall draw myself into no such *delemy*." At which words her lady's bell rung, and Mr. Adams was forced to retire; nor could he gain a second opportunity with her before their London journey, which happened a few days afterwards. However, Andrews behaved very thankfully and gratefully to him for his intended kindness, which he told him he never would forget, and at the same time received from the good man many admonitions concerning the regulation of his future conduct, and his perseverance in innocence and industry.

CHAPTER IV.

What happened after their journey to London.

No sooner was young Andrews arrived at London than he began to scrape an acquaintance with his party-coloured brethren, who endeavoured to make him despise his former course of life. His hair was cut after the newest fashion, and became his chief care: he went abroad with it all the morning in papers, and drest it out in the afternoon. They could not, however, teach him to game, swear, drink, nor any other genteel vice the town abounded with. He applied most of his leisure hours to music, in which he greatly improved himself; and became so perfect a connoisseur in that art, that he led the opinion of all the other footmen at an opera, and they never condemned or applauded a single song contrary to his approbation or dislike. He was a little too forward in riots at the play-houses and assemblies; and when he attended his lady at church (which was but seldom) he behaved with less seeming devotion than formerly: however, if he was outwardly a pretty fellow, his morals remained entirely uncorrupted, though he was at the same time smarter and genteeler than any of the beaus in town, either in or out of livery.

His lady, who had often said of him that Joey was the handsomest and genteelest footman in the kingdom, but that it was pity he wanted spirit, began now to find that fault no longer; on the contrary, she was frequently heard to cry out, "Ay, there is some life in this fellow." She plainly saw the effects which the town-air hath on the soberest constitutions. She would now walk out with him into Hyde Park in a morning, and when tired, which happened almost every minute, would lean on his arm, and converse with him in great familiarity. Whenever she stept out of her coach, she would take him by the hand, and sometimes, for fear of stumbling, press it very hard; she admitted him to deliver messages at her bedside in a morning, leered at him at table, and indulged him in all those innocent freedoms which women of figure may permit without the least sully of their virtue.

But though their virtue remains unsullied, yet now and then some small arrows will glance on the shadow of it, their reputation; and so it fell out to Lady Booby, who happened to be walking arm-in-arm with Joey one morning in Hyde Park, when Lady Tittle and Lady Tattle came accidentally by in their coach. "Bless me," says Lady Tittle, "can I believe my eyes? Is that Lady Booby?" — "Surely," says Tattle. "But what makes you surprised?" — "Why, is not that her footman?" replied Tittle. At which Tattle laughed, and cried, "An old business, I assure you; is it possible you should not have heard it? The whole town hath known it this half-year." The consequence of this interview was a whisper through a hundred visits, which were separately performed by the two ladies* the same afternoon, and might have had a mischievous effect, had it not been stopt by two fresh reputations which were published the day afterwards, and engrossed the whole talk of the town.

But whatever opinion or suspicion the scandalous inclination of defamers might entertain of Lady Booby's innocent freedoms, it is certain they made no impression on young Andrews, who never offered to encroach beyond the liberties which his lady allowed him — a behaviour which she imputed to the violent respect he preserved for her, and which served only to heighten a something she began to conceive, and which the next chapter will open a little farther.

* It may seem an absurdity that Tattle should visit, as she actually did, to spread a known scandal: but the reader may reconcile this, by supposing, with me, that, notwithstanding what she says, this was her first acquaintance with it. — F.

CHAPTER V.

The death of Sir Thomas Booby, with the affectionate and mournful behaviour of his widow, and the great purity of Joseph Andrews.

AT this time, an accident happened which put a stop to those agreeable walks, which probably would have soon puffed up the cheeks of Fame, and caused her to blow her brazen trumpet through the town; and this was no other than the death of Sir Thomas Booby, who, departing this life, left his disconsolate lady confined to her house, as closely as if she herself had been attacked by some violent disease. During the first six days the poor lady admitted none but Mrs. Slipslop, and three female friends, who made a party at cards; but on the seventh she ordered Joey, whom, for a good reason, we shall hereafter call JOSEPH, to bring up her tea-kettle. The lady being in bed, called Joseph to her, bade him sit down, and, having accidentally laid her hand on his, she asked him, "If he had ever been in love?" Joseph answered, with some confusion, it was time enough for one so young as himself to think on such things. "As young as you are," replied the lady, "I am convinced you are no stranger to that passion. Come, Joey," says she, "tell me truly, who is the happy girl whose eyes have made a conquest of you?" Joseph returned, that all the women he had ever seen were equally indifferent to him. "O then," said the lady, "you are a general lover. Indeed, you handsome fellows, like handsome women, are very long and difficult in fixing; but yet you shall never persuade me that your heart is so insusceptible of affection; I rather impute what you say to your secrecy, a very commendable quality, and what I am far from being angry with you for. Nothing can be more unworthy in a young man than to betray any intimacies with the ladies." "Ladies! madam," said Joseph, "I am sure I never had the impudence to think of any that deserve that name." "Don't pretend to too much modesty," said she, "for that sometimes may be impertinent: but pray answer me this question: Suppose a lady should happen to like you; suppose she should prefer you to all your sex, and admit you to the same familiarities as you might have hoped for if you had been born her equal, are you certain that no vanity could tempt you to discover her? Answer me honestly, Joseph; have you so much more sense and so much more virtue than you handsome young fellows generally have, who make no scruple of sacrificing our dear reputation to your pride, without considering the great obligation we lay on you by our condescension and confidence? Can you keep a secret, my Joey?" "Madam," says he, "I hope your ladyship can't tax me with ever betraying the secrets of the family; and I hope, if you was to turn me away, I might have that character of you." "I don't intend to turn you away, Joey," said she, and sighed; "I am afraid it is not in my power." She then raised herself a little in her bed, and discovered one of the whitest necks that ever was seen; at which Joseph blushed. "La!" says she, in an affected surprise, "what am I doing? I have trusted myself with a man alone, naked in bed; suppose you should have any wicked intentions upon my honour, how should I defend myself?" Joseph protested that he never had the least evil design against her. "No," says she, "perhaps you may not call your designs wicked; and perhaps they are not so." — He swore they were not. "You misunderstand me," says she; "I mean if they were against my honour, they may not be wicked; but the world calls them so. But then, say you, the world will never know anything of the matter; yet would not that be trusting to your secrecy? Must not my reputation be then in your power? Would you not then be my master?" Joseph begged her ladyship to be comforted; for that he would never imagine the least wicked thing against her, and that he had rather die a thousand deaths than give her any reason to suspect him. "Yes," said she, "I must have reason to suspect you. Are you not a man? and without vanity I may pretend to some charms. But perhaps you may fear I should prosecute you; indeed I hope you do; and yet Heaven knows I should never have the confidence to appear before a court of justice; and you know, Joey, I am of a forgiving temper. Tell me, Joey, don't you think I should forgive you?" — "Indeed, madam," says Joseph, "I will never do anything to disoblige your ladyship." — "How," says she, "do you think it would not disoblige me then? Do you think I would willingly suffer you?" — "I don't understand you, madam," says Joseph. — "Don't you?" said she, "then you either are a fool, or pretend to be so; I find I was mistaken in you. So get you downstairs, and never let me see your face again; your pretended innocence cannot impose on me." — "Madam," said Joseph, "I would not have your ladyship think any evil of me. I have always endeavoured to be a dutiful servant both to you and my master." — "O thou villain!" answered my lady; "why didst thou mention the name of that dear man, unless to torment me, to bring his precious memory to my mind?" (and then she burst into a fit of tears.) "Get thee from my sight! I shall never endure thee more." At which words she turned away from him; and Joseph retreated from the room in a most disconsolate condition, and writ that letter which the reader will find in the next chapter.

CHAPTER VI.

How Joseph Andrews writ a letter to his sister Pamela.

To Mrs. Pamela Andrews, living with Squire Booby.
DEAR SISTER,

Since I received your letter of your good lady's death, we have had a misfortune of the same kind in our family. My worthy master Sir Thomas died about four days ago; and, what is worse, my poor lady is certainly gone distracted. None of the servants expected her to take it so to heart, because they quarrelled almost every day of their lives: but no more of that, because you know, Pamela, I never loved to tell the secrets of my master's family; but to be sure you must have known they never loved one another; and I have heard her ladyship wish his honour dead above a thousand times; but nobody knows what it is to lose a friend till they have lost him.

Don't tell anybody what I write, because I should not care to have folks say I discover what passes in our family; but if it had not been so great a lady, I should have thought she had had a mind to me. Dear Pamela, don't tell anybody; but she ordered me to sit down by her bedside, when she was naked in bed; and she held my hand, and talked exactly as a lady does to her sweetheart in a stage-play, which I have seen in Covent Garden, while she wanted him to be no better than he should be.

If madam be mad, I shall not care for staying long in the family; so I heartily wish you could get me a place either at the squire's, or some other neighbouring gentleman's, unless it be true that you are going to be married to Parson Williams, as folks talk, and then I should be very willing to be his clerk; for which you know I am qualified, being able to read, and to set a psalm.

I fancy I shall be discharged very soon; and the moment I am, unless I hear from you, I shall return to my old master's country-seat, if it be only to see Parson Adams, who is the best man in the world. London is a bad place, and there is so little good fellowship, that the next-door neighbours don't know one another. Pray give my service to all friends that inquire for me; so I rest

Your loving brother,
JOSEPH ANDREWS.

As soon as Joseph had sealed and directed this letter he walked downstairs, where he met Mrs. Slipslop, with whom we shall take this opportunity to bring the reader a little better acquainted. She was a maiden gentlewoman of about forty-five years of age, who, having made a small slip in her youth, had continued a good maid ever since. She was not at this time remarkably handsome; being very short, and rather too corpulent in body, and somewhat red, with the addition of pimples in the face. Her nose was likewise rather too large, and her eyes too little; nor did she resemble a cow so much in her breath, as in two brown globes which she carried before her; one of her legs was also a little shorter than the other, which occasioned her to limp as she walked. This fair creature had long cast the eyes of affection on Joseph, in which she had not met with quite so good success as she probably wished, though, besides the allurements of her native charms, she had given him tea, sweetmeats, wine, and many other delicacies, of which, by keeping the keys, she had the absolute command. Joseph, however, had not returned the least gratitude to all these favours, not even so much as a kiss; though I would not insinuate she was so easily to be satisfied; for surely then he would have been highly blameable. The truth is, she was arrived at an age when she thought she might indulge herself in any liberties with a man, without the danger of bringing a third person into the world to betray them. She imagined that by so long a self-denial she had not only made amends for the small slip of her youth above hinted at, but had likewise laid up a quantity of merit to excuse any future failings. In a word, she resolved to give a loose to her amorous inclinations, and to pay off the debt of pleasure which she found she owed herself, as fast as possible.

With these charms of person, and in this disposition of mind, she encountered poor Joseph at the bottom of the stairs, and asked him if he would drink a glass of something good this morning. Joseph, whose spirits were not a little cast down, very readily and thankfully accepted the offer; and together they went into a closet, where, having delivered him a full glass of ratifia, and desired him to sit down, Mrs. Slipslop thus began:

"Sure nothing can be a more simple *contract* in a woman than to place her affections on a boy. If I had ever thought it would have been my fate, I should have wished to die a thousand deaths rather than live to see that day. If we like a man, the lightest hint *sophisticates*. Whereas a boy *proposes* upon us to break through all the *regulations* of modesty, before we can make

any *oppression* upon him." Joseph, who did not understand a
word she said, answered, "Yes, madam." — "Yes, madam!" replied
Mrs. Slipslop with some warmth; "do you intend to *result* my
passion? Is it not enough, ungrateful as you are, to make no return to all the favours I have done you; but you must treat me
with *ironing*? Barbarous monster! how have I deserved that my
passion should be *resulted* and treated with *ironing*?" "Madam,"
answered Joseph, "I don't understand your hard words; but I am
certain you have no occasion to call me ungrateful; for, so far from
intending you any wrong, I have always loved you as well as if
you had been my own mother." "How, sirrah!" says Mrs. Slipslop
in a rage: "Your own mother! Do you *assinuate* that I am old
enough to be your mother? I don't know what a stripling may
think, but I believe a man would *refer* me to any green-sickness
silly girl *whatsomdever*: but I ought to despise you rather than
be angry with you, for *referring* the conversation of girls to that
of a woman of sense." — "Madam," says Joseph, "I am sure I have
always valued the honour you did me by your conversation; for
I know you are a woman of learning." — "Yes, but, Joseph," said
she, a little softened by the compliment to her learning, "if you
had a value for me, you certainly would have found some method
of showing it me; for I am *convicted* you must see the value I
have for you. Yes, Joseph, my eyes, whether I would or no, must
have declared a passion I cannot conquer. — Oh! Joseph!"

As when a hungry tigress, who long has traversed the woods in
fruitless search, sees within the reach of her claws a lamb, she
prepares to leap on her prey; or as a voracious pike, of immense
size, surveys through the liquid element a roach or gudgeon,
which cannot escape her jaws, opens them wide to swallow the
little fish; so did Mrs. Slipslop prepare to lay her violent amorous
hands on the poor Joseph, when luckily her mistress's bell rung,
and delivered the intended martyr from her clutches. She was
obliged to leave him abruptly, and to defer the execution of her
purpose till some other time. We shall therefore return to the
Lady Booby, and give our reader some account of her behaviour,
after she was left by Joseph in a temper of mind not greatly
different from that of the inflamed Slipslop.

CHAPTER VII.

Sayings of wise men. A dialogue between the lady and her maid; and a panegyric, or rather satire, on the passion of love, in the sublime style.

It is the observation of some ancient sage, whose name I have forgot, that passions operate differently on the human mind, as diseases on the body, in proportion to the strength or weakness, soundness or rottenness, of the one and the other.

We hope, therefore, a judicious reader will give himself some pains to observe, what we have so greatly laboured to describe, the different operations of this passion of love in the gentle and cultivated mind of the Lady Booby, from those which it effected in the less polished and coarser disposition of Mrs. Slipslop.

Another philosopher, whose name also at present escapes my memory, hath somewhere said, that resolutions taken in the absence of the beloved object are very apt to vanish in its presence; on both which wise sayings the following chapter may serve as a comment.

No sooner had Joseph left the room in the manner we have before related than the lady, enraged at her disappointment, began to reflect with severity on her conduct. Her love was now changed to disdain, which pride assisted to torment her. She despised herself for the meanness of her passion, and Joseph for its ill success. However, she had now got the better of it in her own opinion, and determined immediately to dismiss the object. After much tossing and turning in her bed, and many soliloquies, which, if we had no better matter for our reader, we would give him, she at last rung the bell as above-mentioned, and was presently attended by Mrs. Slipslop, who was not much better pleased with Joseph than the lady herself.

"Slipslop," said Lady Booby, "when did you see Joseph?" The poor woman was so surprised at the unexpected sound of his name, at so critical a time, that she had the greatest difficulty to conceal the confusion she was under from her mistress; whom she answered, nevertheless, with pretty good confidence, though not entirely void of fear of suspicion, that she had not seen him that morning. "I am afraid," said Lady Booby, "he is a wild young fellow." — "That he is," said Slipslop, "and a wicked one too. To my knowledge he games, drinks, swears, and fights eternally; besides, he is horribly *indicted* to wenching." — "Ay!" said the lady, "I never heard that of him." — "O madam!" answered the other, "he is so lewd a rascal, that if your ladyship keeps him much longer, you will not have one virgin in your house except myself. And yet I can't conceive what the wenches see in him, to be so foolishly fond as they are: in my eyes he is as ugly a scarecrow as I ever *upheld.*" — "Nay," said the lady, "the boy is well enough." — "La! ma'am," cries Slipslop, "I think him the *ragmaticallest* fellow in the family." — "Sure, Slipslop," says she, "you are mistaken: but which of the women do you most suspect?" — "Madam," says Slipslop, "there is Betty the chambermaid, I am almost *convicted,* is with child by him." — "Ay!" says the lady, "then pray pay her her wages instantly. I will keep no such sluts in my family. And as for Joseph, you may discard him too." — "Would your ladyship have him paid off immediately?" cries Slipslop, "for perhaps, when Betty is gone, he may mend; and really the boy is a good servant, and a strong healthy *luscious* boy enough." — "This morning," answered the lady with some vehemence. "I wish, madam," cries Slipslop, "your ladyship would be so good as to try him a little longer." — "I will not have my commands disputed," said the lady; "sure you are not fond of him yourself?" — "I, madam?" cries Slipslop, reddening, if not blushing, "I should be sorry to think your ladyship had any reason to *respect* me of fondness for a fellow; and if it be your pleasure, I shall fulfill it with as much *reluctance* as possible." — "As little, I suppose you mean," said the lady; "and so about it instantly." Mrs. Slipslop went out, and the lady had scarce taken two turns, before she fell to knocking and ringing with great violence. Slipslop, who did not travel post haste, soon returned, and was countermanded as to Joseph, but ordered to send Betty about her business without delay. She went out a second time with much greater alacrity than before; when the lady began immediately to accuse herself of want of resolution, and to apprehend the return of her affection with its pernicious consequences; she therefore applied herself again to the bell, and re-summoned Mrs. Slipslop into her presence; who again returned, and was told by her mistress that she had considered better of the matter, and was absolutely resolved to turn away Joseph; which she ordered her to do immediately. Slipslop, who knew the violence of her lady's temper, and would not venture her place for any Adonis or Hercules in the universe, left her a third time; which she had no sooner done, than the little god Cupid, fearing he had not yet done the lady's business, took a fresh arrow with the sharpest point out of his quiver, and shot it directly into her heart: in other and plainer language, the lady's passion got the better of her reason. She called back Slipslop once more, and told her she had resolved to see the boy, and examine him herself; therefore bid her send him up. This wavering in her mistress's temper probably put something into the waiting-gentlewoman's head, not necessary to mention to the sagacious reader.

Lady Booby was going to call her back again, but could not prevail with herself. The next consideration therefore was, how she should behave to Joseph when he came in. She resolved to preserve all the dignity of the woman of fashion to her servant, and to indulge herself in this last view of Joseph (for that she was most certainly resolved it should be) at his own expense, by first insulting, and then discarding him.

O Love, what monstrous tricks dost thou play with thy votaries of both sexes! How dost thou deceive them, and make them deceive themselves! Their follies are thy delight! Their sighs make thee laugh, and their pangs are thy merriment!

Not the great Rich, who turns men into monkeys, wheelbarrows, and whatever else best humours his fancy, hath so strangely metamorphosed the human shape; nor the great Cibber, who confounds all number, gender, and breaks through every rule of grammar at his will, hath so distorted the English language as thou dost metamorphose and distort the human senses.

Thou puttest out our eyes, stoppest up our ears, and takest away the power of our nostrils; so that we can neither see the largest object, hear the loudest noise, nor smell the most poignant perfume. Again, when thou pleasest, thou canst make a molehill appear as a mountain, a Jew's-harp sound like a trumpet, and a daisy smell like a violet. Thou canst make cowardice brave, avarice generous, pride humble, and cruelty tenderhearted. In short, thou turnest the heart of man inside out, as a juggler doth a petticoat, and bringest whatsoever pleaseth thee out from it. If there be anyone who doubts all this, let him read the next chapter.

CHAPTER VIII.

In which, after some very fine writing, the history goes on, and relates the interview between the lady and Joseph; where the latter hath set an example, which we despair of seeing followed by his sex, in this vicious age.

Now the rake Hesperus had called for his breeches, and, having well rubbed his drowsy eyes, prepared to dress himself for all night; by whose example his brother rakes on earth likewise leave those beds in which they had slept away the day. Now Thetis, the good housewife, began to put on the pot, in order to regale the good man Phoebus after his daily labours were over. In vulgar language, it was in the evening when Joseph attended his lady's orders.

But as it becomes us to preserve the character of this lady, who is the heroine of our tale; and as we have naturally a wonderful tenderness for that beautiful part of the human species called the fair sex; before we discover too much of her frailty to our reader, it will be proper to give him a lively idea of the vast temptation, which overcame all the efforts of a modest and virtuous mind; and then we humbly hope his good nature will rather pity than condemn the imperfection of human virtue.

Nay, the ladies themselves will, we hope, be induced, by considering the uncommon variety of charms which united in this young man's person, to bridle their rampant passion for chastity, and be at least as mild as their violent modesty and virtue will permit them, in censuring the conduct of a woman who, perhaps, was in her own disposition as chaste as those pure and sanctified virgins who, after a life innocently spent in the gaieties of the town, begin about fifty to attend twice *per diem* at the polite churches and chapels, to return thanks for the grace which preserved them formerly amongst beaus from temptations perhaps less powerful than what now attacked the Lady Booby.

Mr. Joseph Andrews was now in the one-and-twentieth year of his age. He was of the highest degree of middle stature. His limbs were put together with great elegance and no less strength. His legs and thighs were formed in the exactest proportion. His shoulders were broad and brawny; but yet his arms hung so easily, that he had all the symptoms of strength without the least clumsiness. His hair was of a nut-brown colour, and was displayed in wanton ringlets down his back. His forehead was high, his eyes dark, and as full of sweetness as of fire. His nose a little inclined to the Roman. His teeth white and even. His lips full, red, and soft. His beard was only rough on his chin and upper lip; but his cheeks, in which his blood glowed, were overspread with a thick down. His countenance had a tenderness joined with a sensibility inexpressible. Add to this the most perfect neatness in his dress, and an air which, to those who have not seen many noblemen, would give an idea of nobility.

Such was the person who now appeared before the lady. She viewed him some time in silence, and twice or thrice before she spake, changed her mind as to the manner in which she should begin. At length, she said to him, "Joseph, I am sorry to hear such complaints against you: I am told you behave so rudely to the maids, that they cannot do their business in quiet; I mean those who are not wicked enough to hearken to your solicitations. As to others, they may, perhaps, not call you rude: for there are wicked sluts who make one ashamed of one's own sex, and are as ready to admit any nauseous familiarity as fellows to offer it; nay, there are such in my family, but they shall not stay in it; that impudent trollop who is with child by you is discharged by this time."

As a person who is struck through the heart with a thunderbolt looks extremely surprised, nay, and perhaps is so too — thus the poor Joseph received the false accusation of his mistress; he blushed and looked confounded, which she misinterpreted to be symptoms of his guilt, and thus went on:

"Come hither, Joseph: another mistress might discard you for these offences; but I have a compassion for your youth, and if I could be certain you would be no more guilty — Consider, child" (laying her hand carelessly upon his), "you are a handsome young fellow, and might do better; you might make your fortune—." "Madam," said Joseph, "I do assure your ladyship, I don't know whether any maid in the house is man or woman—." "Oh fie! Joseph," answered the lady, "don't commit another crime in denying the truth. I could pardon the first; but I hate a liar." "Madam," cries Joseph, "I hope your ladyship will not be offended at my asserting my innocence: for by all that is sacred, I have never offered more than kissing." "Kissing!" said the lady, with great discomposure of countenance, and more redness in her cheeks than anger in her eyes; "do you call that no crime?

Kissing, Joseph, is as a prologue to a play. Can I believe a young fellow of your age and complexion will be content with kissing? No, Joseph, there is no woman who grants that, but will grant more; and I am deceived greatly in you, if you would not put her closely to it. What would you think, Joseph, if I admitted you to kiss me?" Joseph replied, "He would sooner die than have any such thought." "And yet, Joseph," returned she, "ladies have admitted their footmen to such familiarities; and footmen, I confess to you, much less deserving them; fellows without half your charms; for such might almost excuse the crime. Tell me, therefore, Joseph, if I should admit you to such freedom, what would you think of me? — tell me freely." "Madam," said Joseph, "I should think your ladyship condescended a great deal below yourself." "Pugh!" said she, "that I am to answer to myself: but would not you insist on more? Would you be contented with a kiss? Would not your inclinations be all on fire rather by such a favour?" "Madam," said Joseph, "if they were, I hope I should be able to control them, without suffering them to get the better of my virtue." — You have heard, reader, poets talk of the "statue of Surprise"; you have heard likewise, or else you have heard very little, how Surprise made one of the sons of Crœsus speak, though he was dumb. You have seen the faces, in the eighteen-penny gallery, when, through the trap-door, to soft or no music, Mr. Bridgewater, Mr. William Mills, or some other of ghostly appearance, hath ascended, with a face all pale with powder, and a shirt all bloody with ribbons; but from none of these, nor from Phidias, or Praxiteles, if they should return to life — no, not from the inimitable pencil of my friend Hogarth, could you receive such an idea of Surprise as would have entered in at your eyes had they beheld the Lady Booby when those last words issued out from the lips of Joseph. — "Your virtue!" (said the lady, recovering after a silence of two minutes) "I shall never survive it. Your virtue! Intolerable confidence! Have you the assurance to pretend, that when a lady demeans herself to throw aside the rules of decency, in order to honour you with the highest favour in her power, your virtue should resist her inclination? That when she had conquered her own virtue, she should find an obstruction in yours?" "Madam," said Joseph, "I can't see why her having no virtue should be a reason against my having any; or why, because I am a man, or because I am poor, my virtue must be subservient to her pleasures." "I am out of patience," cries the lady: "Did ever mortal hear of a man's virtue! Did ever the greatest, or the gravest men pretend to any of this kind! Will magistrates who punish lewdness, or parsons who preach against it, make any scruple of committing it? And can a boy, a stripling, have the confidence to talk of his virtue?" "Madam," says Joseph, "that boy is the brother of Pamela, and would be ashamed that the chastity of his family, which is preserved in her, should be stained in him. If there are such men as your ladyship mentions, I am sorry for it; and I wish they had an opportunity of reading over those letters which my father hath sent me of my sister Pamela's; nor do I doubt but such an example would amend them." "You impudent villain!" cries the lady in a rage, "do you insult me with the follies of my relation, who hath exposed himself all over the country upon your sister's account? a little vixen, whom I have always wondered my late Lady John Booby ever kept in her house. Sirrah! get out of my sight, and prepare to set out this night; for I will order you your wages immediately, and you shall be stripped and turned away." — "Madam," says Joseph, "I am sorry I have offended your ladyship, I am sure I never intended it." "Yes, sirrah," cries she, "you have had the vanity to misconstrue the little innocent freedom I took in order to try whether what I had heard was true. O' my conscience, you have had the assurance to imagine I was fond of you myself." Joseph answered, he had only spoke out of tenderness for his virtue; at which words she flew into a violent passion, and refusing to hear more, ordered him instantly to leave the room.

He was no sooner gone than she burst forth into the following exclamation: "Whither doth this violent passion hurry us? What meannesses do we submit to from its impulse? Wisely we resist its first and least approaches; for it is then only we can assure ourselves the victory. No woman could ever safely say, 'so far only will I go.' Have I not exposed myself to the refusal of my footman? I cannot bear the reflection." Upon which she applied herself to the bell, and rung it with infinite more violence than was necessary; the faithful Slipslop attending near at hand: to say the truth, she had conceived a suspicion at her last interview with her mistress, and had waited ever since in the antechamber, having carefully applied her ears to the keyhole during the whole time that the preceding conversation passed between Joseph and the lady.

CHAPTER IX.

*What passed between the lady and Mrs. Slipslop, in which we
prophesy there are some strokes which everyone will not
truly comprehend at the first reading.*

"SLIPSLOP," said the lady, "I find too much reason to believe all
thou hast told me of this wicked Joseph; I have determined to
part with him instantly; so go you to the steward, and bid him
pay him his wages." Slipslop, who had preserved hitherto a
distance to her lady, rather out of necessity than inclination, and
who thought the knowledge of this secret had thrown down all
distinction between them, answered her mistress very pertly, "She
wished she knew her own mind; and that she was certain she
would call her back again before she was got halfway downstairs." The lady replied, "She had taken a resolution, and was
resolved to keep it." "I am sorry for it," cries Slipslop; "and, if I
had known you would have punished the poor lad so severely, you
should never have heard a *particle* of the matter. Here's a fuss
indeed, about nothing." "Nothing!" returned my lady; "do you
think I will countenance lewdness in my house?" "If you will
turn away every footman," said Slipslop, "that is a lover of the
sport, you must soon open the coach door yourself, or get a set of
mophrodites to wait upon you; and I am sure I hated the sight
of them even singing in an opera." "Do as I bid you," says my
lady, "and don't shock my ears with your beastly language."
"Marry-come-up," cries Slipslop, "people's ears are sometimes the
nicest part about them."

The lady, who began to admire the new style in which her
waiting-gentlewoman delivered herself, and by the conclusion of
her speech, suspected somewhat of the truth, called her back, and
desired to know what she meant by the extraordinary degree of
freedom in which she thought proper to indulge her tongue.
"Freedom!" says Slipslop; "I don't know what you call freedom,
madam; servants have tongues as well as their mistresses." "Yes,
and saucy ones too," answered the lady; "but I assure you I shall
bear no such impertinence." "Impertinence! I don't know that I
am impertinent," says Slipslop. "Yes, indeed you are," cries my
lady; "and unless you mend your manners, this house is no place
for you." "Manners!" cries Slipslop; "I never was thought to want

manners *nor modesty neither;* and for places, there are more places than one; and I know what I know." "What do you know, mistress?" answered the lady. "I am not obliged to tell that to everybody," says Slipslop, "any more than I am obliged to keep it a secret." "I desire you would provide yourself," answered the lady. "With all my heart," replied the waiting-gentlewoman; and so departed in a passion, and slapped the door after her.

The lady too plainly perceived that her waiting-gentlewoman knew more than she would willingly have had her acquainted with; and this she imputed to Joseph's having discovered to her what passed at the first interview. This, therefore, blew up her rage against him, and confirmed her in a resolution of parting with him.

But the dismissing Mrs. Slipslop was a point not so easily to be resolved upon: she had the utmost tenderness for her reputation, as she knew on that depended many of the most valuable blessings of life; particularly cards, making curtsies in public places, and, above all, the pleasure of demolishing the reputations of others, in which innocent amusement she had an extraordinary delight. She therefore determined to submit to any insult from a servant, rather than run a risk of losing the title to so many great privileges.

She therefore sent for her steward, Mr. Peter Pounce, and ordered him to pay Joseph his wages, to strip off his livery, and to turn him out of the house that evening.

She then called Slipslop up, and, after refreshing her spirits with a small cordial which she kept in her closet, she began in the following manner:

"Slipslop, why will you, who know my passionate temper, attempt to provoke me by your answers? I am convinced you are an honest servant, and should be very unwilling to part with you. I believe, likewise, you have found me an indulgent mistress on many occasions, and have as little reason on your side to desire a change. I can't help being surprised, therefore, that you will take the surest method to offend me. I mean repeating my words, which you know I have always detested."

The prudent waiting-gentlewoman had duly weighed the whole matter, and found, on mature deliberation, that a good place in possession was better than one in expectation. As she found her mistress, therefore, inclined to relent, she thought proper also to put on some small condescension, which was as readily accepted;

and so the affair was reconciled, all offences forgiven, and a present of a gown and petticoat made her as an instance of her lady's future favour.

She offered once or twice to speak in favour of Joseph; but found her lady's heart so obdurate, that she prudently dropt all such efforts. She considered there were more footmen in the house, and some as stout fellows, though not quite so handsome, as Joseph; besides, the reader hath already seen her tender advances had not met with the encouragement she might have reasonably expected. She thought she had thrown away a great deal of sack and sweetmeats on an ungrateful rascal; and, being a little inclined to the opinion of that female sect, who hold one lusty young fellow to be near as good as another lusty young fellow, she at last gave up Joseph and his cause, and, with a triumph over her passion highly commendable, walked off with her present, and with great tranquillity paid a visit to a stone-bottle, which is of sovereign use to a philosophical temper.

She left not her mistress so easy. The poor lady could not reflect, without agony, that her dear reputation was in the power of her servants. All her comfort, as to Joseph, was that she hoped he did not understand her meaning; at least, she could say for herself, she had not plainly expressed anything to him; and as to Mrs. Slipslop, she imagined she could bribe her to secrecy.

But what hurt her most was, that in reality she had not so entirely conquered her passion; the little god lay lurking in her heart, though anger and disdain so hoodwinked her, that she could not see him. She was a thousand times on the very brink of revoking the sentence she had passed against the poor youth. Love became his advocate, and whispered many things in his favour. Honour likewise endeavoured to vindicate his crime, and Pity to mitigate his punishment; on the other side, Pride and Revenge spoke as loudly against him; and thus the poor lady was tortured with perplexity, opposite passions distracting and tearing her mind different ways.

So have I seen, in the hall of Westminster, where Serjeant Bramble hath been retained on the right side, and Serjeant Puzzle on the left, the balance of opinion (so equal were their fees) alternately incline to either scale. Now Bramble throws in an argument, and Puzzle's scale strikes the beam; again, Bramble shares the like fate, overpowered by the weight of Puzzle. Here Bramble hits, there Puzzle strikes; here one has you, there t'other has you; till at last all becomes one scene of confusion in the tortured minds of the hearers; equal wagers are laid on the success, and neither judge nor jury can possibly make anything of the matter; all things are so enveloped by the careful serjeants in doubt and obscurity.

Or, as it happens in the conscience, where honour and honesty pull one way, and a bribe and necessity another. — If it was our present business only to make similes, we could produce many more to this purpose; but a simile (as well as a word) to the wise. We shall therefore see a little after our hero, for whom the reader is doubtless in some pain.

CHAPTER X.

Joseph writes another letter: his transactions with Mr. Peter Pounce, &c., with his departure from Lady Booby.

THE disconsolate Joseph would not have had an understanding sufficient for the principal subject of such a book as this, if he had any longer misunderstood the drift of his mistress; and, indeed, that he did not discern it sooner,. the reader will be pleased to apply to an unwillingness in him to discover what he must condemn in her as a fault. Having therefore quitted her presence, he retired into his own garret, and entered himself into an ejaculation on the numberless calamities which attended beauty, and the misfortune it was to be handsomer than one's neighbours.

He then sat down and addressed himself to his sister Pamela in the following words:

DEAR SISTER PAMELA,

Hoping you are well, what news have I to tell you! O Pamela, my mistress is fallen in love with me — that is, what great folks call falling in love — she has a mind to ruin me; but I hope I shall have more resolution and more grace than to part with my virtue to any lady upon earth.

Mr. Adams hath often told me, that chastity is as great a virtue in a man as in a woman. He says he never knew any more than his wife, and I shall endeavour to follow his example. Indeed, it is owing entirely to his excellent sermons and advice, together with your letters, that I have been able to resist a temptation, which he says no man complies with, but he repents in this world, or is damned for it in the next; and why should I trust to repentance on my deathbed, since I may die in my sleep? What fine

things are good advice and good examples! But I am glad she
turned me out of the chamber as she did: for I had once almost
forgotten every word Parson Adams had ever said to me.

I don't doubt, dear sister, but you will have grace to preserve
your virtue against all trials; and I beg you earnestly to pray I
may be enabled to preserve mine; for truly it is very severely
attacked by more than one; but I hope I shall copy your example,
and that of Joseph, my namesake, and maintain my virtue against
all temptations.

Joseph had not finished his letter, when he was summoned
downstairs by Mr. Peter Pounce, to receive his wages; for, besides
that out of eight pounds a year he allowed his father and mother
four, he had been obliged, in order to furnish himself with
musical instruments, to apply to the generosity of the aforesaid
Peter, who, on urgent occasions, used to advance the servants
their wages: not before they were due, but before they were
payable; that is, perhaps, half a year after they were due, and
this at the moderate premium of fifty per cent, or a little more; by
which charitable methods, together with lending money to other
people, and even to his own master and mistress, the honest man
had, from nothing, in a few years amassed a small sum of twenty
thousand pounds or thereabouts.

Joseph having received his little remainder of wages, and
having stript off his livery, was forced to borrow a frock and
breeches of one of the servants (for he was so beloved in the
family, that they would all have lent him anything); and, being
told by Peter that he must not stay a moment longer in the house
than was necessary to pack up his linen, which he easily did in a
very narrow compass, he took a melancholy leave of his fellow-
servants, and set out at seven in the evening.

He had proceeded the length of two or three streets, before he
absolutely determined with himself whether he should leave the
town that night, or, procuring a lodging, wait till the morning. At
last, the moon shining very bright helped him to come to a resolution of beginning his journey immediately, to which likewise he
had some other inducements; which the reader, without being a
conjurer, cannot possibly guess, till we have given him those
hints which it may be now proper to open.

CHAPTER XI.

Of several new matters not expected.

IT is an observation sometimes made, that to indicate our idea of a simple fellow, we say, "He is easily to be seen through": nor do I believe it a more improper denotation of a simple book. Instead of applying this to any particular performance, we choose rather to remark the contrary in this history, where the scene opens itself by small degrees; and he is a sagacious reader who can see two chapters before him.

For this reason, we have not hitherto hinted a matter which now seems necessary to be explained; since it may be wondered at, first, that Joseph made such extraordinary haste out of town, which hath been already shown; and secondly, which will be now shown, that, instead of proceeding to the habitation of his father and mother, or to his beloved sister Pamela, he chose rather to set out full speed to the Lady Booby's country-seat, which he had left on his journey to London.

Be it known, then, that in the same parish where this seat stood, there lived a young girl whom Joseph (though the best of sons and brothers) longed more impatiently to see than his parents or his sister. She was a poor girl, who had formerly been bred up in Sir John's family; whence, a little before the journey to London, she had been discarded by Mrs. Slipslop, on account of her extraordinary beauty: for I never could find any other reason.

This young creature (who now lived with a farmer in the parish) had been always beloved by Joseph, and returned his affection. She was two years only younger than our hero. They had been acquainted from their infancy, and had conceived a very early liking for each other; which had grown to such a degree of affection, that Mr. Adams had with much ado prevented them from marrying, and persuaded them to wait till a few years' service and thrift had a little improved their experience, and enabled them to live comfortably together.

They followed this good man's advice, as indeed his word was little less than a law in his parish; for as he had shown his parishioners, by an uniform behaviour of thirty-five years' duration, that he had their good entirely at heart, so they consulted him on every occasion, and very seldom acted contrary to his opinion.

Nothing can be imagined more tender than was the parting between these two lovers. A thousand sighs heaved the bosom of Joseph, a thousand tears distilled from the lovely eyes of Fanny (for that was her name); though her modesty would only suffer her to admit his eager kisses, her violent love made her more than passive in his embraces; and she often pulled him to her breast with a soft pressure, which, though perhaps it would not have squeezed an insect to death, caused more emotion in the heart of Joseph than the closest Cornish hug could have done.

The reader may perhaps wonder that so fond a pair should, during a twelvemonth's absence, never converse with one another: indeed, there was but one reason which did, or could have prevented them; and this was, that poor Fanny could neither write nor read; nor could she be prevailed upon to transmit the delicacies of her tender and chaste passion by the hands of an amanuensis.

They contented themselves therefore with frequent inquiries after each other's health, with a mutual confidence in each other's fidelity, and the prospect of their future happiness.

Having explained these matters to our reader, and, as far as possible, satisfied all his doubts, we return to honest Joseph, whom we left just set out on his travels by the light of the moon.

Those who have read any romance or poetry, ancient or modern, must have been informed that Love hath wings: by which they are not to understand, as some young ladies by mistake have done, that a lover can fly; the writers, by this ingenious allegory, intending to insinuate no more than that lovers do not march like horseguards; in short, that they put the best leg foremost; which our lusty youth, who could walk with any man, did so heartily on this occasion, that within four hours, he reached a famous house of hospitality well known to the western traveller. It presents you a lion on the sign-post: and the master, who was christened Timotheus, is commonly called plain Tim. Some have conceived that he hath particularly chosen the lion for his sign, as he doth in countenance greatly resemble that magnanimous beast, though his disposition savours more of the sweetness of the lamb. He is a person well received among all sorts of men, being qualified to render himself agreeable to any; as he is well versed in history and politics, hath a smattering in law and divinity, cracks a good jest, and plays wonderfully well on the French horn.

A violent storm of hail forced Joseph to take shelter in this inn, where he remembered Sir Thomas had dined in his way to town.

Joseph had no sooner seated himself by the kitchen fire than Timotheus, observing his livery, began to condole the loss of his late master; who was, he said, his very particular and intimate acquaintance, with whom he had cracked many a merry bottle, ay many a dozen, in his time. He then remarked, that all those things were over now, all past, and just as if they had never been; and concluded with an excellent observation on the certainty of death, which his wife said was indeed very true. A fellow now arrived at the same inn with two horses, one of which he was leading farther down into the country to meet his master; these he put into the stable, and came and took his place by Joseph's side, who immediately knew him to be the servant of a neighbouring gentleman, who used to visit at their house.

This fellow was likewise forced in by the storm; for he had orders to go twenty miles farther that evening, and luckily on the same road which Joseph himself intended to take. He therefore embraced this opportunity of complimenting his friend with his master's horse (notwithstanding he had received express commands to the contrary), which was readily accepted; and so, after they had drank a loving pot, and the storm was over, they set out together.

CHAPTER XII.

Containing many surprising adventures which Joseph Andrews met with on the road, scarce credible to those who have never travelled in a stage-coach.

NOTHING remarkable happened on the road, till their arrival at the inn to which the horses were ordered; whither they came about two in the morning. The moon then shone very bright; and Joseph, making his friend a present of a pint of wine, and thanking him for the favour of his horse, notwithstanding all entreaties to the contrary, proceeded on his journey on foot.

He had not gone above two miles, charmed with the hopes of shortly seeing his beloved Fanny, when he was met by two fellows in a narrow lane, and ordered to stand and deliver. He readily gave them all the money he had, which was somewhat less than two pounds; and told them he hoped they would be so generous as to return him a few shillings, to defray his charges on his way home.

One of the ruffians answered with an oath, "Yes, we'll give you something presently: but first strip and be d—n'd to you." — "Strip," cried the other, "or I'll blow your brains to the devil." Joseph, remembering that he had borrowed his coat and breeches of a friend, and that he should be ashamed of making any excuse for not returning them, replied, he hoped they would not insist on his clothes, which were not worth much, but consider the coldness of the night. "You are cold, are you, you rascal!" says one of the robbers: "I'll warm you with a vengeance"; and, damning his eyes, snapt a pistol at his head; which he had no sooner done than the other levelled a blow at him with his stick, which Joseph, who was expert at cudgel-playing, caught with his, and returned the favour so successfully on his adversary, that he laid him sprawling at his feet, and at the same instant received a blow from behind, with the butt end of a pistol, from the other villain, which felled him to the ground and totally deprived him of his senses.

The thief who had been knocked down had now recovered himself; and both together fell to belabouring poor Joseph with their sticks, till they were convinced they had put an end to his miserable being: they then stript him entirely naked, threw him into a ditch, and departed with their booty.

The poor wretch, who lay motionless a long time, just began to recover his senses as a stage-coach came by. The postilion, hearing a man's groans, stopt his horses, and told the coachman, He was certain there was a *dead* man lying in the ditch; for he heard him groan. "Go on, sirrah," says the coachman; "we are confounded late, and have no time to look after dead men." A lady, who heard what the postilion said, and likewise heard the groan, called eagerly to the coachman to stop and see what was the matter. Upon which he bid the postilion alight, and look into the ditch. He did so, and returned, "That there was a man sitting upright as naked as ever he was born." — "O J—sus!" cried the lady; "a naked man! Dear coachman, drive on and leave him." Upon this the gentlemen got out of the coach; and Joseph begged them to have mercy upon him: for that he had been robbed, and almost beaten to death. "Robbed!" cries an old gentleman: "let us make all the haste imaginable, or we shall be robbed too." A young man who belonged to the law answered, "He wished they had passed by without taking any notice; but that now they might be proved to have been *last in his company*; if he should die, they might be called

to some account for his murder. He therefore thought it advisable
to save the poor creature's life, for their own sakes, if possible;
at least, if he died, to prevent the jury's finding *that they fled
for it*. He was therefore *of opinion* to take the man into the
coach, and carry him to the next inn." The lady insisted, "That
he should not come into the coach. That if they lifted him in,
she would herself alight: for she had rather stay in that place
to all eternity than ride with a naked man." The coachman
objected, "That he could not suffer him to be taken in, unless
somebody would pay a shilling for his carriage the four miles."
Which the two gentlemen refused to do. But the lawyer, who was
afraid of some mischief happening to himself, if the wretch was
left behind in that condition, saying no man could be too cautious
in these matters, and that he remembered very extraordinary cases
in the books, threatened the coachman, and bid him deny taking
him up at his peril; for that, if he died, he should be indicted for
his murder; and if he lived, and brought an action against him,
he would willingly take a brief in it. These words had a sensible
effect on the coachman, who was well acquainted with the person
who spoke them; and the old gentleman above mentioned, thinking the naked man would afford him frequent opportunities of
showing his wit to the lady, offered to join with the company in
giving a mug of beer for his fare; till, partly alarmed by the
threats of the one, and partly by the promises of the other, and
being perhaps *a little* moved with compassion at the poor creature's condition, who stood bleeding and shivering with the cold,
he at length agreed; and Joseph was now advancing to the coach,
where, seeing the lady, who held the sticks of her fan before her
eyes, he absolutely refused, miserable as he was, to enter, unless
he was furnished with sufficient covering to prevent giving the
least offence to decency. So perfectly modest was this young
man; such mighty effects had the spotless example of the amiable
Pamela, and the excellent sermons of Mr. Adams, wrought upon
him.

Though there were several greatcoats about the coach, it was
not easy to get over this difficulty which Joseph had started.
The two gentlemen complained they were cold, and could not
spare a rag; the man of wit saying, with a laugh, "that charity
began at home"; and the coachman, who had two greatcoats
spread under him, refused to lend either, lest they should be made
bloody; the lady's footman desired to be excused for the same
reason, which the lady herself, notwithstanding her abhorrence

of a naked man, approved: and it is more than probable poor
Joseph, who obstinately adhered to his modest resolution, must
have perished, unless the postilion (a lad who hath been since
transported for robbing a hen-roost) had voluntarily stript off
a greatcoat, his only garment, at the same time swearing a great
oath (for which he was rebuked by the passengers), "That he
would rather ride in his shirt all his life than suffer a fellow-
creature to lie in so miserable a condition."

Joseph, having put on the greatcoat, was lifted into the coach,
which now proceeded on its journey. He declared himself almost
dead with the cold, which gave the man of wit an occasion to ask
the lady, if she could not accommodate him with a dram. She
answered with some resentment, "She wondered at his asking
her such a question; but assured him she never tasted any such
thing."

The lawyer was inquiring into the circumstances of the robbery, when the coach stopt, and one of the ruffians, putting a
pistol in, demanded their money of the passengers, who readily
gave it them; and the lady, in her fright, delivered up a little
silver bottle, of about a half-pint size, which the rogue, clapping
it to his mouth, and drinking her health, declared, held some
of the best Nantes he had ever tasted: this the lady afterwards
assured the company was the mistake of her maid, for that she
had ordered her to fill the bottle with Hungary-water.

As soon as the fellows were departed, the lawyer, who had,
it seems, a case of pistols in the seat of the coach, informed the
company, that if it had been daylight, and he could have come
at his pistols, he would not have submitted to the robbery; he
likewise set forth that he had often met highwaymen when he
travelled on horseback, but none ever durst attack him; concluding, that if he had not been more afraid for the lady than
for himself, he should not have now parted with his money so
easily.

As wit is generally observed to love to reside in empty pockets,
so the gentleman whose ingenuity we have above remarked,
as soon as he had parted with his money, began to grow wonderfully facetious. He made frequent allusions to Adam and Eve,
and said many excellent things on figs and fig-leaves; which
perhaps gave more offence to Joseph than to any other in the
company.

The lawyer likewise made several very pretty jests, without
departing from his profession. He said, "If Joseph and the

lady were alone, he would be more capable of making a *conveyance* to her, as his *affairs* were not *fettered* with any *incumbrance*; he'd warrant he soon suffered a *recovery* by a writ of *entry*, which was the proper way to create *heirs in tail*; that, for his own part, he would engage to make so *firm a settlement* in a coach, that there should be no danger of an *ejectment*"; with an inundation of the like gibberish, which he continued to vent till the coach arrived at an inn, where one servant-maid only was up, in readiness to attend the coachman, and furnish him with cold meat and a dram. Joseph desired to alight, and that he might have a bed prepared for him, which the maid readily promised to perform; and, being a good-natured wench, and not so squeamish as the lady had been, she clapt a large fagot on the fire, and, furnishing Joseph with a greatcoat belonging to one of the hostlers, desired him to sit down and warm himself, whilst she made his bed. The coachman, in the meantime, took an opportunity to call up a surgeon, who lived within a few doors; after which, he reminded his passengers how late they were, and, after they had taken leave of Joseph, hurried them off as fast as he could.

The wench soon got Joseph to bed, and promised to use her interest to borrow him a shirt; but imagined, as she afterwards said, by his being so bloody, that he must be a dead man; she ran with all speed to hasten the surgeon, who was more than half drest, apprehending that the coach had been overturned and some gentleman or lady hurt. As soon as the wench had informed him at his window that it was a poor foot-passenger who had been stripped of all he had, and almost murdered, he chid her for disturbing him so early, slipped off his clothes again, and very quietly returned to bed and to sleep.

Aurora now began to show her blooming cheeks over the hills, whilst ten millions of feathered songsters, in jocund chorus, repeated odes a thousand times sweeter than those of our *laureat*, and sung both "the day and the song"; when the master of the inn, Mr. Tow-wouse, arose, and learning from his maid an account of the robbery, and the situation of his poor naked guest, he shook his head, and cried, "Good lack-a-day!" and then ordered the girl to carry him one of his own shirts.

Mrs. Tow-wouse was just awake, and had stretched out her arms in vain to fold her departed husband, when the maid entered the room. "Who's there? Betty?" "Yes, madam." "Where's your master?" "He's without, madam; he hath sent me for a shirt

to lend a poor naked man, who hath been robbed and murdered."
"Touch one, if you dare, you slut," said Mrs. Tow-wouse; "your
master is a pretty sort of a man to take in naked vagabonds, and
clothe them with his own clothes. I shall have no such doings. If
you offer to touch anything, I will throw the chamber-pot at your
head. Go, send your master to me." "Yes, madam," answered
Betty. As soon as he came in, she thus began: "What the devil
do you mean by this, Mr. Tow-wouse? Am I to buy shirts to lend
to a set of scabby rascals?" "My dear," said Mr. Tow-wouse,
"this is a poor wretch." "Yes," says she, "I know it is a poor
wretch; but what the devil have we to do with poor wretches?
The law makes us provide for too many already. We shall
have thirty or forty poor wretches in red coats shortly." "My
dear," cries Tow-wouse, "this man hath been robbed of all he
hath." "Well then," said she, "where's his money to pay his
reckoning? Why doth not such a fellow go to an alehouse? I
shall send him packing as soon as I am up, I assure you." "My
dear," said he, "common charity won't suffer you to do that."
"Common charity, a f—t!" says she, "common charity teaches us
to provide for ourselves, and our families; and I and mine won't
be ruined by your charity, I assure you." "Well," says he, "my
dear, do as you will when you are up; you know I never contradict you." "No," says she, "if the devil was to contradict me, I
would make the house too hot to hold him."

With such like discourses they consumed near half-an-hour,
whilst Betty provided a shirt from the hostler, who was one of
her sweethearts, and put it on poor Joseph. The surgeon had
likewise at last visited him, and washed and drest his wounds,
and was now come to acquaint Mr. Tow-wouse that his guest
was in such extreme danger of his life, that he scarce saw any
hopes of his recovery. — "Here's a pretty kettle of fish," cries
Mrs. Tow-wouse, "you have brought upon us! We are like
to have a funeral at our own expense." Tow-wouse (who, notwithstanding his charity, would have given his vote as freely
as ever he did at an election, that any other house in the kingdom should have quiet possession of his guest) answered, "My
dear, I am not to blame: he was brought hither by the stage-
coach; and Betty had put him to bed before I was stirring."
"I'll Betty her," says she. — At which, with half her garments
on, the other half under her arm, she sallied out in quest of the
unfortunate Betty, whilst Tow-wouse and the surgeon went to

pay a visit to poor Joseph, and inquire into the circumstances of this melancholy affair.

CHAPTER XIII.

What happened to Joseph during his sickness at the inn, with the curious discourse between him and Mr. Barnabas, the parson of the parish.

As soon as Joseph had communicated a particular history of the robbery, together with a short account of himself, and his intended journey, he asked the surgeon if he apprehended him to be in any danger: to which the surgeon very honestly answered, "He feared he was; for that his pulse was very exalted and feverish, and, if his fever should prove more than *symptomatic*, it would be impossible to save him." Joseph, fetching a deep sigh, cried, "Poor Fanny, I would I could have lived to see thee! but God's will be done."

The surgeon then advised him, if he had any worldly affairs to settle, that he would do it as soon as possible; for, though he hoped he might recover, yet he thought himself obliged to acquaint him he was in great danger; and if the malign concoction of his humours should cause a suscitation of his fever, he might soon grow delirious and incapable to make his will. Joseph answered, "That it was impossible for any creature in the universe to be in a poorer condition than himself; for, since the robbery, he had not one thing of any kind whatever which he could call his own." "I had," said he, "a poor little piece of gold which they took away, that would have been a comfort to me in all my afflictions; but surely, Fanny, I want nothing to remind me of thee. I have thy dear image in my heart, and no villain can ever tear it thence."

Joseph desired paper and pens, to write a letter, but they were refused him; and he was advised to use all his endeavours to compose himself. They then left him; and Mr. Tow-wouse sent to a clergyman to come and administer his good offices to the soul of poor Joseph, since the surgeon despaired of making any successful applications to his body.

Mr. Barnabas (for that was the clergyman's name) came as

soon as sent for; and, having first drank a dish of tea with the
landlady, and afterwards a bowl of punch with the landlord,
he walked up to the room where Joseph lay; but, finding him
asleep, returned to take the other sneaker; which when he had
finished, he again crept softly up to the chamber-door, and,
having opened it, heard the sick man talking to himself in the
following manner:

"O most adorable Pamela! most virtuous sister! whose example
could alone enable me to withstand all the temptations of riches
and beauty, and to preserve my virtue pure and chaste for the
arms of my dear Fanny, if it had pleased Heaven that I should
ever have come unto them. What riches, or honours, or pleasures,
can make us amends for the loss of innocence? Doth not that
alone afford us more consolation than all worldly acquisitions?
What but innocence and virtue could give any comfort to such
a miserable wretch as I am? Yet these can make me prefer this
sick and painful bed to all the pleasures I should have found in
my lady's. These can make me face death without fear; and
though I love my Fanny more than ever man loved a woman,
these can teach me to resign myself to the Divine will without
repining. O, thou delightful charming creature! if Heaven had
indulged thee to my arms, the poorest, humblest state would
have been a paradise; I could have lived with thee in the lowest
cottage, without envying the palaces, the dainties, or the riches
of any man breathing. But I must leave thee, leave thee for ever,
my dearest angel! I must think of another world; and I heartily
pray thou may'st meet comfort in this." — Barnabas thought he
had heard enough; so downstairs he went, and told Tow-wouse
he could do his guest no service: for that he was very light-
headed, and had uttered nothing but a rhapsody of nonsense all
the time he stayed in the room.

The surgeon returned in the afternoon, and found his patient
in a higher fever, as he said, than when he left him, though not
delirious; for, notwithstanding Mr. Barnabas's opinion, he had
not been once out of his senses since his arrival at the inn.

Mr. Barnabas was again sent for, and with much difficulty
prevailed on to make another visit. As soon as he entered the
room, he told Joseph, "He was come to pray by him, and to
prepare him for another world: in the first place, therefore, he
hoped he had repented of all his sins." Joseph answered, "He
hoped he had; but there was one thing which he knew not
whether he should call a sin; if it was, he feared he should die in

the commission of it; and that was, the regret of parting with a young woman whom he loved as tenderly as he did his heart-strings." Barnabas bade him be assured, "That any repining at the Divine will was one of the greatest sins he could commit; that he ought to forget all carnal affections, and think of better things." Joseph said, "That neither in this world nor the next could he forget his Fanny; and that the thought, however grievous, of parting from her for ever, was not half so tormenting as the fear of what she would suffer when she knew his misfortune." Barnabas said, "That such fears argued a diffidence and despondence very criminal; that he must divest himself of all human passions, and fix his heart above." Joseph answered, "That was what he desired to do, and should be obliged to him if he would enable him to accomplish it." Barnabas replied, "That must be done by grace." Joseph besought him to discover how he might attain it. Barnabas answered, "By prayer and faith." He then questioned him concerning his forgiveness of the thieves. Joseph answered, "He feared that was more than he could do: for nothing would give him more pleasure than to hear they were taken." "That," cries Barnabas, "is for the sake of justice." "Yes," said Joseph, "but if I was to meet them again, I am afraid I should attack them, and kill them too, if I could." "Doubtless," answered Barnabas, "it is lawful to kill a thief; but can you say you forgive them as a Christian ought?" Joseph desired to know what that forgiveness was. "That is," answered Barnabas, "to forgive them as — as — it is to forgive them as — in short, it is to forgive them as a Christian." Joseph replied, "He forgave them as much as he could." "Well, well," said Barnabas, "that will do." He then demanded of him, "If he remembered any more sins unrepented of; and if he did, he desired him to make haste and repent of them as fast as he could, that they might repeat over a few prayers together." Joseph answered, "He could not recollect any great crimes he had been guilty of, and that those he had committed he was sincerely sorry for." Barnabas said that was enough, and then proceeded to prayer with all the expedition he was master of, some company then waiting for him below in the parlour, where the ingredients for punch were all in readiness; but no one would squeeze the oranges till he came.

Joseph complained he was dry, and desired a little tea; which Barnabas reported to Mrs. Tow-wouse, who answered, "She had just done drinking it, and could not be slopping all day"; but ordered Betty to carry him up some small beer.

Betty obeyed her mistress's commands; but Joseph, as soon as he had tasted it, said, he feared it would increase his fever, and that he longed very much for tea; to which the good-natured Betty answered, he should have tea, if there was any in the land; she accordingly went and bought him some herself, and attended him with it; where we will leave her and Joseph together for some time, to entertain the reader with other matters.

CHAPTER XIV.

Being very full of adventures, which succeeded each other at the inn.

IT was now the dusk of the evening, when a grave person rode into the inn, and, committing his horse to the hostler, went directly into the kitchen, and, having called for a pipe of tobacco, took his place by the fireside, where several other persons were likewise assembled.

The discourse ran altogether on the robbery which was committed the night before, and on the poor wretch who lay above in the dreadful condition in which we have already seen him. Mrs. Tow-wouse said, "She wondered what the devil Tom Whipwell meant by bringing such guests to her house, when there were so many alehouses on the road proper for their reception. But she assured him, if he died, the parish should be at the expense of the funeral." She added, "Nothing would serve the fellow's turn but tea, she would assure him." Betty, who was just returned from her charitable office, answered, she believed he was a gentleman, for she never saw a finer skin in her life. "Pox on his skin!" replied Mrs. Tow-wouse, "I suppose that is all we are like to have for the reckoning. I desire no such gentlemen should ever call at the Dragon" (which it seems was the sign of the inn).

The gentleman lately arrived discovered a great deal of emotion at the distress of this poor creature, whom he observed to be fallen not into the most compassionate hands. And indeed, if Mrs. Tow-wouse had given no utterance to the sweetness of her temper, nature had taken such pains in her countenance, that Hogarth himself never gave more expression to a picture.

Her person was short, thin, and crooked. Her forehead projected in the middle, and thence descended in a declivity to the top of her nose, which was sharp and red, and would have hung over her lips, had not nature turned up the end of it. Her lips were two bits of skin, which, whenever she spoke, she drew together in a purse. Her chin was peaked; and at the upper end of that skin which composed her cheeks, stood two bones, that almost hid a pair of small red eyes. Add to this a voice most wonderfully adapted to the sentiments it was to convey, being both loud and hoarse.

It is not easy to say whether the gentleman had conceived a greater dislike for his landlady, or compassion for her unhappy guest. He inquired very earnestly of the surgeon, who was now come into the kitchen, whether he had any hopes of his recovery? He begged him to use all possible means towards it, telling him, "it was the duty of men of all professions to apply their skill *gratis* for the relief of the poor and necessitous." The surgeon answered, "He should take proper care; but he defied all the surgeons in London to do him any good." "Pray, sir," said the gentleman, "what are his wounds?" — "Why, do you know anything of wounds?" says the surgeon (winking upon Mrs. Tow-wouse). "Sir, I have a small smattering in surgery," answered the gentleman. "A smattering — ho, ho, ho!" said the surgeon; "I believe it is a smattering indeed."

The company were all attentive, expecting to hear the doctor, who was what they call a dry fellow, expose the gentleman.

He began therefore with an air of triumph: "I suppose, sir, you have travelled?" "No, really, sir," said the gentleman. "Ho! then you have practised in the hospitals perhaps?" — "No, sir." "Hum! not that neither? Whence, sir, then, if I may be so bold to inquire, have you got your knowledge in surgery?" "Sir," answered the gentleman, "I do not pretend to much; but the little I know I have from books." "Books!" cries the doctor. "What, I suppose you have read Galen and Hippocrates!" "No, sir," said the gentleman. "How! you understand surgery," answers the doctor, "and not read Galen and Hippocrates?" "Sir," cries the other, "I believe there are many surgeons who have never read these authors." "I believe so too," says the doctor, "more shame for them; but, thanks to my education, I have them by heart, and very seldom go without them both in my pocket." "They are pretty large books," said the gentleman. "Ay," said the doctor, "I believe I know how large they are better than you."

(At which he fell a-winking, and the whole company burst into a laugh.)

The doctor pursuing his triumph, asked the gentleman, "If he did not understand physic as well as surgery." "Rather better," answered the gentleman. "Ay, like enough," cries the doctor, with a wink. "Why, I know a little of physic too." "I wish I knew half so much," said Tow-wouse, "I'd never wear an apron again." "Why, I believe, landlord," cries the doctor, "there are few men, though I say it, within twelve miles of the place, that handle a fever better. — *Veniente accurrite morbo:* that is my method. — I supose, brother, you understand Latin?" "A little," says the gentleman. "Ay, and Greek now, I'll warrant you: *Ton dapomibominos poluflosboio thalasses.* But I have almost forgot these things; I could have repeated Homer by heart once." — "Ifags! the gentleman has caught a *traitor,*" says Mrs. Tow-wouse; at which they all fell a-laughing.

The gentleman, who had not the least affection for joking, very contentedly suffered the doctor to enjoy his victory, which he did with no small satisfaction; and, having sufficiently sounded his depth, told him, "He was thoroughly convinced of his great learning and abilities; and that he would be obliged to him if he would let him know his opinion of his patient's case above-stairs." "Sir," says the doctor, "his case is that of a dead man — The contusion on his head has *perforated* the *internal membrane* of the *occiput,* and *divellicated* that *radical* small *minute* invisible *nerve* which *coheres* to the *pericranium;* and this was attended with a fever at first *symptomatic,* then *pneumatic;* and he is at length grown *deliruus,* or delirious, as the vulgar express it."

He was proceeding in this learned manner, when a mighty noise interrupted him. Some young fellows in the neighbourhood had taken one of the thieves, and were bringing him into the inn. Betty ran upstairs with this news to Joseph, who begged they might search for a little piece of broken gold, which had a ribband tied to it, and which he could swear to amongst all the hoards of the richest men in the universe.

Notwithstanding the fellow's persisting in his innocence, the mob were very busy in searching him, and presently, among other things, pulled out the piece of gold just mentioned; which Betty no sooner saw than she laid violent hands on it, and conveyed it up to Joseph, who received it with raptures of joy, and, hugging it in his bosom, declared, "he could now die contented."

Within a few minutes afterwards came in some other fellows with a bundle which they had found in a ditch, and which was indeed the clothes which had been stripped off from Joseph, and the other things they had taken from him.

The gentleman no sooner saw the coat than he declared he knew the livery; and, if it had been taken from the poor creature above-stairs, desired he might see him; for that he was very well acquainted with the family to whom that livery belonged.

He was accordingly conducted up by Betty: but what, reader, was the surprise on both sides, when he saw Joseph was the person in bed; and when Joseph discovered the face of his good friend Mr. Abraham Adams!

It would be impertinent to insert a discourse which chiefly turned on the relation of matters already well known to the reader; for, as soon as the curate had satisfied Joseph concerning the perfect health of his Fanny, he was on his side very inquisitive into all the particulars which had produced this unfortunate accident.

To return therefore to the kitchen, where a great variety of company were now assembled from all the rooms of the house, as well as the neighbourhood: so much delight do men take in contemplating the countenance of a thief:

Mr. Tow-wouse began to rub his hands with pleasure at seeing so large an assembly; who would, he hoped, shortly adjourn into several apartments, in order to discourse over the robbery, and drink a health to all honest men. But Mrs. Tow-wouse, whose misfortune it was commonly to see things a little perversely, began to rail at those who brought the fellow into her house; telling her husband, "They were very likely to thrive who kept a house of entertainment for beggars and thieves."

The mob had now finished their search, and could find nothing about the captive likely to prove any evidence; for as to the clothes, though the mob were very well satisfied with that proof, yet, as the surgeon observed, they could not convict him, because they were not found in his custody; to which Barnabas agreed, and added that these were *bona waviata,* and belonged to the lord of the manor.

"How," says the surgeon, "do you say these goods belong to the lord of the manor?" "I do," cried Barnabas. "Then I deny it," says the surgeon. "What can the lord of the manor have to do in the case? Will anyone attempt to persuade me that what a man finds is not his own?" "I have heard," says an old fellow in the corner, "Justice Wise-one say, that, if every man had his right, whatever is found belongs to the king of London." "That may be true," says Barnabas, "in some sense: for the law makes a difference between things stolen, and things found; for a thing may be stolen that never is found, and a thing may be found that never was stolen. Now, goods that are both stolen and found are *waviata*; and they belong to the lord of the manor." "So the lord of the manor is the receiver of stolen goods," says the doctor; at which there was a universal laugh, being first begun by himself.

While the prisoner, by persisting in his innocence, had almost (as there was no evidence against him) brought over Barnabas, the surgeon, Tow-wouse, and several others to his side, Betty informed them that they had overlooked a little piece of gold, which she had carried up to the man in bed, and which he offered to swear to amongst a million, ay, amongst ten thousand. This immediately turned the scale against the prisoner; and everyone now concluded him guilty. It was resolved, therefore, to keep him secured that night, and early in the morning to carry him before a justice.

CHAPTER XV.

Showing how Mrs. Tow-wouse was a little mollified; and how officious Mr. Barnabas and the surgeon were to prosecute the thief: with a dissertation accounting for their zeal, and that of many other persons not mentioned in this history.

BETTY told her mistress she believed the man in bed was a greater man than they took him for: for, besides the extreme whiteness of his skin, and the softness of his hands, she observed a very great familiarity between the gentleman and him; and added, she was certain they were intimate acquaintance, if not relations.

This somewhat abated the severity of Mrs. Tow-wouse's countenance. She said, "God forbid she should not discharge the duty of a Christian, since the poor gentleman was brought to her house. She had a natural antipathy to vagabonds; but could pity the misfortunes of a Christian as soon as another." Tow-wouse said, "If the traveller be a gentleman, though he

hath no money about him now, we shall most likely be paid
hereafter; so you may begin to score whenever you will." Mrs.
Tow-wouse answered, "Hold your simple tongue, and don't instruct me in my business. I am sure I am sorry for the gentleman's misfortune with all my heart; and I hope the villain who
hath used him so barbarously will be hanged. Betty, go, see what
he wants. God forbid he should want anything in my house."

Barnabas and the surgeon went up to Joseph to satisfy themselves concerning the piece of gold. Joseph was with difficulty
prevailed upon to show it them, but would by no entreaties be
brought to deliver it out of his own possession. He however
attested this to be the same which had been taken from him;
and Betty was ready to swear to the finding it on the thief.

The only difficulty that remained was, how to produce this gold
before the justice: for as to carrying Joseph himself, it seemed
impossible; nor was there any great likelihood of obtaining it
from him, for he had fastened it with a ribband to his arm, and
solemnly vowed that nothing but irresistible force should ever
separate them; in which resolution, Mr. Adams, clenching a
fist rather less than the knuckle of an ox, declared he would
support him.

A dispute arose on this occasion concerning evidence not
very necessary to be related here; after which the surgeon
dressed Mr. Joseph's head, still persisting in the imminent
danger in which his patient lay, but concluding, with a very
important look, "That he began to have some hopes; that he
should send him a *sanative soporiferous* draught, and would
see him in the morning." After which Barnabas and he departed,
and left Mr. Joseph and Mr. Adams together.

Adams informed Joseph of the occasion of this journey which
he was making to London, namely, to publish three volumes of
sermons; being encouraged, he said, by an advertisement lately
set forth by a society of booksellers, who proposed to purchase
any copies offered to them, at a price to be settled by two
persons; but though he imagined he should get a considerable
sum of money on this occasion, which his family were in urgent
need of, he protested he would not leave Joseph in his present
condition: finally, he told him, "He had nine shillings and three-
pence halfpenny in his pocket, which he was welcome to use as
he pleased."

This goodness of Parson Adams brought tears into Joseph's
eyes; he declared, "He had now a second reason to desire life,

that he might show his gratitude to such a friend." Adams bade him, "Be cheerful; for that he plainly saw the surgeon, besides his ignorance, desired to make a merit of curing him, though the wounds in his head, he perceived, were by no means dangerous; that he was convinced he had no fever, and doubted not but he would be able to travel in a day or two."

These words infused a spirit into Joseph; he said, "He found himself very sore from the bruises, but had no reason to think any of his bones injured, or that he had received any harm in his inside, unless that he felt something very odd in his stomach; but he knew not whether that might not arise from not having eaten one morsel for above twenty-four hours." Being then asked if he had any inclination to eat, he answered in the affirmative. Then Parson Adams desired him to name what he had the greatest fancy for: whether a poached egg, or chicken-broth: he answered, "He could eat both very well; but that he seemed to have the greatest appetite for a piece of boiled beef and cabbage."

Adams was pleased with so perfect a confirmation that he had not the least fever, but advised him to a lighter diet for that evening. He accordingly eat either a rabbit or a fowl, I never could with any tolerable certainty discover which; after this he was, by Mrs. Tow-wouse's order, conveyed into a better bed and equipped with one of her husband's shirts.

In the morning early, Barnabas and the surgeon came to the inn, in order to see the thief conveyed before the justice. They had consumed the whole night in debating what measures they should take to produce the piece of gold in evidence against him: for they were both extremely zealous in the business, though neither of them were in the least interested in the prosecution; neither of them had ever received any private injury from the fellow, nor had either of them ever been suspected of loving the public well enough to give them a sermon or a dose of physic for nothing.

To help our reader, therefore, as much as possible to account for this zeal, we must inform him that, as this parish was so unfortunate as to have no lawyer in it, there had been a constant contention between the two doctors, spiritual and physical, concerning their abilities in a science, in which, as neither of them professed it, they had equal pretensions to dispute each other's opinions. These disputes were carried on with great contempt on both sides, and had almost divided the parish; Mr. Tow-wouse and one half of the neighbours inclining to the surgeon, and Mrs. Tow-wouse with the other half to the parson. The surgeon drew his knowledge from those inestimable fountains, called the *Attorney's Pocket-Companion*, and Mr. Jacob's *Law-Tables;* Barnabas trusted entirely to Wood's *Institutes.* It happened on this occasion, as was pretty frequently the case, that these two learned men differed about the sufficiency of evidence: the doctor being of opinion that the maid's oath would convict the prisoner without producing the gold; the parson, *è contra, totis viribus.* To display their parts, therefore, before the justice and the parish, was the sole motive which we can discover to this zeal which both of them pretended to have for public justice.

O Vanity! how little is thy force acknowledged, or thy operations discerned! How wantonly dost thou deceive mankind under different disguises! Sometimes thou dost wear the face of pity, sometimes of generosity: nay, thou hast the assurance even to put on those glorious ornaments which belong only to heroic virtue. Thou odious, deformed monster! whom priests have railed at, philosophers despised, and poets ridiculed: is there a wretch so abandoned as to own thee for an acquaintance in public? yet, how few will refuse to enjoy thee in private? nay, thou art the pursuit of most men through their lives. The greatest villainies are daily practised to please thee; nor is the meanest thief below, or the greatest hero above, thy notice. Thy embraces are often the sole aim and sole reward of the private robbery and the plundered province. It is to pamper up thee, thou harlot, that we attempt to withdraw from others what we do not want, or to withhold from them what they do. All our passions are thy slaves. Avarice itself is often no more than thy handmaid, and even Lust thy pimp. The bully Fear, like a coward, flies before thee, and Joy and Grief hide their heads in thy presence.

I know thou wilt think that, whilst I abuse thee, I court thee, and that thy love hath inspired me to write this sarcastical panegyric on thee; but thou art deceived: I value thee not of a farthing; nor will it give me any pain if thou shouldst prevail on the reader to censure this digression as arrant nonsense; for know, to thy confusion, that I have introduced thee for no other purpose than to lengthen out a short chapter; and so I return to my history.

CHAPTER XVI.

*The escape of the thief. Mr. Adams's disappointment. The arrival
of two very extraordinary personages, and the introduction
of Parson Adams to Parson Barnabas.*

BARNABAS and the surgeon being returned, as we have said, to
the inn, in order to convey the thief before the justice, were
greatly concerned to find a small accident had happened, which
somewhat disconcerted them; and this was no other than the
thief's escape, who had modestly withdrawn himself by night,
declining all ostentation, and not choosing, in imitation of some
great men, to distinguish himself at the expense of being pointed
at.

When the company had retired the evening before, the thief
was detained in a room where the constable, and one of the
young fellows who took him, were planted as his guard. About
the second watch, a general complaint of drought was made,
both by the prisoner and his keepers. Among whom it was at
last agreed that the constable should remain on duty, and the
young fellow call up the tapster; in which disposition the latter
apprehended not the least danger, as the constable was well
armed, and could besides easily summon him back to his assistance, if the prisoner made the least attempt to gain his liberty.

The young fellow had not long left the room, before it came
into the constable's head that the prisoner might leap on him by
surprise, and, thereby preventing him of the use of his weapons,
especially the long staff in which he chiefly confided, might reduce the success of a struggle to an equal chance. He wisely,
therefore, to prevent this inconvenience, slipt out of the room
himself, and locked the door, waiting without with his staff in
his hand, ready lifted to fell the unhappy prisoner, if by ill
fortune he should attempt to break out.

But human life, as hath been discovered by some great man or
other (for I would by no means be understood to affect the
honour of making any such discovery), very much resembles a
game at chess: for as in the latter, while a gamester is too attentive
to secure himself very strongly on one side the board, he is apt
to leave an unguarded opening on the other; so doth it often
happen in life, and so did it happen on this occasion: for whilst
the cautious constable with such wonderful sagacity had possessed

himself of the door, he most unhappily forgot the window.

The thief, who played on the other side, no sooner perceived this opening than he began to move that way; and, finding the passage easy, he took with him the young fellow's hat, and without any ceremony stepped into the street and made the best of his way.

The young fellow, returning with a double mug of strong beer, was a little surprised to find the constable at the door; but much more so when, the door being opened, he perceived the prisoner had made his escape, and which way. He threw down the beer, and, without uttering anything to the constable, except a hearty curse or two, he nimbly leapt out at the window, and went again in pursuit of his prey, being very unwilling to lose the reward which he had assured himself of.

The constable hath not been discharged of suspicion on this account: it hath been said that, not being concerned in the taking the thief, he could not have been entitled to any part of the reward if he had been convicted; that the thief had several guineas in his pocket; that it was very unlikely he should have been guilty of such an oversight; that his pretence for leaving the room was absurd; that it was his constant maxim, that a wise man never refused money on any conditions; that at every election he always had sold his vote to both parties, &c.

But, notwithstanding these and many other such allegations, I am sufficiently convinced of his innocence; having been positively assured of it by those who received their informations from his own mouth; which, in the opinion of some moderns, is the best and indeed only evidence.

All the family were now up, and with many others assembled in the kitchen, where Mr. Tow-wouse was in some tribulation; the surgeon having declared that by law he was liable to be indicted for the thief's escape, as it was out of his house; he was a little comforted, however, by Mr. Barnabas's opinion, that, as the escape was by night, the indictment would not lie.

Mrs. Tow-wouse delivered herself in the following words: "Sure never was such a fool as my husband! would any other person living have left a man in the custody of such a drunken, drowsy blockhead as Tom Suckbribe?" (which was the constable's name); "and if he could be indicted without any harm to his wife and children, I should be glad of it." (Then the bell rung in Joseph's room.) "Why Betty, John, chamberlain, where the devil are you all? Have you no ears, or no conscience, not to tend the sick better? — See what the gentleman wants; why don't you go yourself, Mr. Tow-wouse? But anyone may die for you; you have no more feeling than a deal board. If a man lived a fortnight in your house without spending a penny, you would never put him in mind of it. See whether he drinks tea or coffee for breakfast." "Yes, my dear," cried Tow-wouse. She then asked the doctor and Mr. Barnabas what morning's draught they chose, who answered, they had a pot of cider-and at the fire; which we will leave them merry over, and return to Joseph.

He had rose pretty early this morning; but, though his wounds were far from threatening any danger, he was so sore with the bruises, that it was impossible for him to think of undertaking a journey yet; Mr. Adams, therefore, whose stock was visibly decreased with the expenses of supper and breakfast, and which could not survive that day's scoring, began to consider how it was possible to recruit it. At last he cried, "He had luckily hit on a sure method, and, though it would oblige him to return himself home together with Joseph, it mattered not much." He then sent for Tow-wouse, and, taking him into another room, told him, "He wanted to borrow three guineas, for which he would put ample security into his hands." Tow-wouse, who expected a watch, or ring, or something of double the value, answered, "He believed he could furnish him." Upon which Adams, pointing to his saddle-bag, told him with a face and voice full of solemnity, "That there were in that bag no less than nine volumes of manu-script sermons, as well worth a hundred pound as a shilling was worth twelve pence, and that he would deposit one of the volumes in his hands by way of pledge, not doubting but that he would have the honesty to return it on his repayment of the money: for otherwise he must be a very great loser, seeing that every volume would at least bring him ten pounds, as he had been informed by a neighbouring clergyman in the country; for," said he, "as to my own part, having never yet dealt in printing, I do not pretend to ascertain the exact value of such things."

Tow-wouse, who was a little surprised at the pawn, said (and not without some truth), "That he was no judge of the price of such kind of goods; and as for money, he really was very short." Adams answered, "Certainly he would not scruple to lend him three guineas on what was undoubtedly worth at least ten." The landlord replied, "He did not believe he had so much money in the house, and besides, he was to make up a sum. He was very confident the books were of much higher value, and heartily sorry it did not suit him." He then cried out, "Coming, sir!" though nobody called; and ran downstairs without any fear of breaking his neck.

Poor Adams was extremely dejected at this disappointment, nor knew he what farther stratagem to try. He immediately applied to his pipe, his constant friend and comfort in his afflictions; and, leaning over the rails, he devoted himself to meditation, assisted by the inspiring fumes of tobacco.

He had on a nightcap drawn over his wig, and a short greatcoat, which half covered his cassock — a dress which, added to something comical enough in his countenance, composed a figure likely to attract the eyes of those who were not over-given to observation.

Whilst he was smoking his pipe in this posture, a coach and six, with a numerous attendance, drove into the inn. There alighted from the coach a young fellow and a brace of pointers, after which another young fellow leapt from the box, and shook the former by the hand; and both, together with the dogs, were instantly conducted by Mr. Tow-wouse into an apartment; whither, as they passed, they entertained themselves with the following short facetious dialogue:

"You are a pretty fellow for a coachman, Jack!" says he from the coach; "you had almost overturned us just now." "Pox take you!" says the coachman; "if I had only broke your neck, it would have been saving somebody else the trouble; but I should have been sorry for the pointers." "Why, you son of a b—," answered the other, "if nobody could shoot better than you, the pointers would be of no use." "D—n me," says the coachman, "I will shoot with you, five guineas a shot." "You be hanged," says the other; "for five guineas you shall shoot at my a—." "Done," says the coachman; "I'll pepper you better than ever you was peppered by Jenny Bouncer." "Pepper your grandmother," says the other; "here's Tow-wouse will let you shoot at him for a shilling a time." "I know his honour better," cries Tow-wouse; "I never saw a surer shot at a partridge. Every man misses now and then; but if I could shoot half as well as his honour, I would desire no better livelihood than I could get by my gun." "Pox on you," said the coachman; "you demolish more game now than your head's worth. There's a bitch, Tow-wouse: by G— she never blinked*

* To *blink* is a term used to signify the dog's passing by a bird without pointing at it. — F.

a bird in her life." "I have a puppy, not a year old, shall hunt with her for a hundred," cries the other gentleman. "Done," says the coachman; "but you will be pox'd before you make the bet. If you have a mind for a bet," cries the coachman, "I will match my spotted dog with your white bitch for a hundred, play or pay." "Done," says the other; "and I'll run Baldface against Slouch with you for another." "No," cries he from the box; "but I'll venture Miss Jenny against Baldface, or Hannibal either." "Go to the devil," cries he from the coach: "I will make every bet your own way, to be sure! I will match Hannibal with Slouch for a thousand, if you dare; and I say done first."

They were now arrived, and the reader will be very contented to leave them, and repair to the kitchen, where Barnabas, the surgeon, and an exciseman were smoking their pipes over some cider-and, and where the servants who attended the two noble gentlemen we have just seen alight, were now arrived.

"Tom," cries one of the footmen, "there's Parson Adams smoking his pipe in the gallery." "Yes," says Tom, "I pulled off my hat to him, and the parson spoke to me."

"Is the gentleman a clergyman, then?" says Barnabas (for his cassock had been tied up when first he arrived). "Yes, sir," answered the footman, "and one there be but few like." "Ay," said Barnabas, "if I had known it sooner, I should have desired his company; I would always show a proper respect for the cloth; but what say you, doctor, shall we adjourn into a room, and invite him to take part of a bowl of punch?"

This proposal was immediately agreed to and executed; and Parson Adams accepting the invitation, much civility passed between the two clergymen, who both declared the great honour they had for the cloth. They had not been long together before they entered into a discourse on small tithes, which continued a full hour, without the doctor or the exciseman's having one opportunity to offer a word.

It was then proposed to begin a general conversation, and the exciseman opened on foreign affairs; but a word unluckily dropping from one of them introduced a dissertation on the hardships suffered by the inferior clergy; which, after a long duration, concluded with bringing the nine volumes of sermons on the carpet.

Barnabas greatly discouraged poor Adams; he said, "The age was so wicked, that nobody read sermons: would you think it, Mr. Adams," said he, "I once intended to print a volume of

sermons myself, and they had the approbation of two or three
bishops; but what do you think a bookseller offered me?" "Twelve
guineas perhaps," cried Adams. "Not twelve pence, I assure you,"
answered Barnabas: "nay, the dog refused me a Concordance in
exchange. — At last I offered to give him the printing them, for
the sake of dedicating them to that very gentleman who just now
drove his own coach into the inn; and, I assure you, he had the
impudence to refuse my offer; by which means I lost a good
living, that was afterwards given away in exchange for a pointer,
to one who — but I will not say anything against the cloth. So
you may guess, Mr. Adams, what you are to expect; for if sermons
would have gone down, I believe — I will not be vain: but to be
concise with you, three bishops said they were the best that ever
were writ; but indeed there are a pretty moderate number printed
already, and not all sold yet." — "Pray, sir," said Adams, "to what
do you think the numbers may amount?" "Sir," answered Barnabas, "a bookseller told me he believed five thousand volumes at
least." "Five thousand!" quoth the surgeon: "what can they be
writ upon? I remember, when I was a boy, I used to read one
Tillotson's sermons; and, I am sure, if a man practised half so
much as is in one of those sermons, he will go to heaven."
"Doctor," cried Barnabas, "you have a profane way of talking,
for which I must reprove you. A man can never have his duty too
frequently inculcated into him. And as for Tillotson, to be sure he
was a good writer, and said things very well: but comparisons
are odious; another man may write as well as he. — I believe
there are some of my sermons," — and then he applied the candle
to his pipe. — "And I believe there are some of my discourses,"
cries Adams, "which the bishops would not think totally unworthy of being printed; and I have been informed I might
procure a very large sum (indeed an immense one) on them."
"I doubt that," answered Barnabas: "however, if you desire to
make some money of them, perhaps you may sell them by adver-
tising 'the manuscript sermons of a clergyman lately deceased,
all warranted originals, and never printed.' And now I think of it,
I should be obliged to you, if there be ever a funeral one among
them, to lend it me; for I am this very day to preach a funeral
sermon, for which I have not penned a line, though I am to have
a double price." Adams answered, "He had but one, which he
feared would not serve his purpose, being sacred to the memory
of a magistrate, who had exerted himself very singularly in the
preservation of the morality of his neighbours, insomuch that he

had neither alehouse nor lewd woman in the parish where he lived." — "No," replied Barnabas, "that will not do quite so well; for the deceased upon whose virtues I am to harangue, was a little too much addicted to liquor, and publicly kept a mistress. — I believe I must take a common sermon, and trust to my memory to introduce something handsome on him." — "To your invention rather," said the doctor: "your memory will be apter to put you out; for no man living remembers anything good of him."

With such kind of spiritual discourse, they emptied the bowl of punch, paid their reckoning, and separated: Adams and the doctor went up to Joseph, Parson Barnabas departed to celebrate the aforesaid deceased, and the exciseman descended into the cellar to gauge the vessels.

Joseph was now ready to sit down to a loin of mutton, and waited for Mr. Adams, when he and the doctor came in. The doctor, having felt his pulse and examined his wounds, declared him much better, which he imputed to *that sanative soporiferous draught,* a medicine "whose virtues," he said, "were never to be sufficiently extolled." And great indeed they must be, if Joseph was so much indebted to them as the doctor imagined; since nothing more than those effluvia which escaped the cork could have contributed to his recovery; for the medicine had stood untouched in the window ever since its arrival.

Joseph passed that day, and the three following, with his friend Adams, in which nothing so remarkable happened as the swift progress of his recovery. As he had an excellent habit of body, his wounds were now almost healed; and his bruises gave him so little uneasiness, that he pressed Mr. Adams to let him depart, told him he should never be able to return sufficient thanks for all his favours, but begged that he might no longer delay his journey to London.

Adams, notwithstanding the ignorance, as he conceived it, of Mr. Tow-wouse, and the envy (for such he thought it) of Mr. Barnabas, had great expectations from his sermons: seeing therefore Joseph in so good a way, he told him he would agree to his setting out the next morning in the stage-coach, that he believed he should have sufficient, after the reckoning paid, to procure him one day's conveyance in it, and afterwards he would be able to get on on foot, or might be favoured with a lift in some neighbour's waggon, especially as there was then to be a fair in the town whither the coach would carry him, to which numbers from

his parish resorted. — And as to himself, he agreed to proceed to
the great city.

They were now walking in the inn-yard, when a fat, fair, short
person rode in, and, alighting from his horse, went directly up to
Barnabas, who was smoking his pipe on a bench. The parson
and the stranger shook one another very lovingly by the hand,
and went into a room together.

The evening now coming on, Joseph retired to his chamber,
whither the good Adams accompanied him, and took this opportunity to expatiate on the great mercies God had lately shown
him, of which he ought not only to have the deepest inward sense,
but likewise to express outward thankfulness for them. They
therefore fell both on their knees, and spent a considerable time
in prayer and thanksgiving.

They had just finished when Betty came in and told Mr. Adams
Mr. Barnabas desired to speak to him on some business of consequence below-stairs. Joseph desired, if it was likely to detain him
long, he would let him know it, that he might go to bed, which
Adams promised, and in that case, they wished one another
good-night.

CHAPTER XVII.

A pleasant discourse between the two parsons and the bookseller,
which was broke off by an unlucky accident happening in
the inn, which produced a dialogue between Mrs. Tow-wouse
and her maid of no gentle kind.

As soon as Adams came into the room, Mr. Barnabas introduced
him to the stranger, who was, he told him, a bookseller, and would
be as likely to deal with him for his sermons as any man whatever. Adams, saluting the stranger, answered Barnabas that he
was very much obliged to him; that nothing could be more
convenient, for he had no other business to the great city, and
was heartily desirous of returning with the young man, who was
just recovered of his misfortune. He then snapt his fingers (as was
usual with him), and took two or three turns about the room in
an ecstasy. And to induce the bookseller to be as expeditious as
possible, as likewise to offer him a better price for his commodity,
he assured him their meeting was extremely lucky to himself; for

that he had the most pressing occasion for money at that time, his own being almost spent, and having a friend then in the same inn who was just recovered from some wounds he had received from robbers, and was in a most indigent condition. "So that nothing," says he, "could be so opportune, for the supplying both our necessities, as my making an immediate bargain with you."

As soon as he had seated himself, the stranger began in these words: "Sir, I do not care absolutely to deny engaging in what my friend Mr. Barnabas recommends; but sermons are mere drugs. The trade is so vastly stocked with them, that really, unless they come out with the name of Whitefield or Wesley, or some other such great man, as a bishop, or those sort of people, I don't care to touch; unless now it was a sermon preached on the '30th of January,' or we could say in the title-page, published at the 'earnest request' of the congregation, or the inhabitants; but, truly, for a dry piece of sermons, I had rather be excused; especially as my hands are so full at present. However, sir, as Mr. Barnabas mentioned them to me, I will, if you please, take the manuscript with me to town, and send you my opinion of it in a very short time."

"O!" said Adams, "if you desire it, I will read two or three discourses as a specimen." This Barnabas, who loved sermons no better than a grocer doth figs, immediately objected to, and advised Adams to let the bookseller have his sermons: telling him, if he gave him a direction, he might be certain of a speedy answer; adding, he need not scruple trusting them in his possession. "No," said the bookseller, "if it was a play that had been acted twenty nights together, I believe it would be safe."

Adams did not at all relish the last expression; he said he was sorry to hear sermons compared to plays. "Not by me, I assure you," cried the bookseller, "though I don't know whether the licensing act may not shortly bring them to the same footing; but I have formerly known a hundred guineas given for a play —." "More shame for those who gave it," cried Barnabas. "Why so?" said the bookseller, "for they got hundreds by it." "But is there no difference between conveying good or ill instructions to mankind?" said Adams; "would not an honest mind rather lose money by the one than gain it by the other?" "If you can find any such, I will not be their hindrance," answered the bookseller; "but I think those persons who get by preaching sermons are the properest to lose by printing them: for my part, the copy that sells best will be always the best copy in my opinion; I am no enemy to sermons but because they don't sell: for I would as soon print one of Whitefield's as any farce whatever."

"Whoever prints such heterodox stuff ought to be hanged," says Barnabas. "Sir," said he, turning to Adams, "this fellow's writings (I know not whether you have seen them) are levelled at the clergy. He would reduce us to the example of the primitive ages, forsooth! and would insinuate to the people that a clergyman ought to be always preaching and praying. He pretends to understand the Scripture literally, and would make mankind believe that the poverty and low estate which was recommended to the Church in its infancy, and was only temporary doctrine adapted to her under persecution, was to be preserved in her flourishing and established state. Sir, the principles of Toland, Woolston, and all the free-thinkers, are not calculated to do half the mischief, as those professed by this fellow and his followers."

"Sir," answered Adams, "if Mr. Whitefield had carried his doctrine no farther than you mention, I should have remained, as I once was, his well-wisher. I am, myself, as great an enemy to the luxury and splendour of the clergy as he can be. I do not, more than he, by the flourishing estate of the Church, understand the palaces, equipages, dress, furniture, rich dainties, and vast fortunes of her ministers. Surely those things, which savour so strongly of this world, become not the servants of one who professed his kingdom was not of it: but when he began to call nonsense and enthusiasm to his aid, and set up the detestable doctrine of faith against good works, I was his friend no longer; for surely, that doctrine was coined in hell, and one would think none but the devil himself could have the confidence to preach it. For can anything be more derogatory to the honour of God than for men to imagine that the all-wise Being will hereafter say to the good and virtuous, 'Notwithstanding the purity of thy life, notwithstanding that constant rule of virtue and goodness in which you walked upon earth, still, as thou didst not believe everything in the true orthodox manner, thy want of faith shall condemn thee'? Or, on the other side, can any doctrine have a more pernicious influence on society, than a persuasion that it will be a good plea for the villain at the last day: 'Lord, it is true, I never obeyed one of thy commandments, yet punish me not, for I believe them all'?" "I suppose, sir," said the bookseller, "your sermons are of a different kind." "Ay, sir," said Adams, "the contrary, I thank Heaven, is inculcated in almost every page, or

I should belie my own opinion, which hath always been, that a virtuous and good Turk, or heathen, are more acceptable in the sight of their Creator than a vicious and wicked Christian, though his faith was as perfectly orthodox as St. Paul's himself." "I wish you success," says the bookseller, "but must beg to be excused, as my hands are so very full at present; and indeed, I am afraid you will find a backwardness in the trade to engage in a book which the clergy would be certain to cry down." "God forbid," says Adams, "any books should be propagated which the clergy would cry down; but if you mean by the clergy, some few designing factious men, who have it at heart to establish some favourite schemes at the price of the liberty of mankind, and the very essence of religion, it is not in the power of such persons to decry ny book they please; witness that excellent book called, *A Plain Account of the Nature and End of the Sacrament;* a book written (if I may venture on the expression) with the pen of an angel, and calculated to restore the true use of Christianity, and of that sacred institution: for what could tend more to the noble purposes of religion than frequent cheerful meetings among the members of a society, in which they should, in the presence of one another, and in the service of the Supreme Being, make promises of being good, friendly, and benevolent to each other? Now, this excellent book was attacked by a party, but unsuccessfully." At these words Barnabas fell a-ringing with all the violence imaginable; upon which a servant attending, he bid him "bring a bill immediately: for that he was in company, for aught he knew, with the devil himself; and he expected to hear the Alcoran, the *Leviathan,* or Woolston commended, if he stayed a few minutes longer." Adams desired, "as he was so much moved at his mentioning a book, which he did without apprehending any possibility of offence, that he would be so kind to propose any objections he had to it, which he would endeavour to answer." "I propose objections!" said Barnabas, "I never read a syllable in any such wicked book; I never saw it in my life, I assure you." — Adams was going to answer, when a most hideous uproar began in the inn. Mrs. Tow-wouse, Mr. Tow-wouse, and Betty, all lifting up their voices together; but Mrs. Tow-wouse's voice, like a bass viol in a concert, was clearly and distinctly distinguished among the rest, and was heard to articulate the following sounds: — "O you damn'd villain! is this the return to all the care I have taken of your family? This the reward of my virtue? Is this the manner in which you behave to one who brought you a fortune, and preferred you to so many matches, all your betters? To abuse my bed, my own bed, with my own servant! but I'll maul the slut, I'll tear her nasty eyes out! Was ever such a pitiful dog, to take up with such a mean trollop? If she had been a gentlewoman like myself, it had been some excuse; but a beggarly, saucy, dirty servant-maid. — Get you out of my house, you whore." To which she added another name, which we do not care to stain our paper with. It was a monosyllable beginning with a b—, and indeed was the same as if she had pronounced the words, *she-dog*. Which term we shall, to avoid offence, use on this occasion, though indeed both the mistress and maid uttered the above-mentioned b—, a word extremely disgustful to females of the lower sort. Betty had borne all hitherto with patience, and had uttered only lamentations; but the last appellation stung her to the quick: "I am a woman as well as yourself," she roared out, "and no she-dog; and if I have been a little naughty, I am not the first; if I have been no better than I should be," cries she, sobbing, "that's no reason you should call me out of my name; my be-betters are wo-worse than me." "Huzzy, huzzy," says Mrs. Tow-wouse, "have you the impudence to answer me? Did I not catch you, you saucy — " and then again repeated the terrible word so odious to female ears. "I can't bear that name," answered Betty; "if I have been wicked, I am to answer for it myself in the other world; but I have done nothing that's unnatural; and I will go out of your house this moment, for I will never be called *she-dog* by any mistress in England." Mrs. Tow-wouse then armed herself with the spit, but was prevented from executing any dreadful purpose by Mr. Adams, who confined her arms with the strength of a wrist which Hercules would not have been ashamed of. Mr. Tow-wouse, being caught, as our lawyers express it, with the manner, and having no defence to make, very prudently withdrew himself; and Betty committed herself to the protection of the hostler, who, though she could not conceive him pleased with what had happened, was in her opinion rather a gentler beast than her mistress.

Mrs. Tow-wouse, at the intercession of Mr. Adams, and finding the enemy vanished, began to compose herself, and at length recovered the usual serenity of her temper, in which we will leave her, to open to the reader the steps which led to a catastrophe, common enough, and comical enough too perhaps, in modern history, yet often fatal to the repose and well-being of families, and the subject of many tragedies, both in life and on the stage.

CHAPTER XVIII.

The history of Betty the chambermaid, and an account of what occasioned the violent scene in the preceding chapter.

BETTY, who was the occasion of all this hurry, had some good qualities. She had good-nature, generosity, and compassion, but unfortunately, her constitution was composed of those warm ingredients which, though the purity of courts or nunneries might have happily controlled them, were by no means able to endure the ticklish situation of a chambermaid at an inn, who is daily liable to the solicitations of lovers of all complexions; to the dangerous addresses of fine gentlemen of the army, who sometimes are obliged to reside with them a whole year together; and, above all, are exposed to the caresses of footmen, stage-coachmen, and drawers; all of whom employ the whole artillery of kissing, flattering, bribing, and every other weapon which is to be found in the whole armoury of love, against them.

Betty, who was but one-and-twenty, had now lived three years in this dangerous situation, during which she had escaped pretty well. An ensign of foot was the first person who made an impression on her heart; he did indeed raise a flame in her which required the care of a surgeon to cool.

While she burnt for him, several others burnt for her. Officers of the army, young gentlemen travelling the western circuit, inoffensive squires, and some of graver character, were set afire by her charms!

At length, having perfectly recovered the effects of her first unhappy passion, she seemed to have vowed a state of perpetual chastity. She was long deaf to all the sufferings of her lovers, till one day at a neighbouring fair, the rhetoric of John the hostler, with a new straw hat and a pint of wine, made a second conquest over her.

She did not, however, feel any of those flames on this occasion which had been the consequence of her former amour; nor, indeed, those other ill effects which prudent young women very justly apprehend from too absolute an indulgence to the pressing endearments of their lovers. This latter, perhaps, was a little owing to her not being entirely constant to John, with whom she permitted Tom Whipwell the stage-coachman, and now and then a handsome young traveller, to share her favours.

Mr. Tow-wouse had for some time cast the languishing eyes of affection on this young maiden. He had laid hold on every opportunity of saying tender things to her, squeezing her by the hand, and sometimes kissing her lips; for, as the violence of his passion had considerably abated to Mrs. Tow-wouse, so, like water, which is stopt from its usual current in one place, it naturally sought a vent in another. Mrs. Tow-wouse is thought to have perceived this abatement, and probably it added very little to the natural sweetness of her temper; for though she was as true to her husband as the dial to the sun, she was rather more desirous of being shone on, as being more capable of feeling his warmth.

Ever since Joseph's arrival, Betty had conceived an extraordinary liking to him, which discovered itself more and more as he grew better and better; till that fatal evening, when, as she was warming his bed, her passion grew to such a height, and so perfectly mastered both her modesty and her reason, that, after many fruitless hints and sly insinuations, she at last threw down the warming-pan, and, embracing him with great eagerness, swore he was the handsomest creature she had ever seen.

Joseph, in great confusion, leapt from her, and told her he was sorry to see a young woman cast off all regard to modesty; but she had gone too far to recede, and grew so very indecent, that Joseph was obliged, contrary to his inclination, to use some violence to her; and, taking her in his arms, he shut her out of the room, and locked the door.

How ought man to rejoice that his chastity is always in his own power; that, if he hath sufficient strength of mind, he hath always a competent strength of body to defend himself, and cannot, like a poor weak woman, be ravished against his will!

Betty was in the most violent agitation at this disappointment. Rage and Lust pulled her heart, as with two strings, two different ways; one moment she thought of stabbing Joseph; the next, of taking him in her arms, and devouring him with kisses; but the latter passion was far more prevalent. Then she thought of revenging his refusal on herself; but, whilst she was engaged in this meditation, happily Death presented himself to her in so many shapes, of drowning, hanging, poisoning, &c., that her distracted mind could resolve on none. In this perturbation of spirit, it accidentally occurred to her memory that her master's bed was not made; she therefore went directly to his room, where he happened at that time to be engaged at his bureau. As soon

as she saw him, she attempted to retire; but he called her back,
and, taking her by the hand, squeezed her so tenderly, at the
same time whispered so many soft things into her ears, and then
pressed her so closely with his kisses, that the vanquished fair
one, whose passions were already raised, and which were not so
whimsically capricious that one man only could lay them, though,
perhaps, she would have rather preferred that one — the vanquished fair one quietly submitted, I say, to her master's will,
who had just attained the accomplishment of his bliss when Mrs.
Tow-wouse unexpectedly entered the room, and caused all that
confusion which we have before seen, and which it is not necessary at present to take any farther notice of; since, without the
assistance of a single hint from us, every reader of any speculation, or experience, though not married himself, may easily
conjecture that it concluded with the discharge of Betty, the submission of Mr. Tow-wouse, with some things to be performed on
his side by way of gratitude for his wife's goodness in being
reconciled to him, with many hearty promises never to offend any
more in the like manner; and, lastly, his quietly and contentedly
bearing to be reminded of his transgressions, as a kind of penance,
once or twice a day during the residue of his life.

BOOK II.

CHAPTER I.

Of divisions in authors.

THERE are certain mysteries or secrets in all trades, from the highest to the lowest, from that of *prime-ministering* to this of *authoring*, which are seldom discovered, unless to members of the same calling. Among those used by us gentlemen of the latter occupation, I take this of dividing our works into books and chapters to be none of the least considerable. Now, for want of being truly acquainted with this secret, common readers imagine that by this art of dividing we mean only to swell our works to a much larger bulk than they would otherwise be extended to. These several places therefore in our paper, which are filled with our books and chapters, are understood as so much buckram, stays, and stay-tape in a tailor's bill, serving only to make up the sum total, commonly found at the bottom of our first page and of his last.

But in reality the case is otherwise, and in this, as well as all other instances, we consult the advantage of our reader, not our own; and indeed, many notable uses arise to him from this method: for, first, those little spaces between our chapters may be looked upon as an inn or resting-place, where he may stop and take a glass, or any other refreshment, as it pleases him. Nay, our fine readers will, perhaps, be scarce able to travel farther than through one of them in a day. As to those vacant pages which are placed between our books, they are to be regarded as those stages where, in long journeys, the traveller stays some time to repose himself, and consider of what he hath seen in the parts he hath already passed through; a consideration which I take the liberty to recommend a little to the reader; for, however swift his capacity may be, I would not advise him to travel through these pages too fast; for if he doth, he may probably miss the seeing some curious productions of nature, which will be observed by the slower and more accurate reader. A volume without any such places of rest resembles the opening of wilds or seas, which tires the eye and fatigues the spirit when entered upon.

Secondly, what are the contents prefixed to every chapter but so many inscriptions over the gates of inns (to continue the same metaphor), informing the reader what entertainment he is to expect, which if he likes not, he may travel on to the next; for, in biography, as we are not tied down to an exact concatenation equally with other historians, so a chapter or two (for instance, this I am now writing) may be often passed over without any injury to the whole. And in these inscriptions I have been as faithful as possible, not imitating the celebrated Montaigne, who promises you one thing and gives you another; nor some title-page authors, who promise a great deal and produce nothing at all.

There are, besides these more obvious benefits, several others which our readers enjoy from this art of dividing; though perhaps most of them too mysterious to be presently understood by any who are not initiated into the science of *authoring*. To mention, therefore, but one which is most obvious, it prevents spoiling the beauty of a book by turning down its leaves, a method otherwise necessary to those readers who (though they read with great improvement and advantage) are apt, when they return to their study after half-an-hour's absence, to forget where they left off.

These divisions have the sanction of great antiquity. Homer not only divided his great work into twenty-four books (in compliment perhaps to the twenty-four letters to which he had very particular obligations), but, according to the opinion of some very sagacious critics, hawked them all separately, delivering only one book at a time (probably by subscription). He was the first inventor of the art which hath so long lain dormant, of publishing by numbers; an art now brought to such perfection, that even dictionaries are divided and exhibited piecemeal to the public; nay, one bookseller hath ("to encourage learning and ease the public") contrived to give them a dictionary in this divided manner, for only fifteen shillings more than it would have cost entire.

Virgil hath given us his poem in twelve books, an argument of his modesty; for by that, doubtless, he would insinuate that he pretends to no more than half the merit of the Greek; for the same reason, our Milton went originally no farther than ten; till, being puffed up by the praise of his friends, he put himself on the same footing with the Roman poet.

I shall not, however, enter so deep into this matter as some very learned critics have done: who have with infinite labour and acute discernment discovered what books are proper for embellishment, and what require simplicity only, particularly with regard to similes, which I think are now generally agreed to become any book but the first.

I will dismiss this chapter with the following observation: that it becomes an author generally to divide a book, as it does a butcher to joint his meat, for such assistance is of great help to both the reader and the carver. And now, having indulged myself a little, I will endeavour to indulge the curiosity of my reader, who is no doubt impatient to know what he will find in the subsequent chapters of this book.

CHAPTER II.

A surprising instance of Mr. Adams's short memory, with the unfortunate consequences which it brought on Joseph.

MR. ADAMS and Joseph were now ready to depart different ways, when an accident determined the former to return with his friend, which Tow-wouse, Barnabas, and the bookseller had not been able to do. This accident was, that those sermons, which the parson was travelling to London to publish, were, O my good reader! left behind; what he had mistaken for them in the saddlebags being no other than three shirts, a pair of shoes, and some other necessaries, which Mrs. Adams, who thought her husband would want shirts more than sermons on his journey, had carefully provided him.

This discovery was now luckily owing to the presence of Joseph at the opening the saddlebags; who, having heard his friend say he carried with him nine volumes of sermons, and not being of that sect of philosophers who can reduce all the matter of the world into a nutshell, seeing there was no room for them in the bags, where the parson had said they were deposited, had the curiosity to cry out, "Bless me, sir, where are your sermons?" The parson answered, "There, there, child; there they are, under my shirts." Now it happened that he had taken forth his last shirt, and the vehicle remained visibly empty. "Sure, sir," says Joseph, "there is nothing in the bags." Upon which Adams, starting, and testifying some surprise, cried, "Hey! fie, fie upon it! they are not here sure enough. Ay, they are certainly left behind."

Joseph was greatly concerned at the uneasiness which he apprehended his friend must feel from this disappointment; he begged him to pursue his journey, and promised he would himself return with the books to him with the utmost expedition. "No, thank you, child," answered Adams; "it shall not be so. What would it avail me, to tarry in the great city, unless I had my discourses with me, which are, *ut ita dicam,* the sole cause, the *aitia monotate* of my peregrination? No, child, as this accident hath happened, I am resolved to return back to my cure, together with you; which indeed my inclination sufficiently leads me to. This disappointment may perhaps be intended for my good." He concluded with a verse out of Theocritus, which signifies no more than, "that sometimes it rains, and sometimes the sun shines."

Joseph bowed with obedience and thankfulness for the inclination which the parson expressed of returning with him; and now the bill was called for, which, on examination, amounted within a shilling to the sum Mr. Adams had in his pocket. Perhaps the reader may wonder how he was able to produce a sufficient sum for so many days: that he may not be surprised, therefore, it cannot be unnecessary to acquaint him that he had borrowed a guinea of a servant belonging to the coach and six, who had been formerly one of his parishioners, and whose master, the owner of the coach, then lived within three miles of him; for so good was the credit of Mr. Adams, that even Mr. Peter, the Lady Booby's steward, would have lent him a guinea with very little security.

Mr. Adams discharged the bill, and they were both setting out, having agreed "to ride and tie": a method of travelling much used by persons who have but one horse between them, and is thus performed. The two travellers set out together, one on horseback, the other on foot: now, as it generally happens that he on horseback outgoes him on foot, the custom is, that, when he arrives at the distance agreed on, he is to dismount, tie the horse to some gate, tree, post, or other thing, and then proceed on foot; when the other comes up to the horse, he unties him, mounts, and gallops on, till, having passed by his fellow-traveller, he likewise arrives at the place of tying. And this is that method of travelling so much in use among our prudent ancestors, who knew that horses had mouths as well as legs, and that they could not use the latter without being at the expense of suffering the beasts themselves to use the former. This was the method in use in those days: when, instead of a coach and six, a member of parliament's lady used to mount a pillion behind her husband; and a grave serjeant at law condescended to amble to Westminster on an easy pad, with his clerk kicking his heels behind him.

Adams was now gone some minutes, having insisted on Joseph's beginning the journey on horseback, and Joseph had his foot in the stirrup, when the hostler presented him a bill for the horse's board during his residence at the inn. Joseph said Mr. Adams had paid all; but this matter, being referred to Mr. Tow-wouse, was by him decided in favour of the hostler, and indeed with truth and justice; for this was a fresh instance of that shortness of memory which did not arise from want of parts, but that continual hurry in which Parson Adams was always involved.

Joseph was now reduced to a dilemma which extremely puzzled him. The sum due for horse-meat was twelve shillings (for Adams, who had borrowed the beast of his clerk, had ordered him to be fed as well as they could feed him), and the cash in his pocket amounted to sixpence (for Adams had divided the last shilling with him). Now, though there have been some ingenious persons who have contrived to pay twelve shillings with sixpence, Joseph was not one of them. He had never contracted a debt in his life, and was consequently the less ready at an expedient to extricate himself. Tow-wouse was willing to give him credit till next time, to which Mrs. Tow-wouse would probably have consented (for such was Joseph's beauty, that it had made some impression even on that piece of flint which that good woman wore in her bosom by way of heart). Joseph would have found, therefore, very likely, the passage free, had he not, when he honestly discovered the nakedness of his pockets, pulled out that little piece of gold which we have mentioned before. This caused Mrs. Tow-wouse's eyes to water; she told Joseph she did not conceive a man could want money whilst he had gold in his pocket. Joseph answered, he had such a value for that little piece of gold, that he would not part with it for a hundred times the riches which the greatest esquire in the county was worth. "A pretty way, indeed," said Mrs. Tow-wouse, "to run in debt, and then refuse to part with your money because you have a value for it! I never knew any piece of gold of more value than as many shillings as it would change for." "Not to preserve my life from starving, nor to redeem it from a robber, would I part with this dear piece!" answered Joseph. "What," says Mrs. Tow-wouse, "I suppose it was given you by some vile trollop, some miss or other; if it had been the present of a virtuous woman, you would not have had such a value for it. My husband is a fool if he parts with the horse without being paid for him." "No, no, I can't part with the horse, indeed, till I have the money," cried Tow-wouse. A resolution highly commended by a lawyer then in the yard, who declared Mr. Tow-wouse might justify the detainer.

As we cannot therefore at present get Mr. Joseph out of the inn, we shall leave him in it, and carry our reader on after Parson Adams, who, his mind being perfectly at ease, fell into a contemplation on a passage in Æschylus, which entertained him for three miles together, without suffering him once to reflect on his fellow-traveller.

At length, having spun out his thread, and being now at the summit of a hill, he cast his eyes backwards, and wondered that he could not see any sign of Joseph. As he left him ready to mount the horse, he could not apprehend any mischief had happened, neither could he suspect that he missed his way, it being so broad and plain; the only reason which presented itself to him was, that he had met with an acquaintance who had prevailed with him to delay some time in discourse.

He therefore resolved to proceed slowly forwards, not doubting but that he should be shortly overtaken; and soon came to a large water, which, filling the whole road, he saw no method of passing unless by wading through, which he accordingly did up to his middle; but was no sooner got to the other side than he perceived, if he had looked over the hedge, he would have found a footpath capable of conducting him without wetting his shoes.

His surprise at Joseph's not coming up grew now very troublesome: he began to fear he knew not what; and as he determined to move no farther, and, if he did not shortly overtake him, to return back, he wished to find a house of public entertainment where he might dry his clothes and refresh himself with a pint; but, seeing no such (for no other reason than because he did not cast his eyes a hundred yards forwards), he sat himself down on a stile, and pulled out his Æschylus.

A fellow passing presently by, Adams asked him if he could direct him to an alehouse. The fellow, who had just left it, and perceived the house and sign to be within sight, thinking he had jeered him, and being of a morose temper, bade him "follow his nose and be d—n'd." Adams told him he was a "saucy jackanapes"; upon which the fellow turned about angrily; but perceiving Adams clench his fist, he thought proper to go on without taking any farther notice.

A horseman, following immediately after, and being asked the same question, answered, "Friend, there is one within a stone's throw; I believe you may see it before you." Adams, lifting up his eyes, cried, "I protest, and so there is"; and, thanking his informer, proceeded directly to it.

CHAPTER III.

The opinion of two lawyers concerning the same gentleman, with Mr. Adams's inquiry into the religion of his host.

HE had just entered the house, had called for his pint, and seated himself, when two horsemen came to the door, and, fastening their horses to the rails, alighted. They said there was a violent shower of rain coming on, which they intended to weather there, and went into a little room by themselves, not perceiving Mr. Adams.

One of these immediately asked the other, If he had seen a more comical adventure a great while? Upon which the other said, "He doubted whether, by law, the landlord could justify detaining the horse for his corn and hay." But the former answered, "Undoubtedly he can; it is an adjudged case, and I have known it tried."

Adams, who, though he was, as the reader may suspect, a little inclined to forgetfulness, never wanted more than a hint to remind him, overhearing their discourse, immediately suggested to himself that this was his own horse, and that he had forgot to pay for him, which, upon inquiry, he was certified of by the gentlemen; who added, that the horse was likely to have more rest than food, unless he was paid for.

The poor parson resolved to return presently to the inn, though he knew no more than Joseph how to procure his horse his liberty; he was, however, prevailed on to stay under covert, till the shower, which was now very violent, was over.

The three travellers then sat down together over a mug of good beer; when Adams, who had observed a gentleman's house as he passed along the road, inquired to whom it belonged; one of the horsemen had no sooner mentioned the owner's name, than the other began to revile him in the most opprobrious terms. The English language scarce affords a single reproachful word which he did not vent on this occasion. He charged him likewise with many particular facts. He said, — "He no more regarded a field of wheat when he was hunting, than he did the highway; that he had injured several poor farmers by trampling their corn under his horse's heels; and if any of them begged him with the utmost submission to refrain, his horsewhip was always ready to do them justice." He said, "That he was the greatest tyrant to the neighbours in every other instance, and would not suffer a farmer to keep a gun, though he might justify it by law; and in his own family so cruel a master, that he never kept a servant a twelve-month. In his capacity as a justice," continued he, "he behaves so partially, that he commits or acquits just as he is in the humour, without any regard to truth or evidence; the devil may carry anyone before him for me; I would rather be tried before some judges, than be a prosecutor before him: if I had an estate in the neighbourhood, I would sell it for half the value rather than live near him."

Adams shook his head and said, "He was sorry such men were suffered to proceed with impunity, and that riches could set any man above law." The reviler, a little after, retiring into the yard, the gentleman who had first mentioned his name to Adams began to assure him, "that his companion was a prejudiced person. It is true," says he, "perhaps, that he may have sometimes pursued his game over a field of corn, but he hath always made the party ample satisfaction; that so far from tyrannizing over his neighbours, or taking away their guns, he himself knew several farmers not qualified, who not only kept guns, but killed game with them. That he was the best of masters to his servants, and several of them had grown old in his service. That he was the best justice of peace in the kingdom, and, to his certain knowledge, had decided many difficult points, which were referred to him, with the greatest equity and the highest wisdom. And he verily believed, several persons would give a year's purchase more for an estate near him, than under the wings of any other great man." He had just finished his encomium when his companion returned and acquainted him the storm was over. Upon which they presently mounted their horses and departed.

Adams, who was in the utmost anxiety at those different characters of the same person, asked his host if he knew the gentleman; for he began to imagine they had by mistake been speaking of two several gentlemen. "No, no, master!" answered the host, a shrewd cunning fellow, "I know the gentleman very well of whom they have been speaking, as I do the gentlemen who spoke of him. As for riding over other men's corn, to my knowledge he hath not been on horseback these two years. I never heard he did any injury of that kind; and as to making reparation, he is not so free of his money as that comes to neither. Nor did I ever hear of his taking away any man's gun; nay, I know several who have guns in their houses; but as for killing game with them, no man is stricter; and I believe he would ruin any who did. You heard one of the gentlemen say he was the worst master in the world, and the other that he is the best; but for my own part, I know all his servants, and never heard from any of them that he was either one or the other. — " "Ay! ay!" says Adams; "and how doth he behave as a justice, pray?" "Faith, friend," answered the host, "I question whether he is in the commission: the only cause I have heard he hath decided a great while, was one between those very two persons who just went out of this house; and I am sure he determined that justly, for I heard the whole matter." "Which did he decide it in favour of?" quoth Adams. "I think I need not answer that question," cried the host, "after the different characters you have heard of him. It is not my business to contradict gentlemen while they are drinking in my house; but I knew neither of them spoke a syllable of truth." "God forbid!" said Adams, "that men should arrive at such a pitch of wickedness to belie the character of their neighbour from a little private affection, or, what is infinitely worse, a private spite. I rather believe we have mistaken them, and they mean two other persons; for there are many houses on the road." "Why, prithee, friend," cries the host, "dost thou pretend never to have told a lie in thy life?" "Never a malicious one, I am certain," answered Adams; "nor with a design to injure the reputation of any man living." "Pugh, malicious! no, no," replied the host; "not malicious with a design to hang a man, or bring him into trouble; but surely, out of love to one's self, one must speak better of a friend than an enemy." "Out of love to yourself, you should confine yourself to truth," says Adams, "for by doing otherwise, you injure the noblest part of yourself, your immortal soul. I can hardly believe any man such an idiot to risk the loss of that by any trifling gain, and the greatest gain in this world is but dirt in comparison of what shall be revealed hereafter." Upon which the host, taking up the cup with a smile, drank a health to hereafter; adding, "He was for something present." "Why," says Adams very gravely, "do not you believe another world?" To which the host answered, "Yes; he was no atheist." "And you believe you have an immortal soul?" cries Adams. He answered, "God forbid he should not." "And heaven and hell?" said the parson. The host then bid him "not to profane: for those were things not to be mentioned nor thought of but in church." Adams asked him, "Why he went to church, if what he learned there had no influence on his conduct in life?" "I go to church," answered the host, "to say my prayers and behave godly." "And dost not thou," cried Adams, "believe what thou hearest at church?" "Most part of it, master," returned the host. "And dost not thou then tremble," cries Adams, "at the thought of eternal punishment?" "As for that, master," said he, "I never once thought about it; but what signifies talking about matters so far off? The mug is out, shall I draw another?"

Whilst he was gone for that purpose, a stage-coach drove up to the door. The coachman, coming into the house, was asked by the mistress what passengers he had in his coach? "A parcel of squinny-gut b—s," says he; "I have a good mind to overturn them; you won't prevail upon them to drink anything, I assure you." Adams asked him, "If he had not seen a young man on horseback on the road" (describing Joseph). "Ay," said the coachman, "a gentlewoman in my coach that is his acquaintance redeemed him and his horse; he would have been here before this time, had not the storm driven him to shelter." "God bless her!" said Adams, in a rapture; nor could he delay walking out to satisfy himself who this charitable woman was; but what was his surprise when he saw his old acquaintance, Madam Slipslop? Hers indeed was not so great, because she had been informed by Joseph that he was on the road. Very civil were the salutations on both sides; and Mrs. Slipslop rebuked the hostess for denying the gentleman to be there when she asked for him; but indeed the poor woman had not erred designedly: for Mrs. Slipslop asked for a clergyman, and she had unhappily mistaken Adams for a person travelling to a neighbouring fair with the thimble and button, or some other such operation: for he marched in a swinging great, but short, white coat with black buttons, a short wig, and a hat which, so far from having a black hatband, had nothing black about it.

Joseph was now come up, and Mrs. Slipslop would have had him quit his horse to the parson, and come himself into the coach;

but he absolutely refused, saying, he thanked Heaven he was well enough recovered to be very able to ride; and added, he hoped he knew his duty better than to ride in a coach while Mr. Adams was on horseback.

Mrs. Slipslop would have persisted longer, had not a lady in the coach put a short end to the dispute, by refusing to suffer a fellow in a livery to ride in the same coach with herself; so it was at length agreed that Adams should fill the vacant place in the coach, and Joseph should proceed on horseback.

They had not proceeded far before Mrs. Slipslop, addressing herself to the parson, spoke thus: "There hath been a strange alteration in our family, Mr. Adams, since Sir Thomas's death." "A strange alteration indeed!" says Adams, "as I gather from some hints which have dropped from Joseph." "Ay," says she, "I could never have believed it, but the longer one lives in the world, the more one sees. So Joseph hath given you hints." — "But of what nature will always remain a perfect secret with me," cries the parson: "he forced me to promise before he would communicate anything. I am indeed concerned to find her ladyship behave in so unbecoming a manner. I always thought her in the main a good lady, and should never have suspected her of thoughts so unworthy a Christian, and with a young lad her own servant." "These things are no secrets to me, I assure you," cries Slipslop; "and I believe they will be none anywhere shortly: for ever since the boy's departure, she hath behaved more like a mad woman than anything else." "Truly, I am heartily concerned," says Adams, "for she was a good sort of a lady; indeed, I have often wished she had attended a little more constantly at the service, but she hath done a great deal of good in the parish." "O Mr. Adams!" says Slipslop, "people that don't see all, often know nothing. Many things have been given away in our family, I do assure you, without her knowledge. I have heard you say in the pulpit we ought not to brag; but indeed I can't avoid saying, if she had kept the keys herself, the poor would have wanted many a cordial which I have let them have. As for my late master, he was as worthy a man as ever lived, and would have done infinite good if he had not been controlled; but he loved a quiet life, Heavens rest his soul! I am confident he is there, and enjoys a quiet life, which some folks would not allow him here." Adams answered, "He had never heard this before, and was mistaken if she herself" (for he remembered she used to commend her mistress and blame her master) "had not formerly

been of another opinion." "I don't know," replied she, "what I
might once think; but now I am *confidous* matters are as I tell
you; the world will shortly see who hath been deceived; for my
part I say nothing, but that it is *wondersome* how some people
can carry all things with a grave face."

Thus Mr. Adams and she discoursed, till they came opposite
to a great house which stood at some distance from the road;
a lady in the coach spying it, cried, "Yonder lives the unfortunate Leonora, if one can justly call a woman unfortunate
whom we must own at the same time guilty and the author of
her own calamity." This was abundantly sufficient to awaken
the curiosity of Mr. Adams, as indeed it did that of the whole
company, who jointly solicited the lady to acquaint them with
Leonora's history, since it seemed, by what she had said, to
contain something remarkable.

The lady, who was perfectly well-bred, did not require many
entreaties, and having only wished their entertainment might
make amends for the company's attention, she began in the following manner.

CHAPTER IV.

The History of Leonora, or the Unfortunate Jilt.

LEONORA was the daughter of a gentleman of fortune; she was
tall and well-shaped, with a sprightliness in her countenance
which often attracts beyond more regular features joined with
an insipid air; nor is this kind of beauty less apt to deceive than
allure; the good humour which it indicates being often mistaken
for good nature, and the vivacity for true understanding.

Leonora, who was now at the age of eighteen, lived with an
aunt of hers in a town in the north of England. She was an
extreme lover of gaiety, and very rarely missed a ball, or any
other public assembly; where she had frequent opportunities
of satisfying a greedy appetite of vanity, with the preference
which was given her by the men to almost every other woman
present.

Among many young fellows who were particular in their
gallantries towards her, Horatio soon distinguished himself in
her eyes beyond all his competitors; she danced with more than

ordinary gaiety when he happened to be her partner; neither the fairness of the evening, nor the music of the nightingale, could lengthen her walk like his company. She affected no longer to understand the civilities of others; whilst she inclined so attentive an ear to every compliment of Horatio, that she often smiled even when it was too delicate for her comprehension.

"Pray, madam," says Adams, "who was this squire Horatio?"

Horatio, says the lady, was a young gentleman of a good family, bred to the law, and had been some few years called to the degree of a barrister. His face and person were such as the generality allowed handsome; but he had a dignity in his air very rarely to be seen. His temper was of the saturnine complexion, but without the least taint of moroseness. He had wit and humour, with an inclination to satire, which he indulged rather too much.

This gentleman, who had contracted the most violent passion for Leonora, was the last person who perceived the probability of its success. The whole town had made the match for him before he himself had drawn a confidence from her actions sufficient to mention his passion to her; for it was his opinion (and perhaps he was there in the right) that it is highly impolitic to talk seriously of love to a woman before you have made such a progress in her affections that she herself expects and desires to hear it.

But whatever diffidence the fears of a lover may create, which are apt to magnify every favour conferred on a rival, and to see the little advances towards themselves through the other end of the perspective, it was impossible that Horatio's passion should so blind his discernment as to prevent his conceiving hopes from the behaviour of Leonora, whose fondness for him was now as visible to an indifferent person in their company as his for her.

"I never knew any of these forward sluts come to good" (says the lady who refused Joseph's entrance into the coach), "nor shall I wonder at anything she doth in the sequel."

The lady proceeded in her story thus: It was in the midst of a gay conversation in the walks one evening, when Horatio whispered Leonora, that he was desirous to take a turn or two with her in private, for that he had something to communicate to her of great consequence. "Are you sure it is of consequence?" said she, smiling. — "I hope," answered he, "you will think so too, since the whole future happiness of my life must depend on the event."

Leonora, who very much suspected what was coming, would have deferred it till another time; but Horatio, who had more than half conquered the difficulty of speaking by the first motion, was so very importunate, that she at last yielded, and, leaving the rest of the company, they turned aside into an unfrequented walk.

They had retired far out of the sight of the company, both maintaining a strict silence. At last Horatio made a full stop, and taking Leonora, who stood pale and trembling, gently by the hand, he fetched a deep sigh, and then, looking on her eyes with all the tenderness imaginable, he cried out in a faltering accent, "O Leonora! is it necessary for me to declare to you on what the future happiness of my life must be founded? Must I say there is something belonging to you which is a bar to my happiness, and which unless you will part with, I must be miserable?" "What can that be?" replied Leonora. — "No wonder," said he, "you are surprised that I should make an objection to anything which is yours; yet sure you may guess, since it is the only one which the riches of the world, if they were mine, should purchase of me. O, it is that which you must part with to bestow all the rest! Can Leonora, or rather will she, doubt longer? — Let me then whisper it in her ears — It is your name, madam. It is by parting with that, by your condescension to be for ever mine, which must at once prevent me from being the most miserable, and will render me the happiest of mankind."

Leonora, covered with blushes, and, with as angry a look as she could possibly put on, told him, "That had she suspected what his declaration would have been, he should not have decoyed her from her company; that he had so surprised and frighted her, that she begged him to convey her back as quick as possible"; which he, trembling very near as much as herself, did.

"More fool he," cried Slipslop; "it is a sign he knew very little of our *sect.*" "Truly, madam," said Adams, "I think you are in the right: I should have insisted to know a piece of her mind, when I had carried matters so far." But Miss Grave-airs desired the lady to omit all such fulsome stuff in her story, for that it made her sick.

Well, then, madam, to be as concise as possible, said the lady, many weeks had not passed after this interview, before Horatio and Leonora were what they call on a good footing together. All ceremonies except the last were now over; the writings were now drawn, and everything was in the utmost forwardness preparative to the putting Horatio in possession of all his wishes. I will, if you please, repeat you a letter from each of them which I have got by heart, and which will give you no small idea of their passion on both sides.

Miss Grave-airs objected to hearing these letters; but being put to the vote, it was carried against her by all the rest in the coach; Parson Adams contending for it with the utmost vehemence.

HORATIO TO LEONORA

"How vain, most adorable creature, is the pursuit of pleasure in the absence of an object to which the mind is entirely devoted, unless it have some relation to that object! I was last night condemned to the society of men of wit and learning, which, however agreeable it might have formerly been to me, now only gave me a suspicion that they imputed my absence in conversation to the true cause. For which reason, when your engagements forbid me the ecstatic happiness of seeing you, I am always desirous to be alone; since my sentiments for Leonora are so delicate, that I cannot bear the apprehension of another's prying into those delightful endearments with which the warm imagination of a lover will sometimes indulge him, and which I suspect my eyes then betray. To fear this discovery of our thoughts may perhaps appear too ridiculous a nicety to minds not susceptible of all the tendernesses of this delicate passion. And surely we shall suspect there are few such, when we consider that it requires every human virtue to exert itself in its full extent. Since the beloved, whose happiness it ultimately respects, may give us charming opportunities of being brave in her defence, generous to her wants, compassionate to her afflictions, grateful to her kindness; and, in the same manner, of exercising every other virtue, which he who would not do to any degree, and that with the utmost rapture, can never deserve the name of a lover: it is, therefore, with a view to the delicate modesty of your mind that I cultivate it so purely in my own; and it is that which will sufficiently suggest to you the uneasiness I bear from those liberties, which men to whom the world allow politeness will sometimes give themselves on these occasions.

"Can I tell you with what eagerness I expect the arrival of that blest day, when I shall experience the falsehood of a common assertion, that the greatest human happiness consists in hope? A doctrine which no person had ever stronger reason to believe than myself at present, since none ever tasted such bliss as fires my bosom with the thoughts of spending my future days with such a companion, and that every action of my life will have the glorious satisfaction of conducing to your happiness."

LEONORA TO HORATIO*

"The refinement of your mind has been so evidently proved by every word and action ever since I had first the pleasure of knowing you, that I thought it impossible my good opinion of Horatio could have been heightened to any additional proof of merit. This very thought was my amusement when I received your last letter, which, when I opened, I confess I was surprised to find the delicate sentiments expressed there so far exceeded what I thought could come even from you (although I know all the generous principles human nature is capable of are centred in your breast), that words cannot paint what I feel on the reflection that my happiness shall be the ultimate end of all your actions.

"Oh, Horatio! what a life must that be, where the meanest domestic cares are sweetened by the pleasing consideration that the man on earth who best deserves, and to whom you are most inclined to give your affections, is to reap either profit or pleasure from all you do! In such a case, toils must be turned into diversions, and nothing but the unavoidable inconveniences of life can make us remember that we are mortal.

"If the solitary turn of your thoughts, and the desire of keeping them undiscovered, makes even the conversation of men of wit and learning tedious to you, what anxious hours must I spend, who am condemned by custom to the conversation of women, whose natural curiosity leads them to pry into all my thoughts, and whose envy can never suffer Horatio's heart to be possessed by any one, without forcing them into malicious designs against the person who is so happy as to possess it: but, indeed, if ever envy can possibly have any excuse, or even alleviation, it is in this case, where the good is so great, and it must be equally natural to all to wish it for themselves, nor am I ashamed to own it; and to your merit, Horatio, I am obliged, that prevents my being in that most uneasy of all the situations

* This letter was written by a young lady on reading the former. — F.

I can figure in my imagination, of being led by inclination to love the person whom my own judgment forces me to condemn."

Matters were in so great forwardness between this fond couple, that the day was fixed for their marriage, and was now within a fortnight, when the sessions chanced to be held for that county in a town about twenty miles' distance from that which is the scene of our story. It seems it is usual for the young gentlemen of the bar to repair to these sessions, not so much for the sake of profit as to show their parts, and learn the law of the justices of peace; for which purpose one of the wisest and gravest of all the justices is appointed speaker, or chairman, as they modestly call it, and he reads them a lecture, and instructs them in the true knowledge of the law.

"You are here guilty of a little mistake," says Adams, "which, if you please, I will correct: I have attended at one of these quarter-sessions, where I observed the counsel taught the justices, instead of learning anything of them."

It is not very material, said the lady. Hither repaired Horatio, who, as he hoped by his profession to advance his fortune, which was not at present very large, for the sake of his dear Leonora, he resolved to spare no pains, nor lose any opportunity of improving or advancing himself in it.

The same afternoon in which he left the town, as Leonora stood at her window, a coach and six passed by, which she declared to be the completest, genteelest, prettiest equipage she ever saw; adding these remarkable words, "O, I am in love with that equipage!" which, though her friend Florella at that time did not greatly regard, she hath since remembered.

In the evening an assembly was held, which Leonora honoured with her company; but intended to pay her dear Horatio the compliment of refusing to dance in his absence.

O, why have not women as good resolution to maintain their vows as they have often good inclinations in making them!

The gentleman who owned the coach and six came to the assembly. His clothes were as remarkably fine as his equipage could be. He soon attracted the eyes of the company; all the smarts, all the silk waistcoats with silver and gold edgings, were eclipsed in an instant.

"Madam," said Adams, "if it be not impertinent, I should be glad to know how this gentleman was drest."

Sir, answered the lady, I have been told he had on a cut velvet coat of a cinnamon colour, lined with a pink satin, embroidered all over with gold; his waistcoat, which was cloth of silver, was embroidered with gold likewise. I cannot be particular as to the rest of his dress: but it was all in the French fashion; for Bellarmine (that was his name) was just arrived from Paris.

This fine figure did not more entirely engage the eyes of every lady in the assembly than Leonora did his. He had scarce beheld her, but he stood motionless and fixed as a statue, or at least would have done so, if good breeding had permitted him. However, he carried it so far before he had power to correct himself, that every person in the room easily discovered where his admiration was settled. The other ladies began to single out their former partners, all perceiving who would be Bellarmine's choice; which they however endeavoured, by all possible means, to prevent: many of them saying to Leonora, "O, madam! I suppose we shan't have the pleasure of seeing you dance tonight"; and then crying out, in Bellarmine's hearing, "O! Leonora will not dance, I assure you: her partner is not here." One maliciously attempted to prevent her, by sending a disagreeable fellow to ask her, that so she might be obliged either to dance with him, or sit down; but this scheme proved abortive.

Leonora saw herself admired by the fine stranger, and envied by every woman present. Her little heart began to flutter within her, and her head was agitated with a convulsive motion; she seemed as if she would speak to several of her acquaintance, but had nothing to say: for, as she would not mention her present triumph, so she could not disengage her thoughts one moment from the contemplation of it: She had never tasted anything like this happiness. She had before known what it was to torment a single woman; but to be hated and secretly cursed by a whole assembly was a joy reserved for this blessed moment. As this vast profusion of ecstasy had confounded her understanding, so there was nothing so foolish as her behaviour: she played a thousand childish tricks, distorted her person into several shapes, and her face into several laughs, without any reason. In a word, her carriage was as absurd as her desires, which were, to affect an insensibility of the stranger's admiration, and at the same time a triumph, from that admiration, over every woman in the room.

In this temper of mind, Bellarmine, having inquired who she was, advanced to her, and, with a low bow, begged the honour of dancing with her, which she, with as low a curtsy, immediately granted. She danced with him all night, and enjoyed perhaps the highest pleasure that she was capable of feeling.

At these words, Adams fetched a deep groan, which frighted the ladies, who told him, "They hoped he was not ill." He answered, "He groaned only for the folly of Leonora."

Leonora retired (continued the lady) about six in the morning, but not to rest. She tumbled and tossed in her bed, with very short intervals of sleep, and those entirely filled with dreams of the equipage and fine clothes she had seen, and the balls, operas, and ridottos, which had been the subject of their conversation.

In the afternoon, Bellarmine, in the dear coach and six, came to wait on her. He was indeed charmed with her person, and was, on inquiry, so well pleased with the circumstances of her father (for he himself, notwithstanding all his finery, was not quite so rich as a Crœsus or an Attǎlus). "Attǎlus," says Mr. Adams: "but pray how came you acquainted with these names?" The lady smiled at the question, and proceeded. — He was so pleased, I say, that he resolved to make his addresses to her directly. He did so accordingly, and that with so much warmth and briskness, that he quickly baffled her weak repulses, and obliged the lady to refer him to her father, who, she knew, would quickly declare in favour of a coach and six.

Thus, what Horatio had by sighs and tears, love and tenderness, been so long obtaining, the French-English Bellarmine with gaiety and gallantry possessed himself of in an instant. In other words, what modesty had employed a full year in raising, impudence demolished in twenty-four hours.

Here Adams groaned a second time; but the ladies, who began to smoke him, took no notice.

From the opening of the assembly till the end of Bellarmine's visit, Leonora had scarce once thought of Horatio; but he now began, though an unwelcome guest, to enter into her mind. She wished she had seen the charming Bellarmine and his charming equipage before matters had gone so far. "Yet why," says she, "should I wish to have seen him before; or what signifies it that I have seen him now? Is not Horatio my lover? almost my husband? Is he not as handsome, nay handsomer than Bellarmine? Ay, but Bellarmine is the genteeler and the finer man; yes, that he must be allowed. Yes, yes, he is that certainly. But did not I, no longer ago than yesterday, love Horatio more than all the world? Ay, but yesterday I had not seen Bellarmine. But doth not Horatio doat on me, and may he not in despair break his heart if I abandon him? Well, and hath not Bellarmine a heart to break too? Yes, but I promised Horatio first; but that was poor Bellarmine's misfortune; if I had seen him first, I should certainly have preferred him. Did not the dear creature prefer me to every woman in the assembly, when every she was laying out for him? When was it in Horatio's power to give me such an instance of affection? Can he give me an equipage, or any of those things which Bellarmine will make me mistress of? How vast is the difference between being the wife of a poor counsellor, and the wife of one of Bellarmine's fortune! If I marry Horatio, I shall triumph over no more than one rival; but by marrying Bellarmine, I shall be the envy of all my acquaintance. What happiness! — But can I suffer Horatio to die? for he hath sworn he cannot survive my loss: but perhaps he may not die; if he should, can I prevent it? Must I sacrifice myself to him? besides, Bellarmine may be as miserable for me too." She was thus arguing with herself, when some young ladies called her to the walks, and a little relieved her anxiety for the present.

The next morning Bellarmine breakfasted with her in presence of her aunt, whom he sufficiently informed of his passion for Leonora; he was no sooner withdrawn than the old lady began to advise her niece on this occasion — "You see, child," says she, "what Fortune hath thrown in your way; and I hope you will not withstand your own preferment." Leonora, sighing, "begged her not to mention any such thing, when she knew her engagements to Horatio." "Engagements to a fig!" cried the aunt; "you should thank Heaven on your knees that you have it yet in your power to break them. Will any woman hesitate a moment whether she shall ride in a coach, or walk on foot all the days of her life? — But Bellarmine drives six, and Horatio not even a pair." "Yes, but, madam, what will the world say?" answered Leonora: "will not they condemn me?" "The world is always on the side of prudence," cries the aunt, "and would surely condemn you if you sacrificed your interest to any motive whatever. O! I know the world very well; and you show your ignorance, my dear, by your objection. O' my conscience! the world is wiser. I have lived longer in it than you; and I assure you there is not anything worth our regard besides money; nor did I ever know one person who married from other considerations, who did not afterwards heartily repent it. Besides, if we examine the two men, can you prefer a sneaking fellow, who hath been bred at a university, to a fine gentleman just come from his travels? — All the world must allow Bellarmine to be a fine gentleman, positively a fine gentleman, and a handsome man." — "Perhaps, madam, I should not doubt, if I knew how to be handsomely off with the other." "O! leave that to me," says the aunt. "You know your father hath not been acquainted with the affair. Indeed, for my part, I thought it might do well enough, not dreaming of such an offer; but I'll disengage you: leave me to give the fellow an answer. I warrant you shall have no farther trouble."

Leonora was at length satisfied with her aunt's reasoning; and Bellarmine supping with her that evening, it was agreed he should the next morning go to her father and propose the match, which she consented should be consummated at his return.

The aunt retired soon after supper; and, the lovers being left together, Bellarmine began in the following manner: "Yes, madam, this coat, I assure you, was made at Paris, and I defy the best English tailor even to imitate it. There is not one of them can cut, madam; they can't cut. If you observe how this skirt is turned, and this sleeve — a clumsy English rascal can do nothing like it. — Pray, how do you like my liveries?" Leonora answered, "She thought them very pretty." "All French," says he, "I assure you, except the greatcoats; I never trust anything more than a greatcoat to an Englishman; you know one must encourage our own people what one can, especially as, before I had a place, I was in the Country Interest, he, he, he! But for myself, I would see the dirty island at the bottom of the sea, rather than wear a single rag of English work about me; and I am sure, after you have made one tour to Paris, you will be of the same opinion with regard to your own clothes. You can't conceive what an addition a French dress would be to your beauty; I positively assure you, at the first opera I saw since I came over, I mistook the English ladies for chambermaids, he, he, he!"

With such sort of polite discourse did the gay Bellarmine entertain his beloved Leonora, when the door opened on a sudden, and Horatio entered the room. Here 'tis impossible to express the surprise of Leonora.

"Poor woman!" says Mrs. Slipslop, "what a terrible *quandary* she must be in!" "Not at all," says Miss Grave-airs, "such sluts can never be confounded." "She must have then more than Corinthian assurance," said Adams; "ay, more than Lais herself."

A long silence, continued the lady, prevailed in the whole company: If the familiar entrance of Horatio struck the greatest astonishment into Bellarmine, the unexpected presence of Bellarmine no less surprised Horatio. At length Leonora, collecting all the spirits she was mistress of, addressed herself to the latter, and pretended to wonder at the reason of so late a visit. "I should, indeed," answered he, "have made some apology for disturbing you at this hour, had not my finding you in company assured me I do not break in on your repose." Bellarmine rose from his chair, traversed the room in a minuet step, and hummed an opera tune, while Horatio, advancing to Leonora, asked her in a whisper if that gentleman was not a relation of hers; to which she answered with a smile, or rather sneer, "No, he is no relation of mine yet"; adding, "she could not guess the meaning of his question." Horatio told her softly, "It did not arise from jealousy." "Jealousy!" cries she, "I assure you; — it would be very strange in a common acquaintance to give himself any of those airs." These words a little surprised Horatio; but, before he had time to answer, Bellarmine danced up to the lady, and told her, "He feared he interrupted some business between her and the gentleman." "I can have no business," said she, "with the gentleman, nor any other, which need be any secret to you."

"You'll pardon me," said Horatio, "if I desire to know who this gentleman is who is to be intrusted with all our secrets." "You'll know soon enough," cries Leonora; "but I can't guess what secrets can ever pass between us of such mighty consequence." "No, madam!" cries Horatio, "I'm sure you would not have me understand you in earnest." "'Tis indifferent to me," says she, "how you understand me; but I think so unseasonable a visit is difficult to be understood at all, at least when people find one engaged; though one's servants do not deny one, one may expect a well-bred person should soon take the hint." "Madam," said Horatio, "I did not imagine any engagement with a stranger, as it seems this gentleman is, would have made my visit impertinent, or that any such ceremonies were to be preserved between persons in our situation." "Sure you are in a dream," says she, "or would persuade me that I am in one. I know no pretensions a common acquaintance can have to lay aside the ceremonies of good breeding." "Sure," said he, "I am in a dream; for it is impossible I should be really esteemed a common acquaintance by Leonora, after what has passed between us!" "Passed between us! Do you intend to affront me before this gentleman?" "D—n me, affront the lady!" says Bellarmine, cocking his hat, and strutting up to Horatio: "does any man dare affront this lady before me, d—n me?" "Hark'ee, sir," says Horatio, "I would advise you to lay aside that fierce air; for I am mightily deceived if this lady has not a violent desire to get your worship a good drubbing." "Sir," said Bellarmine, "I have the honour to be her protector, and, d—n me, if I understand your meaning." "Sir," answered Horatio, "she is rather your protectress; but give yourself no more airs, for you see I am prepared for you" (shaking his whip at him). "O! *serviteur très humble*," says Bellarmine; "*Je vous entends parfaitement bien.*" At which time the aunt, who had heard of Horatio's visit, entered the room, and soon satisfied all his doubts. She convinced him that he was never more awake in his life, and that nothing more extraordinary had happened in his three days' absence than a small alteration in the affections of Leonora; who now burst into tears, and wondered what reason she had given him to use her in so barbarous a manner. Horatio desired Bellarmine to withdraw with him; but the ladies prevented it by laying violent hands on the latter; upon which the former took his leave without any great ceremony, and departed, leaving the lady with his rival to consult for his safety, which Leonora feared her indiscretion might have endangered: but the aunt comforted her with assurances that Horatio would not venture his person against so accomplished a cavalier as Bellarmine, and that, being a lawyer, he would seek revenge in his own way, and the most they had to apprehend from him was an action.

They at length, therefore, agreed to permit Bellarmine to retire to his lodgings, having first settled all matters relating to the journey which he was to undertake in the morning, and their preparations for the nuptials at his return.

But, alas! as wise men have observed, the seat of valour is not the countenance; and many a grave and plain man will, on a just provocation, betake himself to that mischievous metal, cold iron; while men of a fiercer brow, and sometimes with that emblem of courage, a cockade, will more prudently decline it.

Leonora was waked in the morning, from a visionary coach and six, with the dismal account that Bellarmine was run through the body by Horatio; that he lay languishing at an inn, and the surgeons had declared the wound mortal. She immediately leaped out of the bed, danced about the room in a frantic manner, tore her hair and beat her breast in all the agonies of despair; in which sad condition her aunt, who likewise arose at the news, found her. The good old lady applied her utmost art to comfort her niece. She told her, "While there was life, there was hope: but that if he should die, her affliction would be of no service to

Bellarmine, and would only expose herself, which might probably keep her some time without any future offer; that, as matters had happened, her wisest way would be to think no more of Bellarmine, but to endeavour to regain the affections of Horatio." "Speak not to me," cried the disconsolate Leonora; "is it not owing to me that poor Bellarmine has lost his life? Have not these cursed charms" (at which words she looked steadfastly in the glass) "been the ruin of the most charming man of this age? Can I ever bear to contemplate my own face again?" (with her eyes still fixed on the glass). "Am I not the murderess of the finest gentleman? No other woman in the town could have made any impression on him." "Never think of things past," cries the aunt: "think of regaining the affections of Horatio." "What reason," said the niece, "have I to hope he would forgive me? No, I have lost him as well as the other, and it was your wicked advice which was the occasion of all; you seduced me, contrary to my inclinations, to abandon poor Horatio" (at which words she burst into tears); "you prevailed upon me, whether I would or no, to give up my affections for him; had it not been for you, Bellarmine never would have entered into my thoughts; had not his addresses been backed by your persuasions, they never would have made any impression on me; I should have defied all the fortune and equipage in the world; but it was you, it was you, who got the better of my youth and simplicity, and forced me to lose my dear Horatio for ever."

The aunt was almost borne down with this torrent of words; she, however, rallied all the strength she could, and, drawing her mouth up in a purse, began: "I am not surprised, niece, at this ingratitude. Those who advise young women for their interest, must always expect such a return; I am convinced my brother will thank me for breaking off your match with Horatio, at any rate." "That may not be in your power yet," answered Leonora, "though it is very ungrateful in you to desire or attempt it, after the presents you have received from him." (For indeed true it is, that many presents, and some pretty valuable ones, had passed from Horatio to the old lady; but as true it is, that Bellarmine, when he breakfasted with her and her niece, had complimented her with a brilliant from his finger, of much greater value than all she had touched of the other.)

The aunt's gall was on float to reply, when a servant brought a letter into the room, which Leonora, hearing it came from Bellarmine, with great eagerness opened, and read as follows:

MOST DIVINE CREATURE,

The wound which I fe.r you have heard I received from my rival is not like to be so fatal as those shot into my heart, which have been fired from your eyes, *tout brilliant*. Those are the only cannons by which I am to fall: for my surgeon gives me hopes of being soon able to attend your *ruelle*; till when, unless you would do me an honour which I have scarce the *hardiesse* to think of, your absence will be the greatest anguish which can be felt by,

MADAM,

Avec toute le respecte in the world,

Your most obedient, most absolute

Dévoté,

BELLARMINE.

As soon as Leonora perceived such hopes of Bellarmine's recovery, and that the gossip Fame had, according to custom, so enlarged his danger, she presently abandoned all further thoughts of Horatio, and was soon reconciled to her aunt, who received her again into favour, with a more Christian forgiveness than we generally meet with. Indeed, it is possible she might be a little alarmed at the hints which her niece had given her concerning the presents. She might apprehend such rumours, should they get abroad, might injure a reputation which, by frequenting church twice a day, and preserving the utmost rigour and strictness in her countenance and behaviour for many years, she had established.

Leonora's passion returned now for Bellarmine with greater force, after its small relaxation, than ever. She proposed to her aunt to make him a visit in his confinement, which the old lady, with great and commendable prudence, advised her to decline: "For," says she, "should any accident intervene to prevent your intended match, too forward a behaviour with this lover may injure you in the eyes of others. Every woman, till she is married, ought to consider of, and provide against, the possibility of the affair's breaking off." Leonora said, "She should be indifferent to whatever might happen in such a case: for she had now so absolutely placed her affections on this dear man" (so she called him), "that, if it was her misfortune to lose him, she should for ever abandon all thoughts of mankind." She therefore resolved to visit him, notwithstanding all the prudent advice of her aunt to the contrary, and that very afternoon executed her resolution.

The lady was proceeding in her story, when the coach drove into the inn where the company were to dine, sorely to the dissatisfaction of Mr. Adams, whose ears were the most hungry part about him; he being, as the reader may perhaps guess, of an insatiable curiosity, and heartily desirous of hearing the end of this amour, though he professed he could scarce wish success to a lady of so inconstant a disposition.

CHAPTER V.

A dreadful quarrel which happened at the inn where the company dined; with its bloody consequences to Mr. Adams.

As soon as the passengers had alighted from the coach, Mr. Adams, as was his custom, made directly to the kitchen, where he found Joseph sitting by the fire, and the hostess anointing his leg; for the horse which Mr. Adams had borrowed of his clerk had so violent a propensity to kneeling, that one would have thought it had been his trade as well as his master's; nor would he always give any notice of such his intention; he was often found on his knees when the rider least expected it. This foible, however, was of no great inconvenience to the parson, who was accustomed to it; and, as his legs almost touched the ground when he bestrode the beast, had but a little way to fall, and threw himself forward on such occasions with so much dexterity that he never received any mischief; the horse and he frequently rolling many paces' distance, and afterwards both getting up and meeting as good friends as ever.

Poor Joseph, who had not been used to such kind of cattle, though an excellent horseman, did not so happily disengage himself: but, falling with his leg under the beast, received a violent contusion, to which the good woman was, as we have said, applying a warm hand, with some camphorated spirits, just at the time when the parson entered the kitchen.

He had scarce expressed his concern for Joseph's misfortune, before the host likewise entered. He was by no means of Mr. Tow-wouse's gentle disposition; and was, indeed, perfect master of his house, and everything in it but his guests.

This surly fellow, who always proportioned his respect to the appearance of a traveller, from "God bless your honour," down to plain "Coming presently," observing his wife on her knees to a footman, cried out, without considering his circumstances, "What a pox is the woman about? why don't you mind the company in the coach? Go and ask them what they will have for dinner." "My dear," says she, "you know they can have nothing but what is at the fire, which will be ready presently; and really the poor young man's leg is very much bruised." At which words she fell to chafing more violently than before: the bell then happening to ring, he damn'd his wife, and bid her go in to the company, and not stand rubbing there all day; for he did not believe the young fellow's leg was so bad as he pretended; and if it was, within twenty miles he would find a surgeon to cut it off. Upon these words, Adams fetched two strides across the room; and snapping his fingers over his head, muttered aloud, "He would excommunicate such a wretch for a farthing; for he believed the devil had more humanity." These words occasioned a dialogue between Adams and the host, in which there were two or three sharp replies, till Joseph bade the latter know how to behave himself to his betters. At which the host (having first strictly surveyed Adams), scornfully repeating the word "betters," flew into a rage, and, telling Joseph he was as able to walk out of his house as he had been to walk into it, offered to lay violent hands on him; which perceiving, Adams dealt him so sound a compliment over his face with his fist, that the blood immediately gushed out of his nose in a stream. The host, being unwilling to be outdone in courtesy, especially by a person of Adams's figure, returned the favour with so much gratitude, that the parson's nostrils began to look a little redder than usual. Upon which he again assailed his antagonist, and with another stroke laid him sprawling on the floor.

The hostess, who was a better wife than so surly a husband deserved, seeing her husband all bloody and stretched along, hastened presently to his assistance, or rather to revenge the blow, which, to all appearance, was the last he would ever receive; when, lo! a pan full of hog's blood, which unluckily stood on the dresser, presented itself first to her hands. She seized it in her fury, and without any reflection, discharged it into the parson's face; and with so good an aim, that much the greater part first saluted his countenance, and trickled thence in so large a current down to his beard, and over his garments, that a more horrible spectacle was hardly to be seen, or even imagined. All which was perceived by Mrs. Slipslop, who entered the kitchen at that instant. This good gentlewoman, not being of a temper so extremely cool and patient as perhaps was required to ask many questions on this occasion, flew with great impetuosity at the hostess's cap, which, together with some of her hair, she plucked from her head in a moment, giving her at the same time several hearty cuffs in the face, which, by frequent practice on the inferior servants, she had learned an excellent knack of delivering with a good grace. Poor Joseph could hardly rise from his chair; the parson was employed in wiping the blood from his eyes, which had entirely blinded him; and the landlord was but just beginning to stir; whilst Mrs. Slipslop, holding down the landlady's face with her left hand, made so dexterous an use of her right, that the poor woman began to roar, in a key which alarmed all the company in the inn.

There happened to be in the inn, at this time, besides the ladies who arrived in the stage-coach, the two gentlemen who were present at Mr. Tow-wouse's when Joseph was detained for his horse's meat, and whom we have before mentioned to have stopt at the alehouse with Adams. There was likewise a gentleman just returned from his travels to Italy; all whom the horrid outcry of murder presently brought into the kitchen, where the several combatants were found in the postures already described.

It was now no difficulty to put an end to the fray, the conquerors being satisfied with the vengeance they had taken, and the conquered having no appetite to renew the fight. The principal figure, and which engaged the eyes of all, was Adams, who was all over covered with blood, which the whole company concluded to be his own, and consequently imagined him no longer for this world. But the host, who had now recovered from his blow, and was risen from the ground, soon delivered them from this apprehension, by damning his wife for wasting the hog's puddings, and telling her all would have been very well if she had not intermeddled, like a b— as she was; adding, he was very glad the gentlewoman had paid her, though not half what she deserved. The poor woman had indeed fared much the worst; having, besides the unmerciful cuffs received, lost a quantity of hair, which Mrs. Slipslop in triumph held in her left hand.

The traveller, addressing himself to Miss Grave-airs, desired her not to be frightened; for here had been only a little boxing, which he said, to their *disgracia*, the English were *accustomata* to: adding, it must be, however, a sight somewhat strange to him, who was just come from Italy; the Italians not being addicted to the *cuffardo*, but *bastonza*, says he. He then went up to Adams, and telling him he looked like the ghost of Othello, bid him "not shake his gory locks at him, for he could not say he did it."

Adams very innocently answered, "Sir, I am far from accusing you." He then returned to the lady, and cried, "I find the bloody gentleman is *uno insipido del nullo senso*. *Damnata di me*, if I have seen such a *spectaculo* in my way from Viterbo."

One of the gentlemen having learnt from the host the occasion of this bustle, and being assured by him that Adams had struck the first blow, whispered in his ear: "He'd warrant he would *recover*." "Recover! master," said the host, smiling: "yes, yes, I am not afraid of dying with a blow or two neither; I am not such a chicken as that." "Pugh!" said the gentleman, "I mean you will recover damages in that action which undoubtedly you intend to bring, as soon as a writ can be returned from London; for you look like a man of too much spirit and courage to suffer anyone to beat you without bringing your action against him: he must be a scandalous fellow indeed who would put up with a drubbing whilst the law is open to revenge it; besides, he hath drawn blood from you, and spoiled your coat; and the jury will give damages for that too. An excellent new coat upon my word; and now not worth a shilling! I don't care," continued he, "to intermeddle in these cases: but you have a right to my evidence; and if I am sworn, I must speak the truth. I saw you sprawling on the floor, and the blood gushing from your nostrils. You may take your own opinion; but was I in your circumstances, every drop of my blood should convey an ounce of gold into my pocket: remember I don't advise you to go to law; but if your jury were Christians, they must give swinging damages. That's all." "Master," cried the host, scratching his head, "I have no stomach to law, I thank you. I have seen enough of that in the parish, where two of my neighbours have been at law about a house, till they have both lawed themselves into a gaol." At which words he turned about, and began to inquire again after his hog's puddings; nor would it probably have been a sufficient excuse for his wife, that she spilt them in his defence, had not some awe of the company, especially of the Italian traveller, who was a person of great dignity, withheld his rage.

Whilst one of the above-mentioned gentlemen was employed, as we have seen him, on the behalf of the landlord, the other was no less hearty on the side of Mr. Adams, whom he advised to bring his action immediately. He said the assault of the wife was, in law, the assault of the husband; for they were but one person; and he was liable to pay damages, which he said must be considerable, where so bloody a disposition appeared. Adams

answered, If it was true that they were but one person, he had
assaulted the wife; for he was sorry to own he had struck the
husband the first blow. "I am sorry you own it too," cries the
gentleman; "for it could not possibly appear to the court: for
here was no evidence present but the lame man in the chair,
whom I suppose to be your friend, and would consequently say
nothing but what made for you." "How, sir," says Adams, "do
you take me for a villain, who would prosecute revenge in cold
blood, and use unjustifiable means to obtain it? If you knew me
and my order, I should think you affronted both." At the word
order, the gentleman stared (for he was too bloody to be of any
modern order of knights); and, turning hastily about, said,
"Every man knew his own business."

Matters being now composed, the company retired to their
several apartments, the two gentlemen congratulating each other
on the success of their good offices in procuring a perfect reconciliation between the contending parties; and the traveller went
to his repast, crying, as the Italian poet says:

> "*Je voi* very well, *que tutta e pace,*
> So send up dinner, good Boniface."

The coachman began now to grow importunate with his
passengers, whose entrance into the coach was retarded by Miss
Grave-airs insisting, against the remonstrances of all the rest,
that she would not admit a footman into the coach; for poor
Joseph was too lame to mount a horse. A young lady, who was,
as it seems, an earl's grand-daughter, begged it with almost tears
in her eyes. Mr. Adams prayed, and Mrs. Slipslop scolded; but
all to no purpose. She said, "She would not demean herself to
ride with a footman: that there were waggons on the road: that
if the master of the coach desired it, she would pay for two
places; but would suffer no such fellow to come in." "Madam,"
says Slipslop, "I am sure no one can refuse another coming into
a stage-coach." "I don't know, madam," says the lady; "I am
not much used to stage-coaches; I seldom travel in them." "That
may be, madam," replied Slipslop; "very good people do; and
some people's betters, for aught I know." Miss Grave-airs said,
"Some folks might sometimes give their tongues a liberty, to
some people that were their betters, which did not become
them: for her part, she was not used to converse with servants."
Slipslop returned, "Some people kept no servants to converse

with; for her part, she thanked Heaven she lived in a family where there were a great many, and had more under her own command than any paltry little gentlewoman in the kingdom." Miss Grave-airs cried, "She believed her mistress would not encourage such sauciness to her betters." "My betters," says Slipslop, "who is my betters, pray?" "I am your betters," answered Miss Grave-airs, "and I'll acquaint your mistress." — At which Mrs. Slipslop laughed aloud, and told her, "Her lady was one of the great gentry; and such little paltry gentlewomen, as some folks who travelled in stage-coaches, would not easily come at her."

This smart dialogue between some people and some folks was going on at the coach door when a solemn person, riding into the inn, and seeing Miss Grave-airs, immediately accosted her with, "Dear child, how do you?" She presently answered, "O, papa! I am glad you have overtaken me." "So am I," answered he: "for one of our coaches is just at hand; and, there being room for you in it, you shall go no farther in the stage unless you desire it." "How can you imagine I should desire it?" says she; so, bidding Slipslop "ride with her fellow, if she pleased," she took her father by the hand, who was just alighted, and walked with him into a room.

Adams instantly asked the coachman in a whisper, "If he knew who the gentleman was?" The coachman answered, "He was now a gentleman, and kept his horse and man; but times are altered, master," said he; "I remember when he was no better born than myself." "Ay! ay!" says Adams. "My father drove the squire's coach," answered he, "when that very man rode postilion; but he is now his steward, and a great gentleman." Adams then snapped his fingers, and cried, "He thought she was some such trollop."

Adams made haste to acquaint Mrs. Slipslop with this good news, as he imagined it; but it found a reception different from what he expected. The prudent gentlewoman, who despised the anger of Miss Grave-airs whilst she conceived her the daughter of a gentleman of small fortune, now she heard her alliance with the upper servants of a great family in her neighbourhood, began to fear her interest with the mistress. She wished she had not carried the dispute so far, and began to think of endeavouring to reconcile herself to the young lady before she left the inn; when, luckily, the scene at London, which the reader can scarce have forgotten, presented itself to her mind, and comforted her with such assurance, that she no longer apprehended any enemy with her mistress.

Everything being now adjusted, the company entered the coach, which was just on its departure, when one lady recollected she had left her fan, a second her gloves, a third a snuff-box, and a fourth a smelling-bottle behind her; to find all which occasioned some delay, and much swearing to the coachman.

As soon as the coach had left the inn, the women all together fell to the character of Miss Grave-airs, whom one of them declared she had suspected to be some low creature, from the beginning of their journey; and another affirmed had not even the looks of a gentlewoman; a third warranted she was no better than she should be; and, turning to the lady who had related the story in the coach, said, "Did you ever hear, madam, anything so prudish as her remarks? Well, deliver me from the censoriousness of such a prude." The fourth added, "O, madam! all these creatures are censorious; but for my part, I wonder where the wretch was bred; indeed, I must own I have seldom conversed with these mean kind of people, so that it may appear stranger to me; but to refuse the general desire of a whole company had something in it so astonishing, that, for my part, I own I should hardly believe it if my own ears had not been witnesses to it." "Yes, and so handsome a young fellow," cries Slipslop; "the woman must have no *compulsion* in her; I believe she is more of a Turk than a Christian; I am certain, if she had any Christian woman's blood in her veins, the sight of such a young fellow must have warmed it. Indeed, there are some wretched, miserable old objects, that turn one's stomach; I should not wonder if she had refused such a one; I am as nice as herself, and should have cared no more than herself for the company of *stinking* old fellows: but, hold up thy head, Joseph, thou art none of those; and she who hath not *compulsion* for thee is a *Myhummetman*, and I will maintain it." This conversation made Joseph uneasy, as well as the ladies; who, perceiving the spirits which Mrs. Slipslop was in (for indeed she was not a cup too low), began to fear the consequence; one of them therefore desired the lady to conclude the story. — "Ay, madam," said Slipslop, "I beg your ladyship to give us that story you *commensated* in the morning"; which request that well-bred woman immediately complied with.

CHAPTER VI.

Conclusion of the Unfortunate Jilt.

LEONORA, having once broke through the bounds which custom and modesty impose on her sex, soon gave an unbridled indulgence to her passion. Her visits to Bellarmine were more constant, as well as longer, than his surgeon's; in a word, she became absolutely his nurse: made his water-gruel, administered him his medicines, and notwithstanding the prudent advice of her aunt to the contrary, almost entirely resided in her wounded lover's apartment.

The ladies of the town began to take her conduct under consideration: it was the chief topic of discourse at their tea tables, and was very severely censured by the most part; especially by Lindamira, a lady whose discreet and starch carriage, together with a constant attendance at church three times a day, had utterly defeated many malicious attacks on her own reputation; for such was the envy that Lindamira's virtue had attracted, that, notwithstanding her own strict behaviour and strict inquiry into the lives of others, she had not been able to escape being the mark of some arrows herself, which, however, did her no injury; a blessing perhaps owed by her to the clergy, who were her chief male companions, and with two or three of whom she had been barbarously and unjustly calumniated.

"Not so unjustly neither, perhaps," says Slipslop; "for the clergy are men as well as other folks."

The extreme delicacy of Lindamira's virtue was cruelly hurt by those freedoms which Leonora allowed herself: she said, "It was an affront to her sex; that she did not imagine it consistent with any woman's honour to speak to the creature, or to be seen in her company; and that, for her part, she should always refuse to dance at an assembly with her, for fear of contamination by taking her by the hand."

But to return to my story: As soon as Bellarmine was recovered, which was somewhat within a month from his receiving the wound, he set out, according to agreement, for Leonora's father's, in order to propose the match, and settle all matters with him touching settlements, and the like.

A little before his arrival, the old gentleman had received an intimation of the affair by the following letter, which I can repeat *verbatim*, and which, they say, was written neither by Leonora nor her aunt, though it was in a woman's hand. The letter was in these words:

> SIR,
>
> I am sorry to acquaint you that your daughter Leonora hath acted one of the basest, as well as most simple, parts with a young gentleman to whom she had engaged herself, and whom she hath (pardon the word) jilted for another of inferior fortune, notwithstanding his superior figure. You may take what measures you please on this occasion; I have performed what I thought my duty; as I have, though unknown to you, a very great respect for your family.

The old gentleman did not give himself the trouble to answer this kind epistle; nor did he take any notice of it, after he had read it, till he saw Bellarmine. He was, to say the truth, one of those fathers who look on children as an unhappy consequence of their youthful pleasures; which, as he would have been delighted not to have had attended them, so was he no less pleased with any opportunity to rid himself of the incumbrance. He passed, in the world's language, as an exceeding good father; being not only so rapacious as to rob and plunder all mankind to the utmost of his power, but even to deny himself the conveniences, and almost necessaries, of life; which his neighbours attributed to a desire of raising immense fortunes for his children: but in fact it was not so; he heaped up money for its own sake only, and looked on his children as his rivals, who were to enjoy his beloved mistress when he was incapable of possessing her, and which he would have been much more charmed with the power of carrying along with him; nor had his children any other security of being his heirs than that the law would constitute them such without a will, and that he had not affection enough for anyone living to take the trouble of writing one.

To this gentleman came Bellarmine on the errand I have mentioned. His person, his equipage, his family, and his estate, seemed to the father to make him an advantageous match for his daughter; he therefore very readily accepted his proposals: but when Bellarmine imagined the principal affair concluded, and began to open the incidental matters of fortune, the old gentleman presently changed his countenance, saying, "He resolved never to marry his daughter on a Smithfield match; that whoever had love for her to take her would, when he died, find her share of his fortune in his coffers; but he had seen such examples of undutifulness happen from the too early generosity of parents, that he had made a vow never to part with a shilling whilst he lived." He commended the saying of Solomon, "He that spareth the rod, spoileth the child"; but added, "he might have likewise asserted, that 'He that spareth the purse, saveth the child.' " He then ran into a discourse on the extravagance of the youth of the age; whence he launched into a dissertation on horses, and came at length to commend those Bellarmine drove. That fine gentleman, who at another season would have been well enough pleased to dwell a little on that subject, was now very eager to resume the circumstance of fortune. He said, "He had a very high value for the young lady, and would receive her with less than he would any other whatever; but that even his love to her made some regard to worldly matters necessary; for it would be a most distracting sight for him to see her, when he had the honour to be her husband, in less than a coach and six." The old gentleman answered, "Four will do, four will do"; and then took a turn from horses to extravagance, and from extravagance to horses, till he came round to the equipage again: whither he was no sooner arrived than Bellarmine brought him back to the point; but all to no purpose; he made his escape from that subject in a minute; till at last the lover declared, "That in the present situation of his affairs, it was impossible for him, though he loved Leonora more than *tout le monde*, to marry her without any fortune." To which the father answered, "He was sorry then his daughter must lose so valuable a match; that, if he had an inclination, at present it was not in his power to advance a shilling: that he had had great losses, and been at great expenses on projects, which, though he had great expectation from them, had yet produced him nothing; that he did not know what might happen hereafter, as on the birth of a son, or such accident; but he would make no promise, or enter into any article, for he would not break his vow for all the daughters in the world."

In short, ladies, to keep you no longer in suspense, Bellarmine having tried every argument and persuasion which he could invent, and finding them all ineffectual, at length took his leave, but not in order to return to Leonora; he proceeded directly to his own seat, whence, after a few days' stay, he returned to Paris, to the great delight of the French, and the honour of the English nation.

But as soon as he arrived at his home, he presently dispatched a messenger with the following epistle to Leonora:

ADORABLE AND CHARMANTE,

I am sorry to have the honour to tell you I am not the *heureux* person destined for your divine arms. Your papa hath told me so with a *politesse* not often seen on this side of Paris. You may perhaps guess his manner of refusing me. — *Ah, mon Dieu!* You will certainly believe me, madam, incapable myself of delivering this *triste* message, which I intend to try the French air to cure the consequences of. — *A jamais! Cœur! Ange!* — *Au diable!* — If your papa obliges you to a marriage, I hope we shall see you at Paris; till when, the wind that flows from thence will be the warmest *dans le monde*: for it will consist almost entirely of my sighs. *Adieu, ma princesse! Ah, l'amour!*

BELLARMINE.

I shall not attempt, ladies, to describe Leonora's condition when she received this letter. It is a picture of horror, which I should have as little pleasure in drawing as you in beholding. She immediately left the place where she was the subject of conversation and ridicule, and retired to that house I showed you when I began the story; where she hath ever since led a disconsolate life, and deserves, perhaps, pity for her misfortunes, more than our censure for a behaviour to which the artifices of her aunt very probably contributed, and to which very young women are often rendered too liable by that blameable levity in the education of our sex.

"If I was inclined to pity her," said a young lady in the coach, "it would be for the loss of Horatio; for I cannot discern any misfortune in her missing such a husband as Bellarmine."

"Why, I must own," says Slipslop, "the gentleman was a little false-hearted; but *howsumever*, it was hard to have two lovers, and get never a husband at all. — But pray, madam, what became of *Our-asho?*"

He remains, said the lady, still unmarried, and hath applied himself so strictly to his business, that he hath raised, I hear, a very considerable fortune. And what is remarkable, they say, he never hears the name of Leonora without a sigh, nor hath ever uttered one syllable to charge her with her ill-conduct towards him.

CHAPTER VII.

A very short chapter, in which Parson Adams went a great way.

THE lady, having finished her story, received the thanks of the company; and now Joseph, putting his head out of the coach, cried out, "Never believe me, if yonder be not our Parson Adams walking along without his horse!" "On my word, and so he is," says Slipslop; "and as sure as twopence, he hath left him behind at the inn." Indeed, true it is, the parson had exhibited a fresh instance of his absence of mind: for he was so pleased with having got Joseph into the coach, that he never once thought of the beast in the stable; and, finding his legs as nimble as he desired, he sallied out, brandishing a crabstick, and had kept on before the coach, mending and slackening his pace occasionally, so that he had never been much more or less than a quarter of a mile distant from it.

Mrs. Slipslop desired the coachman to overtake him, which he attempted, but in vain: for the faster he drove, the faster ran the parson, often crying out, "Ay, ay, catch me if you can"; till at length the coachman swore he would as soon attempt to drive after a greyhound; and, giving the parson two or three hearty curses, he cried, "Softly, softly, boys," to his horses, which the civil beasts immediately obeyed.

But we will be more courteous to our reader than he was to Mrs. Slipslop; and leaving the coach and its company to pursue their journey, we will carry our reader on after Parson Adams, who stretched forwards without once looking behind him, till, having left the coach full three miles in his rear, he came to a place where, by keeping the extremest track to the right, it was just barely possible for a human creature to miss his way. This track, however, did he keep, as indeed he had a wonderful capacity at these kinds of bare possibilities; and, travelling in it about three miles over the plain, he arrived at the summit of a hill, whence looking a great way backwards, and perceiving no coach in sight, he sat himself down on the turf, and pulling out his Æschylus, determined to wait here for its arrival.

He had not sat long here before a gun going off very near a little startled him; he looked up, and saw a gentleman within a hundred paces taking up a partridge which he had just shot.

Adams stood up and presented a figure to the gentleman which would have moved laughter in many: for his cassock had just again fallen down below his greatcoat, that is to say, it reached his knees, whereas the skirts of his greatcoat descended no lower than half-way down his thighs; but the gentleman's mirth gave way to his surprise at beholding such a personage in such a place.

Adams, advancing to the gentleman, told him he hoped he had good sport; to which the other answered, "Very little." "I see, sir," says Adams, "you have *smote* one partridge"; to which the sportsman made no reply, but proceeded to charge his piece.

Whilst the gun was charging, Adams remained in silence, which he at last broke by observing that it was a delightful evening. The gentleman, who had at first sight conceived a very distasteful opinion of the parson, began, on perceiving a book in his hand, and smoking likewise the information of the cassock, to change his thoughts, and made a small advance to conversation on his side, by saying, "Sir, I suppose you are not one of these parts?"

Adams immediately told him, "No: that he was a traveller, and invited by the beauty of the evening and the place to repose a little, and amuse himself with reading." "I may as well repose myself too," said the sportsman; "for I have been out this whole afternoon, and the devil a bird have I seen till I came hither."

"Perhaps then the game is not very plenty hereabouts?" cries Adams. "No, sir," said the gentleman: "the soldiers, who are quartered in the neighbourhood, have killed it all." "It is very probable," cries Adams; "for shooting is their profession." "Ay, shooting the game," answered the other, "but I don't see they are so forward to shoot our enemies. I don't like that affair of Carthagena; if I had been there, I believe I should have done other-guess things, d——n me; what's a man's life when his country demands it? a man who won't sacrifice his life for his country deserves to be hanged, d——n me." Which words he spoke with so violent a gesture, so loud a voice, so strong an accent, and so fierce a countenance, that he might have frightened a captain of trained-bands at the head of his company; but Mr. Adams was not greatly subject to fear: he told him intrepidly that he very much approved his virtue, but disliked his swearing, and begged him not to addict himself to so bad a custom, without which he said he might fight as bravely as Achilles did. Indeed, he was charmed with this discourse; he told the gentleman he would willingly have gone many miles to have met a man of his generous way of thinking; that, if he pleased to sit down, he should be greatly delighted to commune with him: for, though he was a clergyman, he would himself be ready, if thereto called, to lay down his life for his country.

The gentleman sat down, and Adams by him; and then the latter began, as in the following chapter, a discourse which we have placed by itself, as it is not only the most curious in this, but perhaps in any other book.

CHAPTER VIII.

A notable dissertation by Mr. Abraham Adams; wherein that gentleman appears in a political light.

"I DO assure you, sir," says he, taking the gentleman by the hand, "I am heartily glad to meet with a man of your kidney: for, though I am a poor parson, I will be bold to say I am an honest man, and would not do an ill thing to be made a bishop; nay, though it hath not fallen in my way to offer so noble a sacrifice, I have not been without opportunities of suffering for the sake of my conscience; I thank Heaven for them; for I have had relations, though I say it, who made some figure in the world; particularly a nephew, who was a shopkeeper and an alderman of a corporation. He was a good lad, and was under my care when a boy; and I believe would do what I bade him to his dying day. Indeed, it looks like extreme vanity in me to affect being a man of such consequence as to have so great an interest in an alderman; but others have thought so too, as manifestly appeared by the rector, whose curate I formerly was, sending for me on the approach of an election, and telling me, if I expected to continue in his cure, that I must bring my nephew to vote for one Colonel Courtly, a gentleman whom I had never heard tidings of till that instant. I told the rector I had no power over my nephew's vote (God forgive me for such prevarication!); that I supposed he would give it according to his conscience; that I would by no means endeavour to influence him to give it otherwise. He told me it was in vain to equivocate: that he knew I had already spoke to him in favour of Esquire Fickle, my neighbour; and indeed, it was true I had: for it was at a season when the 'Church was in danger,' and when all good men expected they knew not what would happen to us all. I then answered boldly, if he thought I had given my promise, he affronted me in proposing any breach of it. Not to be too prolix: I persevered, and so did my nephew, in the esquire's interest, who was chose chiefly through his means; and so I lost my curacy. Well, sir, but do you think the esquire ever mentioned a word of the Church? *Ne verbum quidem, ut ita dicam;* within two years he got a place, and hath ever since lived in London; where I have been informed (but God forbid I should believe that), that he never so much as goeth to church. I remained, sir, a considerable time without any cure, and lived a full month on one funeral sermon, which I preached on the indisposition of a clergyman; but this by the bye. At last, when Mr. Fickle got his place, Colonel Courtly stood again; and who should make interest for him but Mr. Fickle himself! that very identical Mr. Fickle, who had formerly told me the colonel was an enemy to both the Church and State, had the confidence to solicit my nephew for him; and the colonel himself offered me to make me chaplain to his regiment, which I refused in favour of Sir Oliver Hearty, who told us he would sacrifice everything to his country; and I believe he would, except his hunting, which he stuck so close to, that in five years together he went but twice up to parliament; and one of those times, I have been told, never was within sight of the House. However, he was a worthy man, and the best friend I ever had: for, by his interest with a bishop, he got me replaced into my curacy, and gave me eight pounds out of his own pocket to buy me a gown and cassock, and furnish my house. He had our interest while he lived, which was not many years. On his death I had fresh applications made to me; for all the world knew the interest I had in my good nephew, who was now a leading man in the corporation; and Sir Thomas Booby, buying the estate which had been Sir Oliver's, proposed himself a candidate. He was then a young gentleman just come from his travels; and it did me good to hear him discourse on affairs which, for my part, I knew nothing of. If I had been master of a thousand votes, he should have had them all. I engaged my nephew in his interest, and he was elected; and a very fine parliament-man he was. They tell me he made speeches of an hour long, and, I have been told, very fine ones; but he could never persuade the parliament to be of his opinion. — *Non omnia possumus omnes.* He promised me a living, poor man; and I believe I should have had it, but an accident happened, which was, that my lady had promised it before, unknown to him. This, indeed, I never heard till afterwards: for my nephew, who died about a month before the incumbent, always told me I might be assured of it. Since that time, Sir Thomas, poor man, had always so much business, that he never could find leisure to see me. I believe it was partly my lady's fault too, who did not think my dress good enough for the gentry at her table. However, I must do him the justice to say he never was ungrateful; and I have always found his kitchen, and his cellar too, open to me: many a time, after service on a Sunday — for I preach at four churches — have I recruited my spirits with a glass of his ale. Since my nephew's death, the corporation is in other hands; and I am not a man of that consequence I was formerly. I have now no longer any talents to lay out in the service of my country; and to whom nothing is given, of him can nothing be required. However, on all proper seasons, such as the approach of an election, I throw a suitable dash or two into my sermons; which I have the pleasure to hear is not disagreeable to Sir Thomas, and the other honest gentlemen my neighbours, who have all promised me these five years to procure an ordination for a son of mine, who is now near thirty, hath an infinite stock of learning, and is, I thank Heaven, of an unexceptionable life; though, as he was never at an university, the bishop refuses to ordain him. Too much care cannot indeed be taken in admitting any to the sacred office; though I hope he will never act so as to be a disgrace to any order, but will serve his God and his country to the utmost of his power, as I have endeavoured to do before him; nay, and will lay down his life whenever called to that purpose. I am sure I have educated him in those principles; so that I have acquitted my duty, and shall have nothing to answer for on that account: but I do not distrust him, for he is a good boy; and, if Providence should throw it in his way to be of as much consequence in a public light as his father once was, I can answer for him he will use his talents as honestly as I have done."

CHAPTER IX.

In which the gentleman descants on bravery and heroic virtue,
till an unlucky accident puts an end to the discourse.

THE gentleman highly commended Mr. Adams for his good
resolutions, and told him, "He hoped his son would tread in his
steps"; adding, "that if he would not die for his country, he
would not be worthy to live in it. I'd make no more of shooting
a man that would not die for his country, than —

"Sir," said he, "I have disinherited a nephew who is in the
army, because he would not exchange his commission and go
to the West Indies. I believe the rascal is a coward, though
he pretends to be in love forsooth. I would have all such fellows
hanged, sir; I would have them hanged." Adams answered,
"That would be too severe; that men did not make themselves;
and if fear had too much ascendance in the mind, the man was
rather to be pitied than abhorred; that reason and time might
teach him to subdue it." He said, "A man might be a coward
at one time, and brave at another. Homer," says he, "who so
well understood and copied Nature, hath taught us this lesson;
for Paris fights, and Hector runs away. Nay, we have a mighty
instance of this in the history of later ages, no longer ago than
the 705th year of Rome, when the great Pompey, who had won so
many battles and been honoured with so many triumphs, and of
whose valour several authors, especially Cicero and Paterculus,
have formed such elogiums; this very Pompey left the battle
of Pharsalia before he had lost it, and retreated to his tent, where
he sat like the most pusillanimous rascal in a fit of despair, and
yielded a victory, which was to determine the empire of the
world, to Cæsar. I am not much travelled in the history of modern times, that is to say, these last thousand years; but those who
are can, I make no question, furnish you with parallel instances."
He concluded, therefore, that, had he taken any such hasty
resolutions against his nephew, he hoped he would consider
better, and retract them. The gentleman answered with great
warmth, and talked much of courage and his country, till, perceiving it grew late, he asked Adams, "What place he intended
for that night?" He told him, "He waited there for the stage-
coach." "The stage-coach! Sir," said the gentleman, "they are

all passed by long ago. You may see the last yourself almost three miles before us." "I protest and so they are," cries Adams; "then I must make haste and follow them." The gentleman told him, "He would hardly be able to overtake them; and that, if he did not know his way, he would be in danger of losing himself on the downs, for it would be presently dark; and he might ramble about all night, and perhaps find himself farther from his journey's end in the morning than he was now." He advised him, therefore, "to accompany him to his house, which was very little out of his way," assuring him "that he would find some country fellow in his parish who would conduct him for sixpence to the city where he was going." Adams accepted this proposal, and on they travelled, the gentleman renewing his discourse on courage, and the infamy of not being ready at all times to sacrifice our lives to our country. Night overtook them much about the same time as they arrived near some bushes; whence, on a sudden, they heard the most violent shrieks imaginable, in a female voice. Adams offered to snatch the gun out of his companion's hand. "What are you doing?" said he. "Doing!" said Adams; "I am hastening to the assistance of the poor creature whom some villains are murdering." "You are not mad enough, I hope," says the gentleman, trembling: "Do you consider this gun is only charged with shot, and that the robbers are most probably furnished with pistols loaded with bullets? This is no business of ours; let us make as much haste as possible out of the way, or we may fall into their hands ourselves." The shrieks now increasing, Adams made no answer, but snapt his fingers, and, brandishing his crabstick, made directly to the place whence the voice issued; and the man of courage made as much expedition towards his own home, whither he escaped in a very short time, without once looking behind him: where we will leave him, to contemplate his own bravery, and to censure the want of it in others; and return to the good Adams, who, on coming up to the place whence the noise proceeded, found a woman struggling with a man, who had thrown her on the ground, and had almost overpowered her. The great abilities of Mr. Adams were not necessary to have formed a right judgment of this affair on the first sight. He did not, therefore, want the entreaties of the poor wretch to assist her; but lifting up his crabstick, he immediately levelled a blow at that part of the ravisher's head where, according to the opinion of the ancients, the brains of some persons are deposited, and which he had undoubtedly let forth, had not Nature (who, as wise men have observed, equips all creatures with what is most expedient for them) taken a provident care (as she always doth with those she intends for encounters) to make this part of the head three times as thick as those of ordinary men, who are designed to exercise talents which are vulgarly called rational, and for whom, as brains are necessary, she is obliged to leave some room for them in the cavity of the skull; whereas, those ingredients being entirely useless to persons of the heroic calling, she hath an opportunity of thickening the bone, so as to make it less subject to any impression, or liable to be cracked or broken; and, indeed, in some who are predestined to the command of armies and empires, she is supposed sometimes to make that part perfectly solid.

As a game cock, when engaged in amorous toying with a hen, if perchance he espies another cock at hand, immediately quits his female, and opposes himself to his rival; so did the ravisher, on the information of the crabstick, immediately leap from the woman, and hasten to assail the man. He had no weapons but what Nature had furnished him with. However, he clenched his fist, and presently darted it at that part of Adams's breast where the heart is lodged. Adams staggered at the violence of the blow, when, throwing away his staff, he likewise clenched that fist which we have before commemorated, and would have discharged it full in the breast of his antagonist, had he not dexterously caught it with his left hand, at the same time darting his head (which some modern heroes, of the lower class, use, like the battering-ram of the ancients, for a weapon of offence; another reason to admire the cunningness of Nature, in composing it of those impenetrable materials); dashing his head, I say, into the stomach of Adams, he tumbled him on his back; and, not having any regard to the laws of heroism, which would have restrained him from any farther attack on his enemy till he was again on his legs, he threw himself upon him, and, laying hold on the ground with his left hand, he with his right belaboured the body of Adams till he was weary, and, indeed, till he concluded (to use the language of fighting) "that he had done his business"; or, in the language of poetry, "that he had sent him to the shades below"; in plain English, "that he was dead."

But Adams, who was no chicken, and could bear a drubbing as well as any boxing champion in the universe, lay still only to watch his opportunity; and now, perceiving his antagonist to pant with his labours, he exerted his utmost force at once, and with such success that he overturned him, and became his superior; when, fixing one of his knees in his breast, he cried out in an exulting voice, "It is my turn now"; and, after a few minutes' constant application, he gave him so dexterous a blow just under his chin that the fellow no longer retained any motion, and Adams began to fear he had struck him once too often; for he often asserted, "he should be concerned to have the blood of even the wicked upon him."

Adams got up and called aloud to the young woman — "Be of good cheer, damsel," said he, "you are no longer in danger of your ravisher, who, I am terribly afraid, lies dead at my feet; but God forgive me what I have done in defence of innocence!" The poor wretch, who had been some time in recovering strength enough to rise, and had afterwards, during the engagement, stood trembling, being disabled by fear even from running away, hearing her champion was victorious, came up to him, but not without apprehensions even of her deliverer; which, however, she was soon relieved from by his courteous behaviour and gentle words. They were both standing by the body, which lay motionless on the ground, and which Adams wished to see stir much more than the woman did, when he earnestly begged her to tell him, "by what misfortune she came, at such a time of night, into so lonely a place?" She acquainted him, "She was travelling towards London, and had accidentally met with the person from whom he had delivered her, who told her he was likewise on his journey to the same place, and would keep her company; an offer which, suspecting no harm, she had accepted; that he told her they were at a small distance from an inn where she might take up her lodging that evening, and he would show her a nearer way to it than by following the road. That if she had suspected him (which she did not, he spoke so kindly to her), being alone on these downs in the dark, she had no human means to avoid him; that therefore she put her whole trust in Providence, and walked on, expecting every moment to arrive at the inn; when, on a sudden, being come to those bushes, he desired her to stop, and after some rude kisses, which she resisted, and some entreaties, which she rejected, he laid violent hands on her, and was attempting to execute his wicked will, when, she thanked G—, he timely came up and prevented him." Adams encouraged her for saying she had put her whole trust in Providence, and told her, "He doubted not but Providence had sent him to her deliverance, as a reward for that trust. He wished indeed he had not deprived the wicked wretch of life, but G—'s will be done"; he said, "he hoped the goodness of his intention would excuse him in the next world, and he trusted in her evidence to acquit him in this." He was then silent, and began to consider with himself whether it would be properer to make his escape, or to deliver himself into the hands of justice; which meditation ended as the reader will see in the next chapter.

CHAPTER X.

Giving an account of the strange catastrophe of the preceding adventure, which drew poor Adams into fresh calamities; and who the woman was who owed the preservation of her chastity to his victorious arm.

THE silence of Adams, added to the darkness of the night and loneliness of the place, struck dreadful apprehensions into the poor woman's mind: she began to fear as great an enemy in her deliverer as he had delivered her from; and as she had not light enough to discover the age of Adams, and the benevolence visible in his countenance, she suspected he had used her as some very honest men have used their country; and had rescued her out of the hands of one rifler, in order to rifle her himself. Such were the suspicions she drew from his silence; but indeed they were ill-grounded. He stood over his vanquished enemy, wisely weighing in his mind the objections which might be made to either of the two methods of proceeding mentioned in the last chapter, his judgment sometimes inclining to the one, and sometimes to the other; for both seemed to him so equally advisable, and so equally dangerous, that probably he would have ended his days, at least two or three of them, on that very spot, before he had taken any resolution: At length he lifted up his eyes, and spied a light at a distance, to which he instantly addressed himself with, "*Heus tu*, traveller, *heus tu!*" He presently heard several voices, and perceived the light approaching toward him. The persons who attended the light began some to laugh, others to sing, and others to hollow, at which the woman testified some fear (for she had concealed her suspicions of the parson himself); but Adams said, "Be of good cheer, damsel, and repose thy trust in the same Providence which hath hitherto protected thee, and never will forsake the innocent." These people, who now approached, were no other, reader, than a set of young fellows, who came to these bushes in pursuit of a diversion which they call "bird-batting." This, if thou art ignorant of it (as perhaps if thou hast never travelled beyond Kensington, Islington, Hackney, or the Borough, thou mayst be), I will inform thee, is performed by holding a large clap-net before a lantern, and at the same time beating the bushes: for the birds, when they are disturbed from their places of rest, or roost, immediately make to the light, and so are enticed within the net. Adams immediately told them what had happened, and desired them "to hold the lantern to the face of the man on the ground, for he feared he had *smote* him fatally." But indeed his fears were frivolous; for the fellow, though he had been stunned by the last blow he received, had long since recovered his senses, and, finding himself quit of Adams, had listened attentively to the discourse between him and the young woman; for whose departure he had patiently waited, that he might likewise withdraw himself, having no longer hopes of succeeding in his desires, which were moreover almost as well cooled by Mr. Adams as they could have been by the young woman herself, had he obtained his utmost wish. This fellow, who had a readiness at improving any accident, thought he might now play a better part than that of a dead man; and, accordingly, the moment the candle was held to his face, he leapt up, and, laying hold on Adams, cried out, "No, villain, I am not dead, though you and your wicked whore might well think me so, after the barbarous cruelties you have exercised on me. Gentlemen," said he, "you are luckily come to the assistance of a poor traveller, who would otherwise have been robbed and murdered by this vile man and woman, who led me hither out of my way from the high-road, and, both falling on me, have used me as you see." Adams was going to answer, when one of the young fellows cried, "D—n them, let's carry them both before the justice." The poor woman began to tremble, and Adams lifted up his voice, but in vain. Three or four of them laid hands on him; and one holding the lantern to his face, they all agreed, "he had the most villainous countenance they ever beheld"; and an attorney's clerk who was of the company declared, "he was sure he had remembered him at the bar." As to the woman, her hair was dishevelled in the struggle, and her nose had bled, so that they could not perceive whether she was handsome or ugly; but they said her fright plainly discovered her guilt. And searching

her pockets, as they did those of Adams, for money, which the
fellow said he had lost, they found in her pocket a purse with
some gold in it, which abundantly convinced them, especially
as the fellow offered to swear to it. Mr. Adams was found to
have no more than one halfpenny about him. This the clerk
said, "was a great presumption that he was an old offender, by
cunningly giving all the booty to the woman." To which all
the rest readily assented.

This accident promising them better sport than what they
had proposed, they quitted their intention of catching birds,
and unanimously resolved to proceed to the justice with the
offenders. Being informed what a desperate fellow Adams was,
they tied his hands behind him; and, having hid their nets among
the bushes, and the lantern being carried before them, they
placed the two prisoners in their front, and then began their
march; Adams not only submitting patiently to his own fate,
but comforting and encouraging his companion under her sufferings.

Whilst they were on their way, the clerk informed the rest that
this adventure would prove a very beneficial one; for that they
would be all entitled to their proportions of £80 for apprehending
the robbers. This occasioned a contention concerning the parts
which they had severally borne in taking them; one insisting he
ought to have the greatest share, for he had first laid his hands
on Adams; another claiming a superior part for having first held
the lantern to the man's face on the ground, by which, he said,
"the whole was discovered." The clerk claimed four-fifths of
the reward for having proposed to search the prisoners, and likewise the carrying them before the justice: he said, indeed, "in
strict justice, he ought to have the whole." These claims, however, they at last consented to refer to a future decision, but
seemed all to agree that the clerk was entitled to a moiety.
They then debated what money should be allotted to the young
fellow who had been employed only in holding the nets. He
very modestly said, "That he did not apprehend any large
proportion would fall to his share, but hoped they would allow
him something; he desired them to consider that they had assigned their nets to his care, which prevented him from being
as forward as any in laying hold of the robbers" (for so these
innocent people were called); "that if he had not occupied the
nets, some other must"; concluding, however, "that he should
be contented with the smallest share imaginable, and should

think that rather their bounty than his merit." But they were all unanimous in excluding him from any part whatever, the clerk particularly swearing, "If they gave him a shilling, they might do what they pleased with the rest; for he would not concern himself with the affair." This contention was so hot, and so totally engaged the attention of all the parties, that a dexterous nimble thief, had he been in Mr. Adams's situation, would have taken care to have given the justice no trouble that evening. Indeed, it required not the art of a Shepherd to escape, especially as the darkness of the night would have so much befriended him; but Adams trusted rather to his innocence than his heels, and, without thinking of flight, which was easy, or resistance (which was impossible, as there were six lusty young fellows, besides the villain himself, present), he walked with perfect resignation the way they thought proper to conduct him.

Adams frequently vented himself in ejaculations during their journey; at last, poor Joseph Andrews occurring to his mind, he could not refrain sighing forth his name, which being heard by his companion in affliction, she cried, with some vehemence, "Sure, I should know that voice; you cannot certainly, sir, be Mr. Abraham Adams?" "Indeed, damsel," says he, "that is my name; there is something also in your voice which persuades me I have heard it before." "La! sir," says she, "don't you remember poor Fanny?" "How, Fanny!" answered Adams: "indeed I very well remember you; what can have brought you hither?" "I have told you, sir," replied she, "I was travelling towards London; but I thought you mentioned Joseph Andrews; pray what is become of him?" "I left him, child, this afternoon," said Adams, "in the stage-coach, in his way towards our parish, whither he is going to see you." "To see me! La! sir," answered Fanny, "sure you jeer me; what should he be going to see me for?" "Can you ask that?" replied Adams. "I hope, Fanny, you are not inconstant; I assure you he deserves much better of you." "La! Mr. Adams," said she, "what is Mr. Joseph to me? I am sure I never had anything to say to him, but as one fellow-servant might to another." "I am sorry to hear this," said Adams; "a virtuous passion for a young man is what no woman need be ashamed of. You either do not tell me truth, or you are false to a very worthy man." Adams then told her what had happened at the inn, to which she listened very attentively; and a sigh often escaped from her, notwithstanding her utmost endeavours to the contrary; nor could she prevent herself from asking a thousand questions, which would have assured anyone but Adams, who never saw farther into people than they desired to let him, of the truth of a passion she endeavoured to conceal. Indeed, the fact was, that this poor girl, having heard of Joseph's misfortune by some of the servants belonging to the coach which we have formerly mentioned to have stopt at the inn while the poor youth was confined to his bed, that instant abandoned the cow she was milking, and, taking with her a little bundle of clothes under her arm, and all the money she was worth in her own purse, without consulting anyone, immediately set forward in pursuit of one whom, notwithstanding her shyness to the parson, she loved with inexpressible violence, though with the purest and most delicate passion. This shyness, therefore, as we trust it will recommend her character to all our female readers, and not greatly surprise such of our males as are well acquainted with the younger part of the other sex, we shall not give ourselves any trouble to vindicate.

CHAPTER XI.

What happened to them while before the justice. A chapter very full of learning.

THEIR fellow-travellers were so engaged in the hot dispute concerning the division of the reward for apprehending these innocent people, that they attended very little to their discourse. They were now arrived at the justice's house, and had sent one of his servants in to acquaint his worship that they had taken two robbers, and brought them before him. The justice, who was just returned from a fox-chase, and had not yet finished his dinner, ordered them to carry the prisoners into the stable, whither they were attended by all the servants in the house, and all the people in the neighbourhood, who flocked together to see them with as much curiosity as if there was something uncommon to be seen, or that a rogue did not look like other people.

The justice, now being in the height of his mirth and his cups, bethought himself of the prisoners; and, telling his company he believed they should have good sport in their examination, he ordered them into his presence. They had no sooner entered the room than he began to revile them, saying, "That robberies

on the highway were now grown so frequent, that people could
not sleep safely in their beds, and assured them they both should
be made examples of at the ensuing assizes." After he had gone
on some time in this manner, he was reminded by his clerk,
"That it would be proper to take the depositions of the witnesses
against them." Which he bid him do, and he would light his
pipe in the meantime. Whilst the clerk was employed in writing
down tho deposition of the fellow who had pretended to be
robbed, the justice employed himself in cracking jests on poor
Fanny, in which he was seconded by all the company at table.
One asked, "Whether she was to be indicted for a *highwayman?*"
Another whispered in her ear, "If she had not provided herself a
great belly, he was at her service." A third said, "He warranted
she was a relation of Turpin." To which one of the company,
a great wit, shaking his head, and then his sides, answered, "He
believed she was nearer related to *Turpis*"; at which there was
an universal laugh. They were proceeding thus with the poor
girl, when somebody, smoking the cassock peeping forth from
under the greatcoat of Adams, cried out, "What have we here,
a parson?" "How, sirrah," says the justice, "do you go robbing
in the dress of a clergyman? let me tell you your habit will not
entitle you to the 'benefit of the clergy.'" "Yes," said the witty
fellow, "he will have one benefit of clergy, he will be exalted
above the heads of the people"; at which there was a second
laugh. And now the witty spark, seeing his jokes take, began to
rise in spirits; and, turning to Adams, challenged him to "cap"
verses, and, provoking him by giving the first blow, he repeated:

Molle meum levibus cord est vilebile telis.

Upon which Adams, with a look full of ineffable contempt, told
him, "He deserved scourging for his pronunciation." The witty
fellow answered, "What do you deserve, doctor, for not being
able to answer the first time? Why, I'll give you one, you block-
head — with an *S*.

Si licet, ut fulvum spectatur in ignibus haurum.

"What, canst not with an *M* neither? Thou art a pretty
fellow for a parson! — Why didst not steal some of the parson's
Latin as well as his gown?" Another at the table then answered,
"If he had, you would have been too hard for him; I remember
you at the college a very devil at this sport; I have seen you
catch a freshman: for nobody that knew you would engage with

you." "I have forgot those things now," cried the wit. "I believe I could have done pretty well formerly. — Let's see, what did I end with? — an *M* again? — ay ——

Mars, Bacchus, Apollo, virorum.

I could have done it once." — "Ah! evil betide you, and so you can now," said the other: "nobody in this country will undertake you." Adams could hold no longer: "Friend," said he, "I have a boy not above eight years old who would instruct thee that the last verse runs thus:

Ut sunt Divorum, Mars, Bacchus, Apollo, virorum."

"I'll hold thee a guinea of that," said the wit, throwing the money on the table. — "And I'll go your halves," cried the other. "Done," answered Adams; but upon applying to his pocket, he was forced to retract, and own he had no money about him; which set them all a-laughing, and confirmed the triumph of his adversary, which was not moderate, any more than the approbation he met with from the whole company, who told Adams he must go a little longer to school before he attempted to attack that gentleman in Latin.

The clerk, having finished the depositions, as well of the fellow himself, as of those who apprehended the prisoners, delivered them to the justice; who, having sworn the several witnesses, without reading a syllable, ordered his clerk to make the *mittimus*.

Adams then said, "He hoped he should not be condemned unheard." "No, no," cries the justice, "you will be asked what you have to say for yourself when you come on your trial: we are not trying you now; I shall only commit you to gaol: if you can prove your innocence at 'size, you will be found *ignoramus*, and so no harm done." "Is it no punishment, sir, for an innocent man to lie several months in gaol?" cries Adams: "I beg you would at least hear me before you sign the *mittimus*." "What signifies all you can say?" says the justice: "is it not here in black and white against you? I must tell you, you are a very impertinent fellow to take up so much of my time. — So make haste with his *mittimus*."

The clerk now acquainted the justice that among other suspicious things, as a penknife, &c., found in Adams's pocket, they had discovered a book written, as he apprehended, in ciphers: for no one could read a word in it. "Ay," says the justice, "the fellow may be more than a common robber, he may be in a plot against the government. — Produce the book." Upon which the poor manuscript of Æschylus, which Adams had transcribed with his own hand, was brought forth; and the justice, looking at it, shook his head, and, turning to the prisoner, asked the meaning of those ciphers. "Ciphers!" answered Adams; "it is a manuscript of Æschylus." "Who? who?" said the justice. Adams repeated, "Æschylus." "That is an outlandish name," cried the clerk. "A fictitious name rather, I believe," said the justice. One of the company declared it looked very much like Greek. "Greek?" said the justice; "why, 'tis all writing." "No," says the other, "I don't positively say it is so: for it is a very long time since I have seen any Greek." "There's one," says he, turning to the parson of the parish, who was present, "will tell us immediately." The parson, taking up the book, and putting on his spectacles and gravity together, muttered some words to himself, and then pronounced aloud — "Ay, indeed, it is a Greek manuscript, a very fine piece of antiquity. I make no doubt but it was stolen from the same clergyman from whom the rogue took the cassock." "What did the rascal mean by his Æschylus?" says the justice. "Pooh!" answered the doctor, with a contemptuous grin, "do you think that fellow knows anything of this book? Æschylus! ho! ho! ho! I see now what it is. — A manuscript of one of the fathers. I know a nobleman who would give a great deal of money for such a piece of antiquity. — Ay, ay, question and answer. The beginning is the catechism in Greek. — Ay, — ay, — *Pollaki toi* — What's your name?" — "Ay, what's your name?" says the justice to Adams; who answered, "It is Æschylus, and I will maintain it." — "O! it is," says the justice: "make Mr. Æschylus his *mittimus*. I will teach you to banter me with a false name."

One of the company, having looked steadfastly at Adams, asked him, "If he did not know Lady Booby?" Upon which Adams, presently calling him to mind, answered in a rapture, "O squire! are you there? I believe you will inform his worship I am innocent." "I can indeed say," replied the squire, "that I am very much surprised to see you in this situation"; and then, addressing himself to the justice, he said, "Sir, I assure you Mr. Adams is a clergyman, as he appears, and a gentleman of a very good character. I wish you would inquire a little farther into this affair; for I am convinced of his innocence." "Nay," says the justice, "if he is a gentleman, and you are sure he is innocent, I don't desire to commit him, not I; I will commit the woman by herself, and take your bail for the gentleman; look into the book, clerk, and see how it is to take bail; come — and make the *mittimus* for the woman as fast as you can." "Sir," cries Adams, "I assure you she is as innocent as myself." "Perhaps," said the squire, "there may be some mistake; pray let us hear Mr. Adams's relation." "With all my heart," answered the justice; "and give the gentleman a glass to whet his whistle before he begins. I know how to behave myself to gentlemen as well as another. Nobody can say I have committed a gentleman since I have been in the commission." Adams then began the narrative, in which, though he was very prolix, he was uninterrupted, unless by several "hums" and "hahs" of the justice, and his desire to repeat those parts which seemed to him most material. When he had finished, the justice, who, on what the squire had said, believed every syllable of his story on his bare affirmation, notwithstanding the depositions on oath to the contrary, began to let loose several "rogues" and "rascals" against the witness, whom he ordered to stand forth, but in vain: the said witness, long since finding what turn matters were like to take, had privily withdrawn, without attending the issue. The justice now flew into a violent passion, and was hardly prevailed with not to commit the innocent fellows who had been imposed on as well as himself. He swore, "They had best find out the fellow who was guilty of perjury, and bring him before him within two days, or he would bind them all over to their good behaviour." They all promised to use their best endeavours to that purpose, and were dismissed. Then the justice insisted that Mr. Adams should sit down and take a glass with him; and the parson of the parish delivered him back the manuscript without saying a word; nor would Adams, who plainly discerned his ignorance, expose it. As for Fanny, she was, at her own request, recommended to the care of a maid-servant of the house, who helped her to new dress and clean herself.

The company in the parlour had not been long seated before they were alarmed with a horrible uproar from without, where the persons who had apprehended Adams and Fanny had been regaling, according to the custom of the house, with the justice's strong beer. These were all fallen together by the ears, and were cuffing each other without any mercy. The justice himself sallied out, and with the dignity of his presence soon put an end to the fray. On his return into the parlour, he reported, "That the occasion of the quarrel was no other than a dispute to whom, if Adams had been convicted, the greater share of the reward for apprehending him had belonged." All the company laughed at this, except Adams, who, taking his pipe from his mouth, fetched a deep groan, and said he was concerned to see so litigious a temper in men. That he remembered a story something like it in one of the parishes where his cure lay: "There was," continued he, "a competition between three young fellows for the place of the clerk, which I disposed of, to the best of my abilities, according to merit: that is, I gave it to him who had the happiest knack at setting a psalm. The clerk was no sooner established in his place than a contention began between the two disappointed candidates concerning their excellence; each contending on whom, had they two been the only competitors, my election would have fallen. This dispute frequently disturbed the congregation, and introduced a discord into the psalmody, till I was forced to silence them both. But, alas! the litigious spirit could not be stifled; and, being no longer able to vent itself in singing, it now broke forth in fighting. It produced many battles (for they were very near a match), and, I believe, would have ended fatally, had not the death of the clerk given me an opportunity to promote one of them to his place; which presently put an end to the dispute, and entirely reconciled the contending parties." Adams then proceeded to make some philosophical observations on the folly of growing warm in disputes in which neither party is interested. He then applied himself vigorously to smoking; and a long silence ensued, which was at length broke by the justice, who began to sing forth his own praises, and to value himself exceedingly on his nice discernment in the cause which had lately been before him. He was quickly interrupted by Mr. Adams, between whom and his worship a dispute now arose, whether he ought not, in strictness of law, to have committed him, the said Adams; in which the latter maintained he ought to have been committed, and the justice as vehemently held he ought not. This had most probably produced a quarrel (for both were very violent and positive in their opinions), had not Fanny accidentally heard that a young fellow was going from the justice's house to the very inn where the stage-coach, in which Joseph was, put up. Upon this news, she immediately sent for the parson out of the parlour. Adams, when he found her resolute to go (though she would not own the reason, but pretended she could not bear to see the faces of those who had suspected her of such a crime), was as fully determined to go with her; he accordingly took leave of the justice and company: and so ended a dispute in

which the law seemed shamefully to intend to set a magistrate
and a divine together by the ears.

CHAPTER XII.

*A very delightful adventure, as well to the persons concerned,
as to the good-natured reader.*

ADAMS, Fanny, and the guide, set out together about one in the
morning, the moon being then just risen. They had not gone
above a mile before a most violent storm of rain obliged them to
take shelter in an inn, or rather alehouse, where Adams immediately procured himslf a good fire, a toast and ale, and a pipe,
and began to smoke with great content, utterly forgetting everything that had happened.

Fanny sat likewise down by the fire; but was much more impatient at the storm. She presently engaged the eyes of the
host, his wife, the maid of the house, and the young fellow who
was their guide; they all conceived they had never seen anything
half so handsome: and indeed, reader, if thou art of an amorous
hue, I advise thee to skip over the next paragraph; which, to
render our history perfect, we are obliged to set down, humbly
hoping that we may escape the fate of Pygmalion; for if it should
happen to us, or to thee, to be struck with this picture, we should
be perhaps in as helpless a condition as Narcissus, and might
say to ourselves, *Quod petis est nusquam.* Or, if the finest
features in it should set Lady ——'s image before our eyes, we
should be still in as bad a situation, and might say to our desires,
Cœlum ipsum petimus stultitia.

Fanny was now in the nineteenth year of her age; she was
tall, and delicately shaped; but not one of those slender young
women who seem rather intended to hang-up in the hall of an
anatomist than for any other purpose. On the contrary, she
was so plump that she seemed bursting through her tight stays,
especially in the part which confined her swelling breasts. Nor
did her hips want the assistance of a hoop to extend them.
The exact shape of her arms denoted the form of those limbs
which she concealed; and though they were a little reddened by
her labour, yet, if her sleeve slipt above her elbow, or her handkerchief discovered any part of her neck, a whiteness appeared

which the finest Italian paint would be unable to reach. Her hair was of a chestnut brown, and nature had been extremely lavish to her of it, which she had cut, and on Sundays used to curl down her neck in the modern fashion. Her forehead was high, her eyebrows arched, and rather full than otherwise. Her eyes black and sparkling; her nose just inclining to the Roman; her lips red and moist, and her underlip, according to the opinion of the ladies, too pouting. Her teeth were white, but not exactly even. The small-pox had left one only mark on her chin, which was so large, it might have been mistaken for a dimple, had not her left cheek produced one so near a neighbour to it, that the former served only for a foil to the latter. Her complexion was fair, a little injured by the sun, but overspread with such a bloom that the finest ladies would have exchanged all their white for it; add to these a countenance in which, though she was extremely bashful, a sensibility appeared almost incredible; and a sweetness, whenever she smiled, beyond either imitation or description. To conclude all, she had a natural gentility, superior to the acquisition of art, and which surprised all who beheld her.

This lovely creature was sitting by the fire with Adams, when her attention was suddenly engaged by a voice from an inner room, which sung the following song:

THE SONG

SAY, Chloe, where must the swain stray
   Who is by thy beauties undone?
To wash their remembrance away,
   To what distant Lethe must run?
The wretch who is sentenc'd to die,
   May escape, and leave justice behind;
From his country perhaps he may fly:
   But O can he fly from his mind!

O rapture! unthought of before,
   To be thus of Chloe possest;
Nor she, nor no tyrant's hard power,
   Her image can tear from my breast.
But felt not Narcissus more joy,
   With his eyes he beheld his lov'd charms?
Yet what he beheld, the fond boy
   More eagerly wish'd in his arms.

How can it thy dear image be,
   Which fills thus my bosom with woe?
Can aught bear resemblance to thee,
   Which grief and not joy can bestow?

This counterfeit snatch from my heart,
    Ye pow'rs, tho' with torment I rave,
Tho' mortal will prove the fell smart,
    I then shall find rest in my grave.

Ah! see the dear nymph o'er the plain
    Comes smiling and tripping along,
A thousand Loves dance in her train;
    The Graces around her all throng.
To meet her soft Zephyrus flies,
    And wafts all the sweets from the flow'rs;
Ah, rogue! whilst he kisses her eyes,
    More sweets from her breath he devours.

My soul, whilst I gaze, is on fire,
    But her looks were so tender and kind:
My hope almost reach'd my desire,
    And left lame Despair far behind.
Transported with madness I flew,
    And eagerly seiz'd on my bliss;
Her bosom but half she withdrew,
    But half she refus'd my fond kiss.

Advances like these made me bold;
    I whisper'd her, "Love, — we're alone";
The rest let immortals unfold:
    No language can tell but their own.
Ah, Chloe, expiring, I cried,
    How long I thy cruelty bore!
Ah! Strephon, she blushing replied,
    You ne'er was so pressing before.

Adams had been ruminating all this time on a passage in Æschylus, without attending in the least to the voice, though one of the most melodious that ever was heard; when, casting his eyes on Fanny, he cried out, "Bless us, you look extremely pale!" "Pale! Mr. Adams," says she; "O Jesus!" and fell backwards in her chair. Adams jumped up, flung his Æschylus into the fire, and fell a-roaring to the people of the house for help. He soon summoned everyone into the room, and the songster among the rest: but, O reader! when this nightingale, who was no other than Joseph Andrews himself, saw his beloved Fanny in the situation we have described her, canst thou conceive the agitations of his mind? If thou canst not, waive that meditation to behold his happiness, when, clasping her in his arms, he found life and blood returning into her cheeks; when he saw her open her beloved eyes, and heard her with the softest accent whisper, "Are you Joseph Andrews?" "Art thou my Fanny?" he answered eagerly; and, pulling her to his heart, he imprinted numberless kisses on her lips, without considering who were present.

If prudes are offended at the lusciousness of this picture, they may take their eyes off from it, and survey Parson Adams dancing about the room in a rapture of joy. Some philosophers may perhaps doubt whether he was not the happiest of the three: for the goodness of his heart enjoyed the blessings which were exulting in the breasts of both the other two, together with his own. But we shall leave such disquisitions, as too deep for us, to those who are building some favourite hypothesis, which they will refuse no metaphysical rubbish to erect and support: for our part, we give it clearly on the side of Joseph, whose happiness was not only greater than the parson's, but of longer duration: for as soon as the first tumults of Adams's rapture were over, he cast his eyes towards the fire, where Æschylus lay expiring; and immediately rescued the poor remains, to wit, the sheepskin covering, of his dear friend, which was the work of his own hands, and had been his inseparable companion for upwards of thirty years.

Fanny had no sooner perfectly recovered herself than she began to restrain the impetuosity of her transports; and, reflecting on what she had done and suffered in the presence of so many, she was immediately covered with confusion; and, pushing Joseph gently from her, she begged him to be quiet, nor would admit of either kiss or embrace any longer. Then, seeing Mrs. Slipslop, she curtsied, and offered to advance to her; but that high woman would not return her curtsies; but, casting her eyes another way, immediately withdrew into another room, muttering as she went, "she wondered who the creature was."

CHAPTER XIII.

A dissertation concerning high people and low people, with Mrs. Slipslop's departure in no very good temper of mind, and the evil plight in which she left Adams and his company.

It will doubtless seem extremely odd to many readers, that Mrs. Slipslop, who had lived several years in the same house with Fanny, should, in a short separation, utterly forget her. And indeed the truth is, that she remembered her very well. As we would not willingly, therefore, that anything should appear unnatural in this our history, we will endeavour to explain the reasons of her conduct; nor do we doubt being able to satisfy the most curious reader that Mrs. Slipslop did not in the least deviate from the common road in this behaviour; and, indeed, had she done otherwise, she must have descended below herself, and would have very justly been liable to censure.

Be it known, then, that the human species are divided into two sorts of people, to wit, "high" people and "low" people. As by high people I would not be understood to mean persons literally born higher in their dimensions than the rest of the species, nor metaphorically those of exalted characters or abilities; so by low people I cannot be construed to intend the reverse. High people signify no other than people of fashion, and low people those of no fashion. Now, this word "fashion" hath by long use lost its original meaning, from which at present it gives us a very different idea: for I am deceived if, by persons of fashion, we do not generally include a conception of birth and accomplishments superior to the herd of mankind; whereas, in reality, nothing more was originally meant by a person of fashion than a person who drest himself in the fashion of the times; and the word really and truly signifies no more at this day. Now, the world being thus divided into people of fashion and people of no fashion, a fierce contention arose between them; nor would those of one party, to avoid suspicion, be seen publicly to speak to those of the other, though they often held a very good correspondence in private. In this contention, it is difficult to say which party succeeded: for, whilst the people of fashion seized several places to their own use, such as courts, assemblies, operas, balls, &c., the people of no fashion, besides one royal place, called his Majesty's Bear-Garden, have been in constant possession of all hops, fairs, revels, &c. Two places have been agreed to be divided between them, namely, the church and the playhouse, where they segregate themselves from each other in a remarkable manner: for, as the people of fashion exalt themselves at church over the heads of the people of no fashion, so in the playhouse they abase themselves in the same degree under their feet. This distinction I have never met with anyone able to account for: it is sufficient that, so far from looking on each other as brethren in the Christian language, they seem scarce to regard each other as of the same species. This, the terms "strange persons, people one does not know, the creature, wretches, beasts, brutes," and many other appellations evidently demonstrate; which Mrs. Slipslop, having often heard her mistress use, thought she had also a right to use in her turn; and perhaps she was not mistaken; for these two parties, especially those bordering nearly on each other, to wit, the lowest of the high, and the highest of the low, often change their parties according to place and time; for those who are people of fashion in one place are often people of no fashion in another. And with regard to time, it may not be unpleasant to survey the picture of dependence like a kind of ladder; as, for instance: early in the morning arises the postilion, or some other boy, which great families, no more than great ships, are without, and falls to brushing the clothes and cleaning the shoes of John the footman; who, being drest himself, applies his hands to the same labours for Mr. Second-hand, the squire's gentleman; the gentleman in the like manner, a little later in the day, attends the squire; the squire is no sooner equipped than he attends the levee of my lord; which is no sooner over than my lord himself is seen at the levee of the favourite, who, after the hour of homage is at an end, appears himself to pay homage to the levee of his sovereign. Nor is there, perhaps, in this whole ladder of dependence, any one step at a greater distance from the other than the first from the second; so that to a philosopher the question might only seem, whether you would choose to be a great man at six in the morning, or at two in the afternoon. And yet there are scarce two of these who do not think the least familiarity with the persons below them a condescension, and, if they were to go one step farther, a degradation.

And now, reader, I hope thou wilt pardon this long digression, which seemed to me necessary to vindicate the great character of Mrs. Slipslop from what low people, who have never seen high people, might think an absurdity; but we who know them must have daily found very high persons know us in one place and not in another, to-day and not to-morrow; all which it is difficult to account for otherwise than I have here endeavoured; and perhaps, if the gods, according to the opinion of some, made men only to laugh at them, there is no part of our behaviour which answers the end of our creation better than this.

But to return to our history: Adams, who knew no more of this than the cat which sat on the table, imagining Mrs. Slipslop's memory had been much worse than it really was, followed her into the next room, crying out, "Madam Slipslop, here is one of your old acquaintance; do but see what a fine woman she is grown since she left Lady Booby's service." "I think I *reflect* something of her," answered she, with great dignity, "but I can't remember all the inferior servants in our family." She then proceeded to satisfy Adams's curiosity, by telling him, "When she arrived at the inn, she found a chaise ready for her; that, her lady being expected very shortly in the country, she was obliged to make the utmost haste; and, in *commensuration* of Joseph's lameness, she had taken him with her"; and lastly, "that the excessive *virulence* of the storm had driven them into the house where he found them." After which, she acquainted Adams with his having left his horse, and exprest some wonder at his having strayed so far out of his way, and at meeting him, as she said, "in the company of that wench, who she feared was no better than she should be."

The horse was no sooner put into Adams's head but he was immediately driven out by this reflection on the character of Fanny. He protested, "He believed there was not a chaster damsel in the universe. I heartily wish, I heartily wish," cried he (snapping his fingers), "that all her betters were as good." He then proceeded to inform her of the accident of their meeting; but when he came to mention the circumstance of delivering her from the rape, she said, "She thought him properer for the army than the clergy: that it did not become a clergyman to lay violent hands on anyone; that he should have rather prayed that she might be strengthened." Adams said, "He was very far from being ashamed of what he had done"; she replied, "Want of shame was not the *currycuristic* of a clergyman." This dialogue might have probably grown warmer, had not Joseph opportunely entered the room, to ask leave of Madam Slipslop to introduce Fanny: but she positively refused to admit any such trollops; and told him, "She would have been burnt before she would have suffered him to get into a chaise with her, if she had once *respected* him of having his sluts waylaid on the road for him"; adding, "that Mr. Adams acted a very pretty part, and she did not doubt but to see him a bishop." He made the best bow he could, and cried out, "I thank you, madam, for that right-reverend appellation, which I shall take all honest means to deserve." "Very honest means," returned she, with a sneer, "to bring good people together." At these words Adams took two or three strides across the room, when the coachman came to inform Mrs. Slipslop, "that the storm was over, and the moon shone very bright." She then sent for Joseph, who was sitting without with his Fanny, and would have had him gone with her; but he peremptorily refused to leave Fanny behind; which threw the good woman into a violent rage. She said, "She would inform her lady what doings were carrying on, and did not doubt but she would rid the parish of all such people"; and concluded a long speech, full of bitterness and very hard words, with some reflections on the clergy not decent to repeat; at last, finding Joseph unmoveable, she flung herself into the chaise, casting a look at Fanny as she went, not unlike that which Cleopatra gives Octavia in the play. To say the truth, she was most disagreeably disappointed by the presence of Fanny: she had, from her first seeing Joseph at the inn, conceived hopes of something which might have been accomplished at an alehouse as well as a palace. Indeed, it is probable Mr. Adams had rescued more than Fanny from the danger of a rape that evening.

When the chaise had carried off the enraged Slipslop, Adams, Joseph, and Fanny assembled over the fire, where they had a great deal of innocent chat, pretty enough; but, as possibly it would not be very entertaining to the reader, we shall hasten to the morning; only observing that none of them went to bed that night. Adams, when he had smoked three pipes, took a comfortable nap in a great chair, and left the lovers, whose eyes were too well employed to permit any desire of shutting them, to enjoy by themselves, during some hours, an happiness which none of my readers who have never been in love are capable of the least conception of, though we had as many tongues as Homer desired, to describe it with, and which all true lovers will represent to their own minds without the least assistance from us.

Let it suffice then to say, that Fanny, after a thousand entreaties, a last gave up her whole soul to Joseph; and, almost fainting in his arms, with a sigh infinitely softer and sweeter too than any Arabian breeze, she whispered to his lips, which were then close to hers, "O Joseph, you have won me: I will be yours for ever." Joseph, having thanked her on his knees, and embraced her with an eagerness which she now almost returned, leapt up in a rapture, and awakened the parson, earnestly begging him "that he would that instant join their hands together." Adams rebuked him for his request, and told him, "He would by no means consent to anything contrary to the forms of the Church; that he had no license, nor indeed would he advise him to obtain one. That the Church had prescribed a form — namely, the publication of banns — with which all good Christians ought to comply, and to the omission of which he attributed the many miseries which befell great folks in marriage"; concluding, "As many as are joined together otherwise than G—'s word doth allow are not joined together by G—, neither is their matrimony lawful." Fanny agreed with the parson, saying to Joseph, with a blush, "She assured him she would not consent to any such thing, and that she wondered at his offering it." In which resolution she was comforted and commended by Adams; and Joseph was obliged to wait patiently till after the third publication of the banns, which, however, he obtained the consent of Fanny, in the presence of Adams, to put in at their arrival.

The sun had been now risen some hours, when Joseph, finding his leg surprisingly recovered, proposed to walk forwards; but when they were all ready to set out, an accident a little retarded them. This was no other than the reckoning, which amounted to seven shillings; no great sum, if we consider the immense quantity of ale which Mr. Adams poured in. Indeed, they had no objection to the reasonableness of the bill, but many to the probability of paying it; for the fellow who had taken poor Fanny's purse had unluckily forgot to return it. So that the account stood thus:

	£	s.	d.
Mr. Adams and company, Dr. . . .	0	7	0
In Mr. Adams's pocket	0	0	6½
In Mr. Joseph's	0	0	0
In Mrs. Fanny's	0	0	0
Balance	0	6	5½

They stood silent some few minutes, staring at each other, when Adams whipt out on his toes, and asked the hostess, "If there was no clergyman in that parish?" She answered, "There was." "Is he wealthy?" replied he; to which she likewise answered in the affirmative. Adams then, snapping his fingers, returned overjoyed to his companions, crying out, "*Heureka, Heureka!*" which not being understood, he told them in plain English, "They need give themselves no trouble; for he had a brother in the parish who would defray the reckoning, and that he would just step to his house and fetch the money, and return to them instantly."

CHAPTER XIV.

An interview between Parson Adams and Parson Trulliber.

PARSON ADAMS came to the house of Parson Trulliber, whom he found stript into his waistcoat, with an apron on, and a pail in his hand, just come from serving his hogs; for Mr. Trulliber was a parson on Sundays, but all the other six might more properly be called a farmer. He occupied a small piece of land of his own, besides which he rented a considerable deal more. His wife milked his cows, managed his dairy, and followed the markets with butter and eggs. The hogs fell chiefly to his care, which he carefully waited on at home, and attended to fairs; on which occasion he was liable to many jokes, his own size being, with much ale, rendered little inferior to that of the beasts he sold. He was indeed one of the largest men you should see, and could have acted the part of Sir John Falstaff without stuffing. Add to this that the rotundity of his belly was considerably increased by the shortness of his stature, his shadow ascending very near as far in height, when he lay on his back, as when he stood on his legs. His voice was loud and hoarse, and his accents extremely broad; to complete the whole, he had a stateliness in his gait, when he walked, not unlike that of a goose, only he stalked slower.

Mr. Trulliber, being informed that somebody wanted to speak with him, immediately slipt off his apron, and clothed himself in an old night-gown, being the dress in which he always saw his company at home. His wife, who informed him of Mr. Adams's arrival, had made a small mistake; for she had told her husband, "She believed here was a man come for some of his hogs." This supposition made Mr. Trulliber hasten with the utmost expedition to attend his guest. He no sooner saw Adams than, not in the least doubting the cause of his errand to be what his wife had imagined, he told him, "He was come in very good time; that he expected a dealer that very afternoon"; and added, "they were all pure and fat, and upwards of twenty score a-piece." Adams answered, "He believed he did not know him." "Yes, yes," cried Trulliber, "I have seen you often at fair; why, we have dealt before now, mun, I warrant you; yes, yes," cries he, "I remember thy face very well, but won't mention a word more till you have seen them, though I have never sold thee a flitch of such bacon as is now in the sty." Upon which he laid violent hands on Adams, and dragged him into the hog-sty, which was indeed but two steps from his parlour window. They were no sooner arrived there than he cried out, "Do but handle them! step in, friend! art welcome to handle them, whether dost buy or no." At which words, opening the gate, he pushed Adams into the pig-sty, insisting on it that he should handle them before he would talk one word with him. Adams, whose natural complacence was beyond any artificial, was obliged to comply before he was suffered to explain himself; and, laying hold on one of their tails, the unruly beast gave such a sudden spring, that he threw poor Adams all along in the mire. Trulliber, instead of assisting him to get up, burst into a laughter, and, entering the sty, said to Adams, with some contempt, "Why, dost not know how to handle a hog?" and was going to lay hold of one himself; but Adams, who thought he had carried his complacence far enough, was no sooner on his legs than he escaped out of the reach of the animals, and cried out, "*Nihil habeo cum porcis:* I am a clergyman, sir, and am not come to buy hogs." Trulliber answered, "He was sorry for the mistake; but that he must blame his wife"; adding, "she was a fool, and always committed blunders." He then desired him to walk in and clean himself; that he would only fasten up the sty and follow him. Adams desired leave to dry his greatcoat, wig, and hat by the fire, which Trulliber granted. Mrs. Trulliber would have brought him a basin of water to wash his face, but her husband bid her be quiet like a fool as she was, or she would commit more blunders, and then directed Adams to the pump. While Adams was thus employed, Trulliber, conceiving no great respect for the appearance of his guest, fastened the parlour door, and now conducted him into the kitchen, telling him he believed a cup of drink would do him no harm, and whispered his wife to draw a little of the worst ale. After a short silence, Adams said, "I fancy, sir, you already perceive me to be a clergyman." "Ay, ay," cries Trulliber, grinning, "I perceive you have some cassock; I will not venture to *caale* it a whole one." Adams answered, "It was indeed none of the best; but he had the misfortune to tear it about ten years ago in passing over a stile." Mrs. Trulliber, returning with the drink, told her husband, "She fancied the gentleman was a traveller, and that he would be glad to eat a bit." Trulliber bid her "hold her impertinent tongue"; and asked her, "If parsons used to travel without horses?" adding, "he supposed the gentleman had none by his having no boots on." "Yes, sir, yes," says Adams; "I have a horse, but I have left him behind me." "I am glad to hear you have one," says Trulliber; "for I assure you I don't love to see clergymen on foot; it is not seemly nor suiting the dignity of the cloth." Here Trulliber made a long oration on the dignity of the cloth (or rather gown) not much worth relating, till his wife had spread the table and set a mess of porridge on it for his breakfast. He then said to Adams, "I don't know, friend, how you came to *caale* on me; however, as you are here, if you think proper to eat a morsel, you may." Adams accepted the invitation, and the two parsons sat down together; Mrs. Trulliber waiting behind her husband's chair, as was, it seems, her custom. Trulliber eat heartily, but scarce put anything in his mouth without finding fault with his wife's cookery. All which the poor woman bore patiently. Indeed, she was so absolute an admirer of her husband's greatness and importance, of which she had frequent hints from his own mouth, that she almost carried her adoration to an opinion of his infallibility. To say the truth, the parson had exercised her more ways than one; and the pious woman had so well edified by her husband's sermons, that she had resolved to receive the bad things of this world together with the good. She had indeed been at first a little contentious; but he had long since got the better; partly by her love for *this*, partly by her fear of *that*, partly by her religion, partly by the respect he paid himself, and partly by that which he received from the parish: She had, in short, absolutely submitted, and now worshipped her husband, as Sarah did Abraham, calling him (not lord, but) master. Whilst they were at table, her husband gave her a fresh example of his greatness; for, as she had just delivered a cup of ale to Adams, he snatched it out of his hand, and, crying out, "I *caal'd vurst*," swallowed down the ale. Adams denied it; it was referred to the wife, who, though her conscience was on the side of Adams, durst not give it against her husband. Upon which he said, "No, sir, no; I should not have been so rude to have taken it from you if you had *caal'd vurst*, but I'd have you know I'm a better man than to suffer the best he in the kingdom to drink before me in my own house when I *caale vurst*."

As soon as their breakfast was ended, Adams began in the following manner: "I think, sir, it is high time to inform you of the business of my embassy. I am a traveller, and am passing this way in company with two young people, a lad and a damsel, my parishioners, towards my own cure; we stopt at a house of hospitality in the parish, where they directed me to you as having the cure." — "Though I am but a curate," says Trulliber, "I believe I am as warm as the vicar himself, or perhaps the rector of the next parish too; I believe I could buy them both." "Sir," cries Adams, "I rejoice thereat. Now, sir, my business is, that we are by various accidents stript of our money, and are not able to pay our reckoning, being seven shillings. I therefore request you to assist me with the loan of those seven shillings, and also seven shillings more, which, peradventure, I shall return to you; but if not, I am convinced you will joyfully embrace such an opportunity of laying up a treasure in a better place than any this world affords."

Suppose a stranger, who entered the chambers of a lawyer, being imagined a client, when the lawyer was preparing his palm for the fee, should pull out a writ against him. Suppose an apothecary, at the door of a chariot containing some great doctor of eminent skill, should, instead of directions to a patient, present him with a potion for himself. Suppose a minister should, instead of a good round sum, treat my Lord ——, or Sir ——, or Esq. —— with a good broomstick. Suppose a civil companion, or a led captain, should, instead of virtue, and honour, and beauty, and parts, and admiration, thunder vice and infamy, and ugliness, and folly, and contempt, in his patron's ears. Suppose, when a tradesman first carries in his bill, the man of fashion should pay it; or suppose, if he did so, the tradesman should abate what he had overcharged on the supposition of waiting. In short — suppose what you will, you never can nor will suppose anything equal to the astonishment which seized on Trulliber, as soon as Adams had ended his speech. A while he rolled his eyes in silence; sometimes surveying Adams, then his wife; then casting them on the ground, then lifting them to heaven. At last, he burst forth in the following accents: "Sir, I believe I know where to lay up my little treasure as well as another; I thank G——, if I am not so warm as some, I am content; that is a blessing greater than riches; and he to whom that is given need ask no more. To be content with a little is greater than to possess the world; which a man may possess without being so. Lay up my treasure! what matters where a man's treasure is whose heart is in the Scriptures? there is the treasure of a Christian." At these words the water ran from Adams's eyes; and, catching Trulliber by the hand in a rapture, "Brother," says he, "heavens bless the accident by which I came to see you! I

would have walked many a mile to have communed with you;
and, believe me, I will shortly pay you a second visit; but my
friends, I fancy, by this time, wonder at my stay; so let me have
the money immediately." Trulliber then put on a stern look, and
cried out, "Thou dost not intend to rob me?" At which the wife,
bursting into tears, fell on her knees and roared out, "O dear sir!
for Heaven's sake don't rob my master; we are but poor people."
"Get up, for a fool as thou art, and go about thy business," said
Trulliber: "dost think the man will venture his life? he is a beggar, and no robber." "Very true, indeed," answered Adams. "I
wish, with all my heart, the tithing-man was here," cries Trulliber;
"I would have thee punished as a vagabond for thy impudence.
Fourteen shillings indeed! I won't give thee a farthing. I believe
thou art no more a clergyman than the woman there" (pointing
to his wife); "but if thou art, dost deserve to have thy gown
stript over thy shoulders for running about the country in such
a manner." "I forgive your suspicions," says Adams; "but suppose
I am not a clergyman, I am nevertheless thy brother; and thou,
as a Christian, much more as a clergyman, art obliged to relieve
my distress." "Dost preach to me?" replied Trulliber: "dost pretend to instruct me in my duty?" "Ifacks, a good story," cries
Mrs. Trulliber, "to preach to my master." "Silence, woman!" cries
Trulliber. "I would have thee know, friend" (addressing himself
to Adams), "I shall not learn my duty from such as thee; I know
what charity is, better than to give to vagabonds." "Besides, if
we were inclined, the poor's rate obliges us to give so much
charity," cries the wife. "Pugh! thou art a fool. Poor's rate! Hold
thy nonsense," answered Trulliber; and then, turning to Adams,
he told him, "he would give him nothing." "I am sorry," answered
Adams, "that you do know what charity is, since you practise it no
better; I must tell you, if you trust to your knowledge for your
justification, you will find yourself deceived, though you should
add faith to it, without good works." "Fellow," cries Trulliber,
"dost thou speak against faith in my house? Get out of my doors:
I will no longer remain under the same roof with a wretch who
speaks wantonly of faith and the Scriptures." "Name not the
Scriptures," says Adams. "How! not name the Scriptures! Do
you disbelieve the Scriptures?" cries Trulliber. "No, but you do,"
answered Adams, "if I may reason from your practice, for their
commands are so explicit, and their rewards and punishments so
immense, that it is impossible a man should steadfastly believe
without obeying. Now, there is no command more express, no

duty more frequently enjoined, than charity. Whoever, therefore, is void of charity, I make no scruple of pronouncing that he is no Christian." "I would not advise thee," says Trulliber, "to say that I am no Christian; I won't take it of you; for I believe I am as good a man as thyself" (and indeed, though he was now rather too corpulent for athletic exercises, he had, in his youth, been one of the best boxers and cudgel-players in the county). His wife, seeing him clench his fist, interposed, and begged him not to fight, but show himself a true Christian, and take the law of him. As nothing could provoke Adams to strike, but an absolute assault on himself or his friend, he smiled at the angry look and gestures of Trulliber; and, telling him he was sorry to see such men in orders, departed without further ceremony.

CHAPTER XV.

An adventure, the consequence of a new instance which Parson Adams gave of his forgetfulness.

WHEN he came back to the inn, he found Joseph and Fanny sitting together. They were so far from thinking his absence long, as he had feared they would, that they never once missed or thought of him. Indeed, I have been often assured by both, that they spent these hours in a most delightful conversation; but, as I never could prevail on either to relate it, so I cannot communicate it to the reader.

Adams acquainted the lovers with the ill success of his enterprise. They were all greatly confounded, none being able to propose any method of departing, till Joseph at last advised calling in the hostess, and desiring her to trust them; which Fanny said she despaired of her doing, as she was one of the sourest-faced women she had ever beheld.

But she was agreeably disappointed; for the hostess was no sooner asked the question than she readily agreed; and, with a curtsy and smile, wished them a good journey. However, lest Fanny's skill in physiognomy should be called in question, we will venture to assign one reason which might probably incline her to this confidence and good-humour. When Adams said he was going to visit his brother, he had unwittingly imposed on Joseph and Fanny, who both believed he had meant his natural brother, and not his brother in divinity, and had so informed the hostess, on her inquiry after him. Now Mr. Trulliber had, by his professions of piety, by his gravity, austerity, reserve, and the opinion of his great wealth, so great an authority in his parish, that they all lived in the utmost fear and apprehension of him. It was therefore no wonder that the hostess, who knew it was in his option whether she should ever sell another mug of drink, did not dare to affront his supposed brother by denying him credit.

They were now just on their departure, when Adams recollected he had left his greatcoat and hat at Mr. Trulliber's. As he was not desirous of renewing his visit, the hostess herself, having no servant at home, offered to fetch it.

This was an unfortunate expedient: for the hostess was soon undeceived in the opinion she had entertained of Adams, whom Trulliber abused in the grossest terms, especially when he heard he had had the assurance to pretend to be his near relation.

At her return, therefore, she entirely changed her note. She said, "Folks might be ashamed of travelling about, and pretending to be what they were not. That taxes were high, and, for her part, she was obliged to pay for what she had; she could not therefore possibly, nor would she, trust anybody; no, not her own father. That money was never scarcer, and she wanted to make up a sum. That she expected, therefore, they should pay their reckoning before they left the house."

Adams was now greatly perplexed; but, as he knew that he could easily have borrowed such a sum in his own parish, and as he knew he would have lent it himself to any mortal in distress, so he took fresh courage, and sallied out all round the parish; but to no purpose; he returned as pennyless as he went, groaning and lamenting that it was possible, in a country professing Christianity, for a wretch to starve in the midst of his fellow-creatures who abounded.

Whilst he was gone, the hostess, who stayed as a sort of guard with Joseph and Fanny, entertained them with the goodness of Parson Trulliber. And, indeed, he had not only a very good character as to other qualities in the neighbourhood, but was reputed a man of great charity: for, though he never gave a farthing, he had always that word in his mouth.

Adams was no sooner returned the second time than the storm grew exceeding high, the hostess declaring, among other things, that, if they offered to stir without paying her, she would soon overtake them with a warrant.

Plato or Aristotle, or somebody else, hath said, THAT WHEN THE MOST EXQUISITE CUNNING FAILS, CHANCE OFTEN HITS THE MARK, AND THAT BY MEANS THE LEAST EXPECTED. Virgil expresses this very boldly:

> *Turne, quod optanti divum promittere nemo*
> *Auderet, volvenda dies, en! attulit ultro.*

I would quote more great men if I could; but my memory not permitting me, I will proceed to exemplify these observations by the following instance:

There chanced (for Adams had not cunning enough to contrive it) to be at that time in the alehouse a fellow who had been formerly a drummer in an Irish regiment, and now travelled the country as a pedlar. This man, having attentively listened to the discourse of the hostess, at last took Adams aside, and asked him what the sum was for which they were detained. As soon as he was informed, he sighed, and said, "He was sorry it was so much; for that he had no more than six shillings and sixpence in his pocket, which he would lend them with all his heart." Adams gave a caper, and cried out, "It would do: for that he had sixpence himself." And thus these poor people, who could not engage the compassion of riches and piety, were at length delivered out of their distress by the charity of a poor pedlar.

I shall refer it to my reader to make what observations he pleases on this incident: it is sufficient for me to inform him that, after Adams and his companions had returned him a thousand thanks, and told him where he might call to be repaid, they all sallied out of the house without any compliments from their hostess, or indeed without paying her any; Adams declaring he would take particular care never to call there again; and she on her side assuring them she wanted no such guests.

CHAPTER XVI.

*A very curious adventure, in which Mr. Adams gave a much
greater instance of the honest simplicity of his heart than of
his experience in the ways of this world.*

Our travellers had walked about two miles from that inn, which
they had more reason to have mistaken for a castle than Don
Quixote ever had any of those in which he sojourned, seeing they
had met with such difficulty in escaping out of its walls, when
they came to a parish, and beheld a sign of invitation hanging
out. A gentleman sat smoking a pipe at the door, of whom
Adams inquired the road, and received so courteous and obliging
an answer, accompanied with so smiling a countenance, that the
good parson, whose heart was naturally disposed to love and
affection, began to ask several other questions: particularly the
name of the parish, and who was the owner of a large house
whose front they then had in prospect. The gentleman answered
as obligingly as before; and as to the house, acquainted him it
was his own. He then proceeded in the following manner:
"Sir, I presume by your habit you are a clergyman; and as you
are travelling on foot, I suppose a glass of good beer will not be
disagreeable to you; and I can recommend my landlord's within
as some of the best in all this county. What say you, will you
halt a little and let us take a pipe together? there is no better
tobacco in the kingdom." This proposal was not displeasing to
Adams, who had allayed his thirst that day with no better liquor
than what Mrs. Trulliber's cellar had produced; and which was
indeed little superior, either in richness or flavour, to that
which distilled from those grains her generous husband bestowed
on his hogs. Having therefore abundantly thanked the gentleman for his kind invitation, and bid Joseph and Fanny follow
him, he entered the alehouse, where a large loaf and cheese and
a pitcher of beer, which truly answered the character given of it,
being set before them, the three travellers fell to eating with
appetites infinitely more voracious than are to be found at the
most exquisite eating-houses in the parish of St. James's.

The gentleman expressed great delight in the hearty and
cheerful behaviour of Adams; and particularly in the familiarity
with which he conversed with Joseph and Fanny, whom he often
called his children; a term he explained to mean no more than

his parishioners; saying, "He looked on all those whom God had entrusted to his cure to stand to him in that relation." The gentleman, shaking him by the hand, highly applauded those sentiments. "They are, indeed," says he, "the true principles of a Christian divine; and I heartily wish they were universal: but, on the contrary, I am sorry to say the parson of our parish, instead of esteeming his poor parishioners as a part of his family, seems rather to consider them as not of the same species with himself. He seldom speaks to any, unless some few of the richest of us; nay, indeed, he will not move his hat to the others. I often laugh when I behold him on Sundays strutting along the churchyard like a turkey-cock through rows of his parishioners, who bow to him with as much submission, and are as unregarded, as a set of servile courtiers by the proudest prince in Christendom. But if such temporal pride is ridiculous, surely the spiritual is odious and detestable; if such a puffed-up empty human bladder, strutting in princely robes, justly moves one's derision, surely in the habit of a priest it must raise our scorn."

"Doubtless," answered Adams, "your opinion is right; but I hope such examples are rare. The clergy whom I have the honour to know maintain a different behaviour; and you will allow me, sir, that the readiness which too many of the laity show to contemn the order may be one reason of their avoiding too much humility." "Very true, indeed," says the gentleman; "I find, sir, you are a man of excellent sense, and am happy in this opportunity of knowing you; perhaps our accidental meeting may not be disadvantageous to you neither. At present, I shall only say to you that the incumbent of this living is old and infirm, and that it is in my gift. Doctor, give me your hand; and assure yourself of it at his decease." Adams told him, "He was never more confounded in his life than at his utter incapacity to make any return to such noble and unmerited generosity." "A mere trifle, sir," cries the gentleman, "scarce worth your acceptance; a little more than three hundred a year. I wish it was double the value for your sake." Adams bowed, and cried from the emotions of his gratitude; when the other asked him, "If he was married, or had any children, besides those in the spiritual sense he had mentioned." "Sir," replied the parson, "I have a wife and six at your service." "That is unlucky," says the gentleman; "for I would otherwise have taken you into my own house as my chaplain; however, I have another in the parish (for the

parsonage-house is not good enough), which I will furnish for
you. Pray, does your wife understand a dairy?" "I can't profess
she does," says Adams. "I am sorry for it," quoth the gentleman;
"I would have given you half-a-dozen cows, and very good
grounds to have maintained them." "Sir," said Adams, in an
ecstasy, "you are too liberal; indeed you are." "Not at all," cries
the gentleman; "I esteem riches only as they give me an opportunity of doing good; and I never saw one whom I had a
greater inclination to serve." At which words he shook him
heartily by the hand, and told him he had sufficient room in
his house to entertain him and his friends. Adams begged he
might give him no such trouble; that they could be very well
accommodated in the house where they were, forgetting they
had not a sixpenny piece among them. The gentleman would
not be denied; and, informing himself how far they were travelling, he said it was too long a journey to take on foot, and begged
that they would favour him by suffering him to lend them a
servant and horses; adding, withal, that, if they would do him
the pleasure of their company only two days, he would furnish
them with his coach and six. Adams, turning to Joseph, said,
"How lucky is this gentleman's goodness to you, who I am afraid
would be scarce able to hold out on your lame leg"; and then,
addressing the person who made him these liberal promises, after
much bowing, he cried out, "Blessed be the hour which first
introduced me to a man of your charity! you are indeed a Christian of the true primitive kind, and an honour to the country
wherein you live. I would willingly have taken a pilgrimage
to the Holy Land to have beheld you: for the advantages which
we draw from your goodness give me little pleasure, in comparison of what I enjoy for your own sake when I consider the treasures you are by these means laying up for yourself in a country
that passeth not away. We will therefore, most generous sir,
accept your goodness, as well the entertainment you have so
kindly offered us at your house this evening, as the accommodation of your horses to-morrow morning." He then began to
search for his hat, as did Joseph for his; and both they and Fanny
were in order of departure, when the gentleman, stopping short,
and seeming to meditate by himself for the space of about a
minute, exclaimed thus: "Sure never anything was so unlucky;
I had forgot that my housekeeper was gone abroad, and hath
locked up all my rooms; indeed, I would break them open for
you, but shall not be able to furnish you with a bed; for she

has likewise put away all my linen. I am glad it entered into my head before I had given you the trouble of walking there; besides, I believe you will find better accommodations here than you expected. Landlord, you can provide good beds for these people, can't you?" "Yes, and please your worship," cries the host, "and such as no lord or justice of the peace in the kingdom need be ashamed to lie in." "I am heartily sorry," says the gentleman, "for this disappointment. I am resolved I will never suffer her to carry away the keys again." "Pray, sir, let it not make you uneasy," cries Adams; "we shall do very well here; and the loan of your horses is a favour we shall be incapable of making any return to." "Ay!" said the squire, "the horses shall attend you here at what hour in the morning you please." And now, after many civilities too tedious to enumerate, many squeezes by the hand, with most affectionate looks and smiles at each other, and after appointing the horses at seven the next morning, the gentleman took his leave of them, and departed to his own house. Adams and his companions returned to the table, where the parson smoked another pipe, and then they all retired to rest.

Mr. Adams rose very early, and called Joseph out of his bed, between whom a very fierce dispute ensued whether Fanny should ride behind Joseph, or behind the gentleman's servant; Joseph insisting on it that he was perfectly recovered, and was as capable of taking care of Fanny as any other person could be. But Adams would not agree to it, and declared he would not trust her behind him; for that he was weaker than he imagined himself to be.

This dispute continued a long time, and had begun to be very hot, when a servant arrived from their good friend, to acquaint them that he was unfortunately prevented from lending them any horses; for that his groom had, unknown to him, put his whole stable under a course of physic.

This advice presently struck the two disputants dumb: Adams cried out, "Was ever anything so unlucky as this poor gentleman? I protest I am more sorry on his account than my own. You see, Joseph, how this good-natured man is treated by his servants; one locks up his linen, another physics his horses, and, I suppose, by his being at this house last night, the butler had locked up his cellar. Bless us! how good-nature is used in this world! I protest I am more concerned on his account than my own." "So am not I," cries Joseph; "not that I am much troubled about walking on foot; all my concern is, how we shall get out of the house, unless God sends another pedlar to redeem us. But certainly, this gentleman has such an affection for you, that he would lend you a larger sum than we owe here, which is not above four or five shillings." "Very true, child," answered Adams; "I will write a letter to him, and will even venture to solicit him for three half-crowns; there will be no harm in having two or three shillings in our pockets; as we have full forty miles to travel, we may possibly have occasion for them."

Fanny being now risen, Joseph paid her a visit, and left Adams to write his letter, which having finished, he dispatched a boy with it to the gentleman, and then seated himself by the door, lighted his pipe, and betook himself to meditation.

The boy staying longer than seemed to be necessary, Joseph, who with Fanny was now returned to the parson, expressed some apprehensions that the gentleman's steward had locked up his purse too. To which Adams answered, "It might very possibly be; and he should wonder at no liberties which the devil might put into the head of a wicked servant to take with so worthy a master"; but added, "that, as the sum was so small, so noble a gentleman would be easily able to procure it in the parish, though he had it not in his own pocket. Indeed," says he, "if it was four or five guineas, or any such large quantity of money, it might be a different matter."

They were now sat down to breakfast over some toast and ale, when the boy returned, and informed them that the gentleman was not at home. "Very well!" cries Adams; "but why, child, did you not stay till his return? Go back again, my good boy, and wait for his coming home: he cannot be gone far, as his horses are all sick; and besides, he had no intention to go abroad; for he invited us to spend this day and to-morrow at his house. Therefore go back, child, and tarry till his return home." The messenger departed, and was back again with great expedition, bringing an account that the gentleman was gone a long journey, and would not be at home again this month. At these words Adams seemed greatly confounded, saying, "This must be a sudden accident, as the sickness or death of a relation, or some such unforeseen misfortune"; and then, turning to Joseph, cried, "I wish you had reminded me to have borrowed this money last night." Joseph, smiling, answered, "He was very much deceived if the gentleman would not have found some excuse to

avoid lending it. I own," says he, "I was never much pleased
with his professing so much kindness for you at first sight: for
I have heard the gentlemen of our cloth in London tell many
such stories of their masters. But when the boy brought the
message back of his not being at home, I presently knew what
would follow; for, whenever a man of fashion doth not care to
fulfil his promises, the custom is to order his servants that he will
never be at home to the person so promised. In London they
call it 'denying him.' I have myself denied Sir Thomas Booby
above a hundred times; and when the man hath danced attendance for about a month, or sometimes longer, he is acquainted
in the end that the gentleman is gone out of town, and could do
nothing in the business." "Good Lord!" says Adams, "what
wickedness is there in the Christian world! I profess almost
equal to what I have read of the heathens. But surely, Joseph,
your suspicions of this gentleman must be unjust; for what
a silly fellow must he be who would do the devil's work for
nothing! and canst thou tell me any interest he could possibly
propose to himself by deceiving us in his professions?" "It is
not for me," answered Joseph, "to give reasons for what men do,
to a gentleman of your learning." "You say right," quoth
Adams; "knowledge of men is only to be learnt from books;
Plato and Seneca for that; and those are authors, I am afraid,
child, you never read." "Not I, sir, truly," answered Joseph;
"all I know is, it is a maxim among the gentlemen of our cloth,
that those masters who promise the most perform the least; and
I have often heard them say they have found the largest vails in
those families where they were not promised any. But, sir,
instead of considering any farther these matters, it would be
our wisest way to contrive some method of getting out of this
house: for the generous gentleman, instead of doing us any service, hath left us the whole reckoning to pay." Adams was
going to answer, when their host came in, and, with a kind of
jeering smile, said, "Well, masters! the squire hath not sent his
horses for you yet. Laud help me! how easily some folks make
promises!" "How!" says Adams; "have you ever known him
do anything of this kind before?" "Ay! marry have I," answered
the host; "it is no business of mine, you know, sir, to say
anything to a gentleman to his face: but now he is not here,
I will assure you, he hath not his fellow within the three next
market-towns. I own I could not help laughing when I heard him
offer you the living, for thereby hangs a good jest. I thought he

would have offered you my house next; for one is no more his to dispose of than the other." At these words, Adams, blessing himself, declared, "He had never read of such a monster; but what vexes me most," says he, "is, that he hath decoyed us into running up a long debt with you, which we are not able to pay; for we have no money about us, and, what is worse, live at such a distance, that if you should trust us, I am afraid you would lose your money for want of our finding any conveniency of sending it." "Trust you, master!" says the host, "that I will with all my heart; I honour the clergy too much to deny trusting one of them for such a trifle; besides, I like your fear of never paying me. I have lost many a debt in my lifetime, but was promised to be paid them all in a very short time. I will score this reckoning for the novelty of it. It is the first, I do assure you, of its kind. But what say you, master, shall we have t'other pot before we part? It will waste but a little chalk more; and if you never pay me a shilling, the loss will not ruin me." Adams liked the invitation very well, especially as it was delivered with so hearty an accent. — He shook his host by the hand, and, thanking him, said, "He would tarry another pot rather for the pleasure of such worthy company than for the liquor"; adding, "he was glad to find some Christians left in the kingdom; for that he almost began to suspect that he was sojourning in a country inhabited only by Jews and Turks."

The kind host produced the liquor, and Joseph with Fanny retired into the garden, where, while they solaced themselves with amorous discourse, Adams sat down with his host; and, both filling their glasses, and lighting their pipes, they began that dialogue which the reader will find in the next chapter.

CHAPTER XVII.

A dialogue between Mr. Abraham Adams and his host, which, by the disagreement in their opinions, seemed to threaten an unlucky catastrophe, had it not been timely prevented by the return of the lovers.

"SIR," said the host, "I assure you you are not the first to whom our squire hath promised more than he hath performed. He is so famous for this practice, that his word will not be taken for much by those who know him. I remember a young fellow whom he promised his parents to make an exciseman. The poor people, who could ill afford it, bred their son to writing and accounts, and other learning, to qualify him for the place; and the boy held up his head above his condition with these hopes; nor would he go to plough, nor to any other kind of work, and went constantly drest as fine as could be, with two clean Holland shirts a week, and this for several years; till at last he followed the squire up to London, thinking there to mind him of his promises; but he could never get sight of him. So that, being out of money and business, he fell into evil company and wicked courses; and in the end came to a sentence of transportation, the news of which broke the mother's heart. I will tell you another true story of him: There was a neighbour of mine, a farmer, who had two sons whom he bred up to the business. Pretty lads they were; nothing would serve the squire but that the youngest must be made a parson. Upon which he persuaded the father to send him to school, promising that he would afterwards maintain him at the university, and, when he was of a proper age, give him a living. But after the lad had been seven years at school, and his father brought him to the squire, with a letter from his master that he was fit for the university, the squire, instead of minding his promise, or sending him thither at his expense, only told his father that the young man was a fine scholar, and it was pity he could not afford to keep him at Oxford for four or five years more, by which time, if he could get him a curacy, he might have him ordained. The farmer said, 'He was not a man sufficient to do any such thing.' 'Why, then,' answered the squire, 'I am very sorry you have given him so much learning; for, if he cannot get his living by that, it will rather spoil him for anything else; and your other son, who can hardly write his name, will do more at ploughing and sowing, and is in a better condition, than he.' And indeed so it proved; for the poor lad, not finding friends to maintain him in his learning as he had expected, and being unwilling to work, fell to drinking, though he was a very sober lad before; and in a short time, partly with grief, and partly with good liquor, fell into a consumption, and died. Nay, I can tell you more still: There was another, a young woman, and the handsomest in all this neighbourhood, whom he enticed up to London, promising to make her a gentlewoman to one of your women of quality: but, instead of keeping his word, we have since heard, after having a child by her himself, she became a common whore; then kept a coffee-house in Covent Garden; and a little after died of the French distemper in a gaol. I could tell you many more stories: but how do you imagine he served me myself? You must know, sir, I was bred a seafaring man, and have been many voyages; till at last I came to be master of a ship myself, and was in a fair way of making a fortune, when I was attacked by one of those cursed *guarda-costas* who took our ships before the beginning of the war; and after a fight, wherein I lost the greater part of my crew, my rigging being all demolished, and two shots received between wind and water, I was forced to strike. The villains carried off my ship, a brigantine of 150 tons — a pretty creature she was — and put me, a man, and a boy, into a little bad pink, in which, with much ado, we at last made Falmouth; though I believe the Spaniards did not imagine she could possibly live a day at sea. Upon my return hither, where my wife, who was of this country, then lived, the squire told me he was so pleased with the defence I had made against the enemy, that he did not fear getting me promoted to a lieutenancy of a man-of-war, if I would accept of it; which I thankfully assured him I would. Well, sir, two or three years passed, during which I had many repeated promises, not only from the squire, but (as he told me) from the lords of the admiralty. He never returned from London but I was assured I might be satisfied now, for I was certain of the first vacancy; and, what surprises me still, when I reflect on it, these assurances were given me with no less confidence, after so many disappointments, than at first. At last, sir, growing weary, and somewhat suspicious, after so much delay, I wrote to a friend in London, who I knew had some acquaintance at the best house in the admiralty, and desired him to back the squire's interest: for indeed I feared he had solicited the affair with more coldness than he pretended. — And what answer do you think my friend sent me? — Truly, sir, he acquainted me that the squire had never mentioned my name at the admiralty in his life; and, unless I had much faithfuller interest, advised me to give over my pretensions; which I immediately did, and, with the concurrence of my wife, resolved to set up an alehouse, where you are heartily welcome: and so my service to you; and may the squire, and all such sneaking rascals, go to the devil together." "O fie!" says Adams, "O fie! He is indeed a wicked man; but G— will, I hope, turn his heart to repentance. Nay, if he could but once see the meanness of this detestable vice; would he but once reflect that he is one of the most scandalous as well as pernicious liars; sure he must despise himself to so intolerable a degree, that it would be impossible for him to continue a moment in such a course. And, to confess the truth, notwithstanding the baseness of this character, which he hath too well deserved, he hath in his countenance sufficient symptoms of that *bona indoles,* that sweetness of disposition, which furnishes out a good Christian." "Ah, master! master!" says the host, "if you had travelled as far as I have, and conversed with the many nations where I have traded, you would not give any credit to a man's countenance. Symptoms in his countenance, quotha! I would look there, perhaps, to see whether a man had had the small-pox, but for nothing else!" He spoke this with so little regard to the parson's observation, that it a good deal nettled him; and, taking the pipe hastily from his mouth, he thus answered: "Master of mine, perhaps I have travelled a great deal farther than you without the assistance of a ship. Do you imagine sailing by different cities or countries is travelling? No.

Cœlum non animum mutant qui trans mare currunt.

I can go farther in an afternoon than you in a twelvemonth. What, I suppose you have seen the Pillars of Hercules, and perhaps the walls of Carthage. Nay, you may have heard Scylla, and seen Charybdis; you may have entered the closet where Archimedes was found at the taking Syracuse. I suppose you have sailed among the Cyclades, and passed the famous straits which take their name from the unfortunate Helle, whose fate is sweetly described by Apollonius Rhodius; you have passed the very spot, I conceive, where Dædalus fell into that sea, his waxen wings being melted by the sun; you have traversed the Euxine sea, I make no doubt; nay, you may have been on the banks of the Caspian, and called at Colchis, to see if there is ever another golden fleece." — "Not I, truly, master," answered the host: "I never touched at any of these places." "But I have been at all these," replied Adams. "Then, I suppose," cries the host, "you have been at the East Indies; for there are no such, I will be sworn, either in the West or the Levant." "Pray where's the Levant?" quoth Adams; "that should be in the East Indies by right." — "O ho! you are a pretty traveller," cries the host, "and not know the Levant! My service to you, master; you must not talk of these things with me! you must not tip us the traveller; it won't go here." "Since thou art so dull to misunderstand me still," quoth Adams, "I will inform thee; the travelling I mean is in books, the only way of travelling by which any knowledge is to be acquired. From them I learn what I asserted just now, that nature generally imprints such a portraiture of the mind in the countenance, that a skilful physiognomist will rarely be deceived. I presume you have never read the story of Socrates to this purpose, and therefore I will tell it you. A certain physiognomist asserted of Socrates, that he plainly discovered by his features that he was a rogue in his nature. A character so contrary to the tenour of all this great man's actions, and the generally received opinion concerning him, incensed the boys of Athens so, that they threw stones at the physiognomist, and would have demolished him for his ignorance, had not Socrates himself prevented them by confessing the truth of his observations, and acknowledging that, though he corrected his disposition by philosophy, he was indeed naturally as inclined to vice as had been predicated of him. Now, pray resolve me — How should a man know this story if he had not read it?" "Well, master," said the host, "and what signifies it whether a man knows it or no? He who goes abroad, as I have done, will always have opportunities enough of knowing the world without troubling his head with Socrates, or any such fellows." — "Friend," cries Adams, "if a man should sail round the world, and anchor in every harbour of it, without learning, he would return home as ignorant as he went out." "Lord help you!" answered the host; "there was my boatswain, poor fellow! he could scarce either write or read, and yet he would navigate a ship with any master of a man-of-war; and a very pretty knowledge of trade he had too." "Trade," answered Adams, "as Aristotle proves in his first chapter of Politics, is below a philosopher, and unnatural as it is managed now." The host looked steadfastly at Adams, and after a minute's silence asked him, "If he was one of the writers of the *Gazetteers?* for I have heard," says he, "they are writ by parsons." "*Gazetteers!*" answered Adams, "what is that?" "It is a dirty newspaper," replied the host, "which hath been given away all over the nation for these many years, to abuse trade and honest men, which I would not suffer to lie on my table, though it hath been offered me for nothing." "Not I truly," said Adams; "I never write anything but sermons; and I assure you I am no enemy to trade, whilst it is consistent with honesty; nay, I have always looked on the tradesman as a very valuable member of society,

and perhaps inferior to none but the man of learning." "No, I
believe he is not, nor to him neither," answered the host. "Of
what use would learning be in a country without trade? What
would all you parsons do to clothe your backs and feed your
bellies? Who fetches you your silks and your linens, and your
wines, and all the other necessaries of life? I speak chiefly with
regard to the sailors." "You should say the extravagancies of life,"
replied the parson; "but admit they were the necessaries, there is
something more necessary than life itself, which is provided by
learning; I mean the learning of the clergy. Who clothes you with
piety, meekness, humility, charity, patience, and all the other
Christian virtues? Who feeds your souls with the milk of
brotherly love, and diets them with all the dainty food of holi-
ness, which at once cleanses them of all impure carnal affections,
and fattens them with the truly rich spirit of grace? — Who doth
this?" "Ay, who, indeed!" cries the host; "for I do not remember
ever to have seen any such clothing or such feeding. And so
in the mean time, master, my service to you." Adams was going
to answer with some severity, when Joseph and Fanny returned,
and pressed his departure so eagerly that he would not refuse
them; and so, grasping his crabstick, he took leave of his host
(neither of them being so well pleased with each other as they
had been at their first sitting down together), and with Joseph
and Fanny, who both expressed much impatience, departed, and
now all together renewed their journey.

BOOK III.

CHAPTER I.

Matter prefatory in praise of biography.

NOTWITHSTANDING the preference which may be vulgarly given
to the authority of those romance-writers who entitle their books
"the History of England, the History of France, of Spain, &c.,"
it is most certain that truth is to be found only in the works of
those who celebrate the lives of great men, and are commonly
called biographers, as the others should indeed be termed topographers or chorographers: words which might well mark the
distinction between them; it being the business of the latter
chiefly to describe countries and cities, which, with the assistance
of maps, they do pretty justly, and may be depended upon; but as
to the actions and characters of men, their writings are not quite
so authentic, of which there needs no other proof than those
eternal contradictions occurring between two topographers who
undertake the history of the same country: for instance, between
my Lord Clarendon and Mr. Whitlock, between Mr. Echard
and Rapin, and many others; where, facts being set forth in a
different light, every reader believes as he pleases; and, indeed,
the more judicious and suspicious very justly esteem the whole
as no other than a romance, in which the writer hath indulged
a happy and fertile invention. But though these widely differ
in the narrative of facts; some ascribing victory to the one,
and others to the other party; some representing the same man
as a rogue, to whom others give a great and honest character;
yet all agree in the scene where the fact is supposed to have
happened, and where the person, who is both a rogue and an
honest man, lived. Now with us biographers the case is different;
the facts we deliver may be relied on, though we often mistake
the age and country wherein they happened: for, though it may
be worth the examination of critics, whether the shepherd
Chrysostom, who, as Cervantes informs us, died for love of the
fair Marcella, who hated him, was ever in Spain, will anyone
doubt but that such a silly fellow hath really existed? Is there in

the world such a sceptic as to disbelieve the madness of Cardenio, the perfidy of Ferdinand, the impertinent curiosity of Anselmo, the weakness of Camilla, the irresolute friendship of Lothario? though perhaps, as to the time and place where those several persons lived, that good historian may be deplorably deficient: but the most known instance of this kind is in the true history of Gil Blas, where the inimitable biographer hath made a notorious blunder in the country of Dr. Sangrado, who used his patients as a vintner doth his wine vessels, by letting out their blood, and filling them up with water. Doth not everyone, who is the least versed in physical history, know that Spain was not the country in which this doctor lived? The same writer hath likewise erred in the country of his archbishop, as well as that of those great personages whose understandings were too sublime to taste anything but tragedy, and in many others. The same mistakes may likewise be observed in Scarron, the *Arabian Nights,* the history of Marianne and *Le Paisan Parvenu,* and perhaps some few other writers of this class, whom I have not read, or do not at present recollect; for I would by no means be thought to comprehend those persons of surprising genius, the authors of immense romances, or the modern novel and Atalantis writers; who, without any assistance from nature or history, record persons who never were, or will be, and facts which never did, nor possibly can, happen; whose heroes are of their own creation, and their brains the chaos whence all their materials are collected. Not that such writers deserve no honour; so far otherwise, that perhaps they merit the highest: for what can be nobler than to be as an example of the wonderful extent of human genius! One may apply to them what Balzac says of Aristotle, that they are "a second nature" (for they have no communication with the first; by which, authors of an inferior class, who cannot stand alone, are obliged to support themselves as with crutches); but these of whom I am now speaking seem to be possessed of "those stilts," which the excellent Voltaire tells us, in his Letters, "carry the genius far off, but with an irregular pace." Indeed, far out of the sight of the reader,

Beyond the realm of Chaos and old Night.

But, to return to the former class, who are contented to copy nature, instead of forming originals from the confused heap of matter in their own brains: is not such a book as that which records the achievements of the renowned Don Quixote more

worthy the name of a history than even Mariana's? for, whereas
the latter is confined to a particular period of time, and to a
particular nation, the former is the history of the world in general,
at least that part which is polished by laws, arts, and sciences;
and of that from the time it was first polished to this day; nay,
and forwards as long as it shall so remain.

I shall now proceed to apply these observations to the work
before us; for indeed I have set them down principally to obviate
some constructions which the good-nature of mankind, who are
always forward to see their friends' virtues recorded, may put
to particular parts. I question not but several of my readers
will know the lawyer in the stage-coach the moment they hear
his voice. It is likewise odds but the wit and the prude meet
with some of their acquaintance, as well as all the rest of my
characters. To prevent, therefore, any such malicious applications, I declare here, once for all, I describe not men, but manners;
not an individual, but a species. Perhaps it will be answered,
Are not the characters then taken from life? To which I answer
in the affirmative; nay, I believe I might aver that I have writ
little more than I have seen. The lawyer is not only alive, but
hath been so these four thousand years; and I hope G— will
indulge his life as many yet to come. He hath not indeed confined himself to one profession, one religion, or one country; but
when the first mean selfish creature appeared upon the human
stage, who made self the centre of the whole creation, would give
himself no pain, incur no danger, advance no money, to assist or
preserve his fellow-creatures; then was our lawyer born; and,
whilst such a person as I have described exists on earth, so
long shall he remain upon it. It is, therefore, doing him little
honour to imagine he endeavours to mimic some little obscure
fellow, because he happens to resemble him in one particular
feature, or perhaps in his profession; whereas his appearance in
the world is calculated for much more general and noble purposes; not to expose one pitiful wretch to the small and contemptible circle of his acquaintance; but to hold the glass to
thousands in their closets, that they may contemplate their deformity, and endeavour to reduce it, and thus by suffering private
mortification may avoid public shame. This places the boundary
between, and distinguishes the satirist from the libeller: for the
former privately corrects the fault for the benefit of the person,
like a parent; the latter publicly exposes the person himself, as
an example to others, like an executioner.

There are, besides, little circumstances to be considered; as the drapery of a picture, which though fashion varies at different times, the resemblance of the countenance is not by those means diminished. Thus, I believe, we may venture to say Mrs. Tow-wouse is coeval with our lawyer: and, though perhaps, during the changes which so long an existence must have passed through, she may in her turn have stood behind the bar at an inn, I will not scruple to affirm she hath likewise in the revolution of ages sat on a throne. In short, where extreme turbulency of temper, avarice, and an insensibility of human misery, with a degree of hypocrisy, have united in a female composition, Mrs. Tow-wouse was that woman; and where a good inclination, eclipsed by a poverty of spirit and understanding, hath glimmered forth in a man, that man hath been no other than her sneaking husband.

I shall detain my reader no longer than to give him one caution more of an opposite kind: for, as in most of our particular characters we mean not to lash individuals, but all of the like sort, so, in our general descriptions, we mean not universals, but would be understood with many exceptions: for instance, in our description of high people, we cannot be intended to include such as, whilst they are an honour to their high rank, by a well-guided condescension make their superiority as easy as possible to those whom fortune chiefly hath placed below them. Of this number I could name a peer no less elevated by nature than by fortune; who, whilst he wears the noblest ensigns of honour on his person, bears the truest stamp of dignity on his mind, adorned with greatness, enriched with knowledge, and embellished with genius. I have seen this man relieve with generosity, while he hath conversed with freedom, and be to the same person a patron and a companion. I could name a commoner, raised higher above the multitude by superior talents than is in the power of his prince to exalt him; whose behaviour to those he hath obliged is more amiable than the obligation itself, and who is so great a master of affability, that, if he could divest himself of an inherent greatness in his manner, he would often make the lowest of his acquaintance forget who was the master of that palace in which they are so courteously entertained. These are pictures which must be, I believe, known: I declare they are taken from the life, and not intended to exceed it. By those high people, therefore, whom I have described, I mean a set of wretches, who, while they are a disgrace to their ancestors, whose honours and fortunes they inherit (or perhaps a greater to their mother, for such degeneracy is scarce credible), have the insolence to treat those with disregard who are at least equal to the founders of their own splendour. It is, I fancy, impossible to conceive a spectacle more worthy of our indignation, than that of a fellow who is not only a blot in the escutcheon of a great family, but a scandal to the human species, maintaining a supercilious behaviour to men who are an honour to their nature and a disgrace to their fortune.

And now, reader, taking these hints along with you, you may, if you please, proceed to the sequel of this our true history.

CHAPTER II

A night scene, wherein several wonderful adventures befell Adams and his fellow-travellers.

It was so late when our travellers left the inn or alehouse (for it might be called either), that they had not travelled many miles before night overtook them, or met them, which you please. The reader must excuse me if I am not particular as to the way they took; for, as we are now drawing near the seat of the Boobies, and as that is a ticklish name, which malicious persons may apply, according to their evil inclinations, to several worthy country squires, a race of men whom we look upon as entirely inoffensive, and for whom we have an adequate regard, we shall lend no assistance to any such malicious purposes.

Darkness had now overspread the hemisphere, when Fanny whispered Joseph "that she begged to rest herself a little; for that she was so tired she could walk no farther." Joseph immediately prevailed with Parson Adams, who was as brisk as a bee, to stop. He had no sooner seated himself than he lamented the loss of his dear Æschylus, but was a little comforted when reminded that, if he had it in his possession, he could not see to read.

The sky was so clouded that not a star appeared. It was indeed, according to Milton, darkness visible. This was a circumstance, however, very favourable to Joseph; for Fanny, not suspicious of being overseen by Adams, gave a loose to her passion which she had never done before, and, reclining her head on his bosom, threw her arm carelessly round him, and suffered him to lay his cheek close to hers. All this infused such happiness into Joseph, that he would not have changed his turf for the finest down in the finest palace in the universe.

Adams sat at some distance from the lovers, and, being unwilling to disturb them, applied himself to meditation; in which he had not spent much time before he discovered a light at some distance that seemed approaching towards him. He immediately hailed it; but, to his sorrow and surprise, it stopped for a moment, and then disappeared. He then called to Joseph, asking him, "if he had not seen the light?" Joseph answered, "he had." "And did you not mark how it vanished?" returned he; "though I am not afraid of ghosts, I do not absolutely disbelieve them."

He then entered into a meditation on those unsubstantial beings; which was soon interrupted by several voices, which he thought almost at his elbow, though in fact they were not so extremely near. However, he could distinctly hear them agree on the murder of anyone they met. And a little after heard one of them say, "he had killed a dozen since that day fortnight."

Adams now fell on his knees, and committed himself to the care of Providence; and poor Fanny, who likewise heard those terrible words, embraced Joseph so closely, that had not he, whose ears were also open, been apprehensive on her account, he would have thought no danger which threatened only himself too dear a price for such embraces.

Joseph now drew forth his penknife, and Adams, having finished his ejaculations, grasped his crabstick, his only weapon, and, coming up to Joseph, would have had him quit Fanny, and place her in the rear: but his advice was fruitless; she clung closer to him, not at all regarding the presence of Adams, and in a soothing voice declared, "she would die in his arms." Joseph, clasping her with inexpressible eagerness, whispered her, "that he preferred death in hers to life out of them." Adams, brandishing his crabstick, said, "he despised death as much as any man," and then repeated aloud:

> *Est hic, est animus lucis contemptor et illum,*
> *Qui vita bene credat emi quo tendis, honorem.*

Upon this the voices ceased for a moment, and then one of them called out, "D—n you, who is there?" To which Adams was prudent enough to make no reply; and of a sudden he observed half-a-dozen lights, which seemed to rise all at once from the ground and advance briskly towards him. This he immediately concluded to be an apparition; and now, beginning to conceive that the voices were of the same kind, he called out, "In the name of the L—d, what wouldst thou have?" He had no sooner spoke than he heard one of the voices cry out, "D—n them, here they come"; and soon after heard several hearty blows, as if a number of men had been engaged at quarterstaff. He was just advancing towards the place of combat, when Joseph, catching him by the skirts, begged him that they might take the opportunity of the dark to convey away Fanny from the danger which threatened her. He presently complied, and, Joseph lifting up Fanny, they all three made the best of their way; and without looking behind them, or being overtaken, they had travelled full two miles, poor Fanny not once complaining of being tired, when they saw far off several lights scattered at a small distance from each other, and at the same time found themselves on the descent of a very steep hill. Adams's foot slipping, he instantly disappeared, which greatly frightened both Joseph and Fanny; indeed, if the light had permitted them to see it, they would scarce have refrained laughing to see the parson rolling down the hill; which he did from top to bottom, without receiving any harm. He then hollowed as loud as he could, to inform them of his safety, and to relieve them from the fears which they had conceived for him. Joseph and Fanny halted some time, considering what to do; at last, they advanced a few paces, where the declivity seemed least steep; and then Joseph, taking his Fanny in his arms, walked firmly down the hill, without making a false step, and at length landed her at the bottom, where Adams soon came to them.

Learn hence, my fair countrywomen, to consider your own weakness, and the many occasions on which the strength of a man may be useful to you; and, duly weighing this, take care that you match not yourselves with the spindle-shanked beaus and *petit-maîtres* of the age, who, instead of being able, like Joseph Andrews, to carry you in lusty arms through the rugged ways and downhill steeps of life, will rather want to support their feeble limbs with your strength and assistance.

Our travellers now moved forwards where the nearest light presented itself; and, having crossed a common field, they came to a meadow, where they seemed to be at a very little distance from the light, when, to their grief, they arrived at the banks of a river. Adams here made a full stop, and declared he could swim, but doubted how it was possible to get Fanny over; to

which Joseph answered, "If they walked along its banks, they
might be certain of soon finding a bridge, especially as by the
number of lights they might be assured a parish was near."
"Odso, that's true indeed," said Adams; "I did not think of that."

Accordingly, Joseph's advice being taken, they passed over
two meadows, and came to a little orchard, which led them to a
house. Fanny begged of Joseph to knock at the door, assuring
him, "She was so weary that she could hardly stand on her feet."
Adams, who was foremost, performed this ceremony; and, the
door being immediately opened, a plain kind of man appeared at
it: Adams acquainted him, "That they had a young woman with
them who was so tired with her journey that he should be much
obliged to him if he would suffer her to come in and rest
herself." The man, who saw Fanny by the light of the candle
which he held in his hand, perceiving her innocent and modest
look, and having no apprehensions from the civil behaviour of
Adams, presently answered, "That the young woman was very
welcome to rest herself in his house, and so were her company."
He then ushered them into a very decent room, where his wife
was sitting at a table: she immediately rose up, and assisted
them in setting forth chairs, and desired them to sit down;
which they had no sooner done than the man of the house
asked them if they would have anything to refresh themselves
with? Adams thanked him, and answered he should be obliged
to him for a cup of his ale, which was likewise chosen by Joseph
and Fanny. Whilst he was gone to fill a very large jug with
this liquor, his wife told Fanny she seemed greatly fatigued, and
desired her to take something stronger than ale; but she refused
with many thanks, saying it was true she was very much tired,
but a little rest she hoped would restore her. As soon as the
company were all seated, Mr. Adams, who had filled himself
with ale, and by public permission had lighted his pipe, turned to
the master of the house, asking him, "If evil spirits did not use
to walk in that neighbourhood?" To which receiving no answer,
he began to inform him of the adventure which they met with
on the downs; nor had he proceeded far in the story when somebody knocked very hard at the door. The company expressed
some amazement, and Fanny and the good woman turned pale:
her husband went forth, and whilst he was absent, which was
some time, they all remained silent, looking at one another, and
heard several voices discoursing pretty loudly. Adams was fully
persuaded that spirits were abroad, and began to meditate some

exorcisms; Joseph a little inclined to the same opinion; Fanny was more afraid of men; and the good woman herself began to suspect her guests, and imagined those without were rogues belonging to their gang. At length the master of the house returned, and laughing, told Adams he had discovered his apparition; that the murderers were sheep-stealers, and the twelve persons murdered were no other than twelve sheep — adding, that the shepherds had got the better of them, had secured two, and were proceeding with them to a justice of peace. This account greatly relieved the fears of the whole company; but Adams muttered to himself, "He was convinced of the truth of apparitions for all that."

They now sat cheerfully round the fire, till the master of the house, having surveyed his guests, and conceiving that the cassock, which, having fallen down, appeared under Adams's greatcoat, and the shabby livery on Joseph Andrews, did not well suit with the familiarity between them, began to entertain some suspicions, not much to their advantage: addressing himself therefore to Adams, he said, "He perceived he was a clergyman by his dress, and supposed that honest man was his footman." "Sir," answered Adams, "I am a clergyman at your service; but as to that young man, whom you have rightly termed honest, he is at present in nobody's service; he never lived in any other family than that of Lady Booby, from whence he was discharged, I assure you, for no crime." Joseph said, "He did not wonder the gentleman was surprised to see one of Mr. Adams's character condescend to so much goodness with a poor man." "Child," said Adams, "I should be ashamed of my cloth if I thought a poor man, who is honest, below my notice or my familiarity. I know not how those who think otherwise can profess themselves followers and servants of Him who made no distinction, unless, peradventure, by preferring the poor to the rich. Sir," said he, addressing himself to the gentleman, "these two poor young people are my parishioners, and I look on them and love them as my children. There is something singular enough in their history, but I have not now time to recount it." The master of the house, notwithstanding the simplicity which discovered itself in Adams, knew too much of the world to give a hasty belief to professions. He was not yet quite certain that Adams had any more of the clergyman in him than his cassock. To try him therefore further, he asked him, "If Mr. Pope had lately published anything new?" Adams answered, "He had heard great commendations of that poet, but that he had never read, nor knew, any of his works." "Ho! ho!" says the gentleman to himself, "have I caught you? — What!" said he, "have you never seen his Homer?" Adams answered, "He had never read any translation of the classics." "Why, truly," replied the gentleman, "there is a dignity in the Greek language which I think no modern tongue can reach." "Do you understand Greek, sir?" said Adams hastily. "A little, sir," answered the gentleman. "Do you know, sir," cried Adams, "where I can buy an Æschylus? an unlucky misfortune lately happened to mine." Æschylus was beyond the gentleman, though he knew him very well by name; he therefore, returning back to Homer, asked Adams, "What part of the *Iliad* he thought most excellent?" Adams returned, "His question would be properer, What kind of beauty was the chief in poetry? for that Homer was equally excellent in them all. And, indeed," continued he, "what Cicero says of a complete orator may well be applied to a great poet: 'He ought to comprehend all perfections.' Homer did this in the most excellent degree; it is not without reason, therefore, that the philosopher, in the 22d chapter of his Poetics, mentions him by no other appellation than that of 'the Poet': He was the father of the drama as well as the epic: not of tragedy only, but of comedy also; for his *Margites*, which is deplorably lost, bore, says Aristotle, the same analogy to comedy as his *Odyssey* and *Iliad* to tragedy. To him, therefore, we owe Aristophanes, as well as Euripides, Sophocles, and my poor Æschylus. But if you please we will confine ourselves (at least for the present) to the *Iliad*, his noblest work; though neither Aristotle nor Horace give it the preference, as I remember, to the *Odyssey*. First, then, as to his subject, can anything be more simple, and at the same time more noble? He is rightly praised by the first of those judicious critics for not choosing the whole war, which, though he says it hath a complete beginning and end, would have been too great for the understanding to comprehend at one view. I have therefore often wondered why so correct a writer as Horace should, in his epistle to Lollius, call him the *Trojani Belli Scriptorem*. Secondly, his action, termed by Aristotle, *Pragmaton Systasis;* is it possible for the mind of man to conceive an idea of such perfect unity, and at the same time so replete with greatness? And here I must observe, what I do not remember to have seen noted by any, the *Harmotton*, that agreement of his action to his subject: for, as the subject is anger, how agreeable is his action, which is war? from which every incident arises, and to which every episode immediately relates. Thirdly, his manners, which Aristotle places second in his description of the several parts of tragedy, and which he says are included in the action; I am at a loss whether I should rather admire the exactness of his judgment in the nice distinction, or the immensity of his imagination in their variety. For, as to the former of these, how accurately is the sedate, injured resentment of Achilles, distinguished from the hot, insulting passion of Agamemnon! How widely doth the brutal courage of Ajax differ from the amiable bravery of Diomedes; and the wisdom of Nestor, which is the result of long reflection and experience, from the cunning of Ulysses, the effect of art and subtlety only! If we consider their variety, we may cry out, with Aristotle in his 24th chapter, that no part of this divine poem is destitute of manners. Indeed, I might affirm that there is scarce a character in human nature untouched in some part or other. And, as there is no passion which he is not able to describe, so is there none in his reader which he cannot raise. If he hath any superior excellence to the rest, I have been inclined to fancy it is in the pathetic. I am sure I never read with dry eyes the two episodes where Andromache is introduced, in the former lamenting the danger, and in the latter the death, of Hector. The images are so extremely tender in these, that I am convinced the poet had the worthiest and best heart imaginable. Nor can I help observing how Sophocles falls short of the beauties of the original, in that imitation of the dissuasive speech of Andromache which he hath put into the mouth of Tecmessa. And yet Sophocles was the greatest genius who ever wrote tragedy; nor have any of his successors in that art, that is to say, neither Euripides nor Seneca the tragedian, been able to come near him. As to his sentiments and diction, I need say nothing: the former are particularly remarkable for the utmost perfection on that head, namely, propriety; and as to the latter, Aristotle, whom doubtless you have read over and over, is very diffuse. I shall mention but one thing more, which that great critic in his division of tragedy calls *Opsis,* or the scenery; and which is as proper to the epic as to the drama, with this difference, that in the former it falls to the share of the poet, and in the latter to that of the painter. But did ever painter imagine a scene like that in the 13th and 14th Iliads? where the reader sees at one view the prospect of Troy, with the army drawn up before it; the Grecian army, camp, and fleet; Jupiter sitting on Mount Ida,

with his head wrapt in a cloud, and a thunderbolt in his hand,
looking towards Thrace; Neptune driving through the sea, which
divides on each side to permit his passage, and then seating
himself on Mount Samos; the heavens opened, and the deities
all seated on their thrones. This is sublime! This is poetry!"
Adams then rapt out a hundred Greek verses, and with such a
voice, emphasis, and action, that he almost frightened the women;
and as for the gentleman, he was so far from entertaining any
further suspicion of Adams, that he now doubted whether he had
not a bishop in his house. He ran into the most extravagant encomiums on his learning; and the goodness of his heart began to
dilate to all the strangers. He said he had great compassion for
the poor young woman, who looked pale and faint with her
journey; and in truth he conceived a much higher opinion of her
quality than it deserved. He said he was sorry he could not
accommodate them all; but if they were contented with his fireside, he would sit up with the men; and the young woman might,
if she pleased, partake his wife's bed, which he advised her to;
for that they must walk upwards of a mile to any house of
entertainment, and that not very good neither. Adams, who
liked his seat, his ale, his tobacco, and his company, persuaded
Fanny to accept this kind proposal, in which solicitation he was
seconded by Joseph. Nor was she very difficultly prevailed on;
for she had slept little the last night, and not at all the preceding;
so that love itself was scarce able to keep her eyes open any
longer. The offer, therefore, being kindly accepted, the good
woman produced everything eatable in her house on the table,
and the guests, being heartily invited, as heartily regaled themselves, especially Parson Adams. As to the other two, they were
examples of the truth of that physical observation, that love,
like other sweet things, is no whetter of the stomach.

Supper was no sooner ended, than Fanny at her own request
retired, and the good woman bore her company. The man of
the house, Adams, and Joseph, who would modestly have withdrawn, had not the gentleman insisted on the contrary, drew
round the fireside, where Adams (to use his own words) replen-
ished his pipe, and the gentleman produced a bottle of excellent
beer, being the best liquor in his house.

The modest behaviour of Joseph, with the gracefulness of his
person, the character which Adams gave of him, and the friendship he seemed to entertain for him, began to work on the
gentleman's affections, and raised in him a curiosity to know the

singularity which Adams had mentioned in his history. This curiosity Adams was no sooner informed of than, with Joseph's consent, he agreed to gratify it; and accordingly related all he knew, with as much tenderness as was possible for the character of Lady Booby; and concluded with the long, faithful, and mutual passion between him and Fanny, not concealing the meanness of her birth and education. These latter circumstances entirely cured a jealousy which had lately risen in the gentleman's mind, that Fanny was the daughter of some person of fashion, and that Joseph had run away with her, and Adams was concerned in the plot. He was now enamoured of his guests, drank their healths with great cheerfulness, and returned many thanks to Adams, who had spent much breath, for he was a circumstantial teller of a story.

Adams told him it was now in his power to return that favour; for his extraordinary goodness, as well as that fund of literature he was master of,* which he did not expect to find under such a roof, had raised in him more curiosity than he had ever known. "Therefore," said he, "if it be not too troublesome, sir, your history, if you please."

The gentleman answered, he could not refuse him what he had so much right to insist on; and after some of the common apologies, which are the usual preface to a story, he thus began.

CHAPTER III.

In which the gentleman relates the history of his life.

Sir, I am descended of a good family, and was born a gentleman. My education was liberal, and at a public school, in which I proceeded so far as to become master of the Latin, and to be

* The author hath by some been represented to have made a blunder here: for Adams had indeed shown some learning (say they), perhaps all the author had; but the gentleman hath shown none, unless his approbation of Mr. Adams be such: but surely it would be preposterous in him to call it so. I have, however, notwithstanding this criticism, which I am told came from the mouth of a great orator in a public coffee-house, left this blunder as it stood in the first edition. I will not have the vanity to apply to anything in this work the observation which M. Dacier makes in her preface to her Aristophanes: *Je tiens pour une maxime constante, qu'une beauté médiocre plaît plus généralement qu'une beauté sans défaut.* Mr. Congreve hath made such another blunder in his *Love for Love*, where Tattle tells Miss Prue, "She should admire him as much for the beauty he commends in her as if he himself was possessed of it." — F.

tolerably versed in the Greek language. My father died when I was sixteen, and left me master of myself. He bequeathed me a moderate fortune, which he intended I should not receive till I attained the age of twenty-five: for he constantly asserted that was full early enough to give up any man entirely to the guidance of his own discretion. However, as this intention was so obscurely worded in his will that the lawyers advised me to contest the point with my trustees, I own I paid so little regard to the inclinations of my dead father, which were sufficiently certain to me, that I followed their advice, and soon succeeded, for the trustees did not contest the matter very obstinately on their side. "Sir," said Adams, "may I crave the favour of your name?" The gentleman answered, "his name was Wilson," and then proceeded.

I stayed a very little while at school after his death; for, being a forward youth, I was extremely impatient to be in the world: for which I thought my parts, knowledge, and manhood thoroughly qualified me. And to this early introduction into life, without a guide, I impute all my future misfortunes; for, besides the obvious mischiefs which attend this, there is one which hath not been so generally observed. The first impression which mankind receives of you will be very difficult to eradicate. How unhappy, therefore, must it be to fix your character in life, before you can possibly know its value, or weigh the consequences of those actions which are to establish your future reputation!

A little under seventeen I left my school, and went to London, with no more than six pounds in my pocket — a great sum, as I then conceived; and which I was afterwards surprised to find so soon consumed.

The character I was ambitious of attaining was that of a fine gentleman; the first requisites to which I apprehended were to be supplied by a tailor, a periwig-maker, and some few more tradesmen, who deal in furnishing out the human body. Notwithstanding the lowness of my purse, I found credit with them more easily than I expected, and was soon equipped to my wish. This I own then agreeably surprised me; but I have since learned that it is a maxim among many tradesmen at the polite end of the town to deal as largely as they can, reckon as high as they can, and arrest as soon as they can.

The next qualifications, namely, dancing, fencing, riding the great horse, and music, came into my head: but, as they required expense and time, I comforted myself, with regard to dancing, that I had learned a little in my youth, and could walk a minuet genteelly enough; as to fencing, I thought my good-humour would preserve me from the danger of a quarrel; as to the horse, I hoped it would not be thought of; and for music, I imagined I could easily acquire the reputation of it; for I had heard some of my schoolfellows pretend to knowledge in operas, without being able to sing or play on the fiddle.

Knowledge of the town seemed another ingredient; this I thought I should arrive at by frequenting public places. Accordingly I paid constant attendance to them all; by which means I was soon master of the fashionable phrases, learned to cry up the fashionable diversions, and knew the names and faces of the most fashionable men and women.

Nothing now seemed to remain but an intrigue, which I was resolved to have immediately; I mean the reputation of it; and indeed I was so successful, that in a very short time I had half-a-dozen with the finest women in town.

At these words Adams fetched a deep groan, and then, blessing himself, cried out, "Good Lord! what wicked times these are!"

Not so wicked as you imagine, continued the gentleman; for I assure you they were all vestal virgins for anything which I knew to the contrary. The reputation of intriguing with them was all I sought, and was what I arrived at; and perhaps I only flattered myself even in that: for very probably the persons to whom I showed their billets knew as well as I that they were counterfeits, and that I had written them to myself.

"*Write letters to yourself!*" said Adams, staring.

O sir, answered the gentleman, *It is the very error of the times*. Half our modern plays have one of these characters in them. It is incredible the pains I have taken, and the absurd methods I employed, to traduce the characters of women of distinction. When another had spoken in raptures of anyone, I have answered, "D—n her, she! We shall have her at H——d's very soon." When he hath replied, "He thought her virtuous," I have answered, "Ay, thou wilt always think a woman virtuous, till she is in the streets; but you and I, Jack or Tom (turning to another in company), know better." At which I have drawn a paper out of my pocket, perhaps a tailor's bill, and kissed it, crying at the same time, "By Gad, I was once fond of her."

"Proceed, if you please, but do not swear any more," said Adams.

Sir, said the gentleman, I ask your pardon. Well, sir, in this course of life I continued full three years. — "What course of life?" answered Adams; "I do not remember you have mentioned any." — Your remark is just, said the gentleman, smiling; I should rather have said, in this course of doing nothing. I remember some time afterwards I wrote the journal of one day, which would serve, I believe, as well for any other during the whole time. I will endeavour to repeat it to you.

In the morning I arose, took my great stick, and walked out in my green frock, with my hair in papers (*a groan from Adams*), and sauntered about till ten.

Went to the auction; told Lady —— she had a dirty face; laughed heartily at something Captain —— said, I can't remember what, for I did not very well hear it; whispered Lord ——; bowed to the Duke of ——; and was going to bid for a snuffbox, but did not, for fear I should have had it.

> From 2 to 4, drest myself.   *A groan.*
>   4 to 6, dined.   *A groan.*
>   6 to 8, coffee-house.
>   8 to 9, Drury-Lane playhouse.
>   9 to 10, Lincoln's Inn Fields.
>   10 to 12, drawing-room.   *A great groan.*

At all which places nothing happened worth remark. At which Adams said, with some vehemence, "Sir, this is below the life of an animal, hardly above vegetation; and I am surprised what could lead a man of your sense into it." What leads us into more follies than you imagine, doctor, answered the gentleman — vanity: for as contemptible a creature as I was, and I assure you, yourself cannot have more contempt for such a wretch than I now have, I then admired myself, and should have despised a person of your present appearance (you will pardon me), with all your learning and those excellent qualities which I have remarked in you. Adams bowed, and begged him to proceed. After I had continued two years in this course of life, said the gentleman, an accident happened which obliged me to change the scene. As I was one day at St. James's coffee-house, making very free with the character of a young lady of quality, an officer of the guards, who was present, thought proper to give me the lie. I answered I might possibly be mistaken; but I intended to tell no more than the truth. To which he made no reply but by a scornful sneer. After this I observed a strange coldness in all

my acquaintance; none of them spoke to me first, and very few
returned me even the civility of a bow. The company I used to
dine with left me out, and within a week I found myself in as
much solitude at St. James's as if I had been in a desert. An
honest elderly man, with a great hat and long sword, at last told
me he had a compassion for my youth, and therefore advised me
to show the world I was not such a rascal as they thought me to
be. I did not at first understand him; but he explained himself,
and ended with telling me, if I would write a challenge to the
captain, he would, out of pure charity, go to him with it. "A
very charitable person, truly!" cried Adams. I desired till the
next day, continued the gentleman, to consider on it, and, retiring to my lodgings, I weighed the consequences on both sides as
fairly as I could. On the one, I saw the risk of this alternative,
either losing my own life, or having on my hands the blood of a
man with whom I was not in the least angry. I soon determined
that the good which appeared on the other was not worth this
hazard. I therefore resolved to quit the scene, and presently
retired to the Temple, where I took chambers. Here I soon got
a fresh set of acquaintance, who knew nothing of what had
happened to me. Indeed, they were not greatly to my approbation; for the beaus of the Temple are only the shadows of the
others. They are the affectation of affectation. The vanity of
these is still more ridiculous, if possible, than of the others. Here
I met with smart fellows, who drank with lords they did not
know, and intrigued with women they never saw. Covent
Garden was now the farthest stretch of my ambition; where I
shone forth in the balconies at the playhouses, visited whores,
made love to orange-wenches, and damned plays. This career
was soon put a stop to by my surgeon, who convinced me of
the necessity of confining myself to my room for a month. At
the end of which, having had leisure to reflect, I resolved to quit
all further conversation with beaus and smarts of every kind, and
to avoid, if possible, any occasion of returning to this place of
confinement. "I think," said Adams, "the advice of a month's
retirement and reflection was very proper; but I should rather
have expected it from a divine than a surgeon." The gentleman
smiled at Adams's simplicity, and, without explaining himself
farther on such an odious subject, went on thus: I was no sooner
perfectly restored to health than I found my passion for women,
which I was afraid to satisfy as I had done, made me very uneasy;
I determined, therefore, to keep a mistress. Nor was I long be-

fore I fixed my choice on a young woman, who had before been kept by two gentlemen, and to whom I was recommended by a celebrated bawd. I took her home to my chambers, and made her a settlement during cohabitation. This would, perhaps, have been very ill paid: however, she did not suffer me to be perplexed on that account; for, before quarter-day, I found her at my chambers in too familiar conversation with a young fellow who was drest like an officer, but was indeed a City apprentice. Instead of excusing her inconstancy, she rapped out half-a-dozen oaths, and, snapping her fingers at me, swore she scorned to confine herself to the best man in England. Upon this we parted, and the same bawd presently provided her another keeper. I was not so much concerned at our separation as I found, within a day or two, I had reason to be for our meeting: for I was obliged to pay a second visit to my surgeon. I was now forced to do penance for some weeks, during which time I contracted an acquaintance with a beautiful young girl, the daughter of a gentleman who, after having been forty years in the army, and in all the campaigns under the Duke of Marlborough, died a lieutenant on half-pay, and had left a widow, with this only child, in very distrest circumstances: they had only a small pension from the government, with what little the daughter could add to it by her work; for she had great excellence at her needle. This girl was, at my first acquaintance with her, solicited in marriage by a young fellow in good circumstances. He was apprentice to a linendraper, and had a little fortune, sufficient to set up his trade. The mother was greatly pleased with this match, as indeed she had sufficient reason. However, I soon prevented it. I represented him in so low a light to his mistress, and made so good an use of flattery, promises, and presents, that, not to dwell longer on this subject than is necessary, I prevailed with the poor girl, and conveyed her away from her mother! In a word, I debauched her. — (At which words Adams started up, fetched three strides 'cross the room, and then replaced himself in his chair.) You are not more affected with this part of my story than myself; I assure you it will never be sufficiently repented of in my own opinion: but, if you already detest it, how much more will your indignation be raised when you hear the fatal consequences of this barbarous, this villainous action! If you please, therefore, I will here desist. — "By no means," cries Adams; "go on, I beseech you; and Heaven grant you may sincerely repent of this and many other things you have related!"

— I was now, continued the gentleman, as happy as the possession of a fine young creature, who had a good education, and was endued with many agreeable qualities, could make me. We lived some months with vast fondness together, without any company or conversation, more than we found in one another: but this could not continue always; and, though I still preserved a great affection for her, I began more and more to want the relief of other company, and consequently to leave her by degrees — at last, whole days to herself. She failed not to testify some uneasiness on these occasions, and complained of the melancholy life she led; to remedy which, I introduced her into the acquaintance of some other kept mistresses, with whom she used to play at cards, and frequent plays and other diversions. She had not lived long in this intimacy before I perceived a visible alteration in her behaviour; all her modesty and innocence vanished by degrees, till her mind became thoroughly tainted. She affected the company of rakes, gave herself all manner of airs, was never easy but abroad, or when she had a party at my chambers. She was rapacious of money, extravagant to excess, loose in her conversation; and, if ever I demurred to any of her demands, oaths, tears, and fits were the immediate consequences. As the first raptures of fondness were long since over, this behaviour soon estranged my affections from her; I began to reflect with pleasure that she was not my wife, and to conceive an intention of parting with her; of which, having given her a hint, she took care to prevent me the pains of turning her out of doors, and accordingly departed herself, having first broken open my escrutore, and taken with her all she could find, to the amount of about £200. In the first heat of my resentment, I resolved to pursue her with all the vengeance of the law: but, as she had the good luck to escape me during that ferment, my passion afterwards cooled; and, having reflected that I had been the first aggressor, and had done her an injury for which I could make her no reparation, by robbing her of the innocence of her mind; and hearing at the same time that the poor old woman her mother had broke her heart on her daughter's elopement from her, I, concluding myself her murderer ("As you very well might," cries Adams with a groan), was pleased that God Almighty had taken this method of punishing me, and resolved quietly to submit to the loss. Indeed, I could wish I had never heard more of the poor creature, who became in the end an abandoned profligate; and, after being some years a common prostitute, at last ended her miserable life in Newgate. — Here the gentleman fetched a deep sigh, which Mr. Adams echoed very loudly; and both continued silent, looking on each other for some minutes. At last the gentleman proceeded thus: I had been perfectly constant to this girl during the whole time I kept her: but she had scarce departed before I discovered more marks of her infidelity to me than the loss of my money. In short, I was forced to make a third visit to my surgeon, out of whose hands I did not get a hasty discharge.

I now forswore all future dealings with the sex, complained loudly that the pleasure did not compensate the pain, and railed at the beautiful creatures in as gross language as Juvenal himself formerly reviled them in. I looked on all the town harlots with a detestation not easy to be conceived; their persons appeared to me as painted palaces, inhabited by Disease and Death: nor could their beauty make them more desirable objects in my eyes than gilding could make me covet a pill, or golden plates a coffin. But though I was no longer the absolute slave, I found some reasons to own myself still the subject, of love. My hatred for women decreased daily; and I am not positive but time might have betrayed me again to some common harlot, had I not been secured by a passion for the charming Sapphira, which, having once entered upon, made a violent progress in my heart. Sapphira was wife to a man of fashion and gallantry, and one who seemed, I own, every way worthy of her affections; which, however, he had not the reputation of having. She was indeed a *coquette achevée.* "Pray, sir," says Adams, "what is a coquette? I have met with the word in French authors, but never could assign any idea to it. I believe it is the same with *une sotte,* Anglicè, *a fool.*" Sir, answered the gentleman, perhaps you are not much mistaken; but, as it is a particular kind of folly, I will endeavour to describe it. Were all creatures to be ranked in the order of creation according to their usefulness, I know few animals that would not take place of a coquette; nor indeed hath this creature much pretence to anything beyond instinct: for, though sometimes we might imagine it was animated by the passion of vanity, yet far the greater part of its actions fall beneath even that low motive; for instance, several absurd gestures and tricks, infinitely more foolish than what can be observed in the most ridiculous birds and beasts, and which would persuade the beholder that the silly wretch was aiming at our contempt. Indeed its characteristic is affectation, and this led and governed by whim only: for as beauty, wisdom, wit, good-nature, politeness, and health are sometimes affected by this creature, so are ugliness, folly, nonsense, ill-nature, ill-breeding, and sickness likewise put on by it in their turn. Its life is one constant lie; and the only rule by which you can form any judgment of them is, that they are never what they seem. If it was possible for a coquette to love (as it is not, for if ever it attains this passion, the coquette ceases instantly), it would wear the face of indifference, if not of hatred, to the beloved object; you may therefore be assured, when they endeavour to persuade you of their liking, that they are indifferent to you at least. And indeed this was the case of my Sapphira, who no sooner saw me in the number of her admirers than she gave me what is commonly called encouragement: she would often look at me, and, when she perceived me meet her eyes, would instantly take them off, discovering at the same time as much surprise and emotion as possible. These arts failed not of the success she intended; and, as I grew more particular to her than the rest of her admirers, she advanced, in proportion, more directly to me than to the others. She affected the low voice, whisper, lisp, sigh, start, laugh, and many other indications of passion which daily deceive thousands. When I played at whisk with her, she would look earnestly at me, and at the same time lose deal or revoke; then burst into a ridiculous laugh, and cry, "La! I can't imagine what I was thinking of." To detain you no longer, after I had gone through a sufficient course of gallantry, as I thought, and was thoroughly convinced I had raised a violent passion in my mistress, I sought an opportunity of coming to an *eclaircissement* with her. She avoided this as much as possible; however, great assiduity at length presented me one. I will not describe all the particulars of this interview; let it suffice that, when she could no longer pretend not to see my drift, she first affected a violent surprise, and immediately after as violent a passion: she wondered what I had seen in her conduct which could induce me to affront her in this manner; and, breaking from me the first moment she could, told me I had no other way to escape the consequence of her resentment than by never seeing, or at least speaking to her more. I was not contented with this answer; I still pursued her, but to no purpose; and was at length convinced that her husband had the sole possession of her person, and that neither he nor any other had made any impression on her heart. I was taken off from following this *ignis fatuus* by some advances

which were made me by the wife of a citizen, who, though
neither very young nor handsome, was yet too agreeable to be
rejected by my amorous constitution. I accordingly soon satisfied
her that she had not cast away her hints on a barren or cold
soil: on the contrary, they instantly produced her an eager and
desiring lover. Nor did she give me any reason to complain; she
met the warmth she had raised with equal ardour. I had no
longer a coquette to deal with, but one who was wiser than to
prostitute the noble passion of love to the ridiculous lust of
vanity. We presently understood one another; and, as the
pleasures we sought lay in a mutual gratification, we soon found
and enjoyed them. I thought myself at first greatly happy in the
possession of this new mistress, whose fondness would have
quickly surfeited a more sickly appetite; but it had a different
effect on mine: she carried my passion higher by it than youth
or beauty had been able. But my happiness could not long continue uninterrupted. The apprehensions we lay under from the
jealousy of her husband gave us great uneasiness. "Poor wretch!
I pity him," cried Adams. He did indeed deserve it, said the
gentleman; for he loved his wife with great tenderness; and, I
assure you, it is a great satisfaction to me that I was not the
man who first seduced her affections from him. These apprehensions appeared also too well grounded, for in the end he discovered us, and procured witnesses of our caresses. He then
prosecuted me at law, and recovered £3000 damages, which
much distressed my fortune to pay; and, what was worse, his
wife, being divorced, came upon my hands. I led a very uneasy
life with her; for, besides that my passion was now much abated,
her excessive jealousy was very troublesome. At length death
delivered me from an inconvenience which the consideration of
my having been the author of her misfortunes would never
suffer me to take any other method of discarding.

I now bade adieu to love, and resolved to pursue other less
dangerous and expensive pleasures. I fell into the acquaintance
of a set of jolly companions, who slept all day and drank all
night; fellows who might rather be said to consume time than to
live. Their best conversation was nothing but noise: singing,
hollowing, wrangling, drinking, toasting, sp—wing, smoking,
were the chief ingredients of our entertainment. And yet, bad
as these were, they were more tolerable than our graver scenes,
which were either excessive tedious narratives of dull common
matters of fact, or hot disputes about trifling matters, which

commonly ended in a wager. This way of life the first serious reflection put a period to; and I became member of a club frequented by young men of great abilities. The bottle was now only called in to the assistance of our conversation, which rolled on the deepest points of philosophy. These gentlemen were engaged in a search after truth, in the pursuit of which they threw aside all the prejudices of education, and governed themselves only by the infallible guide of human reason. This great guide, after having shown them the falsehood of that very ancient but simple tenet, that there is such a being as a Deity in the universe, helped them to establish in his stead a certain "Rule of Right," by adhering to which they all arrived at the utmost purity of morals. Reflection made me as much delighted with this society as it had taught me to despise and detest the former. I began now to esteem myself a being of a higher order than I had ever before conceived; and was the more charmed with this Rule of Right, as I really found in my own nature nothing repugnant to it. I held in utter contempt all persons who wanted any other inducement to virtue besides her intrinsic beauty and excellence; and had so high an opinion of my present companions, with regard to their morality, that I would have trusted them with whatever was nearest and dearest to me. Whilst I was engaged in this delightful dream, two or three accidents happened successively, which at first much surprised me. For one of our greatest philosophers, or "Rule-of-Right men," withdrew himself from us, taking with him the wife of one of his most intimate friends. Secondly, another of the same society left the club without remembering to take leave of his bail. A third, having borrowed a sum of money of me, for which I received no security, when I asked him to repay it, absolutely denied the loan. These several practices, so inconsistent with our golden rule, made me begin to suspect its infallibility; but when I communicated my thoughts to one of the club, he said, "There was nothing absolutely good or evil in itself; that actions were denominated good or bad by the circumstances of the agent. That possibly the man who ran away with his neighbour's wife might be one of very good inclinations, but over-prevailed on by the violence of an unruly passion, and, in other particulars, might be a very worthy member of society; that if the beauty of any woman created in him an uneasiness, he had a right from nature to relieve himself"; with many other things, which I then detested so much, that I took leave of the society that very

evening, and never returned to it again. Being now reduced to
a state of solitude which I did not like, I became a great fre-
quenter of the playhouses, which indeed was always my favourite
diversion; and most evenings passed away two or three hours behind the scenes, where I met with several poets, with whom I
made engagements at the taverns. Some of the players were
likewise of our parties. At these meetings we were generally
entertained by the poets with reading their performances, and
by the players with repeating their parts: upon which occasions,
I observed the gentleman who furnished our entertainment was
commonly the best pleased of the company; who, though they
were pretty civil to him to his face, seldom failed to take the
first opportunity of his absence to ridicule him. Now I made
some remarks, which probably are too obvious to be worth relating. "Sir," says Adams, "your remarks, if you please." First
then, says he, I concluded that the general observation, that wits
are most inclined to vanity, is not true. Men are equally vain of
riches, strength, beauty, honours, &c. But these appear of themselves to the eyes of the beholders, whereas the poor wit is
obliged to produce his performance to show you his perfection;
and on his readiness to do this, that vulgar opinion I have before
mentioned is grounded; but doth not the person who expends
vast sums in the furniture of his house, or in the ornaments of
his person, who consumes much time and employs great pains
in dressing himself, or who thinks himself paid for self-denial,
labour, or even villainy, by a title or a ribbon, sacrifice as much
to vanity as the poor wit who is desirous to read you his poem or
his play? My second remark was, that vanity is the worst of
passions, and more apt to contaminate the mind than any other:
for, as selfishness is much more general than we please to allow
it, so it is natural to hate and envy those who stand between us
and the good we desire. Now, in lust and ambition these are
few; and even in avarice we find many who are no obstacles to
our pursuits; but the vain man seeks pre-eminence; and everything which is excellent or praiseworthy in another renders him
the mark of his antipathy. Adams now began to fumble in his
pockets, and soon cried out, "O la! I have it not about me." —
Upon this, the gentleman asking him what he was searching for,
he said he searched after a sermon, which he thought his masterpiece, against vanity. "Fie upon it, fie upon it!" cries he, "why
do I ever leave that sermon out of my pocket? I wish it was
within five miles; I would willingly fetch it, to read it to you."

The gentleman answered that there was no need, for he was cured of the passion. "And for that very reason," quoth Adams, "I would read it, for I am confident you would admire it: indeed, I have never been a greater enemy to any passion than that silly one of vanity." The gentleman smiled, and proceeded — From this society I easily passed to that of the gamesters, where nothing remarkable happened but the finishing my fortune, which those gentlemen soon helped me to the end of. This opened scenes of life hitherto unknown; Poverty and Distress, with their horrid train of duns, attorneys, bailiffs, haunted me day and night. My clothes grew shabby, my credit bad, my friends and acquaintance of all kinds cold. In this situation, the strangest thought imaginable came into my head; and what was this but to write a play? for I had sufficient leisure: fear of bailiffs confined me every day to my room; and, having always had a little inclination, and something of a genius that way, I set myself to work, and within few months produced a piece of five acts, which was accepted of at the theatre. I remembered to have formerly taken tickets of other poets for their benefits, long before the appearance of their performances; and, resolving to follow a precedent which was so well suited to my present circumstances, I immediately provided myself with a large number of little papers. Happy indeed would be the state of poetry, would these tickets pass current at the bakehouse, the alehouse, and the chandler's shop: but alas! far otherwise; no tailor will take them in payment for buckram, stays, stay-tape; nor no bailiff for civility-money. They are, indeed, no more than a passport to beg with; a certificate that the owner wants five shillings, which induces well-disposed Christians to charity. I now experienced what is worse than poverty, or rather what is the worst consequence of poverty: I mean attendance and dependence on the great. Many a morning have I waited hours in the cold parlours of men of quality; where, after seeing the lowest rascals in lace and embroidery, the pimps and buffoons in fashion, admitted, I have been sometimes told, on sending in my name, that my lord could not possibly see me this morning: a sufficient assurance that I should never more get entrance into that house. Sometimes I have been at last admitted; and the great man hath thought proper to excuse himself, by telling me he was "tied up." " 'Tied up,' " says Adams, "pray what's that?" Sir, says the gentleman, the profit which booksellers allowed authors for the best works was so very small, that certain men of birth and fortune some years ago, who were the patrons of wit and learning, thought fit to encourage them farther by entering into voluntary subscriptions for their encouragement. Thus Prior, Rowe, Pope, and some other men of genius, received large sums for their labours from the public. This seemed so easy a method of getting money, that many of the lowest scribblers of the times ventured to publish their works in the same way; and many had the assurance to take in subscriptions for what was not writ, nor ever intended. Subscriptions in this manner growing infinite, and a kind of tax on the public, some persons, finding it not so easy a task to discern good from bad authors, or to know what genius was worthy encouragement and what was not, to prevent the expense of subscribing to so many, invented a method to excuse themselves from all subscriptions whatever; and this was to receive a small sum of money in consideration of giving a large one if ever they subscribed; which many have done, and many more have pretended to have done, in order to silence all solicitation. The same method was likewise taken with playhouse tickets, which were no less a public grievance; and this is what they call being "tied up" from subscribing. "I can't say but the term is apt enough, and somewhat typical," said Adams; "for a man of large fortune, who ties himself up, as you call it, from the encouragement of men of merit, ought to be tied up in reality." Well, sir, says the gentleman, to return to my story. Sometimes I have received a guinea from a man of quality, given with as ill a grace as alms are generally to the meanest beggar; and purchased too with as much time spent in attendance as, if it had been spent in honest industry, might have brought me more profit with infinitely more satisfaction. After about two months spent in this disagreeable way, with the utmost mortification, when I was pluming my hopes on the prospect of a plentiful harvest from my play, upon applying to the prompter to know when it came into rehearsal, he informed me he had received orders from the managers to return me the play again, for that they could not possibly act it that season; but, if I would take it and revise it against the next, they would be glad to see it again. I snatched it from him with great indignation, and retired to my room, where I threw myself on the bed in a fit of despair — "You should rather have thrown yourself on your knees," says Adams, "for despair is sinful." As soon, continued the gentleman, as I had indulged the first tumult of my passion, I began to consider coolly what course I should take, in a situation without friends, money, credit, or reputation of any kind. After revolving many things in my mind, I could see no other possibility of furnishing myself with the miserable necessaries of life than to retire to a garret near the Temple, and commence hackney-writer to the lawyers; for which I was well qualified, being an excellent penman. This purpose I resolved on, and immediately put it in execution. I had an acquaintance with an attorney who had formerly transacted affairs for me, and to him I applied; but, instead of furnishing me with any business, he laughed at my undertaking, and told me, "He was afraid I should turn his deeds into plays, and he should expect to see them on the stage." Not to tire you with instances of this kind from others, I found that Plato himself did not hold poets in greater abhorrence than these men of business do. Whenever I durst venture to a coffee-house, which was on Sundays only, a whisper ran round the room, which was constantly attended with a sneer — "That's poet Wilson": for I know not whether you have observed it, but there is a malignity in the nature of man, which, when not weeded out, or at least covered by a good education and politeness, delights in making another uneasy or dissatisfied with himself. This abundantly appears in all assemblies, except those which are filled by people of fashion, and especially among the younger people of both sexes whose birth and fortunes place them just without the polite circles; I mean the lower class of the gentry, and the higher of the mercantile world, who are, in reality, the worst-bred part of mankind. Well, sir, whilst I continued in this miserable state, with scarce sufficient business to keep me from starving, the reputation of a poet being my bane, I accidentally became acquainted with a bookseller, who told me, "It was pity a man of my learning and genius should be obliged to such a method of getting his livelihood; that he had a compassion for me, and, if I would engage with him, he would undertake to provide handsomely for me." A man in my circumstances, as he very well knew, had no choice. I accordingly accepted his proposal with his conditions, which were none of the most favourable, and fell to translating with all my might. I had no longer reason to lament the want of business; for he furnished me with so much, that in half a year I almost writ myself blind. I likewise contracted a distemper by my sedentary life, in which no part of my body was exercised but my right arm, which rendered me incapable of writing for a long time. This unluckily happening to delay the publication of a work, and my last performance not having sold well, the bookseller declined any further engagement, and aspersed me to

his brethren as a careless, idle fellow. I had, however, by having
half worked and half starved myself to death during the time I
was in his service, saved a few guineas, with which I bought a
lottery-ticket, resolving to throw myself into Fortune's lap, and
try if she would make me amends for the injuries she had done
me at the gaming-table. This purchase, being made, left me
almost pennyless; when, as if I had not been sufficiently miserable, a bailiff in woman's clothes got admittance to my chamber,
whither he was directed by the bookseller. He arrested me at
my tailor's suit for thirty-five pounds; a sum for which I could
not procure bail; and was therefore conveyed to his house, where
I was locked up in an upper chamber. I had now neither health
(for I was scarce recovered from my indisposition), liberty,
money, or friends; and had abandoned all hopes, and even the
desire of life. "But this could not last long," said Adams; "for
doubtless the tailor released you the moment he was truly acquainted with your affairs, and knew that your circumstances
would not permit you to pay him." O, sir, answered the gentleman, he knew that before he arrested me; nay, he knew that
nothing but incapacity could prevent me paying my debts; for
I had been his customer many years, had spent vast sums of
money with him, and had always paid most punctually in my
prosperous days; but when I reminded him of this, with assurances that, if he would not molest my endeavours, I would pay
him all the money I could by my utmost labour and industry
procure, reserving only what was sufficient to preserve me alive,
he answered, His patience was worn out; that I had put him off
from time to time; that he wanted the money; that he had put
it into a lawyer's hands; and if I did not pay him immediately,
or find security, I must lie in gaol and expect no mercy. "He may
expect mercy," cries Adams, starting from his chair, "where he will
find none! How can such a wretch repeat the Lord's Prayer;
where the word, which is translated, I know not for what
reason, 'trespasses,' is in the original, 'debts'? And as surely as we
do not forgive others their debts, when they are unable to pay
them, so surely shall we ourselves be unforgiven when we are
in no condition of paying." He ceased, and the gentleman proceeded. While I was in this deplorable situation, a former
acquaintance, to whom I had communicated my lottery-ticket,
found me out, and, making me a visit, with great delight in his
countenance, shook me heartily by the hand, and wished me
joy of my good fortune: for, says he, your ticket is come up a

prize of £3000. Adams snapt his fingers at these words in an
ecstasy of joy; which, however, did not continue long: for the
gentleman thus proceeded. Alas! sir, this was only a trick of
Fortune to sink me the deeper: for I had disposed of this lottery-
ticket two days before to a relation, who refused lending me a
shilling without it, in order to procure myself bread. As soon as
my friend was acquainted with my unfortunate sale, he began to
revile me, and to remind me of all the ill-conduct and miscarriages
of my life. He said, "I was one whom Fortune could not save if
she would; that I was now ruined without any hopes of retrieval,
nor must expect any pity from my friends; that it would be
extreme weakness to compassionate the misfortunes of a man
who ran headlong to his own destruction." He then painted to
me, in as lively colours as he was able, the happiness I should
have now enjoyed, had I not foolishly disposed of my ticket.
I urged the plea of necessity; but he made no answer to that,
and began again to revile me, till I could bear it no longer, and
desired him to finish his visit. I soon exchanged the bailiff's
house for a prison; where, as I had not money sufficient to
procure me a separate apartment, I was crowded in with a great
number of miserable wretches, in common with whom I was
destitute of every convenience of life, even that which all the
brutes enjoy, wholesome air. In these dreadful circumstances
I applied by letter to several of my old acquaintance, and such
to whom I had formerly lent money without any great prospect
of its being returned, for their assistance; but in vain. An excuse,
instead of a denial, was the gentlest answer I received. —
Whilst I languished in a condition too horrible to be described,
and which, in a land of humanity, and, what is much more,
Christianity, seems a strange punishment for a little inadvertency
and indiscretion; whilst I was in this condition, a fellow came
into the prison, and, inquiring me out, delivered me the following letter:

SIR,
   My father, to whom you sold your ticket in the last lottery, died
the same day in which it came up a prize, as you have possibly
heard, and left me sole heiress of all his fortune. I am so much
touched with your present circumstances, and the uneasiness you
must feel at having been driven to dispose of what might have
made you happy, that I must desire your acceptance of the
inclosed, and am
                                             Your humble servant,
                                             HARRIET HEARTY.

And what do you think was inclosed? "I don't know," cried
Adams; "not less than a guinea, I hope." — Sir, it was a bank-
note for £200. — "£200!" says Adams, in a rapture. — No less,
I assure you, answered the gentleman; a sum I was not half so
delighted with as with the dear name of the generous girl that
sent it me; and who was not only the best, but the handsomest
creature in the universe; and for whom I had long had a passion
which I never durst disclose to her. I kissed her name a thousand
times, my eyes overflowing with tenderness and gratitude; I repeated — But not to detain you with these raptures, I immediately acquired my liberty; and, having paid all my debts, departed, with upwards of fifty pounds in my pocket, to thank my
kind deliverer. She happened to be then out of town, a circumstance which, upon reflection, pleased me; for by that means I
had an opportunity to appear before her in a more decent dress.
At her return to town, within a day or two, I threw myself at her
feet with the most ardent acknowledgments, which she rejected
with an unfeigned greatness of mind, and told me I could not
oblige her more than by never mentioning, or if possible thinking
on, a circumstance which must bring to my mind an accident
that might be grievous to me to think on. She proceeded thus:
"What I have done is in my own eyes a trifle, and perhaps infinitely less than would have become me to do. And if you think
of engaging in any business where a larger sum may be serviceable to you, I shall not be over-rigid either as to the security or
interest." I endeavoured to express all the gratitude in my power
to this profusion of goodness, though perhaps it was my enemy,
and began to afflict my mind with more agonies than all the
miseries I had underwent; it affected me with severer reflections
than poverty, distress, and prisons united had been able to make
me feel: for, sir, these acts and professions of kindness, which
were sufficient to have raised in a good heart the most violent
passion of friendship to one of the same, or to age and ugliness
in a different sex, came to me from a woman, a young and
beautiful woman; one whose perfections I had long known, and
for whom I had long conceived a violent passion, though with
a despair which made me endeavour rather to curb and conceal, than to nourish or acquaint her with it. In short, they
came upon me united with beauty, softness, and tenderness:
such bewitching smiles! — O Mr. Adams, in that moment I lost
myself, and, forgetting our different situations, nor considering
what return I was making to her goodness by desiring her, who

had given me so much, to bestow her all, I laid gently hold on
her hand, and, conveying it to my lips, I prest it with inconceivable ardour; then, lifting up my swimming eyes, I saw her
face and neck overspread with one blush; she offered to withdraw her hand, yet not so as to deliver it from mine, though
I held it with the gentlest force. We both stood trembling: her
eyes cast on the ground, and mine steadfastly fixed on her. Good
G—d, what was then the condition of my soul! burning with
love, desire, admiration, gratitude, and every tender passion, all
bent on one charming object. Passion at last got the better of
both reason and respect, and, softly letting go her hand, I offered
madly to clasp her in my arms; when, a little recovering herself,
she started from me, asking me, with some show of anger, "If she
had any reason to expect this treatment from me?" I then fell
prostrate before her, and told her, "If I had offended, my life
was absolutely in her power, which I would in any manner lose
for her sake. Nay, madam," said I, "you shall not be so ready
to punish me as I to suffer. I own my guilt. I detest the reflection that I would have sacrificed your happiness to mine. Believe
me, I sincerely repent my ingratitude; yet, believe me too, it was
my passion, my unbounded passion for you, which hurried me
so far: I have loved you long and tenderly, and the goodness you
have shown me hath innocently weighed down a wretch undone
before. Acquit me of all mean, mercenary views; and, before
I take my leave of you for ever, which I am resolved instantly
to do, believe me that Fortune could have raised me to no
height to which I could not have gladly lifted you. O, curst
be Fortune!"—"Do not," says she, interrupting me with the
sweetest voice, "do not curse Fortune, since she hath made me
happy; and, if she hath put your happiness in my power, I
have told you you shall ask nothing in reason which I will
refuse." "Madam," said I, "you mistake me if you imagine, as
you seem, my happiness is in the power of Fortune now. You
have obliged me too much already; if I have any wish, it is for
some blest accident, by which I may contribute with my life
to the least augmentation of your felicity. As for myself, the
only happiness I can ever have will be hearing of yours; and
if Fortune will make that complete, I will forgive her all her
wrongs to me." "You may, indeed," answered she, smiling,
"for your own happiness must be included in mine. I have
long known your worth; nay, I must confess," said she, blushing,
"I have long discovered that passion for me you profess, not-

withstanding those endeavours, which I am convinced were unaffected, to conceal it; and if all I can give with reason will
not suffice, — take reason away, — and now I believe you cannot
ask me what I will deny." — She uttered these words with a
sweetness not to be imagined. I immediately started; my blood,
which lay freezing at my heart, rushed tumultuously through
every vein. I stood for a moment silent; then, flying to her, I
caught her in my arms, no longer resisting, — and softly told
her she must give me then herself. — O, sir! — Can I describe
her look? She remained silent, and almost motionless, several
minutes. At last, recovering herself a little, she insisted on my
leaving her, and in such a manner that I instantly obeyed;
you may imagine, however, I soon saw her again. — But I ask
pardon: I fear I have detained you too long in relating the
particulars of the former interview. "So far otherwise," said
Adams, licking his lips, "that I could willingly hear it over again."
Well, sir, continued the gentleman, to be as concise as possible,
within a week she consented to make me the happiest of mankind. We were married shortly after; and when I came to examine the circumstances of my wife's fortune (which, I do assure
you, I was not presently at leisure enough to do), I found it
amounted to about six thousand pounds, most part of which lay
in effects; for her father had been a wine merchant, and she
seemed willing, if I liked it, that I should carry on the same
trade. I readily, and too inconsiderately, undertook it: for, not
having been bred up to the secrets of the business, and endeavouring to deal with the utmost honesty and uprightness, I
soon found our fortune in a declining way, and my trade de-
creasing by little and little: for my wines, which I never adul-
terated after their importation, and were sold as neat as they
came over, were universally decried by the vintners, to whom
I could not allow them quite as cheap as those who gained
double the profit by a less price. I soon began to despair of improving our fortune by these means; nor was I at all easy at the
visits and familiarity of many who had been my acquaintance in
my prosperity, but had denied and shunned me in my adversity,
and now very forwardly renewed their acquaintance with me.
In short, I had sufficiently seen that the pleasures of the world
are chiefly folly, and the business of it mostly knavery; and both
nothing better than vanity: the men of pleasure tearing one another to pieces from the emulation of spending money, and the
men of business from envy in getting it. My happiness consisted

entirely in my wife, whom I loved with an inexpressible fondness, which was perfectly returned; and my prospects were no other than to provide for our growing family; for she was now big of her second child: I therefore took an opportunity to ask her opinion of entering into a retired life, which, after hearing my reasons, and perceiving my affection for it, she readily embraced. We soon put our small fortune, now reduced under three thousand pounds, into money, with part of which we purchased this little place, whither we retired soon after her delivery, from a world full of bustle, noise, hatred, envy, and ingratitude, to ease, quiet, and love. We have here lived almost twenty years, with little other conversation than our own, most of the neighbourhood taking us for very strange people; the squire of the parish representing me as a madman, and the parson as a Presbyterian; because I will not hunt with the one nor drink with the other. "Sir," says Adams, "Fortune hath, I think, paid you all her debts in this sweet retirement." Sir, replied the gentleman, I am thankful to the great Author of all things for the blessings I here enjoy. I have the best of wives, and three pretty children, for whom I have the true tenderness of a parent; but no blessings are pure in this world. Within three years of my arrival here I lost my eldest son. (*Here he sighed bitterly.*) "Sir," says Adams, "we must submit to Providence, and consider death as common to all." We must submit, indeed, answered the gentleman; and if he had died, I could have borne the loss with patience; but alas! sir, he was stolen away from my door by some wicked travelling people whom they call "gipsies", nor could I ever, with the most diligent search, recover him. Poor child! he had the sweetest look — the exact picture of his mother; at which some tears unwittingly dropt from his eyes, as did likewise from those of Adams, who always sympathized with his friends on those occasions. Thus, sir, said the gentleman, I have finished my story, in which if I have been too particular, I ask your pardon; and now, if you please, I will fetch you another bottle; which proposal the parson thankfully accepted.

CHAPTER IV.

A description of Mr. Wilson's way of living. The tragical adventure of the dog, and other grave matters.

THE gentleman returned with the bottle; and Adams and he sat some time silent, when the former started up, and cried, *"No, that won't do."* The gentleman inquired into his meaning; he answered, "He had been considering that it was possible the late famous King Theodore might have been that very son whom he had lost"; but added, "that his age could not answer that imagination. However," says he, "G— disposes all things for the best; and very probably he may be some great man, or duke, and may, one day or other, revisit you in that capacity." The gentleman answered, he should know him amongst ten thousand; for he had a mark on his left breast of a strawberry, which his mother had given him by longing for that fruit.

That beautiful young lady the Morning now rose from her bed, and with a countenance blooming with fresh youth and sprightliness, like Miss ——,* with soft dews hanging on her pouting lips, began to take her early walk over the eastern hills; and presently after, that gallant person the sun stole softly from his wife's chamber to pay his addresses to her; when the gentleman asked his guest if he would walk forth and survey his little garden, which he readily agreed to, and Joseph at the same time awaking from a sleep in which he had been two hours buried, went with them. No parterres, no fountains, no statues, embellished this little garden. Its only ornament was a short walk, shaded on each side by a filbert-hedge, with a small alcove at one end, whither in hot weather the gentleman and his wife used to retire, and divert themselves with their children, who played in the walk before them: but, though vanity had no votary in this little spot, here was variety of fruit and everything useful for the kitchen, which was abundantly sufficient to catch the admiration of Adams, who told the gentleman he had certainly a good gardener. Sir, answered he, that gardener is now before you: whatever you see here is the work solely of my own hands. Whilst I am providing necessaries for my table, I likewise procure myself an appetite for them. In fair seasons, I seldom pass less than six hours of the twenty-four in this place, where I am

* Whoever the reader pleases. — F.

not idle; and by these means I have been able to preserve my health ever since my arrival here, without assistance from physic. Hither I generally repair at the dawn, and exercise myself whilst my wife dresses her children and prepares our breakfast; after which we are seldom asunder during the residue of the day; for, when the weather will not permit them to accompany me here, I am usually within with them; for I am neither ashamed of conversing with my wife, nor of playing with my children: to say the truth, I do not perceive that inferiority of understanding which the levity of rakes, the dulness of men of business, or the austerity of the learned, would persuade us of in women. As for my woman, I declare I have found none of my own sex capable of making juster observations on life, or of delivering them more agreeably; nor do I believe anyone possessed of a faithfuller or braver friend. And sure as this friendship is sweetened with more delicacy and tenderness, so is it confirmed by dearer pledges than can attend the closest male alliance: for what union can be so fast as our common interest in the fruits of our embraces? Perhaps, sir, you are not yourself a father; if you are not, be assured you cannot conceive the delight I have in my little ones. Would you not despise me if you saw me stretched on the ground, and my children playing round me? "I should reverence the sight," quoth Adams; "I myself am now the father of six, and have been of eleven, and I can say I never scourged a child of my own, unless as his schoolmaster, and then have felt every stroke on my own posteriors. And as to what you say concerning women, I have often lamented my own wife did not understand Greek." — The gentleman smiled, and answered, he would not be apprehended to insinuate that his own had an understanding above the care of her family; on the contrary, says he, my Harriet, I assure you, is a notable housewife, and the housekeepers of few gentlemen understand cookery or confectionery better; but these are arts which she hath no great occasion for now: however, the wine you commended so much last night at supper was of her own making, as is indeed all the liquor in my house, except my beer, which falls to my province. ("And I assure you it is as excellent," quoth Adams, "as ever I tasted.") We formerly kept a maid-servant, but since my girls have been growing up, she is unwilling to indulge them in idleness; for as the fortunes I shall give them will be very small, we intend not to breed them above the rank they are likely to fill hereafter, nor to teach them to despise, or ruin a plain husband.

Indeed, I could wish a man of my own temper, and a retired life, might fall to their lot: for I have experienced that calm serene happiness, which is seated in content, is inconsistent with the hurry and bustle of the world. He was proceeding thus when the little things, being just risen, ran eagerly towards him and asked his blessing. They were shy to the strangers, but the eldest acquainted her father, that her mother and the young gentlewoman were up, and that breakfast was ready. They all went in, where the gentleman was surprised at the beauty of Fanny, who had now recovered herself from her fatigue, and was entirely clean drest; for the rogues who had taken away her purse had left her her bundle. But if he was so much amazed at the beauty of this young creature, his guests were no less charmed at the tenderness which appeared in the behaviour of the husband and wife to each other, and to their children, and at the dutiful and affectionate behaviour of these to their parents. These instances pleased the well-disposed mind of Adams equally with the readiness which they exprest to oblige their guests, and their forwardness to offer them the best of everything in their house; and what delighted him still more was an instance or two of their charity: for whilst they were at breakfast, the good woman was called for to assist her sick neighbour, which she did with some cordials made for the public use; and the good man went into his garden at the same time to supply another with something which he wanted thence; for they had nothing which those who wanted it were not welcome to. These good people were in the utmost cheerfulness, when they heard the report of a gun; and immediately afterwards a little dog, the favourite of the eldest daughter, came limping in all bloody, and laid himself at his mistress's feet: the poor girl, who was about eleven years old, burst into tears at the sight; and presently one of the neighbours came in and informed them that the young squire, the son of the lord of the manor, had shot him as he passed by, swearing at the same time he would prosecute the master of him for keeping a spaniel; for that he had given notice he would not suffer one in the parish. The dog, whom his mistress had taken into her lap, died in a few minutes, licking her hand. She exprest great agony at her loss; and the other children began to cry for their sister's misfortune; nor could Fanny herself refrain. Whilst the father and mother attempted to comfort her, Adams grasped his crabstick and would have sallied out after the squire had not Joseph withheld him. He could not however bridle his tongue — he pronounced the word "rascal" with great emphasis; said he deserved to be hanged more than a highwayman, and wished he had the scourging him. The mother took her child, lamenting and carrying the dead favourite in her arms, out of the room, when the gentleman said this was the second time this squire had endeavoured to kill the little wretch, and had wounded him smartly once before; adding, he could have no motive but ill-nature, for the little thing, which was not near as big as one's fist, had never been twenty yards from the house in the six years his daughter had had it. He said he had done nothing to deserve this usage, but his father had too great a fortune to contend with. That he was as absolute as any tyrant in the universe, and had killed all the dogs, and taken away all the guns in the neighbourhood; and not only that, but he trampled down hedges, and rode over corn and gardens, with no more regard than if they were the highway. "I wish I could catch him in my garden," said Adams; "though I would rather forgive him riding through my house than such an ill-natured act as this."

The cheerfulness of their conversation being interrupted by this accident, in which the guests could be of no service to their kind entertainer; and as the mother was taken up in administering consolation to the poor girl, whose disposition was too good hastily to forget the sudden loss of her little favourite, which had been fondling with her a few minutes before; and as Joseph and Fanny were impatient to get home and begin those previous ceremonies to their happiness which Adams had insisted on, they now offered to take their leave. The gentleman importuned them much to stay dinner; but when he found their eagerness to depart, he summoned his wife; and accordingly, having performed all the usual ceremonies of bows and curtsies more pleasant to be seen than to be related, they took their leave, the gentleman and his wife heartily wishing them a good journey, and they as heartily thanking them for their kind entertainment. The then departed, Adams declaring that this was the manner in which the people had lived in the Golden Age.

CHAPTER V.

A disputation on schools, held on the road between Mr. Abraham Adams and Joseph; and a discovery not unwelcome to them both.

OUR travellers, having well refreshed themselves at the gentleman's house, Joseph and Fanny with sleep, and Mr. Abraham Adams with ale and tobacco, renewed their journey with great alacrity; and, pursuing the road into which they were directed, travelled many miles before they met with any adventure worth relating. In this interval, we shall present our readers with a very curious discourse, as we apprehend it, concerning public schools, which passed between Mr. Joseph Andrews and Mr. Abraham Adams.

They had not gone far before Adams, calling to Joseph, asked him, If he had attended to the gentleman's story? He answered, "To all the former part." "And don't you think," says he, "he was a very unhappy man in his youth?" "A very unhappy man, indeed," answered the other. "Joseph," cries Adams, screwing up his mouth, "I have found it; I have discovered the cause of all the misfortunes which befell him. A public school, Joseph, was the cause of all the calamities which he afterwards suffered. Public schools are the nurseries of all vice and immorality. All the wicked fellows whom I remember at the university were bred at them. — Ah, Lord! I can remember as well as if it was but yesterday, a knot of them; they called them King's Scholars, I forget why — very wicked fellows! Joseph, you may thank the Lord you were not bred at a public school; you would never have preserved your virtue as you have. The first care I always take is of a boy's morals; I had rather he should be a blockhead than an atheist or a Presbyterian. What is all the learning in the world compared to his immortal soul? What shall a man take in exchange for his soul? But the masters of great schools trouble themselves about no such thing. I have known a lad of eighteen at the university, who hath not been able to say his catechism; but for my own part, I always scourged a lad sooner for missing that than any other lesson. Believe me, child, all that gentleman's misfortunes arose from his being educated at a public school."

"It doth not become me," answered Joseph, "to dispute anything, sir, with you, especially a matter of this kind; for to be sure you must be allowed by all the world to be the best teacher of a school in all our county." "Yes, that," says Adams, "I believe, is granted me; that I may without much vanity pretend to — nay, I believe I may go to the next county too — but *gloriari non est meum —*" "However, sir, as you are pleased to bid me speak," says Joseph, "you know my late master, Sir Thomas Booby, was bred at a public school, and he was the finest gentleman in all the neighbourhood. And I have often heard him say, if he had a hundred boys he would breed them all at the same place. It was his opinion, and I have often heard him deliver it, that a boy taken from a public school and carried into the world, will learn more in one year there than one of a private education will in five. He used to say the school itself initiated him a great way (I remember that was his very expression), for great schools are little societies, where a boy of any observation may see in epitome what he will afterwards find in the world at large." "*Hinc illæ lachrymæ:* for that very reason," quoth Adams, "I prefer a private school, where boys may be kept in innocence and ignorance; for, according to that fine passage in the play of Cato, the only English tragedy I ever read,

> If knowledge of the world must make men villains,
> May Juba ever live in ignorance.

Who would not rather preserve the purity of his child than wish him to attain the whole circle of arts and sciences; which, by the bye, he may learn in the classes of a private school? For I would not be vain, but I esteem myself to be second to none, *nulli secundum*, in teaching these things; so that a lad may have as much learning in a private as in a public education." "And, with submission," answered Joseph, "he may get as much vice: witness several country gentlemen, who were educated within five miles of their own houses, and are as wicked as if they had known the world from their infancy. I remember when I was in the stable, if a young horse was vicious in his nature, no correction would make him otherwise; I take it to be equally the same among men: if a boy be of a mischievous, wicked inclination, no school, though ever so private, will ever make him good, on the contrary, if he be of a righteous temper, you may trust him to London, or wherever else you please — he will be in no danger of being corrupted. Besides, I have often heard my master say that the discipline practised in public schools was much better than that in private." — "You talk like a jackanapes," says Adams, "and so did your master. Discipline indeed! Because one man scourges twenty or thirty boys more in a morning than another, is he therefore a better disciplinarian? I do presume to confer in this point with all who have taught from Chiron's time to this day; and, if I was master of six boys only, I would preserve as good discipline amongst them as the master of the greatest school in the world. I say nothing, young man; remember, I say nothing; but if Sir Thomas himself had been educated nearer home, and under the tuition of somebody — remember I name nobody — it might have been better for him, — but his father must institute him in the knowledge of the world. *Nemo mortalium omnibus horis sapit.*" Joseph, seeing him run on in this manner, asked pardon many times, assuring him he had no intention to offend. "I believe you had not, child," said he, "and I am not angry with you: but for maintaining good discipline in a school; for this" — And then he ran on as before, named all the masters who are recorded in old books, and preferred himself to them all. Indeed, if this good man had an enthusiasm, or what the vulgar call a blind side, it was this: he thought a schoolmaster the greatest character in the world, and himself the greatest of all school-masters; neither of which points he would have given up to Alexander the Great at the head of his army.

Adams continued his subject till they came to one of the beautifullest spots of ground in the universe. It was a kind of natural amphitheatre, formed by the winding of a small rivulet, which was planted with thick woods, and the trees rose gradually above each other by the natural ascent of the ground they stood on; which ascent as they hid with their boughs, they seemed to have been disposed by the design of the most skilful planter. The soil was spread with a verdure which no paint could imitate; and the whole place might have raised romantic ideas in elder minds than those of Joseph and Fanny, without the assistance of love.

Here they arrived about noon, and Joseph proposed to Adams that they should rest awhile in this delightful place, and refresh themselves with some provisions which the good-nature of Mrs. Wilson had provided them with. Adams made no objection to the proposal; so down they sat, and, pulling out a cold fowl, and a bottle of wine, they made a repast with a cheerfulness which might have attracted the envy of more splendid tables. I should not omit that they found among their provision a little paper containing a piece of gold, which Adams imagining had been put there by mistake, would have returned back to restore it; but he was at last convinced by Joseph that Mr. Wilson had taken this handsome way of furnishing them with a supply for their journey, on his having related the distress which they had been in, when they were relieved by the generosity of the pedlar. Adams said he was glad to see such an instance of goodness, not so much for the conveniency which it brought them as for the sake of the doer, whose reward would be great in heaven. He likewise comforted himself with a reflection that he should shortly have an opportunity of returning it him; for the gentleman was within a week to make a journey into Somersetshire, to pass through Adams's parish, and had faithfully promised to call on him; a circumstance which we thought too immaterial to mention before; but which those who have as great an affection for that gentleman as ourselves will rejoice at, as it may give them hopes of seeing him again. Then Joseph made a speech on charity which the reader, if he is so disposed, may see in the next chapter; for we scorn to betray him into any such reading, without first giving him warning.

CHAPTER VI.

Moral reflections by Joseph Andrews, with the hunting adventure, and Parson Adams's miraculous escape.

"I HAVE often wondered, sir," said Joseph, "to observe so few instances of charity among mankind; for though the goodness of a man's heart did not incline him to relieve the distresses of his fellow-creatures, methinks the desire of honour should move him to it. What inspires a man to build fine houses, to purchase fine furniture, pictures, clothes, and other things, at a great expense, but an ambition to be respected more than other people? Now, would not one great act of charity, one instance of redeeming a poor family from all the miseries of poverty, restoring an unfortunate tradesman by a sum of money to the means of procuring a livelihood by his industry, discharging an undone debtor from his debts or a gaol, or any such like example of goodness, create a man more honour and respect than he could acquire by the finest house, furniture, pictures, or clothes, that were ever beheld? For not only the object himself who was thus relieved, but all who heard the name of such a person, must, I imagine, reverence him infinitely more than the possessor of all those other things; which when we so admire, we rather praise the builder, the workman, the painter, the lace-maker, the tailor, and the rest, by whose ingenuity they are produced, than the person who by his money makes them his own. For my own part, when I have waited behind my lady in a room hung with fine pictures, while I have been looking at them I have never once thought of their owner, nor hath anyone else, as I ever observed; for when it hath been asked whose picture that was, it was never once answered, the master's of the house; but Ammyconni, Paul Varnish, Hannibal Scratchi, or Hogarthi, which I suppose were the names of the painters; but if it was asked, Who redeemed such a one out of prison? Who lent such a ruined tradesman money to set up? Who clothed that family of poor small children? it is very plain what must be the answer. And besides, these great folks are mistaken if they imagine they get any honour at all by these means; for I do not remember I ever was with my lady at any house where she commended the house or furniture but I have heard her at her return home make sport and jeer at whatever she had before commended; and I have been told by other gentlemen in livery that it is the same in their families: but I defy the wisest man in the world to turn a true good action into ridicule. I defy him to do it. He who should endeavour it would be laughed at himself, instead of making others laugh. Nobody scarce doth any good, yet they all agree in praising those who do. Indeed, it is strange that all men should consent in commending goodness, and no man endeavour to deserve that commendation; whilst, on the contrary, all rail at wickedness, and all are as eager to be what they abuse. This I know not the reason of; but it is as plain as daylight to those who converse in the world, as I have done these three years." "Are all the great folks wicked then?" says Fanny. "To be sure there are some exceptions," answered Joseph. "Some gentlemen of our cloth report charitable actions done by their lords and masters; and I have heard Squire Pope, the great poet, at my lady's table, tell stories of a man that lived at a place called Ross, and another at the Bath, one Al— Al— I forget his name, but it is in the book of verses. This gentleman hath built up a stately house too, which the squire likes very well; but his charity is seen farther than his house, though it stands on a hill,—ay, and brings him more honour too. It was his charity that put him in the book, where the squire says he puts all those who deserve it; and to be sure, as he lives among all the great people, if there were any such, he would know them." — This was all of Mr. Joseph Andrews's speech which I could get him to recollect, which I have delivered as near as was possible in his own words, with a very small embellishment. But I believe the reader hath not been a little surprised at the long silence of Parson Adams, especially as so many occasions offered themselves to exert his curiosity and observation. The truth is, he was fast asleep, and had so been from the beginning of the preceding narrative; and, indeed, if the reader considers that so many hours had passed since he had closed his eyes, he will not wonder at his repose, though even Henley himself, or as great an orator (if any such be), had been in his rostrum or tub before him.

Joseph, who, whilst he was speaking, had continued in one attitude, with his head reclining on one side, and his eyes cast on the ground, no sooner perceived, on looking up, the position of Adams, who was stretched on his back, and snored louder than the usual braying of the animal with long ears, than he turned towards Fanny, and, taking her by the hand, began a dalliance, which, though consistent with the purest innocence and decency, neither he would have attempted, nor she permitted, before any witness. Whilst they amused themselves in this harmless and delightful manner, they heard a pack of hounds approaching in full cry towards them, and presently afterwards saw a hare pop forth from the wood, and, crossing the water, land within a few yards of them in the meadows. The hare was no sooner on shore than it seated itself on its hinder legs, and listened to the sound of the pursuers. Fanny was wonderfully pleased with the little wretch, and eagerly longed to have it in her arms that she might preserve it from the dangers which seemed to threaten it; but the rational part of the creation do not always aptly distinguish their friends from their foes; what wonder then if this silly creature, the moment it beheld her, fled from the friend who would have protected it, and, traversing the meadows again, passed the little rivulet on the opposite side. It was, however, so spent and weak, that it fell down twice or thrice in its way. This affected the tender heart of Fanny, who exclaimed, with tears in her eyes, against the barbarity of worrying a poor innocent defenceless animal out of its life, and putting it to the extremest torture for diversion.

She had not much time to make reflections of this kind; for on a sudden the hounds rushed through the wood, which resounded with their throats, and the throats of their *retinue*, who *attended* on them on horseback. The dogs now passed the rivulet, and pursued the footsteps of the hare; five horsemen attempted to leap over, three of whom succeeded, and two were in the attempt thrown from their saddles into the water; their companions, and their own horses too, proceeded after their sport, and left their friends and riders to invoke the assistance of Fortune, or to employ the more active means of strength and agility for their deliverance. Joseph, however, was not so unconcerned on this occasion: he left Fanny for a moment to herself, and ran to the gentlemen, who were immediately on their legs, shaking their ears, and easily, with the help of his hand, attained the bank (for the rivulet was not at all deep); and, without staying to thank their kind assister, ran dripping across the meadow, calling to their brother sportsmen to stop their horses; but they heard them not.

The hounds were now very little behind their poor reeling, staggering prey, which, fainting almost at every step, crawled through the wood, and had almost got round to the place where Fanny stood, when it was overtaken by its enemies, and being driven out of the covert, was caught, and instantly tore to pieces before Fanny's face, who was unable to assist it with any aid more powerful than pity; nor could she prevail on Joseph, who had been himself a sportsman in his youth, to attempt anything contrary to the laws of hunting in favour of the hare, which he said was killed fairly.

The hare was caught within a yard or two of Adams, who lay asleep at some distance from the lovers; and the hounds in devouring it, and pulling it backwards and forwards, had drawn it so close to him, that some of them (by mistake perhaps for the hare's skin) laid hold of the skirts of his cassock; others at the same time applying their teeth to his wig, which he had with a handkerchief fastened to his head, began to pull him about; and had not the motion of his body had more effect on him than seemed to be wrought by the noise, they must certainly have tasted his flesh, which delicious flavour might have been fatal to him; but being roused by these tuggings, he instantly awaked and with a jerk delivering his head from his wig, he with most admirable dexterity recovered his legs, which now seemed the only members he could entrust his safety to. Having, therefore,

escaped likewise from at least a third part of his cassock, which
he willingly left as his *exuviæ* or spoils to the enemy, he fled
with the utmost speed he could summon to his assistance. Nor
let this be any detraction from the bravery of his character: let
the number of the enemies, and the surprise in which he was
taken, be considered; and if there be any modern so outrageously
brave that he cannot admit of flight in any circumstance whatever, I say (but I whisper that softly, and, I solemnly declare,
without any intention of giving offence to any brave man in the
nation), I say, or rather I whisper, that he is an ignorant fellow,
and hath never read Homer nor Virgil, nor knows he anything
of Hector or Turnus; nay, he is unacquainted with the history of
some great men living, who, though as brave as lions, ay, as
tigers, have run away, the Lord knows how far, and the Lord
knows why, to the surprise of their friends, and the entertainment of their enemies. But if persons of such heroic disposition
are a little offended at the behaviour of Adams, we assure them
they shall be as much pleased with what we shall immediately
relate of Joseph Andrews. The master of the pack was just
arrived, or, as the sportsmen call it, "come in," when Adams set
out, as we have before mentioned. This gentleman was generally
said to be a great lover of humour; but, not to mince the matter,
especially as we are upon this subject, he was a great "hunter
of men": indeed, he had hitherto followed the sport only with
dogs of his own species; for he kept two or three couple of
barking curs for that use only. However, as he thought he had
now found a man nimble enough, he was willing to indulge
himself with other sport, and accordingly crying out, "Stole
away," encouraged the hounds to pursue Mr. Adams, swearing
it was the largest jack-hare he ever saw; at the same time
hallooing and hooping as if a conquered foe was flying before
him; in which he was imitated by these two or three couple
of human, or rather two-legged, curs on horseback which we
have mentioned before.

Now, thou, whoever thou art, whether a muse, or by what
other name soever thou choosest to be called, who presidest
over biography, and hast inspired all the writers of lives in
these our times: thou who didst infuse such wonderful humour
into the pen of immortal Gulliver; who hast carefully guided
the judgment, whilst thou hast exalted the nervous manly style
of thy Mallet: thou who hadst no hand in that Dedication and
Preface, or the translations, which thou wouldst willingly have

struck out of the Life of Cicero: lastly, thou who, without the assistance of the least spice of literature, and even against his inclination, hast, in some pages of his book, forced Colley Cibber to write English; do thou assist me in what I find myself unequal to. Do thou introduce on the plain the young, the gay, the brave Joseph Andrews, whilst men shall view him with admiration and envy, tender virgins with love and anxious concern for his safety.

No sooner did Joseph Andrews perceive the distress of his friend, when first the quick-scenting dogs attacked him, than he grasped his cudgel in his right hand, a cudgel which his father had of his grandfather, to whom a mighty strong man of Kent had given it for a present in that day when he broke three heads on the stage. It was a cudgel of mighty strength and wonderful art, made by one of Mr. Deard's best workmen, whom no other artificer can equal, and who hath made all those sticks which the beaus have lately walked with about the Park in a morning; but this was far his masterpiece: on its head was engraved a nose and chin, which might have been mistaken for a pair of nut-crackers. The learned have imagined it designed to represent the Gorgon; but it was in fact copied from the face of a certain long English baronet, of infinite wit, humour, and gravity. He did intend to have engraved here many histories: as the first night of Captain B——'s play, where you would have seen critics in embroidery transplanted from the boxes to the pit, whose ancient inhabitants were exalted to the galleries, where they played on catcalls. He did intend to have painted an auction room, where Mr. Cock would have appeared aloft in his pulpit, trumpeting forth the praises of a china basin, and with astonishment wondering that "Nobody bids more for that fine, that superb——" He did intend to have engraved many other things, but was forced to leave all out for want of room.

No sooner had Joseph grasped his cudgel in his hands than lightning darted from his eyes; and the heroic youth, swift of foot, ran with the utmost speed to his friend's assistance. He overtook him just as Rockwood had laid hold of the skirt of his cassock, which, being torn, hung to the ground. Reader, we would make a simile on this occasion, but for two reasons: the first is, it would interrupt the description, which should be rapid in this part; but that doth not weigh much, many precedents occurring for such an interruption: the second, and much the greater, reason is, that we could find no simile adequate to our purpose: for indeed, what instance could we bring to set before our reader's eyes at once the idea of friendship, courage, youth, beauty, strength, and swiftness? all which blazed in the person of Joseph Andrews. Let those, therefore, that describe lions and tigers, and heroes fiercer than both, raise their poems or plays with the simile of Joseph Andrews, who is himself above the reach of any simile.

Now Rockwood had laid fast hold on the parson's skirts, and stopt his flight; which Joseph no sooner perceived than he levelled his cudgel at his head, and laid him sprawling. Jowler and Ringwood then fell on his greatcoat, and had undoubtedly brought him to the ground, had not Joseph, collecting all his force, given Jowler such a rap on the back, that, quitting his hold, he ran howling over the plain: A harder fate remained for thee, O Ringwood! Ringwood the best hound that ever pursued a hare, who never threw his tongue but where the scent was undoubtedly true; good at "trailing," and "sure in a highway"; no "babler," no "overrunner"; respected by the whole pack: for, whenever he opened, they knew the game was at hand. He fell by the stroke of Joseph. Thunder, and Plunder, and Wonder, and Blunder, were the next victims of his wrath, and measured their lengths on the ground. Then Fairmaid, a bitch which Mr. John Temple had bred up in his house, and fed at his own table, and lately sent the squire fifty miles for a present, ran fiercely at Joseph, and bit him by the leg; no dog was ever fiercer than she, being descended from an Amazonian breed, and had worried bulls in her own country, but now waged an unequal fight, and had shared the fate of those we have mentioned before, had not Diana (the reader may believe it or not, as he pleases) in that instant interposed, and, in the shape of the huntsman, snatched her favourite up in her arms.

The parson now faced about, and with his crabstick felled many to the earth, and scattered others, till he was attacked by Cæsar, and pulled to the ground. Then Joseph flew to his rescue, and with such might fell on the victor, that, O eternal blot to his name! Cæsar ran yelping away.

The battle now raged with the most dreadful violence, when lo! the huntsman, a man of years and dignity, lifted his voice, and called his hounds from the fight; telling them, in a language they understood, that it was in vain to contend longer, for that fate had decreed the victory to their enemies.

Thus far the muse hath with her usual dignity related this prodigious battle, a battle we apprehend never equalled by any poet, romance- or life-writer whatever, and, having brought it to a conclusion, she ceased; we shall therefore proceed in our ordinary style with the continuation of this history. The squire and his companions, whom the figure of Adams, and the gallantry of Joseph, had at first thrown into a violent fit of laughter, and who had hitherto beheld the engagement with more delight than any chase, shooting-match, race, cock-fighting, bull- or bear-baiting, had ever given them, began now to apprehend the danger of their hounds, many of which lay sprawling in the fields. The squire, therefore, having first called his friends about him, as guards for safety of his person, rode manfully up to the combatants, and, summoning all the terror he was master of into his countenance, demanded with an authoritative voice of Joseph, what he meant by assaulting his dogs in that manner? Joseph answered, with great intrepidity, that they had first fallen on his friend; and if they had belonged to the greatest man in the kingdom, he would have treated them in the same way; for, whilst his veins contained a single drop of blood, he would not stand idle by and see that gentleman (*pointing to Adams*) abused either by man or beast; and, having so said, both he and Adams brandished their wooden weapons, and put themselves into such a posture, that the squire and his company thought proper to preponderate before they offered to revenge the cause of their four-footed allies.

At this instant Fanny, whom the apprehension of Joseph's danger had alarmed so much that, forgetting her own, she had made the utmost expedition, came up. The squire and all the horsemen were so surprised with her beauty that they imme-diately fixed both their eyes and thoughts solely on her, every-one declaring he had never seen so charming a creature. Neither mirth nor anger engaged them a moment longer; but all sat in silent amaze. The huntsman only was free from her attraction, who was busy in cutting the ears of the dogs and endeavouring to recover them to life; in which he succeeded so well, that only two of no great note remained slaughtered on the field of action. Upon this the huntsman declared, "'Twas well it was no worse; for his part he could not blame the gentleman, and wondered his master would encourage the dogs to hunt *Christians;* that it was the surest way to spoil them, to make them follow *vermin* instead of sticking to a hare."

The squire being informed of the little mischief that had been done, and perhaps having more mischief of another kind in his head, accosted Mr. Adams with a more favourable aspect than before: he told him he was sorry for what had happened; that he had endeavoured all he could to prevent it the moment he was acquainted with his cloth, and greatly commended the courage of his servant; for so he imagined Joseph to be. He then invited Mr. Adams to dinner, and desired the young woman might come with him. Adams refused a long while; but the invitation was repeated with so much earnestness and courtesy, that at length he was forced to accept it. His wig and hat, and other spoils of the field, being gathered together by Joseph (for otherwise probably they would have been forgotten), he put himself into the best order he could; and then the horse and foot moved forward in the same pace towards the squire's house, which stood at a very little distance.

Whilst they were on the road, the lovely Fanny attracted the eyes of all: they endeavoured to outvie one another in encomiums on her beauty; which the reader will pardon my not relating, as they had not anything new or uncommon in them: so must he likewise my not setting down the many curious jests which were made on Adams; some of them declaring that parson-hunting was the best sport in the world; others commending his standing at bay, which they said he had done as well as any badger; with such like merriment, which, though it would ill become the dignity of this history, afforded much laughter and diversion to the squire and his facetious companions.

CHAPTER VII.

A scene of roasting very nicely adapted to the present taste and times.

THEY arrived at the squire's house just as his dinner was ready. A little dispute arose on the account of Fanny, whom the squire, who was a bachelor, was desirous to place at his own table; but she would not consent, nor would Mr. Adams permit her to be parted from Joseph: so that she was at length with him consigned over to the kitchen, where the servants were ordered to make him drunk; a favour which was likewise intended for Adams: which design being executed, the squire thought he should easily accomplish what he had, when he first saw her, intended to perpetrate with Fanny.

It may not be improper, before we proceed farther, to open a little the character of this gentleman, and that of his friends. The master of this house, then, was a man of a very considerable fortune; a bachelor, as we have said, and about forty years of age: he had been educated (if we may here use that expression) in the country, and at his own home, under the care of his mother, and a tutor who had orders never to correct him, nor to compel him to learn more than he liked, which it seems was very little, and that only in his childhood; for from the age of fifteen he addicted himself entirely to hunting and other rural amusements, for which his mother took care to equip him with horses, hounds, and all other necessaries; and his tutor, endeavouring to ingratiate himself with his young pupil, who would, he knew, be able handsomely to provide for him, became his companion, not only at these exercises, but likewise over a bottle, which the young squire had a very early relish for. At the age of twenty his mother began to think she had not fulfilled the duty of a parent; she therefore resolved to persuade her son, if possible, to that which she imagined would well supply all that he might have learned at a public school or university. This is what they commonly call "travelling"; which, with the help of the tutor, who was fixed on to attend him, she easily succeeded in. He made in three years the tour of Europe, as they term it, and returned home well furnished with French clothes, phrases, and servants, with a hearty contempt for his own country; especially what had any savour of the plain spirit and honesty of our ancestors. His mother greatly applauded herself at his return; and now, being master of his own fortune, he soon procured himself a seat in Parliament, and was in the common opinion one of the finest gentlemen of his age: but what distinguished him chiefly was a strange delight which he took in everything which is ridiculous, odious, and absurd in his own species; so that he never chose a companion without one or more of these ingredients, and those who were marked by nature in the most eminent degree with them were most his favourites:

if he ever found a man who either had not, or endeavoured to
conceal, these imperfections, he took great pleasure in inventing
methods of forcing him into absurdities which were not natural
to him, or in drawing forth and exposing those that were; for
which purpose he was always provided with a set of fellows,
whom we have before called curs, and who did, indeed, no
great honour to the canine kind; their business was to hunt out
and display everything that had any savour of the above-
mentioned qualities, and especially in the gravest and best characters; but if they failed in their search, they were to turn even
virtue and wisdom themselves into ridicule, for the diversion
of their master and feeder. The gentlemen of curlike disposition
who were now at his house, and whom he had brought with him
from London, were, an old half-pay officer, a player, a dull poet,
a quack-doctor, a scraping fiddler, and a lame German dancing-
master.

As soon as dinner was served, while Mr. Adams was saying
grace, the captain conveyed his chair from behind him; so that
when he endeavoured to seat himself, he fell down on the ground;
and this completed joke the first, to the great entertainment of
the whole company. The second joke was performed by the
poet, who sat next him on the other side, and took an opportunity, while poor Adams was respectfully drinking to the master
of the house, to overturn a plate of soup into his breeches; which,
with the many apologies he made, and the parson's gentle answers, caused much mirth in the company. Joke the third was
served up by one of the waiting-men, who had been ordered
to convey a quantity of gin into Mr. Adams's ale, which he
declaring to be the best liquor he ever drank, but rather too rich
of the malt, contributed again to their laughter. Mr. Adams,
from whom we had most of this relation, could not recollect all
the jests of this kind practised on him, which the inoffensive
disposition of his own heart made him slow in discovering; and
indeed, had it not been for the information which we received
from a servant of the family, this part of our history, which we
take to be none of the least curious, must have been deplorably
imperfect; though we must own it probable that some more
jokes were (as they call it) "cracked" during their dinner; but we
have by no means been able to come at the knowledge of them.
When dinner was removed, the poet began to repeat some verses,
which he said were made *extempore*. The following is a copy
of them, procured with the greatest difficulty:

An extempore *Poem on Parson Adams.*

Did ever mortal such a parson view;
His cassock old, his wig not over-new?
Well might the hounds have him for fox mistaken,
In smell more like to that than rusty bacon.*
But would it not make any mortal stare,
To see this parson taken for a hare?
Could Phœbus err thus grossly, even he
For a good player might have taken thee.

At which words the bard whipt off the player's wig, and received the approbation of the company, rather perhaps for the dexterity of his hand than his head. The player, instead of retorting the jest on the poet, began to display his talents on the same subject. He repeated many scraps of wit out of plays, reflecting on the whole body of the clergy, which were received with great acclamations by all present. It was now the dancing-master's turn to exhibit his talents; he therefore, addressing himself to Adams in broken English, told him, "He was a man ver well made for de dance, and he suppose by his walk, dat he had learn of some great master." He said, "It was ver pretty quality in clergyman to dance"; and concluded with desiring him to dance a minuet, telling him, "his cassock would serve for petticoats; and that he would himself be his partner." At which words, without waiting for an answer, he pulled out his gloves, and the fiddler was preparing his fiddle. The company all offered the dancing-master wagers that the parson out-danced him, which he refused, saying, "He believed so too; for he had never seen any man in his life who looked de dance so well as de gentleman": he then stepped forwards to take Adams by the hand, which the latter hastily withdrew, and, at the same time clenching his fist, advised him not to carry the jest too far, for he would not endure being put upon. The dancing-master no sooner saw the fist than he prudently retired out of its reach, and stood aloof, mimicking Adams, whose eyes were fixed on him, not guessing what he was at, but to avoid his laying hold on him, which he had once attempted. In the meanwhile, the captain, perceiving an opportunity, pinned a cracker or devil to the cassock, and then lighted it with their little smoking-candle. Adams, being a stranger to this sport, and believing he had been blown up in reality, started from his chair, and jumped about the room, to the infinite

* All hounds that will hunt fox or other vermin will hunt a piece of rusty bacon trailed on the ground. — F.

joy of the beholders, who declared he was the best dancer in the universe. As soon as the devil had done tormenting him, and he had a little recovered his confusion, he returned to the table, standing up in the posture of one who intended to make a speech. They all cried out, "Hear him, hear him!" and he then spoke in the following manner: "Sir, I am sorry to see one to whom Providence hath been so bountiful in bestowing his favours make so ill and ungrateful a return for them; for though you have not insulted me yourself, it is visible you have delighted in those that do it, nor have once discouraged the many rudenesses which have been shown towards me; indeed, towards yourself if you rightly understood them; for I am your guest, and by the laws of hospitality entitled to your protection. One gentleman hath thought proper to produce some poetry upon me, of which I shall only say, that I had rather be the subject than the composer. He hath pleased to treat me with disrespect as a parson. I apprehend my order is not the subject of scorn, nor that I can become so, unless by being a disgrace to it, which I hope poverty will never be called. Another gentleman, indeed, hath repeated some sentences, where the order itself is mentioned with contempt. He says they are taken from plays. I am sure such plays are a scandal to the government which permits them, and cursed will be the nation where they are represented. How others have treated me I need not observe; they themselves, when they reflect, must allow the behaviour to be as improper to my years as to my cloth. You found me, sir, travelling with two of my parishioners (I omit your hounds falling on me; for I have quite forgiven it, whether it proceeded from the wantonness or negligence of the huntsman): my appearance might very well persuade you that your invitation was an act of charity, though in reality we were well provided; yes, sir, if we had an hundred miles to travel, we had sufficient to bear our expenses in a noble manner." (At which words he produced the half-guinea which was found in the basket.) "I do not show you this out of ostentation of riches, but to convince you I speak truth. Your seating me at your table was an honour which I did not ambitiously affect. When I was here, I endeavoured to behave towards you with the utmost respect; if I have failed, it was not with design; nor could I, certainly, so far be guilty as to deserve the insults I have suffered. If they were meant, therefore, either to my order or my poverty (and you see I am not very poor), the shame doth not lie at my door, and I heartily pray that the sin may be

averted from yours." He thus finished, and received a general
clap from the whole company. Then the gentleman of the house
told him, "He was sorry for what had happened; that he could not
accuse him of any share in it: that the verses were, as himself
had well observed, so bad, that he might easily answer them; and
for the serpent, it was undoubtedly a very great affront done him
by the dancing-master, for which, if he well thrashed him, as he
deserved, the gentleman said he should be very much pleased to
see it" (in which, probably, he spoke truth). Adams answered,
"Whoever had done it, it was not his profession to punish him
that way; but for the person whom he had accused, I am a witness," says he, "of his innocence; for I had my eye on him all the
while. Whoever he was, God forgive him, and bestow on him a
little more sense as well as humanity." The captain answered
with a surly look and accent, "That he hoped he did not mean
to reflect on him; d—n him, he had as much *imanity* as
another, and, if any man said he had not, he would convince him
of his mistake by cutting his throat." Adams, smiling, said, "He
believed he had spoke right by accident." To which the captain
returned, "What do you mean by my speaking right? If you
was not a parson, I would not take these words; but your gown
protects you. If any man who wears a sword had said so much,
I had pulled him by the nose before this." Adams replied, "If he
attempted any rudeness to his person, he would not find any protection for himself in his gown"; and, clenching his fist, declared
he had thrashed many a stouter man. The gentleman did all he
could to encourage this warlike disposition in Adams, and was
in hopes to have produced a battle: but he was disappointed;
for the captain made no other answer than, "It is very well you
are a parson"; and so, drinking off a bumper to old mother
Church, ended the dispute.

Then the doctor, who had hitherto been silent, and who was
the gravest but most mischievous dog of all, in a very pompous
speech highly applauded what Adams had said, and as much
discommended the behaviour to him. He proceeded to encomiums on the Church and poverty; and, lastly, recommended
forgiveness of what had passed to Adams, who immediately
answered, "That everything was forgiven"; and in the warmth
of his goodness he filled a bumper of strong beer (a liquor he
preferred to wine), and drank a health to the whole company,
shaking the captain and the poet heartily by the hand, and
addressing himself with great respect to the doctor; who, indeed,

had not laughed outwardly at anything that passed, as he had a
perfect command of his muscles, and could laugh inwardly without betraying the least symptoms in his countenance. The
doctor now began a second formal speech, in which he declaimed
against all levity of conversation, and what is usually called mirth.
He said, "There were amusements fitted for persons of all ages
and degrees, from the rattle to the discussing a point of philosophy; and that men discovered themselves in nothing more than
in the choice of their amusements; for," says he, "as it must
greatly raise our expectation of the future conduct in life of
boys whom in their tender years we perceive, instead of taw or
balls, or other childish playthings, to choose, at their leisure hours,
to exercise their genius in contentions of wit, learning, and such
like; so must it inspire one with equal contempt of a man, if we
should discover him playing at taw or other childish play."
Adams highly commended the doctor's opinion, and said, "He
had often wondered at some passages in ancient authors, where
Scipio, Lælius, and other great men were represented to have
passed many hours in amusements of the most trifling kind." The
doctor replied, "He had by him an old Greek manuscript where a
favourite diversion of Socrates was recorded." "Ay!" says the
parson eagerly; "I should be most infinitely obliged to you for
the favour of perusing it." The doctor promised to send it him,
and farther said, "That he believed he could describe it. I think,"
says he, "as near as I can remember, it was this. There was a
throne erected, on one side of which sat a king, and on the other
a queen, with their guards and attendants ranged on both sides;
to them was introduced an ambassador, which part Socrates
always used to perform himself; and when he was led up to the
footsteps of the throne, he addressed himself to the monarchs in
some grave speech, full of virtue, and goodness, and morality,
and such like. After which, he was seated between the king and
queen, and royally entertained. This I think was the chief
part. — Perhaps I may have forgot some particulars; for it is long
since I read it." Adams said, "It was, indeed, a diversion worthy
the relaxation of so great a man; and thought something resembling it should be instituted among our great men, instead
of cards and other idle pastime, in which, he was informed, they
trifled away too much of their lives." He added, "The Christian
religion was a nobler subject for these speeches than any Socrates
could have invented." The gentleman of the house approved what
Mr. Adams said, and declared, "he was resolved to perform the

ceremony this very evening." To which the doctor objected, as no one was prepared with a speech, "unless," said he (turning to Adams with a gravity of countenance which would have deceived a more knowing man), "you have a sermon about you, doctor." — "Sir," says Adams, "I never travel without one, for fear of what may happen." He was easily prevailed on by his worthy friend, as he now called the doctor, to undertake the part of the ambassador; so that the gentleman sent immediate orders to have the throne erected, which was performed before they had drank two bottles: and, perhaps, the reader will hereafter have no great reason to admire the nimbleness of the servants. Indeed, to confess the truth, the throne was no more than this: there was a great tub of water provided, on each side of which were placed two stools raised higher than the surface of the tub, and over the whole was laid a blanket; on these stools were placed the king and queen, namely, the master of the house and the captain. And now the ambassador was introduced between the poet and the doctor; who, having read his sermon, to the great entertainment of all present, was led up to his place, and seated between their majesties. They immediately rose up, when the blanket, wanting its supports at either end, gave way, and soused Adams over head and ears in the water; the captain made his escape, but, unluckily, the gentleman himself not being as nimble as he ought, Adams caught hold of him before he descended from his throne, and pulled him in with him, to the entire secret satisfaction of all the company. Adams, after ducking the squire twice or thrice, leapt out of the tub, and looked sharp for the doctor, whom he would certainly have conveyed to the same place of honour; but he had wisely withdrawn: he then searched for his crabstick, and having found that, as well as his fellow-travellers, he declared he would not stay a moment longer in such a house. He then departed, without taking leave of his host, whom he had exacted a more severe revenge on than he intended: for, as he did not use sufficient care to dry himself in time, he caught a cold by the accident, which threw him into a fever that had like to have cost him his life.

CHAPTER VIII.

Which some readers will think too short, and others too long.

ADAMS, and Joseph, who was no less enraged than his friend at the treatment he met with, went out with their sticks in their hands, and carried off Fanny, notwithstanding the opposition of the servants, who did all, without proceeding to violence, in their power to detain them. They walked as fast as they could, not so much from any apprehension of being pursued as that Mr. Adams might, by exercise, prevent any harm from the water. The gentleman, who had given such orders to his servants concerning Fanny that he did not in the least fear her getting away, no sooner heard that she was gone, than he began to rave, and immediately dispatched several with orders either to bring her back or never return. The poet, the player, and all but the dancing-master and doctor, went on this errand.

The night was very dark in which our friends began their journey; however, they made such expedition, that they soon arrived at an inn, which was at seven miles' distance. Here they unanimously consented to pass the evening, Mr. Adams being now as dry as he was before he had set out on his embassy.

This inn, which indeed we might call an ale-house, had not the words, The New Inn, been writ on the sign, afforded them no better provision than bread and cheese and ale; on which, however, they made a very comfortable meal; for hunger is better than a French cook.

They had no sooner supped, than Adams, returning thanks to the Almighty for his food, declared he had eat his homely commons with much greater satisfaction than his splendid dinner; and expressed great contempt for the folly of mankind, who sacrificed their hopes of heaven to the acquisition of vast wealth, since so much comfort was to be found in the humblest state and the lowest provision. "Very true, sir," says a grave man who sat smoking his pipe by the fire, and who was a traveller as well as himself. "I have often been as much surprised as you are, when I consider the value which mankind in general set on riches, since every day's experience shows us how little is in their power; for what, indeed, truly desirable, can they bestow on us? Can they give beauty to the deformed, strength to the weak, or health to the infirm? Surely if they

could, we should not see so many ill-favoured faces haunting
the assemblies of the great, nor would such numbers of feeble
wretches languish in their coaches and palaces. No, not the
wealth of a kingdom can purchase any paint to dress pale
Ugliness in the bloom of that young maiden, nor any drugs to
equip Disease with the vigour of that young man. Do not
riches bring us solicitude instead of rest, envy instead of affection, and danger instead of safety? Can they prolong their own
possession, or lengthen his days who enjoys them? So far otherwise, that the sloth, the luxury, the care which attend them,
shorten the lives of millions, and bring them with pain and
misery to an untimely grave. Where, then, is their value if they
can neither embellish or strengthen our forms, sweeten or
prolong our lives? Again — Can they adorn the mind more
than the body? Do they not rather swell the heart with vanity,
puff up the cheeks with pride, shut our ears to every call of
virtue, and our bowels to every motive of compassion?" "Give
me your hand, brother," said Adams, in a rapture; "for I suppose
you are a clergyman." "No, truly," answered the other (indeed,
he was a priest of the Church of Rome; but those who understand
our laws will not wonder he was not over-ready to own it).
"Whatever you are," cries Adams, "you have spoken my sentiments: I believe I have preached every syllable of your speech
twenty times over: for it hath always appeared to me easier for
a cable-rope (which by the way is the true rendering of that
word we have translated "camel") to go through the eye of a
needle than for a rich man to get into the kingdom of heaven."
"That, sir," said the other, "will be easily granted you by divines,
and is deplorably true; but as the prospect of our good at a distance doth not so forcibly affect us, it might be of some service to
mankind to be made thoroughly sensible — which I think they
might be with very little serious attention — that even the blessings of this world are not to be purchased with riches: a
doctrine, in my opinion, not only metaphysically, but, if I may
so say, mathematically demonstrable; and which I have been
always so perfectly convinced of that I have a contempt for
nothing so much as for gold." Adams now began a long discourse; but as most which he said occurs among many authors
who have treated this subject, I shall omit inserting it. During
its continuance Joseph and Fanny retired to rest, and the host
likewise left the room. When the English parson had concluded,
the Romish resumed the discourse, which he continued with

great bitterness and invective; and at last ended by desiring Adams to lend him eighteen-pence to pay his reckoning; promising, if he never paid him, he might be assured of his prayers. The good man answered that eighteen-pence would be too little to carry him any very long journey; that he had half a guinea in his pocket, which he would divide with him. He then fell to searching his pockets, but could find no money: for indeed the company with whom he dined had passed one jest upon him which we did not then enumerate, and had picked his pocket of all that treasure which he had so ostentatiously produced.

"Bless me!" cried Adams, "I have certainly lost it; I can never have spent it. Sir, as I am a Christian, I had a whole half-guinea in my pocket this morning, and have not now a single halfpenny of it left. Sure the devil must have taken it from me." "Sir," answered the priest, smiling, "you need make no excuses; if you are not willing to lend me the money, I am contented." "Sir," cries Adams, "if I had the greatest sum in the world — ay, if I had ten pounds about me — I would bestow it all to rescue any Christian from distress. I am more vexed at my loss on your account than my own. Was ever anything so unlucky? Because I have no money in my pocket, I shall be suspected to be no Christian." "I am more unlucky," quoth the other, "if you are as generous as you say: for really a crown would have made me happy, and conveyed me in plenty to the place I am going, which is not above twenty miles off, and where I can arrive by to-morrow night. I assure you I am not accustomed to travel pennyless. I am but just arrived in England; and we were forced by a storm in our passage to throw all we had overboard. I don't suspect but this fellow will take my word for the trifle I owe him; but I hate to appear so mean as to confess myself without a shilling to such people: for these, and indeed too many others, know little difference in their estimation between a beggar and a thief." However, he thought he should deal better with the host that evening than the next morning: he therefore resolved to set out immediately, notwithstanding the darkness; and accordingly, as soon as the host returned, he communicated to him the situation of his affairs; upon which the host, scratching his head, answered, "Why, I do not know, master; if it be so, and you have no money, I must trust, I think, though I had rather always have ready money if I could; but, marry, you look like so honest a gentleman that I don't fear your paying me if it was twenty times as much." The priest made no reply, but, taking leave of him and Adams as fast as he could, not without confusion, and perhaps with some distrust of Adams's sincerity, departed.

He was no sooner gone than the host fell a-shaking his head, and declared, if he had suspected the fellow had no money, he would not have drawn him a single drop of drink; saying, he despaired of ever seeing his face again, for that he looked like a confounded rogue. "Rabbit the fellow," cries he, "I thought, by his talking so much about riches, that he had a hundred pounds at least in his pocket." Adams chid him for his suspicions, which he said were not becoming a Christian; and then, without reflecting on his loss, or considering how he himself should depart in the morning, he retired to a very homely bed, as his companions had before; however, health and fatigue gave them a sweeter repose than is often in the power of velvet and down to bestow.

CHAPTER IX.

Containing as surprising and bloody adventures as can be found in this, or perhaps any other authentic history.

IT was almost morning when Joseph Andrews, whose eyes the thoughts of his dear Fanny had opened, as he lay fondly meditating on that lovely creature, heard a violent knocking at the door over which he lay. He presently jumped out of bed, and, opening the window, was asked if there were no travellers in the house; and presently, by another voice, if two men and a young woman had not taken up their lodgings there that night. Though he knew not the voices, he began to entertain a suspicion of the truth — for indeed he had received some information from one of the servants of the squire's house of his design — and answered in the negative. One of the servants, who knew the host well, called out to him by his name just as he had opened another window, and asked him the same question; to which he answered in the affirmative. "O ho!" said another, "have we found you?" and ordered the host to come down and open his door. Fanny, who was as wakeful as Joseph, no sooner heard all this than she leaped from her bed, and, hastily putting on her gown and petticoats, ran as fast as possible to Joseph's room, who then was almost drest; he immediately let her in, and, embracing her with the most passionate tenderness, bid her fear nothing: for he would die in her defence. "Is that a reason why I should not fear," says she, "when I should lose what is dearer to me than the whole world?" Joseph then, kissing her hand, said he could almost thank the occasion which had extorted from her a tenderness she would never indulge him with before. He then ran and waked his bedfellow Adams, who was yet fast asleep, notwithstanding many calls from Joseph; but was no sooner made sensible of their danger than he leaped from his bed, without considering the presence of Fanny, who hastily turned her face from him, and enjoyed a double benefit from the dark, which, as it would have prevented any offence to an innocence less pure, or a modesty less delicate, so it concealed even those blushes which were raised in her.

Adams had soon put on all his clothes but his breeches, which in the hurry he forgot; however, they were pretty well supplied by the length of his other garments; and now, the house-door being opened, the captain, the poet, the player, and three servants came in. The captain told the host that two fellows, who were in his house, had run away with a young woman, and desired to know in which room she lay. The host, who presently believed the story, directed them, and instantly the captain and poet, jostling one another, ran up. The poet, who was the nimblest, entering the chamber first, searched the bed, and every other part, but to no purpose; the bird was flown, as the impatient reader, who might otherwise have been in pain for her, was before advertised. They then inquired where the men lay, and were approaching the chamber, when Joseph roared out, in a loud voice, that he would shoot the first man who offered to attack the door. The captain inquired what fire-arms they had; to which the host answered, he believed they had none; nay, he was almost convinced of it: for he had heard one ask the other in the evening what they should have done if they had been overtaken, when they had no arms; to which the other answered, they would have defended themselves with their sticks as long as they were able, and God would assist a just cause. This satisfied the captain, but not the poet, who prudently retreated downstairs, saying, it was his business to record great actions, and not to do them. The captain was no sooner well satisfied that there were no fire-arms than, bidding defiance to gunpowder, and swearing he loved the smell of it, he ordered the servants to follow him, and, marching boldly up, immediately attempted to force the door, which the servants soon helped him to accomplish. When it was opened, they discovered the enemy drawn up three deep; Adams in the front, and Fanny in the rear. The captain told Adams, that if they would go all back to the house again, they should be civilly treated; but unless they consented, he had orders to carry the young lady with him, whom there was great reason to believe they had stolen from her parents; for, notwithstanding her disguise, her air, which she could not conceal, sufficiently discovered her birth to be infinitely superior to theirs. Fanny, bursting into tears, solemnly assured him he was mistaken; that she was a poor helpless foundling, and had no relation in the world which she knew of; and, throwing herself on her knees, begged that he would not attempt to take her from her friends, who, she was convinced, would die before they would lose her; which Adams confirmed with words not far from amounting to an oath. The captain swore he had no leisure to talk, and, bidding them thank themselves for what happened, he ordered the servants to fall on, at the same time endeavouring to pass by Adams, in order to lay hold on Fanny; but the parson, interrupting him, received a blow from one of them, which, without considering whence it came, he returned to the captain, and gave him so dexterous a knock in that part of the stomach which is vulgarly called the pit, that he staggered some paces backwards. The captain, who was not accustomed to this kind of play, and who wisely apprehended the consequence of such another blow, two of them seeming to him equal to a thrust through the body, drew forth his hanger, as Adams approached him, and was levelling a blow at his head, which would probably have silenced the preacher for ever, had not Joseph in that instant lifted up a certain huge stone pot of the chamber with one hand, which six beaus could not have lifted with both, and discharged it, together with the contents, full in the captain's face. The uplifted hanger dropped from his hand, and he fell prostrate on the floor *with a lumpish noise, and his halfpence rattled in his pocket*; the red liquor which his veins contained, and the white liquor which the pot contained, ran in one stream down his face and his clothes. Nor had Adams quite escaped, some of the water having in its passage shed its honours on his head, and began to trickle down the wrinkles or rather furrows of his cheeks, when one of the servants, snatching a mop out of a pail of water which had already done its duty in washing the house, pushed it in the parson's face; yet could not he bear him down; for the parson, wresting the mop from the fellow with one hand, with the other brought his enemy as low as the earth, having given him a stroke over that part of the face where, in some men of pleasure, the natural and artificial noses are conjoined.

Hitherto, Fortune seemed to incline the victory on the travellers' side, when, according to her custom, she began to show the fickleness of her disposition: for now the host entering the field, or rather chamber, of battle, flew directly at Joseph, and, darting his head into his stomach (for he was a stout fellow, and an expert boxer), almost staggered him, but Joseph, stepping one leg back, did with his left hand so chuck him under the chin that he reeled. The youth was pursuing his blow with his right hand when he received from one of the servants such a stroke with a cudgel on his temples, that it instantly deprived him of sense, and he measured his length on the ground.

Fanny rent the air with her cries, and Adams was coming to the assistance of Joseph; but the two serving-men and the host now fell on him, and soon subdued him, though he fought like a madman, and looked so black with the impressions he had received from the mop, that Don Quixote would certainly have taken him for an enchanted Moor. But now follows the most tragical part; for the captain was risen again, and, seeing Joseph on the floor. and Adams secured, he instantly laid hold on Fanny, and, with the assistance of the poet and player, who, hearing the battle was over, were now come up, dragged her, crying and tearing her hair, from the sight of her Joseph, and, with a perfect deafness to all her entreaties, carried her downstairs by violence, and fastened her on the player's horse; and the captain, mounting his own, and leading that on which this poor miserable wretch was, departed without any more consideration of her cries than a butcher hath of those of a lamb; for indeed his thoughts were entertained only with the degree of favour which he promised himself from the squire on the success of this adventure.

The servants, who were ordered to secure Adams and Joseph as safe as possible, that the squire might receive no interruption to his design on poor Fanny, immediately, by the poet's advice, tied Adams to one of the bed-posts, as they did Joseph on the other side, as soon as they could bring him to himself; and then, leaving them together, back to back, and desiring the host not to set them at liberty, nor to go near them till he had farther orders, they departed towards their master; but happened to take a different road from that which the captain had fallen into.

CHAPTER X.

A discourse between the poet and player; of no other use in this history, but to divert the reader.

BEFORE we proceed any farther in this tragedy, we shall leave Mr. Joseph and Mr. Adams to themselves, and imitate the wise conductors of the stage, who in the midst of a grave action entertain you with some excellent piece of satire or humour called a dance. Which piece, indeed, is therefore danced, and not spoke, as it is delivered to the audience by persons whose thinking faculty is by most people held to lie in their heels; and to whom, as well as heroes, who think with their hands, Nature hath only given heads for the sake of conformity, and as they are of use in dancing, to hang their hats on.

The poet, addressing the player, proceeded thus: "As I was saying" (for they had been at this discourse all the time of the engagement above-stairs), "the reason you have no good new plays is evident; it is from your discouragement of authors. Gentlemen will not write, sir, they will not write without the expectation of fame or profit, or perhaps both. Plays are like trees, which will not grow without nourishment; but, like mushrooms, they shoot up spontaneously, as it were, in a rich soil. The muses, like vines, may be pruned, but not with a hatchet. The town, like a peevish child, knows not what it desires, and is always best pleased with a rattle. A farce-writer hath indeed some chance for success; but they have lost all taste for the sublime. Though I believe one reason of their depravity is the badness of the actors. If a man writes like an angel, sir, those fellows know not how to give a sentiment utterance." "Not so fast," says the player: "the modern actors are as good at least as their authors, nay, they come nearer their illustrious predecessors; and I expect a Booth on the stage again, sooner than a Shakespear or an Otway; and indeed I may turn your observation against you, and with truth say, that the reason no authors are encouraged is because we have no good new plays." "I have not affirmed the contrary," said the poet; "but I am surprised you grow so warm; you cannot imagine yourself interested in this dispute; I hope you have a better opinion of my taste than to apprehend I squinted at yourself. No, sir, if we had six such actors as you, we should soon rival the Bettertons and Sandfords of former times; for, without a compliment to you, I think it impossible for anyone to have excelled you in most of your parts. Nay, it is solemn truth, and I have heard many, and all great judges, express as much; and you will pardon me if I tell you, I think every time I have seen you lately, you have constantly acquired some new excellence, like a snowball. You have deceived me in my estimation of perfection, and have outdone what I thought inimitable." "You are as little interested," answered the player, "in what I have said of other poets; for d—n me if there are not manly strokes, ay, whole scenes, in your last tragedy, which at least equal Shakespear. There is a delicacy of sentiment, a dignity of expression in it, which I will own many of our gentlemen did not do adequate justice to. To confess the truth, they are bad enough, and I pity an author who is present at the murder of his works." — "Nay, it is but seldom that it can happen," returned the poet: "the works of most modern authors, like dead-born children, cannot be murdered. It is such wretched, half-begotten, half-writ, lifeless, spiritless, low, groveling stuff, that I almost pity the actor who is obliged to get it by heart, which must be almost as difficult to remember as words in a language you don't understand." "I am sure," said the player, "if the sentences have little meaning when they are writ, when they are spoken they have less. I know scarce one who ever lays an emphasis right, and much less adapts his action to his character. I have seen a tender lover in an attitude of fighting with his mistress, and a brave hero suing to his enemy with his sword in his hand. — I don't care to abuse my profession, but rot me if in my heart I am not inclined to the poet's side." "It is rather generous in you than just," said the poet; "and, though I hate to speak ill of any person's production — nay, I never do it, nor will — but yet, to do justice to the actors, what could Booth or Betterton have made of such horrible stuff as Fenton's *Mariamne*,

Frowd's *Philotas,* or Mallet's *Eurydice;* or those low, dirty,
last-dying-speeches, which a fellow in the City or Wapping,
your Dillo or Lillo, what was his name, called tragedies?" —
"Very well," says the player; "and pray what do you think
of such fellows as Quin and Delane, or that face-making puppy
young Cibber, that ill-looked dog Macklin, or that saucy slut
Mrs. Clive? What work would they make with your Shake-
spears, Otways, and Lees? How would those harmonious lines
of the last come from their tongues?

> —— No more; for I disdain
> All pomp when thou art by — far be the noise
> Of kings and crowns from us, whose gentle souls
> Our kinder fates have steer'd another way.
> Free as the forest birds we'll pair together,
> Without rememb'ring who our fathers were:
> Fly to the arbors, grots, and flow'ry meads,
> There in soft murmurs interchange our souls,
> Together drink the crystal of the stream,
> Or taste the yellow fruit which autumn yields.
> And when the golden evening calls us home,
> Wing to our downy nests, and sleep till morn.

Or how would this disdain of Otway,

> Who'd be that foolish, sordid thing, call'd man?"

"Hold! hold! hold!" said the poet: "Do repeat that tender
speech in the third act of my play which you made such a
figure in." — "I would willingly," said the player, "but I have
forgot it." — "Ay, you was not quite perfect enough in it when
you played it," cries the poet, "or you would have had such an
applause as was never given on the stage; an applause I was
extremely concerned for your losing." — "Sure," says the player,
"if I remember, that was hissed more than any passage in the
whole play." — "Ay, your speaking it was hissed," said the
poet. "My speaking it!" said the player. — "I mean your not
speaking it," said the poet. "You was out, and then they
hissed." — "They hissed, and then I was out, if I remember,"
answered the player; "and I must say this for myself, that
the whole audience allowed I did your part justice: so don't
lay the damnation of your play to my account." "I don't
know what you mean by damnation," replied the poet. "Why,
you know it was acted but one night," cried the player. "No,"
said the poet, "you and the whole town were my enemies;

the pit were all my enemies, fellows that would cut my throat, if the fear of hanging did not restrain them. All tailors, sir, all tailors." — "Why should the tailors be so angry with you?" cries the player. "I suppose you don't employ so many in making your clothes." "I admit your jest," answered the poet; "but you remember the affair as well as myself; you know there was a party in the pit and upper gallery that would not suffer it to be given out again; though much, ay infinitely, the majority, all the boxes in particular, were desirous of it; nay, most of the ladies swore they never would come to the house till it was acted again. — Indeed, I must own their policy was good in not letting it be given out a second time; for the rascals knew if it had gone a second night, it would have run fifty: for if ever there was distress in a tragedy — I am not fond of my own performance; but if I should tell you what the best judges said of it — Nor was it entirely owing to my enemies neither that it did not succeed on the stage as well as it hath since among the polite readers; for you can't say it had justice done it by the performers." — "I think," answered the player, "the performers did the distress of it justice: for I am sure we were in distress enough, who were pelted with oranges all the last act; we all imagined it would have been the last act of our lives."

The poet, whose fury was now raised, had just attempted to answer when they were interrupted, and an end put to their discourse, by an accident, which, if the reader is impatient to know, he must skip over the next chapter, which is a sort of counterpart to this, and contains some of the best and gravest matters in the whole book, being a discourse between Parson Abraham Adams and Mr. Joseph Andrews.

CHAPTER XI.

Containing the exhortations of Parson Adams to his friend in affliction; calculated for the instruction and improvement of the reader.

JOSEPH no sooner came perfectly to himself than, perceiving his mistress gone, he bewailed her loss with groans which would have pierced any heart but those which are possessed by some people, and are made of a certain composition not unlike flint in its hardness and other properties; for you may strike fire from them, which will dart through the eyes, but they can never distil one drop of water the same way. His own, poor youth, was of a softer composition; and at those words, "O my dear Fanny! O my love! shall I never, never see thee more?" his eyes overflowed with tears, which would have become any but a hero. In a word, his despair was more easy to be conceived than related. —

Mr. Adams, after many groans, sitting with his back to Joseph, began thus in a sorrowful tone: "You cannot imagine, my good child, that I entirely blame these first agonies of your grief; for, when misfortunes attack us by surprise, it must require infinitely more learning than you are master of to resist them; but it is the business of a man and a Christian to summon Reason as quickly as he can to his aid; and she will presently teach him patience and submission. Be comforted, therefore, child; I say be comforted. It is true, you have lost the prettiest, kindest, loveliest, sweetest young woman: one with whom you might have expected to have lived in happiness, virtue, and innocence. By whom you might have promised yourself many little darlings, who would have been the delight of your youth, and the comfort of your age. You have not only lost her, but have reason to fear the utmost violence which lust and power can inflict upon her. Now, indeed, you may easily raise ideas of horror, which might drive you to despair." — "O I shall run mad!" cries Joseph. "O that I could but command my hands to tear my eyes out and my flesh off!" — "If you would use them to such purposes, I am glad you can't," answered Adams. "I have stated your misfortune as strong as I possibly can; but, on the other side, you are to consider you are a Christian; that no accident happens to us without the Divine permission, and that it is the duty of a man, much more of a Christian, to submit. We did not make ourselves; but the same Power which made us rules over us, and we are absolutely at his disposal; he may do with us what he pleases, nor have we any right to complain. A second reason against our complaint is our ignorance; for, as we know not future events, so neither can we tell to what purpose any accident tends; and that which at first threatens us with evil may in the end produce our good. I should indeed have said our ignorance is twofold (but I have not at present time to divide properly), for, as we know not to what purpose any event is ultimately directed, so neither can we affirm from what cause it originally sprung. You are a man, and consequently a sinner; and this may be a punishment to you for your sins: indeed in this sense it may be esteemed as a good, yea, as the greatest good, which satisfies the anger of Heaven, and averts that wrath which cannot continue without our destruction. Thirdly, our impotency of relieving ourselves demonstrates the folly and absurdity of our complaints: for whom do we resist, or against whom do we complain, but a Power from whose shafts no armour can guard us, no speed can fly? A Power which leaves us no hope but in submission." — "O sir!" cried Joseph, "all this is very true, and very fine, and I could hear you all day, if I was not so grieved at heart as now I am." "Would you take physic," says Adams, "when you are well, and refuse it when you are sick? Is not comfort to be administered to the afflicted, and not to those who rejoice, or those who are at ease?" — "O! you have not spoken one word of comfort to me yet!" returned Joseph. "No!" cries Adams; "what am I then doing? what can I say to comfort you?" — "O tell me," cries Joseph, "that Fanny will escape back to my arms, that they shall again inclose that lovely creature, with all her sweetness, all her untainted innocence about her!" — "Why, perhaps you may," cries Adams; "but I can't promise you what's to come. You must, with perfect resignation, wait the event: if she be restored to you again, it is your duty to be thankful, and so it is if she be not: Joseph, if you are wise, and truly know your own interest, you will peaceably and quietly submit to all the dispensations of Providence, being thoroughly assured that all the misfortunes, how great soever, which happen to the righteous, happen to them for their own good. — Nay, it is not your interest only, but your duty, to abstain from immoderate grief; which if you indulge, you are not worthy the name of a Christian." — He spoke these last words with an accent a little severer than usual; upon which Joseph begged him not to be angry, saying, he mistook him if he thought he denied it was his duty; for he had known that long ago. "What signifies knowing your duty, if you do not perform it?" answered Adams. "Your knowledge increases your guilt. — O Joseph! I never thought you had this stubbornness in your mind." Joseph replied, "He fancied he misunderstood him; which I assure you," says he, "you do, if you imagine I endeavour to grieve; upon my soul I don't." Adams rebuked him for swearing, and then proceeded to enlarge on the folly of grief, telling him, all the wise men and philosophers, even among the heathens, had written against it, quoting several passages from Seneca, and the *Consolation*, which, though it was not Cicero's, was, he said, as good almost as any of his works; and concluded all by hinting that immoderate grief in this case might incense that Power which alone could restore him his Fanny. This reason, or indeed rather the idea which it raised of the restoration of his mistress, had more effect than all which the parson had said before, and for a moment abated his agonies; but, when his fears sufficiently set before his eyes the danger that poor creature was in, his grief returned again with repeated violence, nor could Adams in the least assuage it; though it may be doubted in his behalf whether Socrates himself could have prevailed any better.

They remained some time in silence; and groans and sighs issued from them both; at length Joseph burst out into the following soliloquy:

> Yes, I will bear my sorrows like a man,
> But I must also feel them as a man.
> I cannot but remember such things were,
> And were most dear to me. —

Adams asked him what stuff that was he repeated? — To which he answered, they were some lines he had gotten by heart out of a play. — "Ay, there is nothing but heathenism to be learned from plays," replied he. — "I never heard of any plays fit for a Christian to read, but *Cato* and the *Conscious Lovers;* and, I must own, in the latter there are some things almost solemn enough for a sermon." But we shall now leave them a little, and inquire after the subject of their conversation.

CHAPTER XII.

More adventures, which we hope will as much please as surprise the reader.

NEITHER the facetious dialogue which passed between the poet and the player, nor the grave and truly solemn discourse of Mr. Adams, will, we conceive, make the reader sufficient amends

for the anxiety which he must have felt on the account of poor
Fanny, whom we left in so deplorable a condition. We shall
therefore now proceed to the relation of what happened to that
beautiful and innocent virgin, after she fell into the wicked
hands of the captain.

The man of war, having conveyed his charming prize out of
the inn a little before day, made the utmost expedition in his
power towards the squire's house, where this delicate creature
was to be offered up a sacrifice to the lust of a ravisher. He
was not only deaf to all her bewailings and entreaties on the
road, but accosted her ears with impurities which, having been
never before accustomed to them, she happily for herself very
little understood. At last he changed his note, and attempted
to soothe and mollify her, by setting forth the splendour and
luxury which would be her fortune with a man who would
have the inclination, and power too, to give her whatever
her utmost wishes could desire; and told her he doubted not but
she would soon look kinder on him, as the instrument of her
happiness, and despise that pitiful fellow whom her ignorance
only could make her fond of. She answered, she knew not
whom he meant; she never was fond of any pitiful fellow.
"Are you affronted, madam," says he, "at my calling him so?
But what better can be said of one in a livery, notwithstanding
your fondness for him?" She returned, that she did not understand him, that the man had been her fellow-servant, and she
believed was as honest a creature as any alive; but as for
fondness for men — "I warrant ye," cries the captain, "we
shall find means to persuade you to be fond; and I advise you
to yield to gentle ones; for you may be assured that it is not
in your power, by any struggles whatever, to preserve your
virginity two hours longer. It will be your interest to consent:
for the squire will be much kinder to you if he enjoys you
willingly than by force." — At which words she began to call
aloud for assistance (for it was now open day), but, finding
none, she lifted her eyes to heaven, and supplicated the Divine
assistance to preserve her innocence. The captain told her, if
she persisted in her vociferation, he would find a means of
stopping her mouth. And now the poor wretch, perceiving no
hope of succour, abandoned herself to despair, and, sighing
out the name of Joseph! Joseph! a river of tears ran down her
lovely cheeks, and wet the handkerchief which covered her
bosom. A horseman now appeared in the road, upon which

the captain threatened her violently if she complained; however, the moment they approached each other, she begged him with the utmost earnestness to relieve a distressed creature who was in the hands of a ravisher. The fellow stopt at those words; but the captain assured him it was his wife, and that he was carrying her home from her adulterer: which so satisfied the fellow, who was an old one (and perhaps a married one too), that he wished him a good journey, and rode on. He was no sooner passed than the captain abused her violently for breaking his commands, and threatened to gag her, when two more horsemen, armed with pistols, came into the road just before them. She again solicited their assistance, and the captain told the same story as before. Upon which one said to the other — "That's a charming wench, Jack! I wish I had been in the fellow's place, whoever he is." But the other, instead of answering him, cried out eagerly, "Zounds, I know her!" and then, turning to her, said, "Sure, you are not Fanny Goodwill?" — "Indeed, indeed, I am," she cried — "O John, I know you now — Heaven hath sent you to my assistance, to deliver me from this wicked man, who is carrying me away for his vile purposes — O for God's sake rescue me from him!" A fierce dialogue immediately ensued between the captain and these two men, who, being both armed with pistols, and the chariot which they attended being now arrived, the captain saw both force and stratagem were vain, and endeavoured to make his escape; in which, however, he could not succeed. The gentleman who rode in the chariot ordered it to stop, and with an air of authority examined into the merits of the cause; of which being advertised by Fanny, whose credit was confirmed by the fellow who knew her, he ordered the captain, who was all bloody from his encounter at the inn, to be conveyed as a prisoner behind the chariot, and very gallantly took Fanny into it; for to say the truth, this gentleman (who was no other than the celebrated Mr. Peter Pounce, and who preceded the Lady Booby only a few miles, by setting out earlier in the morning) was a very gallant person, and loved a pretty girl better than anything, besides his own money, or the money of other people.

The chariot now proceeded towards the inn, which, as Fanny was informed, lay in their way, and where it arrived at that very time while the poet and player were disputing below-stairs, and Adams and Joseph were discoursing back to back above: just at that period to which we brought them both in the two preceding chapters, the chariot stopt at the door, and in an instant Fanny, leaping from it, ran up to her Joseph. — O reader! conceive, if thou canst, the joy which fired the breasts of these lovers on this meeting; and if thy own heart doth not sympathetically assist thee in this conception, I pity thee sincerely from my own; for let the hard-hearted villain know this, that there is a pleasure in a tender sensation beyond any which he is capable of tasting.

Peter, being informed by Fanny of the presence of Adams, stopt to see him, and receive his homage; for, as Peter was an hypocrite, a sort of people whom Mr. Adams never saw through, the one paid that respect to his seeming goodness which the other believed to be paid to his riches; hence Mr. Adams was so much his favourite, that he once lent him four pounds thirteen shillings and sixpence to prevent his going to gaol, on no greater security than a bond and judgment, which probably he would have made no use of, though the money had not been (as it was) paid exactly at the time.

It is not perhaps easy to describe the figure of Adams; he had risen in such a violent hurry, that he had on neither breeches nor stockings; nor had he taken from his head a red spotted handkerchief, which by night bound his wig, that was turned inside out, around his head. He had on his torn cassock and his greatcoat; but, as the remainder of his cassock hung down below his greatcoat, so did a small stripe of white, or rather whitish, linen appear below that; to which we may add the several colours which appeared on his face, where a long piss-burnt beard served to retain the liquor of the stone-pot, and that of a blacker hue which distilled from the mop. — This figure, which Fanny had delivered from his captivity, was no sooner spied by Peter than it disordered the composed gravity of his muscles; however, he advised him immediately to make himself clean, nor would accept his homage in that pickle.

The poet and player no sooner saw the captain in captivity than they began to consider of their own safety, of which flight presented itself as the only means; they therefore both of them mounted the poet's horse, and made the most expeditious retreat in their power.

The host, who well knew Mr. Pounce and the Lady Booby's livery, was not a little surprised at this change of the scene: nor was his confusion much helped by his wife, who was now just risen, and, having heard from him the account of what had passed, comforted him with a decent number of fools and blockheads; asked him why he did not consult her, and told him he would never leave following the nonsensical dictates of his own numskull till she and her family were ruined.

Joseph, being informed of the captain's arrival, and seeing his Fanny now in safety, quitted her a moment, and, running downstairs, went directly to him, and stripping off his coat, challenged him to fight; but the captain refused, saying he did not understand boxing. He then grasped a cudgel in one hand, and, catching the captain by the collar with the other, gave him a most severe drubbing, and ended with telling him he had now had some revenge for what his dear Fanny had suffered.

When Mr. Pounce had a little regaled himself with some provision which he had in his chariot, and Mr. Adams had put on the best appearance his clothes would allow him, Pounce ordered the captain into his presence; for he said he was guilty of felony, and the next justice of peace should commit him; but the servants (whose appetite for revenge is soon satisfied), being sufficiently contented with the drubbing which Joseph had inflicted on him, and which was indeed of no very moderate kind, had suffered him to go off, which he did, threatening a severe revenge against Joseph, which I have never heard he thought proper to take.

The mistress of the house made her voluntary appearance before Mr. Pounce, and with a thousand curtsies told him, "She hoped his honour would pardon her husband, who was a very *nonsense* man, for the sake of his poor family; that indeed if he could be ruined alone, she would be very willing of it; *for because as why,* his worship very well knew he deserved it; but she had three poor small children, who were not capable to get their own living; and if her husband was sent to gaol, they must all come to the parish; for she was a poor weak woman, continually a-breeding, and had no time to work for them. She therefore hoped his honour would take it into his worship's consideration, and forgive her husband this time; for she was sure he never intended any harm to man, woman, or child; and if it was not for that block-head of his own, the man in some things was well enough; for she had had three children by him in less than three years, and was almost ready to cry out the fourth time." She would have proceeded in this manner much longer, had not Peter stopt her tongue, by telling her he had nothing to say to her husband, nor her neither. So, as Adams and the rest had assured her of forgiveness, she cried and curtsied out of the room.

Mr. Pounce was desirous that Fanny should continue her journey with him in the chariot; but she absolutely refused, saying she would ride behind Joseph on a horse which one of Lady Booby's servants had equipped him with. But, alas! when the horse appeared, it was found to be no other than that identical beast which Mr. Adams had left behind him at the inn, and which these honest fellows, who knew him, had redeemed. Indeed, whatever horse they had provided for Joseph, they would have prevailed with him to mount none, no, not even to ride before his beloved Fanny, till the parson was supplied; much less would he deprive his friend of the beast which belonged to him, and which he knew the moment he saw, though Adams did not; however, when he was reminded of the affair, and told that they had brought the horse with them which he had left behind, he answered — "Bless me! and so I did."

Adams was very desirous that Joseph and Fanny should mount this horse, and declared he could very easily walk home. "If I walked alone," says he, "I would wage a shilling that the *pedestrian* outstripped the *equestrian* travellers; but, as I intend to take the company of a pipe, peradventure I may be an hour later." One of the servants whispered Joseph to take him at his word, and suffer the old put to walk if he would: this proposal was answered with an angry look, and a peremptory refusal by Joseph, who, catching Fanny up in his arms, averred he would rather carry her home in that manner, than take away Mr. Adams's horse and permit him to walk on foot.

Perhaps, reader, thou hast seen a contest between two gentlemen, or two ladies, quickly decided, though they have both asserted they would not eat such a nice morsel, and each insisted on the other's accepting it; but in reality both were very desirous to swallow it themselves. Do not therefore conclude hence that this dispute would have come to a speedy decision: for here both parties were heartily in earnest, and it is very probable they would have remained in the inn-yard to this day, had not the good Peter Pounce put a stop to it; for, finding he had no longer hopes of satisfying his old appetite with Fanny, and being desirous of having some one to whom he might communicate his grandeur, he told the parson he would convey him home in his chariot. This favour was by Adams, with many bows and acknowledgments, accepted, though he afterwards said, "he ascended the chariot rather that he might not offend than from any desire of riding in it, for that in his heart he preferred the *pedestrian* even to the *vehicular* expedition." All matters being now settled, the chariot, in which rode Adams and Pounce, moved forwards; and Joseph having borrowed a pillion from the host, Fanny had just seated herself thereon, and had laid hold of the girdle which her lover wore for that purpose, when the wise beast, who concluded that one at a time was sufficient, that two to one were odds, &c., discovered much uneasiness at his double load, and began to consider his hinder as his fore legs, moving the direct contrary way to that which is called forwards. Nor could Joseph, with all his horsemanship, persuade him to advance; but, without having any regard to the lovely part of the lovely girl which was on his back, he used such agitations, that, had not one of the men come immediately to her assistance, she had, in plain English, tumbled backwards on the ground. This inconvenience was presently remedied by an exchange of horses; and then Fanny being again placed on her pillion, on a better-natured and somewhat a better-fed beast, the parson's horse, finding he had no longer odds to contend with, agreed to march; and the whole procession set forwards for Booby-Hall, where they arrived in a few hours without anything remarkable happening on the road, unless it was a curious dialogue between the parson and the steward: which, to use the language of a late Apologist, a pattern to all biographers, "waits for the reader in the next chapter."

CHAPTER XIII.

A curious dialogue which passed between Mr. Abraham Adams and Mr. Peter Pounce, better worth reading than all the works of Colley Cibber and many others.

THE chariot had not proceeded far before Mr. Adams observed it was a very fine day. "Ay, and a very fine country too," answered Pounce. "I should think so more," returned Adams, "if I had not lately travelled over the Downs, which I take to exceed this and all other prospects in the universe." "A fig for prospects!" answered Pounce; "one acre here is worth ten there; and, for my own part, I have no delight in the prospect of any land but my own." "Sir," said Adams, "you can indulge yourself with many fine prospects of that kind." "I thank God I have a little," replied the other, "with which I am content, and envy no man: I have a little, Mr. Adams, with which I do as much good as I can." Adams answered, that riches without charity were nothing worth; for that they were a blessing only to him who made them a blessing to others. "You and I," said Peter, "have different notions of charity. I own, as it is generally used, I do not like the word, nor do I think it becomes one of us gentlemen; it is a mean parson-like quality; though I would not infer many parsons have it neither." "Sir," said Adams, "my definition of charity is, a generous disposition to relieve the distressed." "There is something in that definition," answered Peter, "which I like well enough; it is, as you say, a disposition — and does not so much consist in the act as in the disposition to do it; but, alas, Mr. Adams, who are meant by the distressed? Believe me, the distresses of mankind are mostly imaginary, and it would be rather folly than goodness to relieve them." "Sure, sir," replied Adams, "hunger and thirst, cold and nakedness, and other distresses which attend the poor, can never be said to be imaginary evils." "How can any man complain of hunger," said Peter, "in a country where such excellent salads are to be gathered in almost every field? Or of thirst, where every river and stream produce such delicious potations? And as for cold and nakedness, they are evils introduced by luxury and custom. A man naturally wants clothes no more than a horse or any other animal; and there are whole nations who go without them; but these are things perhaps which you, who do not know the world ——" "You will pardon me, sir," returned Adams; "I have read of the Gymnosophists." "A plague of your Jehosaphats!" cried Peter; "the greatest fault in our constitution is the provision made for the poor, except that perhaps made for some others. Sir, I have not an estate which doth not contribute almost as much again to the poor as to the land-tax; and I do assure you I expect to come myself to the parish in the end." To which Adams giving a dissenting smile, Peter thus proceeded: "I fancy, Mr. Adams, you are one of those who imagine I am a lump of money; for there are many who, I fancy, believe that not only my pockets, but my whole clothes, are lined with bank-bills; but I assure you, you are all mistaken: I am not the man the world esteems me. If I can hold my head above water, it *is* all I can. I have injured myself by purchasing. I have been too liberal of my money. Indeed, I fear my heir will find my affairs in a worse condition than they are reputed to be. Ah! he will have reason to wish I had loved money more, and land less. Pray, my good neighbour, where should I have that quantity of riches the world is so liberal to bestow on me? Where could I possibly, without I had stole it, acquire such a treasure?" "Why, truly," says Adams, "I have been always of your opinion; I have wondered as well as yourself with what confidence they could report such things of you, which have to me appeared as mere impossibilities; for you know, sir, and I have often heard you say it, that your wealth is of your own acquisition; and can it be credible that in your short time you should have amassed such a heap of treasure as these people will have you worth? Indeed, had you inherited an estate like Sir Thomas Booby, which had descended in your family for many generations, they might have had a colour for their assertations." "Why, what do they say I am worth?" cries Peter, with a malicious sneer. "Sir," answered Adams, "I have heard some aver you are not worth less than twenty thousand pounds." At which Peter frowned. "Nay, sir," said Adams, "you ask me only the opinion of others; for my own part, I have always denied it, nor did I ever believe you could possibly be worth half that sum." "However, Mr. Adams," said he, squeezing him by the hand, "I would not sell them all I am worth for double that sum; and as to what you believe, or they believe, I care not a fig, no not a fart. I am not poor because you think me so, nor because you attempt to undervalue me in the country. I know the envy of mankind very well; but I thank Heaven I am above them. It is true, my wealth is of my own acquisition. I have not an estate like Sir Thomas Booby, that has descended in my family through many generations; but I know heirs of such estates who are forced to travel about the country like some people in torn cassocks, and might be glad to accept of a pitiful curacy for what I know. Yes, sir, as shabby fellows as yourself, whom no man of my figure, without that vice of good-nature about him, would suffer to ride in a chariot with him." "Sir," said Adams, "I value not your chariot of a rush; and if I had known you had intended to affront me, I would have walked to the world's end on foot ere I would have accepted a place in it. However, sir, I will soon rid you of that inconvenience"; and, so saying, he opened the chariot door, without calling to the coachman, and leapt out into the highway, forgetting to take his hat along with him; which, however, Mr. Pounce threw after him with great violence. Joseph and Fanny stopt to bear him company the rest of the way, which was not above a mile.

BOOK IV.

CHAPTER I.

The arrival of Lady Booby and the rest at Booby-Hall.

THE coach and six, in which Lady Booby rode, overtook the other travellers as they entered the parish. She no sooner saw Joseph than her cheeks glowed with red, and immediately after became as totally pale. She had in her surprise almost stopt her coach; but recollected herself timely enough to prevent it. She entered the parish amidst the ringing of bells, and the acclamations of the poor, who were rejoiced to see their patroness returned after so long an absence, during which time all her rents had been drafted to London, without a shilling being spent among them, which tended not a little to their utter impoverishing; for, if the court would be severely missed in such a city as London, how much more must the absence of a person of great fortune be felt in a little country village, for whose inhabitants such a family finds a constant employment and supply; and with the offals of whose table the infirm, aged, and infant poor are abundantly fed, with a generosity which hath scarce a visible effect on their benefactor's pockets!

But, if their interest inspired so public a joy into every countenance, how much more forcibly did the affection which they bore Parson Adams operate upon all who beheld his return! They flocked about him like dutiful children round an indulgent parent, and vied with each other in demonstrations of duty and love. The parson on his side shook everyone by the hand, inquiring heartily after the healths of all that were absent, of their children and relations; and exprest a satisfaction in his face which nothing but benevolence made happy by its objects could infuse.

Nor did Joseph and Fanny want a hearty welcome from all who saw them. In short, no three persons could be more kindly received, as, indeed, none ever more deserved to be universally beloved.

Adams carried his fellow-travellers home to his house, where he insisted on their partaking whatever his wife, whom, with his children, he found in health and joy, could provide: where we shall leave them enjoying perfect happiness over a homely meal, to view scenes of greater splendour, but infinitely less bliss.

Our more intelligent readers will doubtless suspect, by this second appearance of Lady Booby on the stage, that all was not ended by the dismission of Joseph; and, to be honest with them, they are in the right: the arrow had pierced deeper than she imagined; nor was the wound so easily to be cured. The removal of the object soon cooled her rage, but it had a different effect on her love: that departed with his person, but this remained lurking in her mind with his image. Restless, interrupted slumbers, and confused horrible dreams were her portion the first night. In the morning, fancy painted her a more delicious scene; but to delude, not delight her: for, before she could reach the promised happiness, it vanished, and left her to curse, not bless, the vision.

She started from her sleep, her imagination being all on fire with the phantom, when, her eyes accidentally glancing towards the spot where yesterday the real Joseph had stood, that little circumstance raised his idea in the liveliest colours in her memory. Each look, each word, each gesture rushed back on her mind with charms which all his coldness could not abate. Nay, she imputed that to his youth, his folly, his awe, his religion, to everything but what would instantly have produced contempt, want of passion for the sex; or that which would have roused her hatred, want of liking to her.

Reflection then hurried her farther, and told her she must see this beautiful youth no more; nay, suggested to her that she herself had dismissed him for no other fault than probably that of too violent an awe and respect for herself; and which she ought rather to have esteemed a merit, the effects of which were besides so easily and surely to have been removed; she then blamed, she cursed the hasty rashness of her temper; her fury was vented all on herself, and Joseph appeared innocent in her eyes. Her passion at length grew so violent, that it forced her on seeking relief, and now she thought of recalling him; but Pride forbade that: Pride, which soon drove all softer passions from her soul, and represented to her the meanness of him she was fond of. That thought soon began to obscure his beauties; Contempt succeeded next, and then Disdain, which presently introduced her hatred of the creature who had given her so much uneasiness. These enemies of Joseph had no sooner taken possession of her mind than they insinuated to her a thousand things in his disfavour; everything but dislike of her person; a thought which, as it would have been intolerable to bear, she checked the moment it endeavoured to arise. Revenge came now to her assistance; and she considered her dismission of him, stript, and without a character, with the utmost pleasure. She rioted in the several kinds of misery which her imagination suggested to her might be his fate; and, with a smile composed of anger, mirth, and scorn, viewed him in the rags in which her fancy had drest him.

Mrs. Slipslop, being summoned, attended her mistress, who had now in her own opinion totally subdued this passion. Whilst she was dressing, she asked if that fellow had been turned away according to her orders. Slipslop answered, she had told her ladyship so (as indeed she had). — "And how did he behave?" replied the lady. "Truly, madam," cries Slipslop, "in such a manner that *infected* everybody who saw him. The poor lad had but little wages to receive: for he constantly allowed his father and mother half his income; so that, when your ladyship's livery was stript off, he had not wherewithal to buy a coat, and must have gone naked if one of the footmen had not *incommodated* him with one; and whilst he was standing in his shirt (and, to say truth, he was an *amorous* figure), being told your ladyship would not give him a character, he sighed, and said he had done nothing willingly to offend; that for his part, he should always give your ladyship a good character wherever he went; and he prayed God to bless you; for you was the best of ladies, though his enemies had set you against him: I wish you had not turned him away; for I believe you have not a faithfuller servant in the house." — "How came you then," replied the lady, "to advise me to turn him away?" "I, madam!" said Slipslop; "I am sure you will do me the justice to say, I did all in my power to prevent it; but I saw your ladyship was angry; and it is not the business of us upper servants to *hint or fear* on these occasions." — "And was it not you, audacious wretch!" cried the lady, "who made me angry? Was it not your tittle-tattle, in which I believe you belied the poor fellow, which incensed me against him? He may thank you for all that hath happened; and so may I for the loss of a good servant, and one who probably had more merit than all of you. Poor fellow! I am charmed with his goodness to his parents. Why did not you tell me of that, but suffer me to dismiss so good a creature without a character? I see the reason of your whole behaviour now as well as of your complaint; you was jealous of the wenches." "I jealous!" said Slipslop; "I assure you, I look upon myself as his betters; I am not meat for a footman, I hope." These words threw the lady into a violent passion, and she sent Slipslop from her presence, who departed, tossing her nose, and crying, "Marry, come up! there are some people more jealous than I, I believe." Her lady affected not to hear the words, though in reality she did, and understood them too. Now ensued a second conflict, so like the former, that it might savour of repetition to relate it minutely. It may suffice to say that Lady Booby found good reason to doubt whether she had so absolutely conquered her passion as she had flattered herself; and, in order to accomplish it quite, took a resolution, more common than wise, to retire immediately into the country. The reader hath long ago seen the arrival of Mrs. Slipslop, whom no pertness could make her mistress resolve to part with; lately, that of Mr. Pounce, her forerunners; and, lastly, that of the lady herself.

The morning after her arrival being Sunday, she went to church, to the great surprise of everybody, who wondered to see her ladyship, being no very constant churchwoman, there so suddenly upon her journey. Joseph was likewise there; and I have heard it was remarked that she fixed her eyes on him much more than on the parson; but this I believe to be only a malicious rumour. When the prayers were ended Mr. Adams stood up, and with a loud voice pronounced: "I publish the banns of marriage between Joseph Andrews and Frances Goodwill, both of this parish," &c. Whether this had any effect on Lady Booby or no, who was then in her pew, which the congregation could not see into, I could never discover: but certain it is that in about a quarter of an hour she stood up, and directed her eyes to that part of the church where the women sat, and persisted in looking that way during the remainder of the sermon, in so scrutinising a manner, and with so angry a countenance, that most of the women were afraid she was offended at them. The moment she returned home she sent for Slipslop into her chamber, and told her she wondered what that impudent fellow Joseph did in that parish? Upon which Slipslop gave her an account of her meeting Adams with him on the road, and likewise the adventure with Fanny. At the relation of which, the lady often changed her countenance; and when she had heard all, she ordered Mr. Adams into her presence, to whom she behaved as the reader will see in the next chapter.

CHAPTER II.

A dialogue between Mr. Abraham Adams and the Lady Booby.

MR. ADAMS was not far off; for he was drinking her ladyship's health below in a cup of her ale. He no sooner came before her than she began in the following manner: "I wonder, sir, after the many great obligations you have had to this family" (with all which the reader hath, in the course of this history, been minutely acquainted), "that you will ungratefully show any respect to a fellow who hath been turned out of it for his misdeeds. Nor doth it, I can tell you, sir, become a man of your character, to run about the country with an idle fellow and wench. Indeed, as for the girl, I know no harm of her. Slipslop tells me she was formerly bred up in my house, and behaved as she ought, till she hankered after this fellow, and he spoiled her. Nay, she may still, perhaps, do very well, if he will let her alone. You are therefore doing a monstrous thing in endeavouring to procure a match between these two people, which will be to the ruin of them both." — "Madam," said Adams, "if your ladyship will but hear me speak, I protest I never heard any harm of Mr. Joseph Andrews; if I had, I should have corrected him for it: for I never have, nor will, encourage the faults of those under my cure. As for the young woman, I assure your ladyship I have as good an opinion of her as your ladyship yourself, or any other can have. She is the sweetest-tempered, honestest, worthiest young creature; indeed, as to her beauty, I do not commend her on that account, though all men allow she is the handsomest woman, gentle or simple, that ever appeared in the parish." "You are very impertinent," says she, "to talk such fulsome stuff to me. It is mighty becoming truly in a clergyman to trouble himself about handsome women, and you are a delicate judge of beauty, no doubt. A man who hath lived all his life in such a parish as this is a rare judge of beauty! Ridiculous! beauty indeed! — a country wench a beauty! — I shall be sick whenever I hear beauty mentioned again. — And so this wench is to stock the parish with beauties, I hope. — But, sir, our poor are numerous enough already; I will have no more vagabonds settled here." "Madam," says Adams, "your ladyship is offended with me, I protest, without any reason. This couple were desirous to consummate long ago, and I dis-

suaded them from it; nay, I may venture to say, I believe, I was
the sole cause of their delaying it." "Well," says she, "and you
did very wisely and honestly too, notwithstanding she is the
greatest beauty in the parish." — "And now, madam," continued
he, "I only perform my office to Mr. Joseph." — "Pray, don't
mister such fellows to me," cries the lady. "He," said the parson,
"with the consent of Fanny, before my face, put in the banns."
— "Yes," answered the lady, "I suppose the slut is forward
enough; Slipslop tells me how her head runs on fellows; that is
one of her beauties, I suppose. But if they have put in the banns,
I desire you will publish them no more without my orders."
"Madam," cries Adams, "if anyone puts in a sufficient caution,
and assigns a proper reason against them, I am willing to sur-
cease." — "I tell you a reason," says she: "he is a vagabond, and
he shall not settle here, and bring a nest of beggars into the
parish; it will make us but little amends that they will be
beauties." "Madam," answered Adams, "with the utmost submission to your ladyship, I have been informed by Lawyer Scout
that any person who serves a year gains a settlement in the parish
where he serves." "Lawyer Scout," replied the lady, "is an impudent coxcomb; I will have no Lawyer Scout interfere with me.
I repeat to you again, I will have no more incumbrances brought
on us: so I desire you will proceed no farther." "Madam," returned Adams, "I would obey your ladyship in everything that
is lawful; but surely the parties being poor is no reason against
their marrying. God forbid there should be any such law! The
poor have little share enough of this world already; it would be
barbarous indeed to deny them the common privileges, and
innocent enjoyments which nature indulges to the animal creation." "Since you understand yourself no better," cries the lady,
"nor the respect due from such as you to a woman of my distinction, than to affront my ears by such loose discourse, I shall
mention but one short word: it is my orders to you that you
publish these banns no more; and if you dare, I will recommend it to your master, the doctor, to discard you from his
service. I will, sir, notwithstanding your poor family; and then
you and the greatest beauty in the parish may go and beg together." "Madam," answered Adams, "I know not what your
ladyship means by the terms 'master' and 'service.' I am in
the service of a Master who will never discard me for doing
my duty; and if the doctor (for indeed I have never been able
to pay for a licence) thinks proper to turn me out from my cure,

God will provide me, I hope, another. At least, my family, as well as myself, have hands; and he will prosper, I doubt not, our endeavours to get our bread honestly with them. Whilst my conscience is pure, I shall never fear what man can do unto me." — "I condemn my humility," said the lady, "for demeaning myself to converse with you so long. I shall take other measures; for I see you are a confederate with them. But the sooner you leave me, the better; and I shall give orders that my doors may no longer be open to you. I will suffer no parsons who run about the country with beauties to be entertained here." — "Madam," said Adams, "I shall enter into no persons' doors against their will; but I am assured, when you have inquired farther into this matter, you will applaud, not blame, my proceeding; and so I humbly take my leave": which he did with many bows, or at least many attempts at a bow.

CHAPTER III.

What passed between the lady and Lawyer Scout.

IN the afternoon the lady sent for Mr. Scout, whom she attacked most violently for intermeddling with her servants, which he denied, and indeed with truth; for he had only asserted accidentally, and perhaps rightly, that a year's service gained a settlement; and so far he owned he might have formerly informed the parson, and believed it was law. "I am resolved," said the lady, "to have no discarded servants of mine settled here; and so, if this be your law, I shall send to another lawyer." Scout said, "If she sent to a hundred lawyers, not one or all of them could alter the law. The utmost that was in the power of a lawyer was to prevent the law's taking effect; and that he himself could do for her ladyship as well as any other; and I believe," says he, "madam, your ladyship, not being conversant in these matters, hath mistaken a difference: for I asserted only that a man who served a year was settled. Now there is a material difference between being settled in law and settled in fact; and as I affirmed generally he was settled, and law is preferable to fact, my settlement must be understood in law, and not in fact. And suppose, madam, we admit he was settled in law, what use will they make of it? how doth that relate to fact? He is not settled in fact; and if he be not settled in fact, he is not an inhabitant; and if he is not an inhabitant, he is not of this parish; and then undoubtedly he ought not to be published here; for Mr. Adams hath told me your ladyship's pleasure, and the reason, which is a very good one, to prevent burdening us with the poor; we have too many already, and I think we ought to have an act to hang or transport half of them. If we can prove in evidence that he is not settled in fact, it is another matter. What I said to Mr. Adams was on a supposition that he was settled in fact; and indeed, if that was the case, I should doubt —" "Don't tell me your 'facts' and your 'ifs'," said the lady; "I don't understand your gibberish; you take too much upon you, and are very impertinent, in pretending to direct in this parish; and you shall be taught better, I assure you, you shall. But as to the wench, I am resolved she shall not settle here; I will not suffer such beauties as these to produce children for us to keep." — "Beauties, indeed! your ladyship is pleased to be merry," answered Scout. — "Mr. Adams described her so to me," said the lady. — "Pray, what sort of dowdy is it, Mr. Scout?" — "The ugliest creature almost I ever beheld: a poor dirty drab, your ladyship never saw such a wretch." — "Well, but, dear Mr. Scout, let her be what she will, — these ugly women will bring children, you know; so that we must prevent the marriage." — "True, madam," replied Scout, "for the subsequent marriage, co-operating with the law, will carry law into fact. When a man is married, he is settled in fact; and then he is not removable. I will see Mr. Adams, and I make no doubt of prevailing with him. His only objection is, doubtless, that he shall lose his fee; but that being once made easy, as it shall be, I am confident no farther objection will remain. No, no, it is impossible; but your ladyship can't discommend his unwillingness to depart from his fee. Every man ought to have a proper value for his fee. As to the matter in question, if your ladyship pleases to employ me in it, I will venture to promise you success. The laws of this land are not so vulgar to permit a mean fellow to contend with one of your ladyship's fortune. We have one sure card, which is, to carry him before Justice Frolick, who, upon hearing your ladyship's name, will commit him without any farther questions. As for the dirty slut, we shall have nothing to do with her: for, if we get rid of the fellow, the ugly jade will ——" "Take what measures you please, good Mr. Scout," answered the lady; "but I wish you could rid the parish of both; for Slipslop tells me such stories of this wench, that I abhor the thoughts of her; and, though you say she is such an ugly slut, yet you know, dear Mr. Scout, these forward creatures, who run after men, will always find some as forward as themselves: so that, to prevent the increase of beggars, we must get rid of her." — "Your ladyship is very much in the right," answered Scout; "but I am afraid the law is a little deficient in giving us any such power of prevention; however, the justice will stretch it as far as he is able, to oblige your ladyship. To say truth, it is a great blessing to the country that he is in the commission: for he hath taken several poor off our hands that the law would never have lain hold on. I know some justices who make as much of committing a man to Bridewell as his lordship at 'size would of hanging him; but it would do a man good to see his worship, our justice, commit a fellow to Bridewell, he takes so much pleasure in it; and when once we ha'un there, we seldom hear any more o'un. He's either starved or eat up by vermin in a month's time." — Here the arrival of a visitor put an end to the conversation, and Mr. Scout, having undertaken the cause, and promised it success, departed.

This Scout was one of those fellows who, without any knowledge of the law, or being bred to it, take upon them, in defiance of an act of Parliament, to act as lawyers in the country, and are called so. They are the pests of society, and a scandal to a profession, to which indeed they do not belong, and which owes to such kind of rascallions the ill-will which weak persons bear towards it. With this fellow, to whom a little before she would not have condescended to have spoken, did a certain passion for Joseph, and the jealousy and the disdain of poor innocent Fanny, betray the Lady Booby into a familiar discourse, in which she inadvertently confirmed many hints with which Slipslop, whose gallant he was, had preacquainted him; and whence he had taken an opportunity to assert those severe falsehoods of little Fanny, which possibly the reader might not have been well able to account for if we had not thought proper to give him this information.

CHAPTER IV.

A short chapter, but very full of matter; particularly the arrival
of Mr. Booby and his lady.

ALL that night, and the next day, the Lady Booby passed with
the utmost anxiety; her mind was distracted, and her soul tossed
up and down by many turbulent and opposite passions. She
loved, hated, pitied, scorned, admired, despised the same person
by fits, which changed in a very short interval. On Tuesday
morning, which happened to be a holiday, she went to church,
where, to her surprise, Mr. Adams published the banns again with
as audible a voice as before. It was lucky for her that, as there
was no sermon, she had an immediate opportunity of returning
home to vent her rage, which she could not have concealed from
the congregation five minutes; indeed, it was not then very
numerous, the assembly consisting of no more than Adams, his
clerk, his wife, the lady, and one of her servants. At her return
she met Slipslop, who accosted her in these words: — "O meam,
what doth your ladyship think? To be sure, Lawyer Scout hath
carried Joseph and Fanny both before the justice. All the parish
are in tears, and say they will certainly be hanged: for nobody
knows what it is for." — "I suppose they deserve it," says the lady.
"What dost thou mention such wretches to me?" — "O dear
madam," answered Slipslop, "is it not a pity such a *graceless*
young man should die a *virulent* death? I hope the judge will
take *commensuration* on his youth. As for Fanny, I don't think
it signifies much what becomes of her; and if poor Joseph hath
done anything, I could venture to swear she *traduced* him to it:
few men ever come to a *fragrant* punishment but by those nasty
creatures, who are a scandal to our *sect*." The lady was no more
pleased at this news, after a moment's reflection, than Slipslop
herself: for, though she wished Fanny far enough, she did not
desire the removal of Joseph, especially with her. She was
puzzled how to act, or what to say on this occasion, when a coach
and six drove into the court, and a servant acquainted her with
the arrival of her nephew Booby and his lady. She ordered them
to be conducted into a drawing-room, whither she presently repaired, having composed her countenance as well as she could.
and being a little satisfied that the wedding would by these means
be at least interrupted, and that she should have an opportunity

to execute any resolution she might take, for which she saw herself provided with an excellent instrument in Scout.

The Lady Booby apprehended her servant had made a mistake when he mentioned Mr. Booby's lady; for she had never heard of his marriage; but how great was her surprise when, at her entering the room, her nephew presented his wife to her! saying, "Madam, this is that charming Pamela, of whom I am convinced you have heard so much." The lady received her with more civility than he expected; indeed with the utmost: for she was perfectly polite, nor had any vice inconsistent with good-breeding. They passed some little time in ordinary discourse, when a servant came and whispered Mr. Booby, who presently told the ladies he must desert them a little on some business of consequence; and, as their discourse during his absence would afford little improvement or entertainment to the reader, we will leave them for a while to attend Mr. Booby.

CHAPTER V.

Containing justice business: curious precedents of depositions, and other matters necessary to be perused by all justices of the peace and their clerks.

THE young squire and his lady were no sooner alighted from their coach than the servants began to inquire after Mr. Joseph, from whom they said their lady had not heard a word, to her great surprise, since he had left Lady Booby's. Upon this they were instantly informed of what had lately happened, with which they hastily acquainted their master, who took an immediate resolution to go himself, and endeavour to restore his Pamela her brother, before she even knew she had lost him.

The justice before whom the criminals were carried, and who lived within a short mile of the lady's house, was luckily Mr. Booby's acquaintance, by his having an estate in his neighbourhood. Ordering therefore his horses to his coach, he set out for the judgment-seat, and arrived when the justice had almost finished his business. He was conducted into a hall, where he was acquainted that his worship would wait on him in a moment; for he had only a man and a woman to commit to Bridewell first. As he was now convinced he had not a minute to lose, he insisted on the servant's introducing him directly into the room where the justice was then executing his office, as he called it. Being brought thither, and the first compliments being passed between the squire and his worship, the former asked the latter what crime those two young people had been guilty of. "No great crime," answered the justice; "I have only ordered them to Bridewell for a month." "But what is their crime?" repeated the squire. "Larceny, an't please your honour," said Scout. "Ay," says the justice, "a kind of felonious larcenous thing. I believe I must order them a little correction too, a little stripping and whipping." (Poor Fanny, who had hitherto supported all with the thoughts of Joseph's company, trembled at that sound; but, indeed, without reason, for none but the devil himself would have executed such a sentence on her.) "Still," said the squire, "I am ignorant of the crime — the fact I mean." "Why, there it is in peaper," answered the justice, showing him a deposition which, in the absence of his clerk, he had writ himself, of which we have with great difficulty procured an authentic copy; and here it follows *verbatim* & *literatim*:

> The *depusition of* James Scout, *layer, and* Thomas Trotter, *yeoman, taken befor mee, on of his magesty's justasses of the piece for* Zumersetshire.
>
> THESE deponants saith, and first Thomas Trotter for himself saith, that on the   of this instant October, being Sabbathday, betwin the ours of 2 and 4 in the afternoon, he zeed Joseph Andrews and Francis Goodwill walk akross a certane felde belunging to Layer Scout, and out of the path which ledes thru the said felde, and there he zede Joseph Andrews with a nife cut one hassel-twig, of the value, as he believes, of 3 half pence, or thereabouts; and he saith, that the said Francis Goodwill was likewise walking on the grass out of the said path in the said felde, and did receive and karry in her hand the said twig, and so was cumfarting, eading and abatting to the said Joseph therein. And the said James Scout for himself says, that he verily believes the said twig to be his own proper twig, &c.

"Jesu!" said the squire, "would you commit two persons to Bridewell for a twig?" "Yes," said the lawyer, "and with great lenity too; for if we had called it a young tree, they would have been both hanged." — "Harkee," (says the justice, taking aside the squire) "I should not have been so severe on this occasion, but Lady Booby desires to get them out of the parish; so Lawyer Scout will give the constable orders to let them run away, if they

please, but it seems they intend to marry together, and the lady
hath no other means, as they are legally settled there, to prevent
their bringing an incumbrance on her own parish." "Well," said
the squire, "I will take care my aunt shall be satisfied in this point;
and likewise I promise you, Joseph here shall never be any incumbrance on her. I shall be obliged to you, therefore, if, instead
of Bridewell, you will commit them to my custody." — "O! to be
sure, sir, if you desire it," answered the justice; and without more
ado, Joseph and Fanny were delivered over to Squire Booby,
whom Joseph very well knew, but little guessed how nearly he
was related to him. The justice burnt his mittimus: the constable
was sent about his business: the lawyer made no complaint for
want of justice; and the prisoners, with exulting hearts, gave a
thousand thanks to his honour Mr. Booby, who did not intend
their obligations to him should cease here; for, ordering his man
to produce a cloak-bag, which he had caused to be brought
from Lady Booby's on purpose, he desired the justice that he
might have Joseph with him into a room; where, ordering his
servant to take out a suit of his own clothes, with linen and
other necessaries, he left Joseph to dress himself, who, not yet
knowing the cause of all this civility, excused his accepting such
a favour as long as decently he could. Whilst Joseph was dressing, the squire repaired to the justice, whom he found talking
with Fanny; for, during the examination, she had looped her
hat over her eyes, which were also bathed in tears, and had by
that means concealed from his worship what might perhaps have
rendered the arrival of Mr. Booby unnecessary, at least for herself. The justice no sooner saw her countenance cleared up, and
her bright eyes shining through her tears, than he secretly cursed
himself for having once thought of Bridewell for her. He would
willingly have sent his own wife thither, to have had Fanny in
her place. And, conceiving almost at the same instant desires and
schemes to accomplish them, he employed the minutes whilst the
squire was absent with Joseph in assuring her how sorry he was
for having treated her so roughly before he knew her merit; and
told her, that since Lady Booby was unwilling that she should
settle in her parish, she was heartily welcome to his, where he
promised her his protection, adding that he would take Joseph
and her into his own family, if she liked it; which assurance he
confirmed with a squeeze by the hand. She thanked him very
kindly, and said, "She would acquaint Joseph with the offer,
which he would certainly be glad to accept; for that Lady Booby

was angry with them both; though she did not know either had done anything to offend her, but imputed it to Madam Slipslop, who had always been her enemy."

The squire now returned, and prevented any farther continuance of this conversation; and the justice, out of a pretended respect to his guest, but in reality from an apprehension of a rival (for he knew nothing of his marriage), ordered Fanny into the kitchen, whither she gladly retired; nor did the squire, who declined the trouble of explaining the whole matter, oppose it.

It would be unnecessary, if I was able, which indeed I am not, to relate the conversation between these two gentlemen, which rolled, as I have been informed, entirely on the subject of horse-racing. Joseph was soon drest in the plainest dress he could find, which was a blue coat and breeches, with a gold edging, and a red waistcoat with the same; and as this suit, which was rather too large for the squire, exactly fitted him, so he became it so well, and looked so genteel, that no person would have doubted its being as well adapted to his quality as his shape; nor have suspected, as one might, when my Lord ——, or Sir ——, or Mr. ——, appear in lace or embroidery, that the tailor's man wore those clothes home on his back which he should have carried under his arm.

The squire now took leave of the justice; and, calling for Fanny, made her and Joseph, against their wills, get into the coach with him, which he then ordered to drive to Lady Booby's. — It had moved a few yards only, when the squire asked Joseph if he knew who that man was crossing the field; for, added he, "I never saw one take such strides before." Joseph answered eagerly, "O, sir, it is Parson Adams!" — "O la, indeed, and so it is," said Fanny; "poor man, he is coming to do what he could for us. Well, he is the worthiest, best-natured creature." — "Ay," said Joseph; "God bless him! for there is not such another in the universe." — "The best creature living sure," cries Fanny. "Is he?" says the squire; "then I am resolved to have the best creature living in my coach"; and so saying, he ordered it to stop, whilst Joseph, at his request, hollowed to the parson, who, well knowing his voice, made all the haste imaginable, and soon came up with them. He was desired by the master, who could scarce refrain from laughter at his figure, to mount into the coach, which he with many thanks refused, saying he could walk by its side, and he'd warrant he kept up with it; but he was at length overprevailed on. The squire now acquainted Joseph with his mar-

riage; but he might have spared himself that labour; for his
servant, whilst Joseph was dressing, had performed that office
before. IIe continued to express the vast happiness he enjoyed
in his sister, and the value he had for all who belonged to her.
Joseph made many bows, and exprest as many acknowledgments;
and Parson Adams, who now first perceived Joseph's new apparel,
burst into tears with joy, and fell to rubbing his hands and snapping his fingers, as if he had been mad.

They were now arrived at the Lady Booby's, and the squire,
desiring them to wait a moment in the court, walked in to his
aunt, and calling her out from his wife, acquainted her with
Joseph's arrival; saying, "Madam, as I have married a virtuous
and worthy woman, I am resolved to own her relations, and show
them all a proper respect; I shall think myself therefore infinitely
obliged to all mine who will do the same. It is true, her brother
hath been your servant, but he is now become my brother; and
I have one happiness, that neither his character, his behaviour
or appearance, give me any reason to be ashamed of calling him
so. In short, he is now below, dressed like a gentleman, in which
light I intend he shall hereafter be seen; and you will oblige me
beyond expression if you will admit him to be of our party; for
I know it will give great pleasure to my wife, though she will not
mention it."

This was a stroke of Fortune beyond the Lady Booby's hopes
or expectation; she answered him eagerly, "Nephew, you know
how easily I am prevailed on to do anything which Joseph
Andrews desires — Phoo, I mean which you desire me; and, as
he is now your relation, I cannot refuse to entertain him as
such." The squire told her he knew his obligation to her for
her compliance; and going three steps, returned and told her
— he had one more favour, which he believed she would easily
grant, as she had accorded him the former. "There is a young
woman ——" "Nephew," says she, "don't let my good-nature
make you desire, as is too commonly the case, to impose on
me. Nor think, because I have with so much condescension
agreed to suffer your brother-in-law to come to my table, that
I will submit to the company of all my own servants, and all
the dirty trollops in the country." "Madam," answered the
squire, "I believe you never saw this young creature. I never
beheld such sweetness and innocence, joined with such beauty,
and withal so genteel." "Upon my soul I won't admit her," replied the lady in a passion; "the whole world shan't prevail on

me; I resent even the desire as an affront, and ——" The squire, who knew her inflexibility, interrupted her, by asking pardon, and promising not to mention it more. He then returned to Joseph, and she to Pamela. He took Joseph aside and told him he would carry him to his sister, but could not prevail as yet for Fanny. Joseph begged that he might see his sister alone, and then be with his Fanny; but the squire, knowing the pleasure his wife would have in her brother's company, would not admit it, telling Joseph there would be nothing in so short an absence from Fanny, whilst he was assured of her safety; adding, he hoped he could not so easily quit a sister whom he had not seen so long, and who so tenderly loved him. — Joseph immediately complied; for indeed no brother could love a sister more; and, recommending Fanny, who rejoiced that she was not to go before Lady Booby, to the care of Mr. Adams, he attended the squire upstairs, whilst Fanny repaired with the parson to his house, where she thought herself secure of a kind reception.

CHAPTER VI.

Of which you are desired to read no more than you like.

THE meeting between Joseph and Pamela was not without tears of joy on both sides; and their embraces were full of tenderness and affection. They were, however, regarded with much more pleasure by the nephew than by the aunt, to whose flame they were fuel only; and this was increased by the addition of dress, which was indeed not wanted to set off the lively colours in which Nature had drawn health, strength, comeliness, and youth. In the afternoon Joseph, at their request, entertained them with the account of his adventures; nor could Lady Booby conceal her dissatisfaction at those parts in which Fanny was concerned, especially when Mr. Booby launched forth into such rapturous praises of her beauty. She said, applying to her niece, that she wondered her nephew, who had pretended to marry for love, should think such a subject proper to amuse his wife with; adding, that, for her part, she should be jealous of a husband who spoke so warmly in praise of another woman. Pamela answered, indeed she thought she had cause; but it was an instance of Mr. Booby's aptness to see more beauty in women than they were

mistresses of. At which words both the women fixed their eyes
on two looking-glasses; and Lady Booby replied, that men were,
in the general, very ill judges of beauty; and then, whilst both
contemplated only their own faces, they paid a cross compliment
to each other's charms. When the hour of rest approached, which
the lady of the house deferred as long as decently she could, she
informed Joseph (whom for the future we shall call Mr. Joseph,
he having as good a title to that appellation as many others — I
mean that incontested one of good clothes) that she had ordered
a bed to be provided for him. He declined this favour to his
utmost; for his heart had long been with his Fanny; but she
insisted on his accepting it, alleging that the parish had no proper
accommodation for such a person as he was now to esteem
himself. The squire and his lady both joining with her, Mr.
Joseph was at last forced to give over his design of visiting
Fanny that evening; who, on her side, as impatiently expected
him till midnight, when, in complacence to Mr. Adams's family,
who had sat up two hours out of respect to her, she retired to
bed, but not to sleep; the thoughts of her love kept her waking,
and his not returning according to his promise filled her with
uneasiness; of which, however, she could not assign any other
cause than merely that of being absent from him.

Mr. Joseph rose early in the morning, and visited her in whom
his soul delighted. She no sooner heard his voice in the parson's
parlour than she leapt from her bed, and, dressing herself in a
few minutes, went down to him. They passed two hours with
inexpressible happiness together; and then, having appointed
Monday, by Mr. Adams's permission, for their marriage, Mr.
Joseph returned, according to his promise, to breakfast at the
Lady Booby's, with whose behaviour since the evening we shall
now acquaint the reader.

She was no sooner retired to her chamber than she asked
Slipslop, what she thought of this wonderful creature her nephew
had married. "Madam?" said Slipslop, not yet sufficiently understanding what answer she was to make. "I ask you," answered
the lady, "what you think of the dowdy, my niece, I think I am
to call her?" Slipslop, wanting no further hint, began to pull her
to pieces, and so miserably defaced her, that it would have been
impossible for anyone to have known the person. The lady gave
her all the assistance she could, and ended with saying, — "I
think, Slipslop, you have done her justice; but yet, bad as she
is, she is an angel compared to this Fanny." Slipslop then fell

on Fanny, whom she hacked and hewed in the like barbarous manner, concluding with an observation that there was always something in those low-life creatures which must eternally distinguish them from their betters. "Really," said the lady, "I think there is one exception to your rule; I am certain you may guess who I mean." — "Not I, upon my word, madam," said Slipslop. — "I mean a young fellow; sure you are the dullest wretch," said the lady. — "O la! I am indeed. — Yes, truly, madam, he is an *accession*," answered Slipslop. — "Ay, is he not, Slipslop?" returned the lady. "Is he not so genteel that a prince might, without a blush, acknowledge him for his son? His behaviour is such that would not shame the best education. He borrows from his station a condescension in everything to his superiors, yet unattended by that mean servility which is called good behaviour in such persons. Everything he doth hath no mark of the base motive of fear, but visibly shows some respect and gratitude, and carries with it the persuasion of love. — And then for his virtues: such piety to his parents, such tender affection to his sister, such integrity in his friendship, such bravery, such goodness, that, if he had been born a gentleman, his wife would have possessed the most invaluable blessing." — "To be sure, ma'am," says Slipslop. — "But as he is," answered the lady, "if he had a thousand more good qualities, it must render a woman of fashion contemptible even to be suspected of thinking of him; yes, I should despise myself for such a thought." "To be sure, ma'am," said Slipslop. "And why to be sure?" replied the lady; "thou art always one's echo. Is he not more worthy of affection than a dirty country clown, though born of a family as old as the flood? or an idle worthless rake, or little puisny beau of quality? And yet these we must condemn ourselves to, in order to avoid the censure of the world; to shun the contempt of others, we must ally ourselves to those we despise; we must prefer birth, title, and fortune, to real merit. It is a tyranny of custom, a tyranny we must comply with: for we people of fashion are the slaves of custom." — "Marry come up!" said Slipslop, who now well knew which party to take; "if I was a woman of your ladyship's fortune and quality, I would be a slave to nobody." — "Me!" said the lady; "I am speaking if a young woman of fashion, who had seen nothing of the world, should happen to like such a fellow. — Me, indeed! I hope thou dost not imagine——" "No, ma'am, to be sure," cries Slipslop. — "No! what no?" cried the lady. "Thou art always ready to answer before thou hast heard one. So far I must allow he is a charming fellow. Me, indeed! No, Slipslop, all thoughts of men are over with me. — I have lost a husband who — but if I should reflect, I should run mad. — My future ease must depend upon forgetfulness. Slipslop, let me hear some of thy nonsense, to turn my thoughts another way. What dost thou think of Mr. Andrews?" "Why, I think," says Slipslop, "he is the handsomest, most properest man I ever saw; and if I was a lady of the greatest degree, it would be well for some folks. Your ladyship may talk of custom, if you please; but I am *confidous* there is no more comparison between young Mr. Andrews and most of the young gentlemen who come to your ladyship's house in London; a parcel of *whipper-snapper* sparks: I would sooner marry our old Parson Adams: never tell me what people say, whilst I am happy in the arms of him I love. Some folks rail against other folks because other folks have what some folks would be glad of." — "And so," answered the lady, "if you was a woman of condition, you would really marry Mr. Andrews?" — "Yes, I assure your ladyship," replied Slipslop, "if he would have me." — "Fool, idiot!" cries the lady; "if he would have a woman of fashion! Is that a question?" "No, truly, madam," said Slipslop, "I believe it would be none if Fanny was out of the way; and I am *confidous*, if I was in your ladyship's place, and liked Mr. Joseph Andrews, she should not stay in the parish a moment. I am sure Lawyer Scout would send her packing if your ladyship would but say the word." This last speech of Slipslop raised a tempest in the mind of her mistress. She feared Scout had betrayed her, or rather that she had betrayed herself. After some silence, and a double change of her complexion, first to pale and then to red, she thus spoke: "I am astonished at the liberty you give your tongue. Would you insinuate that I employed Scout against this wench on account of the fellow?" "La, ma'am," said Slipslop, frighted out of her wits, "I *assassinate* such a thing!" "I think you dare not," answered the lady; "I believe my conduct may defy malice itself to assert so cursed a slander. If I had ever discovered any wantonness, any lightness in my behaviour: if I had followed the example of some whom thou hast, I believe, seen, in allowing myself indecent liberties, even with a husband; but the dear man who is gone" (*here she began to sob*), "was he alive again" (*then she produced tears*), "could not upbraid me with any one act of tenderness or passion. No, Slipslop, all the time I cohabited with him, he never obtained even a kiss from me without my expressing reluctance in the granting it. I am sure

he himself never suspected how much I loved him. Since his
death, thou knowest, though it is almost six weeks (it wants but
a day) ago, I have not admitted one visitor till this fool my
nephew arrived. I have confined myself quite to one party of
friends. — And can such a conduct as this fear to be arraigned?
To be accused not only of a passion which I have always despised,
but of fixing it on such an object, a creature so much beneath my
notice!" — "Upon my word, ma'am," says Slipslop, "I do not
understand your ladyship; nor know I anything of the matter." —
"I believe indeed thou dost not understand me. — These are delicacies which exist only in superior minds; thy coarse ideas cannot comprehend them. Thou art a low creature, of the Andrews
breed, a reptile of a lower order, a weed that grows in the common garden of the creation." — "I assure your ladyship," says
Slipslop, whose passions were almost of as high an order as her
lady's, "I have no more to do with *Common Garden* than other
folks. Really, your ladyship talks of servants as if they were not
born of the Christian *specious*. Servants have flesh and blood as
well as quality; and Mr. Andrews himself is a proof that they have
as good, if not better. And for my own part, I can't perceive my
*dears** are coarser than other people's; and I am sure, if Mr.
Andrews was a *dear* of mine, I should not be ashamed of him
in company with gentlemen; for whoever hath seen him in his
new clothes must confess he looks as much like a gentleman as
anybody. Coarse, quotha! I can't bear to hear the poor young
fellow run down neither; for I will say this, I never heard him
say an ill word of anybody in his life. I am sure his coarseness
doth not lie in his heart; for he is the best-natured man in the
world; and as for his skin, it is no coarser than other people's,
I am sure. His bosom, when a boy, was as white as driven
snow; and, where it is not covered with hairs, is so still. Ifaukins!
if I was Mrs. Andrews, with a hundred a year, I should not
envy the best she who wears a head. A woman that could not
be happy with such a man ought never to be so: for if he can't
make a woman happy, I never yet beheld the man who could.
I say again, I wish I was a great lady for his sake. I believe
when I had made a gentleman of him, he'd behave so, that
nobody should *deprecate* what I had done; and I fancy few
would venture to tell him he was no gentleman to his face, nor
to mine neither." At which words, taking up the candles, she
asked her mistress, who had been some time in her bed, if she

---

* Meaning perhaps ideas. — F.

had any farther commands; who mildly answered, she had none; and, telling her she was a comical creature, bid her good-night.

CHAPTER VII.

Philosophical reflections, the like not to be found in any light French romance. Mr. Booby's grave advice to Joseph, and Fanny's encounter with a beau.

HABIT, my good reader, hath so vast a prevalence over the human mind, that there is scarce anything too strange or too strong to be asserted of it. The story of the miser, who, from long accustoming to cheat others, came at last to cheat himself, and with great delight and triumph picked his own pocket of a guinea to convey to his hoard, is not impossible or improbable. In like manner it fares with the practisers of deceit, who, from having long deceived their acquaintance, gain at last a power of deceiving themselves, and acquire that very opinion (however false) of their own abilities, excellencies, and virtues, into which they have for years perhaps endeavoured to betray their neighbours. Now, reader, to apply this observation to my present purpose, thou must know, that as the passion generally called love exercises most of the talents of the female or fair world, so in this they now and then discover a small inclination to deceit; for which thou wilt not be angry with the beautiful creatures when thou hast considered that at the age of seven, or something earlier, miss is instructed by her mother that master is a very monstrous kind of animal, who will, if she suffers him to come too near her, infallibly eat her up, and grind her to pieces. That so far from kissing or toying with him of her own accord, she must not admit him to kiss or toy with her. And lastly, that she must never have any affection towards him; for if she should, all her friends in petticoats would esteem her a traitress, point at her, and hunt her out of their society. These impressions, being first received, are farther and deeper inculcated by their school-mistresses and companions; so that by the age of ten they have contracted such a dread and abhorrence of the above-named monster, that, whenever they see him, they fly from him as the innocent hare doth from the greyhound. Hence, to the age of fourteen or fifteen, they entertain a mighty antipathy to master; they resolve, and

frequently profess, that they will never have any commerce
with him, and entertain fond hopes of passing their lives out
of his reach, of the possibility of which they have so visible an
example in their good maiden aunt. But when they arrive at
this period, and have now passed their second climacteric, when
their wisdom, grown riper, begins to see a little farther, and,
from almost daily falling in master's way, to apprehend the great
difficulty of keeping out of it; and when they observe him look
often at them, and sometimes very eagerly and earnestly too (for
the monster seldom takes any notice of them till at this age),
they then begin to think of their danger; and, as they perceive
they cannot easily avoid him, the wiser part bethink themselves
of providing by other means for their security. They endeavour,
by all the methods they can invent, to render themselves so
amiable in his eyes, that he may have no inclination to hurt them;
in which they generally succeed so well, that his eyes, by frequent
languishing, soon lessen their idea of his fierceness, and so far
abate their fears, that they venture to parley with him; and when
they perceive him so different from what he hath been described,
all gentleness, softness, kindness, tenderness, fondness, their
dreadful apprehensions vanish in a moment; and now (it being
usual with the human mind to skip from one extreme to its opposite, as easily, and almost as suddenly, as a bird from one bough
to another) love instantly succeeds to fear: but, as it happens to
persons who have in their infancy been thoroughly frightened
with certain no-persons called ghosts, that they retain their dread
of those beings after they are convinced that there are no such
things, so these young ladies, though they no longer apprehend
devouring, cannot so entirely shake off all that hath been instilled
into them; they still entertain the idea of that censure which was
so strongly imprinted on their tender minds, to which the declara-
tions of abhorrence they every day hear from their companions
greatly contribute. To avoid this censure, therefore, is now their
only care; for which purpose they still pretend the same aversion
to the monster: and the more they love him, the more ardently
they counterfeit the antipathy. By the continual and constant
practice of which deceit on others, they at length impose on
themselves, and really believe they hate what they love. Thus,
indeed, it happened to Lady Booby, who loved Joseph long
before she knew it; and now loved him much more than she
suspected. She had indeed, from the time of his sister's arrival
in the quality of her niece, and from the instant she viewed him

in the dress and character of a gentleman, began to conceive secretly a design which love had concealed from herself, till a dream betrayed it to her.

She had no sooner risen than she sent for her nephew; when he came to her, after many compliments on his choice, she told him, "He might perceive, in her condescension to admit her own servant to her table, that she looked on the family of Andrews as his relations, and indeed hers; that, as he had married into such a family, it became him to endeavour by all methods to raise it as much as possible. At length she advised him to use all his art to dissuade Joseph from his intended match, which would still enlarge their relation to meanness and poverty; concluding that, by a commission in the army, or some other genteel employment, he might soon put young Mr. Andrews on the foot of a gentleman; and, that being once done, his accomplishments might quickly gain him an alliance which would not be to their discredit."

Her nephew heartily embraced this proposal; and, finding Mr. Joseph with his wife, `at his return to her chamber, he immediately began thus: "My love to my dear Pamela, brother, will extend to all her relations; nor shall I show them less respect than if I had married into the family of a duke. I hope I have given you some early testimonies of this, and shall continue to give you daily more. You will excuse me therefore, brother, if my concern for your interest makes me mention what may be, perhaps, disagreeable to you to hear: but I must insist upon it, that, if you have any value for my alliance or my friendship, you will decline any thoughts of engaging farther with a girl who is, as you are a relation of mine, so much beneath you. I know there may be at first some difficulty in your compliance, but that will daily diminish; and you will in the end sincerely thank me for my advice. I own, indeed, the girl is handsome; but beauty alone is a poor ingredient, and will make but an uncomfortable marriage." "Sir," said Joseph, "I assure you her beauty is her least perfection; nor do I know a virtue which that young creature is not possest of." "As to her virtues," answered Mr. Booby, "you can be yet but a slender judge of them; but, if she had never so many, you will find her equal in these among her superiors in birth and fortune, which now you are to esteem on a footing with yourself; at least I will take care they shall shortly be so, unless you prevent me by degrading yourself with such a match, a match I have hardly patience to think of, and which would break the hearts of your parents, who now rejoice in the expectation of seeing you make a figure in the world." "I know not," replied Joseph, "that my parents have any power over my inclinations; nor am I obliged to sacrifice my happiness to their whim or ambition: besides, I shall be very sorry to see that the unexpected advancement of my sister should so suddenly inspire them with this wicked pride, and make them despise their equals. I am resolved on no account to quit my dear Fanny; no, though I could raise her as high above her present station as you have raised my sister." "Your sister, as well as myself," said Booby, "are greatly obliged to you for the comparison: but, sir, she is not worthy to be compared in beauty to my Pamela; nor hath she half her merit. And besides, sir, as you civilly throw my marriage with your sister in my teeth, I must teach you the wide difference between us: my fortune enabled me to please myself; and it would have been as overgrown a folly in me to have omitted it as in you to do it." "My fortune enables me to please myself likewise," said Joseph; "for all my pleasure is centered in Fanny; and whilst I have health, I shall be able to support her with my labour in that station to which she was born, and with which she is content." "Brother," said Pamela, "Mr. Booby advises you as a friend; and no doubt my papa and mamma will be of his opinion, and will have great reason to be angry with you for destroying what his goodness hath done, and throwing down our family again, after he hath raised it. It would become you better, brother, to pray for the assistance of grace against such a passion than to indulge it." — "Sure, sister, you are not in earnest; I am sure she is your equal, at least." — "She was my equal," answered Pamela, "but I am no longer Pamela Andrews; I am now this gentleman's lady, and as such am above her — I hope I shall never behave with an unbecoming pride; but, at the same time, I shall always endeavour to know myself, and question not the assistance of grace to that purpose." They were now summoned to breakfast, and thus ended their discourse for the present, very little to the satisfaction of any of the parties.

Fanny was now walking in an avenue at some distance from the house, where Joseph had promised to take the first opportunity of coming to her. She had not a shilling in the world, and had subsisted ever since her return entirely on the charity of Parson Adams. A young gentleman, attended by many servants, came up to her, and asked her if that was not the Lady Booby's house before him? This, indeed, he well knew;

but had framed the question for no other reason than to make
her look up, and discover if her face was equal to the delicacy
of her shape. He no sooner saw it than he was struck with
amazement. He stopt his horse, and swore she was the most
beautiful creature he ever beheld. Then, instantly alighting,
and delivering his horse to his servant, he rapt out half a dozen
oaths that he would kiss her; to which she at first submitted,
begging he would not be rude; but he was not satisfied with the
civility of a salute, nor even with the rudest attack he could
make on her lips, but caught her in his arms, and endeavoured
to kiss her breasts, which with all her strength she resisted, and,
as our spark was not of the Herculean race, with some difficulty
prevented. The young gentleman, being soon out of breath in
the struggle, quitted her, and, remounting his horse, called one
of his servants to him, whom he ordered to stay behind with
her, and make her any offers whatever to prevail on her to
return home with him in the evening; and to assure her he would
take her into keeping. He then rode on with his other servants,
and arrived at the lady's house, to whom he was a distant relation, and was come to pay a visit.

The trusty fellow, who was employed in an office he had been
long accustomed to, discharged his part with all the fidelity and
dexterity imaginable; but to no purpose. She was entirely deaf
to his offers, and rejected them with the utmost disdain. At
last the pimp, who had perhaps more warm blood about him
than his master, began to solicit for himself; he told her, though
he was a servant, he was a man of some fortune, which he would
make her mistress of — and this without any insult to her virtue,
for that he would marry her. She answered, if his master himself, or the greatest lord in the land, would marry her, she would
refuse him. At last, being weary with persuasions, and on fire
with charms which would have almost kindled a flame in the
bosom of an ancient philosopher, or modern divine, he fastened
his horse to the ground, and attacked her with much more force
than the gentleman had exerted. Poor Fanny would not have
been able to resist his rudeness any long time, but the deity who
presides over chaste love sent her Joseph to her assistance. He
no sooner came within sight, and perceived her struggling with
a man, than, like a cannon-ball, or like lightning, or anything
that is swifter, if anything be, he ran towards her, and, coming
up just as the ravisher had torn her handkerchief from her breast,
before his lips had touched that seat of innocence and bliss, he

dealt him so lusty a blow in that part of his neck which a rope
would have become with the utmost propriety, that the fellow
staggered backwards, and, perceiving he had to do with something rougher than the little, tender, trembling hand of Fanny,
he quitted her, and, turning about, saw his rival, with fire flash-
ing from his eyes, again ready to assail him; and indeed before
he could well defend himself, or return the first blow, he received
a second, which, had it fallen on that part of the stomach to which
it was directed, would have been probably the last he would have
had any occasion for; but the ravisher, lifting up his hand, drove
the blow upwards to his mouth, whence it dislodged three of
his teeth; and now, not conceiving any extraordinary affection
for the beauty of Joseph's person, nor being extremely pleased
with this method of salutation, he collected all his force, and
aimed a blow at Joseph's breast, which he artfully parried with
one fist, so that it lost its force entirely in air; and, stepping one
foot backward, he darted his fist so fiercely at his enemy, that,
had he not caught it in his hand (for he was a boxer of no
inferior fame), it must have tumbled him on the ground. And
now the ravisher meditated another blow, which he aimed at
that part of the breast where the heart is lodged; Joseph did
not catch it as before, yet so prevented its aim that it fell
directly on his nose, but with abated force. Joseph then, moving
both fist and foot forwards at the same time, threw his head so
dexterously into the stomach of the ravisher that he fell a lifeless
lump on the field, where he lay many minutes breathless and
motionless.

When Fanny saw her Joseph receive a blow in his face, and
blood running in a stream from him, she began to tear her hair,
and invoke all human and divine power to his assistance. She
was not, however, long under this affliction before Joseph, having
conquered his enemy, ran to her, and assured her he was not
hurt; she then instantly fell on her knees, and thanked God that
he had made Joseph the means of her rescue, and at the same
time preserved him from being injured in attempting it. She
offered with her handkerchief to wipe his blood from his face;
but he, seeing his rival attempting to recover his legs, turned to
him, and asked him if he had enough? To which the other
answered he had; for he believed he had fought with the devil
instead of a man; and, loosening his horse, said he should not
have attempted the wench if he had known she had been so
well provided for.

Fanny now begged Joseph to return with her to Parson Adams, and to promise that he would leave her no more; these were propositions so agreeable to Joseph, that, had he heard them, he would have given an immediate assent: but indeed his eyes were now his only sense; for you may remember, reader, that the ravisher had tore her handkerchief from Fanny's neck, by which he had discovered such a sight, that Joseph hath declared all the statues he ever beheld were so much inferior to it in beauty, that it was more capable of converting a man into a statue than of being imitated by the greatest master of that art. This modest creature, whom no warmth in summer could ever induce to expose her charms to the wanton sun, a modesty to which perhaps they owed their inconceivable whiteness, had stood many minutes bare-necked in the presence of Joseph before her apprehension of his danger, and the horror of seeing his blood, would suffer her once to reflect on what concerned herself; till at last, when the cause of her concern had vanished, an admiration at his silence, together with observing the fixed position of his eyes, produced an idea in the lovely maid which brought more blood into her face than had flowed from Joseph's nostrils. The snowy hue of her bosom was likewise exchanged to vermilion at the instant when she clapped her handkerchief round her neck. Joseph saw the uneasiness she suffered, and immediately removed his eyes from an object, in surveying which he had felt the greatest delight which the organs of sight were capable of conveying to his soul. So great was his fear of offending her, and so truly did his passion for her deserve the noble name of love.

Fanny, being recovered from her confusion, which was almost equalled by what Joseph had felt from observing it, again mentioned her request; this was instantly and gladly complied with; and together they crossed two or three fields, which brought them to the habitation of Mr. Adams.

CHAPTER VIII.

*A discourse which happened between Mr. Adams, Mrs. Adams,
Joseph and Fanny; with some behaviour of Mr. Adams,
which will be called by some few readers very low, absurd,
and unnatural.*

THE parson and his wife had just ended a long dispute when
the lovers came to the door. Indeed, this young couple had
been the subject of the dispute; for Mrs. Adams was one of
those prudent people who never do anything to injure their
families, or perhaps one of those good mothers who would
even stretch their conscience to serve their children. She had
long entertained hopes of seeing her eldest daughter succeed
Mrs. Slipslop, and of making her second son an exciseman by
Lady Booby's interest. These were expectations she could not
endure the thoughts of quitting, and was therefore very uneasy
to see her husband so resolute to oppose the lady's intention in
Fanny's affair. She told him, "It behoved every man to take the
first care of his family; that he had a wife and six children, the
maintaining and providing for whom would be business enough
for him without intermeddling in other folks' affairs; that he had
always preached up submission to superiors, and would do ill to
give an example of the contrary behaviour in his own conduct;
that if Lady Booby did wrong, she must answer for it herself, and
the sin would not lie at their door; that Fanny had been a servant,
and bred up in the lady's own family, and consequently she
must have known more of her than they did, and it was very
improbable, if she had behaved herself well, that the lady
would have been so bitterly her enemy; that perhaps he was
too much inclined to think well of her because she was handsome, but handsome women were often no better than they
should be; that G— made ugly women as well as handsome
ones; and that if a woman had virtue, it signified nothing
whether she had beauty or no." For all which reasons she concluded he should oblige the lady, and stop the future publication of the banns. But all these excellent arguments had
no effect on the parson, who persisted in doing his duty without
regarding the consequence it might have on his worldly interest;
he endeavoured to answer her as well as he could; to which
she had just finished her reply (for she had always the last

word everywhere but at church) when Joseph and Fanny entered their kitchen, where the parson and his wife then sat at breakfast over some bacon and cabbage. There was a coldness in the civility of Mrs. Adams which persons of accurate speculation might have observed, but escaped her present guests; indeed, it was a good deal covered by the heartiness of Adams, who no sooner heard that Fanny had neither eat nor drank that morning than he presented her a bone of bacon he had just been gnawing, being the only remains of his provision, and then ran nimbly to the tap, and produced a mug of small beer, which he called ale; however, it was the best in his house. Joseph, addressing himself to the parson, told him the discourse which had passed between Squire Booby, his sister, and himself concerning Fanny; he then acquainted him with the dangers whence he had rescued her, and communicated some apprehensions on her account. He concluded that he should never have an easy moment till Fanny was absolutely his, and begged that he might be suffered to fetch a licence, saying he could easily borrow the money. The parson answered, that he had already given his sentiments concerning a licence, and that a very few days would make it unnecessary. "Joseph," says he, "I wish this haste doth not arise rather from your impatience than your fear; but, as it certainly springs from one of these causes, I will examine both. Of each of these therefore in their turn; and first, for the first of these, namely, impatience. Now, child, I must inform you that, if in your purposed marriage with this young woman, you have no intention but the indulgence of carnal appetites, you are guilty of a very heinous sin. Marriage was ordained for nobler purposes, as you will learn when you hear the service provided on that occasion read to you. Nay, perhaps, if you are a good lad, I shall give you a sermon *gratis*, wherein I shall demonstrate how little regard ought to be had to the flesh on such occasions. The text will be, child, Matthew the 5th, and part of the 28th verse: 'Whosoever looketh on a woman so as to lust after her.' The latter part I shall omit, as foreign to my purpose. Indeed, all such brutal lusts and affections are to be greatly subdued, if not totally eradicated, before the vessel can be said to be consecrated to honour. To marry with a view of gratifying those inclinations is a prostitution of that holy ceremony, and must entail a curse on all who so lightly undertake it. If, therefore, this haste arises from impatience, you are to correct, and not give way to it. Now, as to the second head which I proposed to speak to, namely, fear: it argues a diffidence, highly criminal, of that Power in which alone we should put our trust, seeing we may be well assured that he is able, not only to defeat the designs of our enemies, but even to turn their hearts. Instead of taking, therefore, any unjustifiable or desperate means to rid ourselves of fear, we should resort to prayer only on these occasions; and we may be then certain of obtaining what is best for us. When any accident threatens us, we are not to despair, nor, when it overtakes us, to grieve; we must submit in all things to the will of Providence, and not set our affections so much on anything here, as not to be able to quit it without reluctance. You are a young man, and can know but little of this world; I am older, and have seen a great deal. All passions are criminal in their excess; and even love itself, if it is not subservient to our duty, may render us blind to it. Had Abraham so loved his son Isaac as to refuse the sacrifice required, is there any of us who would not condemn him? Joseph, I know your many good qualities, and value you for them; but, as I am to render an account of your soul, which is committed to my cure, I cannot see any fault without reminding you of it. You are too much inclined to passion, child, and have set your affections so absolutely on this young woman, that, if G— required her at your hands, I fear you would reluctantly part with her. Now, believe me, no Christian ought so to set his heart on any person or thing in this world, but that, whenever it shall be required or taken from him in any manner by Divine Providence, he may be able, peaceably, quietly, and contentedly, to resign it." At which words one came hastily in, and acquainted Mr. Adams that his youngest son was drowned. He stood silent a moment, and soon began to stamp about the room and deplore his loss with the bitterest agony. Joseph, who was overwhelmed with concern likewise, recovered himself sufficiently to endeavour to comfort the parson; in which attempt he used many arguments that he had at several times remembered out of his own discourses, both in private and public (for he was a great enemy to the passions, and preached nothing more than the conquest of them by reason and grace), but he was not at leisure now to hearken to his advice. "Child, child," said he, "do not go about impossibilities. Had it been any other of my children, I could have borne it with patience; but my little prattler, the darling and comfort of my old age — the little wretch to be snatched out of life just at his entrance into it; the

sweetest, best-tempered boy, who never did a thing to offend
me. It was but this morning I gave him his first lesson in *Quæ
Genus*. This was the very book he learnt; poor child! it is of no
further use to thee now. He would have made the best scholar,
and have been an ornament to the Church; — such parts and
such goodness never met in one so young." "And the handsomest
lad too," says Mrs. Adams, recovering from a swoon in Fanny's
arms. — "My poor Jacky, shall I never see thee more?" cries the
parson. — "Yes, surely," says Joseph, "and in a better place; you
will meet again, never to part more." — I believe the parson did
not hear these words, for he paid little regard to them, but went
on lamenting, whilst the tears trickled down into his bosom. At
last he cried out, "Where is my little darling?" and was sallying
out, when, to his great surprise and joy, in which I hope the
reader will sympathize, he met his son in a wet condition indeed,
but alive and running towards him. The person who brought
the news of his misfortune had been a little too eager, as people
sometimes are, from, I believe, no very good principle, to relate
ill news; and, having seen him fall into the river, instead of
running to his assistance, directly ran to acquaint his father of
a fate which he had concluded to be inevitable, but whence the
child was relieved by the same poor pedlar who had relieved
his father before from a less distress. The parson's joy was now
as extravagant as his grief had been before; he kissed and embraced his son a thousand times, and danced about the room
like one frantic; but as soon as he discovered the face of his old
friend the pedlar, and heard the fresh obligation he had to him,
what were his sensations? not those which two courtiers feel in
one another's embraces; not those with which a great man
receives the vile, treacherous engines of his wicked purposes; not
those with which a worthless younger brother wishes his elder
joy of a son, or a man congratulates his rival on his obtaining a
mistress, a place, or an honour. — No, reader, he felt the ebulli-
tion, the overflowings of a full, honest, open heart, towards the
person who had conferred a real obligation, and of which, if
thou canst not conceive an idea within, I will not vainly endeavour to assist thee.

When these tumults were over, the parson, taking Joseph
aside, proceeded thus — "No, Joseph, do not give too much way
to thy passions, if thou dost expect happiness." — The patience
of Joseph, nor perhaps of Job, could bear no longer; he interrupted the parson, saying, "It was easier to give advice than to

take it; nor did he perceive he could so entirely conquer himself, when he apprehended he had lost his son, or when he found him recovered." — "Boy," replied Adams, raising his voice, "it doth not become green heads to advise grey hairs. — Thou art ignorant of the tenderness of fatherly affection; when thou art a father, thou wilt be capable then only of knowing what a father can feel. No man is obliged to impossibilities; and the loss of a child is one of those great trials where our grief may be allowed to become immoderate." "Well, sir," cries Joseph, "and if I love a mistress as well as you your child, surely her loss would grieve me equally." "Yes, but such love is foolishness, and wrong in itself, and ought to be conquered," answered Adams; "it savours too much of the flesh." "Sure, sir," says Joseph, "it is not sinful to love my wife, no, not even to doat on her to distraction!" "Indeed but it is," says Adams. "Every man ought to love his wife, no doubt; we are commanded so to do; but we ought to love her with moderation and discretion." — "I am afraid I shall be guilty of some sin, in spite of all my endeavours," says Joseph; "for I shall love without any moderation, I am sure." — "You talk foolishly and childishly," cries Adams. "Indeed," says Mrs. Adams, who had listened to the latter part of their conversation, "you talk more foolishly yourself. I hope, my dear, you will never preach any such doctrine as that husbands can love their wives too well. If I knew you had such a sermon in the house, I am sure I would burn it; and I declare, if I had not been convinced you had loved me as well as you could, I can answer for myself I should have hated and despised you. Marry come up! Fine doctrine, indeed! A wife hath a right to insist on her husband's loving her as much as ever he can; and he is a sinful villain who doth not. Doth he not promise to love her, and to comfort her, and to cherish her, and all that? I am sure I remember it all as well as if I had repeated it over but yesterday, and shall never forget it. Besides, I am certain you do not preach as you practise; for you have been a loving and a cherishing husband to me, that's the truth on't; and why you should endeavour to put such wicked nonsense into this young man's head, I cannot devise. Don't hearken to him, Mr. Joseph; be as good a husband as you are able, and love your wife with all your body and soul too." Here a violent rap at the door put an end to their discourse, and produced a scene which the reader will find in the next chapter.

CHAPTER IX.

A visit which the good Lady Booby and her polite friend paid to the parson.

THE Lady Booby had no sooner had an account from the gentleman of his meeting a wonderful beauty near her house, and perceived the raptures with which he spoke of her, than, immediately concluding it must be Fanny, she began to meditate a design of bringing them better acquainted; and to entertain hopes that the fine clothes, presents, and promises of this youth, would prevail on her to abandon Joseph: she therefore proposed to her company a walk in the fields before dinner, when she led them towards Mr. Adams's house; and, as she approached it, told them if they pleased she would divert them with one of the most ridiculous sights they had ever seen, which was an old foolish parson, who, she said laughing, kept a wife and six brats on a salary of about twenty pounds a year; adding, that there was not such another ragged family in the parish. They all readily agreed to this visit, and arrived whilst Mrs. Adams was declaiming as in the last chapter. Beau Didapper, which was the name of the young gentleman we have seen riding towards Lady Booby's, with his cane mimicked the rap of a London footman at the door. The people within, namely, Adams, his wife and three children, Joseph, Fanny, and the pedlar, were all thrown into confusion by this knock; but Adams went directly to the door, which being opened, the Lady Booby and her company walked in, and were received by the parson with about two hundred bows; and by his wife with as many curtsies; the latter telling the lady, "She was ashamed to be seen in such a pickle, and that her house was in such a litter; but that if she had expected such an honour from her ladyship, she should have found her in a better manner." The parson made no apologies, though he was in his half-cassock and a flannel night-cap. He said, "They were heartily welcome to his poor cottage," and turning to Mr. Didapper, cried out, *"Non mea renidet in domo lacunar."* The beau answered, "He did not understand Welsh"; at which the parson stared, and made no reply.

Mr. Didapper, or Beau Didapper, was a young gentleman of about four foot five inches in height. He wore his own hair,

though the scarcity of it might have given him sufficient excuse
for a periwig. His face was thin and pale; the shape of his
body and legs none of the best, for he had very narrow shoulders,
and no calf; and his gait might more properly be called hopping
than walking. The qualifications of his mind were well adapted
to his person. We shall handle them first negatively. He was
not entirely ignorant; for he could talk a little French, and sing
two or three Italian songs: he had lived too much in the world
to be bashful, and too much at court to be proud: he seemed
not much inclined to avarice; for he was profuse in his expenses:
nor had he all the features of prodigality; for he never gave a
shilling: — no hater of women; for he always dangled after them;
yet so little subject to lust, that he had, among those who knew
him best, the character of great moderation in his pleasures. No
drinker of wine; nor so addicted to passion but that a hot word
or two from an adversary made him immediately cool.

Now, to give him only a dash or two on the affirmative side:
"Though he was born to an immense fortune, he chose, for the
pitiful and dirty consideration of a place of little consequence,
to depend entirely on the will of a fellow whom they call a great
man; who treated him with the utmost disrespect, and exacted
of him a plenary obedience to his commands; which he implicitly
submitted to, at the expense of his conscience, his honour, and
of his country, in which he had himself so very large a share."
And to finish his character: "As he was entirely well satisfied
with his own person and parts, so he was very apt to ridicule
and laugh at any imperfection in another." Such was the little
person, or rather thing, that hopped after Lady Booby into
Mr. Adams's kitchen.

The parson and his company retreated from the chimney-
side, where they had been seated, to give room to the lady and
hers. Instead of returning any of the curtsies or extraordinary
civility of Mrs. Adams, the lady, turning to Mr. Booby, cried
out, *"Quelle Bête! Quel Animal!"* And presently after discovering Fanny (for she did not need the circumstance of her
standing by Joseph to assure the identity of her person), she
asked the beau, "Whether he did not think her a pretty girl?"
— "Begad, madam," answered he, " 'tis the very same I met."
"I did not imagine," replied the lady, "you had so good a
taste." "Because I never liked you, I warrant," cries the beau.
"Ridiculous!" said she, "you know you was always my aversion."

"I would never mention aversion," answered the beau, "with that face;* dear Lady Booby, wash your face before you mention aversion, I beseech you." He then laughed, and turned about to coquet it with Fanny.

Mrs. Adams had been all this time begging and praying the ladies to sit down, a favour which she at last obtained. The little boy to whom the accident had happened, still keeping his place by the fire, was chid by his mother for not being more mannerly: but Lady Booby took his part, and, commending his beauty, told the parson he was his very picture. She then, seeing a book in his hand, asked, "if he could read?" "Yes," cried Adams, "a little Latin, madam: he is just got into *Quæ Genus.*" "A fig for *quere genius!*" answered she, "let me hear him read a little English." — "*Lege*, Dick, *lege*," said Adams; but the boy made no answer, till he saw the parson knit his brows; and then cried, "I don't understand you, father." "How, boy!" says Adams, "what doth *lego* make in the imperative mood? *Legito*, doth it not?" "Yes," answered Dick. — "And what besides?" says the father. "*Lege*," quoth the son, after some hesitation. "A good boy," says the father: "and now, child, what is the English of *lego?*" — To which the boy, after long puzzling, answered, he could not tell. "How!" cries Adams, in a passion, — "what, hath the water washed away your learning? Why, what is Latin for the English verb *read?* Consider before you speak." — The child considered some time, and then the parson cried twice or thrice, "Le —, Le —." Dick answered, "*Lego.*" — "Very well; — and then, what is the English," says the parson, "of the verb *lego?*" — "To read," cried Dick. — "Very well," said the parson; "a good boy: you can do well, if you will take pains. — I assure your ladyship he is not much above eight years old, and is out of his *Propria quæ Maribus* already. — Come, Dick, read to her ladyship"; — which she again desiring, in order to give the beau time and opportunity with Fanny, Dick began as in the following chapter.

* Lest this should appear unnatural to some readers, we think proper to acquaint them, that it is taken *verbatim* from very polite conversation. — F.

CHAPTER X.

The History of two Friends, which may afford an useful lesson to all those persons who happen to take up their residence in married families.

"LEONARD and Paul were two friends." — "Pronounce it *Lennard,* child," cried the parson. — "Pray, Mr. Adams," says Lady Booby, "let your son read without interruption." Dick then proceeded. "Lennard and Paul were two friends, who, having been educated together at the same school, commenced a friendship which they preserved a long time for each other. It was so deeply fixed in both their minds, that a long absence, during which they had maintained no correspondence, did not eradicate nor lessen it: but it revived in all its force at their first meeting, which was not till after fifteen years' absence, most of which time Lennard had spent in the East Indi-es." — "Pronounce it short, *Indies,*" says Adams. — "Pray, sir, be quiet," says the lady. — The boy repeated — "in the East Indies, whilst Paul had served his king and country in the army. In which different services, they had found such different success, that Lennard was now married, and retired with a fortune of thirty thousand pound; and Paul was arrived to the degree of a lieutenant of foot; and was not worth a single shilling.

"The regiment in which Paul was stationed happened to be ordered into quarters within a small distance from the estate which Lennard had purchased, and where he was settled. This latter, who was now become a country gentleman, and a justice of peace, came to attend the quarter-sessions in the town where his old friend was quartered, soon after his arrival. Some affair in which a soldier was concerned occasioned Paul to attend the justices. Manhood, and time, and the change of climate, had so much altered Lennard, that Paul did not immediately recollect the features of his old acquaintance; but it was otherwise with Lennard. He knew Paul the moment he saw him; nor could he contain himself from quitting the bench, and running hastily to embrace him. Paul stood at first a little surprised; but had soon sufficient information from his friend, whom he no sooner remembered than he returned his embrace with a passion which made many of the spectators laugh, and gave to some few a much higher and more agreeable sensation.

"Not to detain the reader with minute circumstances, Lennard insisted on his friend's returning with him to his house that evening; which request was complied with, and leave for a month's absence for Paul obtained of the commanding officer.

"If it was possible for any circumstance to give any addition to the happiness which Paul proposed in this visit, he received that additional pleasure by finding, on his arrival at his friend's house, that his lady was an old acquaintance which he had formerly contracted at his quarters, and who had always appeared to be of a most agreeable temper: a character she had ever maintained among her intimates, being of that number, every individual of which is called quite the best sort of woman in the world.

"But, good as this lady was, she was still a woman; that is to say, an angel, and not an angel." — "You must mistake, child," cries the parson, "for you read nonsense." "It is so in the book," answered the son. Mr. Adams was then silenced by authority, and Dick proceeded. — "For though her person was of that kind to which men attribute the name of angel, yet in her mind she was perfectly woman. Of which a great degree of obstinacy gave the most remarkable, and perhaps most pernicious, instance.

"A day or two passed after Paul's arrival before any instances of this appeared; but it was impossible to conceal it long. Both she and her husband soon lost all apprehension from their friend's presence, and fell to their disputes with as much vigour as ever. These were still pursued with the utmost ardour and eagerness, however trifling the causes were whence they first arose. Nay, however incredible it may seem, the little consequence of the matter in debate was frequently given as a reason for the fierceness of the contention, as thus: 'If you loved me, sure you would never dispute with me such a trifle as this.' The answer to which is very obvious; for the argument would hold equally on both sides, and was constantly retorted with some addition, as — 'I am sure I have much more reason to say so, who am in the right.' During all these disputes, Paul always kept strict silence, and preserved an even countenance, without showing the least visible inclination to either party. One day, however, when madam had left the room in a violent fury, Lennard could not refrain from referring his cause to his friend. Was ever anything so unreasonble, says he, as this woman? What shall I do with her? I doat on her to distraction; nor have I any cause to complain of, more than this obstinacy in her temper; whatever she asserts, she will maintain against all the reason and conviction in the world. Pray give me your advice. — First, says Paul, I will give my opinion, which is, flatly, that you are in the wrong; for, supposing she is in the wrong, was the subject of your contention any ways material? What signified it whether you was married in a red or a yellow waistcoat? for that was your dispute. Now, suppose she was mistaken: as you love her you say so tenderly, and I believe she deserves it, would it not have been wiser to have yielded, though you certainly knew yourself in the right, than to give either her or yourself any uneasiness? For my own part, if ever I marry, I am resolved to enter into an agreement with my wife, that in all disputes (especially about trifles) that party who is most convinced they are right shall always surrender the victory: by which means we shall both be forward to give up the cause. I own, said Lennard, my dear friend, shaking him by the hand, there is great truth and reason in what you say; and I will for the future endeavour to follow your advice. They soon after broke up the conversation, and Lennard, going to his wife, asked her pardon, and told her his friend had convinced him he had been in the wrong. She immediately began a vast encomium on Paul, in which he seconded her, and both agreed he was the worthiest and wisest man upon earth. When next they met, which was at supper, though she had promised not to mention what her husband told her, she could not forbear casting the kindest and most affectionate looks on Paul, and asked him with the sweetest voice, whether she should help him to some potted woodcock? — Potted partridge, my dear, you mean, says the husband. My dear, says she, I ask your friend if he will eat any potted woodcock; and I am sure I must know, who potted it. I think I should know too, who shot them, replied the husband, and I am convinced that I have not seen a woodcock this year; however, though I know I am in the right, I submit, and the potted partridge is potted woodcock if you desire to have it so. It is equal to me, says she, whether it is one or the other; but you would persuade one out of one's senses; to be sure, you are always in the right in your own opinion; but your friend, I believe, knows which he is eating. Paul answered nothing, and the dispute continued, as usual, the greatest part of the evening. The next morning the lady, accidentally meeting Paul, and being convinced he was her friend, and of her side, accosted him thus: I am certain, sir, you have long since wondered at the unreasonableness of my husband. He

is indeed, in other respects, a good sort of man; but so positive,
that no woman but one of my complying temper could possibly
live with him. Why, last night, now, was ever any creature so
unreasonable? — I am certain you must condemn him. — Pray,
answer me, was he not in the wrong? Paul, after a short silence,
spoke as follows: I am sorry, madam, that, as good manners
obliges me to answer against my will, so an adherence to truth
forces me to declare myself of a different opinion. To be plain
and honest, you was entirely in the wrong; the cause I own not
worth disputing, but the bird was undoubtedly a partridge. O
sir! replied the lady, I cannot possibly help your taste. — Madam,
returned Paul, that is very little material; for, had it been otherwise, a husband might have expected submission. — Indeed! sir,
says she, I assure you! — Yes, madam, cried he, he might, from
a person of your excellent understanding; and pardon me for
saying, such a condescension would have shown a superiority of
sense even to your husband himself. — But, dear sir, said she,
why should I submit, when I am in the right? — For that very
reason, answered he; it would be the greatest instance of
affection imaginable: for can anything be a greater object of our
compassion than a person we love in the wrong? Ay, but I
should endeavour, said she, to set him right. Pardon me, madam,
answered Paul; I will apply to your own experience if you ever
found your arguments had that effect. The more our judgments
err, the less we are willing to own it: for my own part, I have
always observed the persons who maintain the worst side in any
contest are the warmest. Why, says she, I must confess there is
truth in what you say, and I will endeavour to practise it. The
husband then coming in, Paul departed. And Lennard, approaching his wife with an air of good humour, told her he was
sorry for their foolish dispute the last night; but he was now
convinced of his error. She answered, smiling, she believed she
owed his condescension to his complacence; that she was ashamed
to think a word had passed on so silly an occasion, especially as
she was satisfied she had been mistaken. A little contention
followed, but with the utmost good-will to each other, and was
concluded by her asserting that Paul had thoroughly convinced
her she had been in the wrong. Upon which they both united
in the praises of their common friend.

"Paul now passed his time with great satisfaction, these disputes being much less frequent, as well as shorter than usual;
but the devil, or some unlucky accident in which perhaps the

devil had no hand, shortly put an end to his happiness. He was now eternally the private referee of every difference; in which, after having perfectly, as he thought, established the doctrine of submission, he never scrupled to assure both privately that they were in the right in every argument, as before he had followed the contrary method. One day a violent litigation happened in his absence, and both parties agreed to refer it to his decision. The husband professing himself sure the decision would be in his favour; the wife answered, he might be mistaken; for she believed his friend was convinced how seldom she was to blame — and that if he knew all —— The husband replied — My dear, I have no desire of any retrospect; but I believe, if you knew all too, you would not imagine my friend so entirely on your side. Nay, says she, since you provoke me, I will mention one instance. You may remember our dispute about sending Jacky to school in cold weather, which point I gave up to you from mere compassion, knowing myself to be in the right; and Paul himself told me afterwards he thought me so. My dear, replied the husband, I will not scruple your veracity; but I assure you solemnly, on my applying to him, he gave it absolutely on my side, and said he would have acted in the same manner. They then proceeded to produce numberless other instances, in all which Paul had, on vows of secrecy, given his opinion on both sides. In the conclusion, both believing each other, they fell severely on the treachery of Paul, and agreed that he had been the occasion of almost every dispute which had fallen out between them. They then became extremely loving, and so full of condescension on both sides, that they vied with each other in censuring their own conduct, and jointly vented their indignation on Paul, whom the wife, fearing a bloody consequence, earnestly entreated her husband to suffer quietly to depart the next day, which was the time fixed for his return to quarters, and then drop his acquaintance.

"However ungenerous this behaviour in Lennard may be esteemed, his wife obtained a promise from him (though with difficulty) to follow her advice; but they both expressed such unusual coldness that day to Paul, that he, who was quick of apprehension, taking Lennard aside, pressed him so home, that he at last discovered the secret. Paul acknowledged the truth, but told him the design with which he had done it. — To which the other answered, he would have acted more friendly to have let him into the whole design; for that he might have assured

himself of his secrecy. Paul replied, with some indignation, he
had given him a sufficient proof how capable he was of concealing a secret from his wife. Lennard returned with some
warmth — he had more reason to upbraid him, for that he had
caused most of the quarrels between them by his strange conduct, and might (if they had not discovered the affair to each
other) have been the occasion of their separation. Paul then
said" —— But something now happened which put a stop to
Dick's reading, and of which we shall treat in the next chapter.

CHAPTER XI.

In which the history is continued

JOSEPH ANDREWS had borne with great uneasiness the impertinence of Beau Didapper to Fanny, who had been talking
pretty freely to her, and offering her settlements; but the
respect to the company had restrained him from interfering
whilst the beau confined himself to the use of his tongue only;
but the said beau, watching an opportunity whilst the ladies'
eyes were disposed another way, offered a rudeness to her
with his hands; which Joseph no sooner perceived than he
presented him with so sound a box on the ear, that it conveyed
him several paces from where he stood. The ladies immediately
screamed out, rose from their chairs; and the beau, as soon as he
recovered himself, drew his hanger: which Adams observing,
snatched up the lid of a pot in his left hand, and, covering himself with it as with a shield, without any weapon of offence in
his other hand, stept in before Joseph, and exposed himself to the
enraged beau, who threatened such perdition and destruction,
that it frighted the women, who were all got in a huddle together,
out of their wits, even to hear his denunciations of vengeance.
Joseph was of a different complexion, and begged Adams to let
his rival come on; for he had a good cudgel in his hand, and
did not fear him. Fanny now fainted into Mrs. Adams's arms,
and the whole room was in confusion, when Mr. Booby, passing
by Adams, who lay snug under the pot-lid, came up to Didapper,
and insisted on his sheathing his hanger, promising he should
have satisfaction; which Joseph declared he would give him,
and fight him at any weapon whatever. The beau now sheathed

his hanger, and taking out a pocket-glass, and vowing vengeance all the time, re-adjusted his hair; the parson deposited his shield; and Joseph, running to Fanny, soon brought her back to life. Lady Booby chid Joseph for his insult on Didapper; but he answered, he would have attacked an army in the same cause. "What cause?" said the lady. "Madam," answered Joseph, "he was rude to that young woman." — "What," says the lady, "I suppose he would have kissed the wench; and is a gentleman to be struck for such an offer? I must tell you, Joseph, these airs do not become you." — "Madam," said Mr. Booby, "I saw the whole affair, and I do not commend my brother; for I cannot perceive why he should take upon him to be this girl's champion." — "I can commend him," says Adams: "he is a brave lad; and it becomes any man to be the champion of the innocent; and he must be the basest coward who would not vindicate a woman with whom he is on the brink of marriage." — "Sir," says Mr. Booby, "my brother is not a proper match for such a young woman as this." — "No," says Lady Booby, "nor do you, Mr. Adams, act in your proper character by encouraging any such doings; and I am very much surprised you should concern yourself in it. I think your wife and family your properer care." — "Indeed, madam, your ladyship says very true," answered Mrs. Adams: "he talks a pack of nonsense, that the whole parish are his children. I am sure I don't understand what he means by it; it would make some women suspect he had gone astray, but I acquit him of that; I can read Scripture as well as he, and I never found that the parson was obliged to provide for other folks' children; and besides, he is but a poor curate, and hath little enough, as your ladyship knows, for me and mine." — "You say very well, Mrs. Adams," quoth the Lady Booby, who had not spoke a word to her before; "you seem to be a very sensible woman; and I assure you, your husband is acting a very foolish part, and opposing his own interest, seeing my nephew is violently set against this match: and indeed I can't blame him; it is by no means one suitable to our family." In this manner the lady proceeded with Mrs. Adams, whilst the beau hopped about the room, shaking his head, partly from pain, and partly from anger; and Pamela was chiding Fanny for her assurance in aiming at such a match as her brother. — Poor Fanny answered only with her tears, which had long since begun to wet her handkerchief; which Joseph perceiving, took her by the arm, and, wrapping it in his, carried her off, swearing he would own no relation to anyone who was an

enemy to her he loved more than all the world. He went out with
Fanny under his left arm, brandishing a cudgel in his right, and
neither Mr. Booby nor the beau thought proper to oppose him.
Lady Booby and her company made a very short stay behind
him; for the lady's bell now summoned them to dress; for which
they had just time before dinner.

Adams seemed now very much dejected, which his wife perceiving, began to apply some matrimonial balsam. She told
him he had reason to be concerned, for that he had probably
ruined his family with his foolish tricks: but perhaps he was
grieved for the loss of his two children, Joseph and Fanny.
His eldest daughter went on: — "Indeed, father, it is very hard
to bring strangers here to eat your children's bread out of their
mouths. — You have kept them ever since they came home; and,
for anything I see to the contrary, may keep them a month
longer: are you obliged to give her meat, tho'f she was never so
handsome? But I don't see she is so much handsomer than other
people. If people were to be kept for their beauty, she would
scarce fare better than her neighbours, I believe. — As for Mr.
Joseph, I have nothing to say; he is a young man of honest
principles, and will pay some time or other for what he hath:
but for the girl — why doth she not return to her place she ran
away from? I would not give such a vagabond slut a halfpenny,
though I had a million of money; no, though she was starving."
"Indeed but I would," cries little Dick; "and, father, rather than
poor Fanny shall be starved, I will give her all this bread and
cheese." — (*offering what he held in his hand*). Adams smiled
on the boy, and told him he rejoiced to see he was a Christian;
and that if he had a halfpenny in his pocket, he would have
given it him; telling him it was his duty to look upon all his
neighbours as his brothers and sisters, and love them accordingly.
"Yes, papa," says he, "I love her better than my sisters: for she
is handsomer than any of them." "Is she so, saucebox?" says the
sister, giving him a box on the ear; which the father would
probably have resented, had not Joseph, Fanny, and the pedlar
at that instant returned together. — Adams bid his wife prepare
some food for their dinner; she said, "Truly she could not, she
had something else to do." Adams rebuked her for disputing his
commands, and quoted many texts of Scripture to prove, "That
the husband is the head of the wife, and she is to submit and
obey." The wife answered, "It was blasphemy to talk Scripture
out of church; that such things were very proper to be said in

the pulpit, but that it was profane to talk them in common discourse." Joseph told Mr. Adams, "He was not come with any design to give him or Mrs. Adams any trouble; but to desire the favour of all their company to the George (an ale-house in the parish), where he had bespoke a piece of bacon and greens for their dinner." Mrs. Adams, who was a very good sort of woman, only rather too strict in œconomics, readily accepted this invitation, as did the parson himself by her example; and away they all walked together, not omitting little Dick, to whom Joseph gave a shilling when he heard of his intended liberality to Fanny.

CHAPTER XII.

Where the good-natured reader will see something which will give him no great pleasure.

THE pedlar had been very inquisitive from the time he had first heard that the great house in this parish belonged to the Lady Booby, and had learnt that she was the widow of Sir Thomas, and that Sir Thomas had bought Fanny, at about the age of three or four years, of a travelling woman; and, now their homely but hearty meal was ended, he told Fanny he believed he could acquaint her with her parents. The whole company, especially she herself, started at this offer of the pedlar's. — He then proceeded thus, while they all lent their strictest attention: "Though I am now contented with this humble way of getting my livelihood, I was formerly a gentleman; for so all those of my profession are called. In a word, I was a drummer in an Irish regiment of foot. Whilst I was in this honourable station, I attended an officer of our regiment into England a-recruiting. In our march from Bristol to Froome (for since the decay of the woolen trade, the clothing towns have furnished the army with a great number of recruits) we overtook on the road a woman, who seemed to be about thirty years old or thereabouts, not very handsome, but well enough for a soldier. As we came up to her, she mended her pace, and falling into discourse with our ladies (for every man of the party, namely, a serjeant, two private men, and a drum, were provided with their woman except myself), she continued to travel on with us. I, perceiving she must fall to my lot, advanced presently to her, made love to her in our military

way, and quickly succeeded to my wishes. We struck a bargain
within a mile, and lived together as man and wife to her dying
day." — "I suppose," says Adams, interrupting him, "you were
married with a licence: for I don't see how you could contrive
to have the banns published while you were marching from
place to place." — "No, sir," said the pedlar, "we took a licence
to go to bed together without any banns." — "Ay! ay!" said
the parson; "*ex necessitate*, a licence may be allowable enough;
but surely, surely, the other is the more regular and eligible
way." — The pedlar proceeded thus: "She returned with me to
our regiment, and removed with us from quarters to quarters,
till at last, whilst we lay at Galloway, she fell ill of a fever, and
died. When she was on her death-bed she called me to her,
and, crying bitterly, declared she could not depart this world
without discovering a secret to me, which she said was the only
sin which sat heavy on her heart. She said she had formerly
travelled in a company of gipsies, who had made a practice of
stealing away children; that for her own part, she had been only
once guilty of the crime; which she said she lamented more than
all the rest of her sins, since probably it might have occasioned
the death of the parents: for, added she, it is almost impossible
to describe the beauty of the young creature, which was about
a year and a half old when I kidnapped it. We kept her (for she
was a girl) above two years in our company, when I sold her
myself for three guineas to Sir Thomas Booby in Somersetshire.
Now, you know whether there are any more of that name in
this county." — "Yes," says Adams, "there are several Boobys
who are squires, but I believe no baronet now alive; besides, it
answers so exactly in every point, there is no room for doubt; but
you have forgot to tell us the parents from whom the child was
stolen." — "Their name," answered the pedlar, "was Andrews.
They lived about thirty miles from the squire; and she told me
that I might be sure to find them out by one circumstance; for
that they had a daughter of a very strange name, Paměla, or
Paměla; some pronounced it one way, and some the other."
Fanny, who had changed colour at the first mention of the name,
now fainted away; Joseph turned pale, and poor Dicky began to
roar; the parson fell on his knees, and ejaculated many thanksgivings that this discovery had been made before the dreadful
sin of incest was committed; and the pedlar was struck with
amazement, not being able to account for all this confusion; the
cause of which was presently opened by the parson's daughter,

who was the only unconcerned person (for the mother was chafing Fanny's temples, and taking the utmost care of her): and, indeed, Fanny was the only creature whom the daughter would not have pitied in her situation; wherein, though we compassionate her ourselves, we shall leave her for a little while, and pay a short visit to Lady Booby.

CHAPTER XIII.

The history, returning to the Lady Booby, gives some account of the terrible conflict in her breast between love and pride; with what happened on the present discovery.

THE lady sat down with her company to dinner, but eat nothing. As soon as her cloth was removed, she whispered Pamela that she was taken a little ill, and desired her to entertain her husband and Beau Didapper. She then went up into her chamber, sent for Slipslop, threw herself on the bed, in the agonies of love, rage, and despair; nor could she conceal these boiling passions longer without bursting. Slipslop now approached her bed, and asked how her ladyship did; but, instead of revealing her disorder, as she intended, she entered into a long encomium on the beauty and virtues of Joseph Andrews; ending at last with expressing her concern that so much tenderness should be thrown away on so despicable an object as Fanny. Slipslop, well knowing how to humour her mistress's frenzy, proceeded to repeat, with exaggeration, if possible, all her mistress had said, and concluded with a wish that Joseph had been a gentleman, and that she could see her lady in the arms of such a husband. The lady then started from the bed, and, taking a turn or two 'cross the room, cried out, with a deep sigh, — "Sure he would make any woman happy!" — "Your ladyship," says she, "would be the happiest woman in the world with him. — A fig for custom and nonsense! What *vails* what people say? Shall I be afraid of eating sweetmeats because people may say I have a sweet tooth? If I had a mind to marry a man, all the world should not hinder me. Your ladyship hath no parents to *tutelar* your *infections;* besides, he is of your ladyship's family now, and as good a gentleman as any in the country; and why should not a woman follow her mind as well as man? Why should not your ladyship marry the brother, as well as your nephew the sister? I am sure, if it was a *fragrant* crime, I would not persuade your ladyship to it." — "But, dear Slipslop," answered the lady, "if I could prevail on myself to commit such a weakness, there is that cursed Fanny in the way, whom the idiot — O how I hate and despise him!" — "She! a little ugly minx," cries Slipslop; "leave her to me. — I suppose your ladyship hath heard of Joseph's *fitting* with one of Mr. Didapper's servants about her; and his master hath ordered them to carry her away by force this evening. I'll take care they shall not want assistance. I was talking with this gentleman, who was below just when your ladyship sent for me." — "Go back," says the Lady Booby, "this instant; for I expect Mr. Didapper will soon be going. Do all you can; for I am resolved this wench shall not be in our family; I will endeavour to return to the company; but let me know as soon as she is carried off." Slipslop went away; and her mistress began to arraign her own conduct in the following manner:

"What am I doing? How do I suffer this passion to creep imperceptibly upon me? How many days are passed since I could have submitted to ask myself the question? — Marry a footman! Distraction! Can I afterwards bear the eyes of my acquaintance? But I can retire from them; retire with one in whom I propose more happiness than the world without him can give me! Retire — to feed continually on beauties which my inflamed imagination sickens with eagerly gazing on; to satisfy every appetite, every desire, with their utmost wish. — Ha! and do I doat thus on a footman! I despise, I detest my passion. — Yet why? Is he not generous, gentle, kind? — Kind to whom? to the meanest wretch, a creature below my consideration. Doth he not? — Yes, he doth prefer her; curse his beauties, and the little low heart that possesses them; which can basely descend to this despicable wench, and be ungratefully deaf to all the honours I do him. — And can I then love this monster? No, I will tear his image from my bosom, tread on him, spurn him. I will have those pitiful charms, which now I despise, mangled in my sight; for I will not suffer the little jade I hate to riot in the beauties I contemn. No, though I despise him myself; though I would spurn him from my feet, was he to languish at them, no other should taste the happiness I scorn. Why do I say happiness? To me it would be misery. — To sacrifice my reputation, my character, my rank in life, to the indulgence of a mean and a vile appetite. — How I detest the thought! How much more exquisite is the pleasure resulting from the reflection of virtue and prudence than the faint relish of what flows from vice and folly! Whither did I suffer this improper, this mad passion to hurry me, only by neglecting to summon the aids of reason to my assistance? Reason, which hath now set before me my desires in their proper colours, and immediately helped me to expel them. Yes, I thank Heaven and my pride, I have now perfectly conquered this unworthy passion; and if there was no obstacle in its way, my pride would disdain any pleasures which could be the consequence of so base, so mean, so vulgar——" Slipslop returned at this instant in a violent hurry, and with the utmost eagerness, cried out, — "O, madam! I have strange news. Tom the footman is just come from the George; where it seems Joseph and the rest of them are a-*jinketting;* and he says there is a strange man who hath discovered that Fanny and Joseph are brother and sister." — "How, Slipslop!" cries the lady, in a surprise. — "I had not time, madam," cries Slipslop, "to inquire about *particles,* but Tom says it is most certainly true."

This unexpected account entirely obliterated all those admirable reflections which the supreme power of reason had so wisely made just before. In short, when despair, which had more share in producing the resolutions of hatred we have seen taken, began to retreat, the lady hesitated a moment, and then, forgetting all the purport of her soliloquy, dismissed her woman again, with orders to bid Tom attend her in the parlour, where she now hastened to acquaint Pamela with the news. Pamela said she could not believe it; for she had never heard that her mother had lost any child, or that she had ever had any more than Joseph and herself. The lady flew into a violent rage with her, and talked of upstarts and disowning relations who had so lately been on a level with her. Pamela made no answer; but her husband, taking up her cause, severely reprimanded his aunt for her behaviour to his wife: he told her, if it had been earlier in the evening she should not have stayed a moment longer in her house; that he was convinced, if this young woman could be proved her sister, she would readily embrace her as such; and he himself would do the same: he then desired the fellow might be sent for, and the young woman with him, which Lady Booby immediately ordered; and, thinking proper to make some apology to Pamela for what she had said, it was readily accepted, and all things reconciled.

The pedlar now attended, as did Fanny and Joseph, who would

not quit her; the parson likewise was induced, not only by curiosity, of which he had no small portion, but by his duty, as he apprehended it, to follow them: for he continued all the way to exhort them, who were now breaking their hearts, to offer up thanksgivings, and be joyful for so miraculous an escape.

When they arrived at Booby-Hall, they were presently called into the parlour, where the pedlar repeated the same story he had told before, and insisted on the truth of every circumstance; so that all who heard him were extremely well satisfied of the truth, except Pamela, who imagined, as she had never heard either of her parents mention such an accident, that it must be certainly false; and except the Lady Booby, who suspected the falsehood of the story from her ardent desire that it should be true; and Joseph, who feared its truth from his earnest wishes that it might prove false.

Mr. Booby now desired them all to suspend their curiosity and absolute belief or disbelief till the next morning, when he expected old Mr. Andrews and his wife to fetch himself and Pamela home in his coach, and then they might be certain of perfectly knowing the truth or falsehood of this relation; in which, he said, as there were many strong circumstances to induce their credit, so he could not perceive any interest the pedlar could have in inventing it, or in endeavouring to impose such a falsehood on them.

The Lady Booby, who was very little used to such company, entertained them all — *viz.* her nephew, his wife, her brother and sister, the beau, and the parson — with great good humour at her own table. As to the pedlar, she ordered him to be made as welcome as possible by her servants. All the company in the parlour, except the disappointed lovers, who sat sullen and silent, were full of mirth: for Mr. Booby had prevailed on Joseph to ask Mr. Didapper's pardon, with which he was perfectly satisfied. Many jokes passed between the beau and the parson, chiefly on each other's dress; these afforded much diversion to the company. Pamela chid her brother Joseph for the concern which he exprest at discovering a new sister. She said, if he loved Fanny as he ought, with a pure affection, he had no reason to lament being related to her. — Upon which Adams began to discourse on Platonic love; whence he made a quick transition to the joys in the next world, and concluded with strongly asserting that there was no such thing as pleasure in this. At which Pamela and her husband smiled on one another.

This happy pair proposing to retire (for no other person gave the least symptom of desiring rest), they all repaired to several beds provided for them in the same house; nor was Adams himself suffered to go home, it being a stormy night. Fanny indeed often begged she might go home with the parson; but her stay was so strongly insisted on, that she at last, by Joseph's advice, consented.

CHAPTER XIV.

Containing several curious night-adventures, in which Mr. Adams fell into many hair-breadth 'scapes, partly owing to his goodness, and partly to his inadvertency.

ABOUT an hour after they had all separated (it being now past three in the morning), Beau Didapper, whose passion for Fanny permitted him not to close his eyes, but had employed his imagination in contrivances how to satisfy his desires, at last hit on a method by which he hoped to effect it. He had ordered his servant to bring him word where Fanny lay, and had received his information; he therefore arose, put on his breeches and nightgown, and stole softly along the gallery which led to her apartment; and, being come to the door, as he imagined it, he opened it with the least noise possible, and entered the chamber. A savour now invaded his nostrils which he did not expect in the room of so sweet a young creature, and which might have probably had no good effect on a cooler lover. However, he groped out the bed with difficulty, for there was not a glimpse of light, and, opening the curtains, he whispered in Joseph's voice (for he was an excellent mimic), "Fanny, my angel, I am come to inform thee that I have discovered the falsehood of the story we last night heard. I am no longer thy brother, but thy lover; nor will I be delayed the enjoyment of thee one moment longer. You have sufficient assurances of my constancy not to doubt of my marrying you, and it would be want of love to deny me the possession of thy charms." — So saying, he disencumbered himself from the little clothes he had on, and, leaping into bed, embraced his angel, as he conceived her, with great rapture. If he was surprised at receiving no answer, he was no less pleased to find his hug returned with equal ardour. He remained not long in this sweet confusion; for both he and his paramour presently discovered their error. Indeed it was no other than the accomplished Slipslop whom he had engaged; but, though she immediately knew the person whom she had mistaken for Joseph, he was at a loss to guess at the representative of Fanny. He had so little seen or taken notice of this gentlewoman, that light itself would have afforded him no assistance in his conjecture. Beau Didapper no sooner had perceived his mistake than he attempted to escape from the bed with much greater haste than he had made to it; but the watchful Slipslop prevented him. For that prudent woman, being disappointed of those delicious offerings which her fancy had promised her pleasure, resolved to make an immediate sacrifice to her virtue. Indeed she wanted an opportunity to heal some wounds which her late conduct had, she feared, given her reputation; and, as she had a wonderful presence of mind, she conceived the person of the unfortunate beau to be luckily thrown in her way to restore her lady's opinion of her impregnable chastity. At that instant, therefore, when he offered to leap from the bed, she caught fast hold of his shirt, at the same time roaring out, "O thou villain! who hast attacked my chastity, and, I believe, ruined me in my sleep; I will swear a rape against thee, I will prosecute thee with the utmost vengeance." The beau attempted to get loose, but she held him fast, and when he struggled, she cried out, "Murther! murther! rape! robbery! ruin!" At which words, Parson Adams, who lay in the next chamber, wakeful, and meditating on the pedlar's discovery, jumped out of bed, and, without staying to put a rag of clothes on, hastened into the apartment whence the cries proceeded. He made directly to the bed in the dark, where, laying hold of the beau's skin (for Slipslop had tore his shirt almost off), and finding his skin extremely soft, and hearing him in a low voice begging Slipslop to let him go, he no longer doubted but this was the young woman in danger of ravishing, and immediately falling on the bed, and laying hold on Slipslop's chin, where he found a rough beard, his belief was confirmed; he therefore rescued the beau, who presently made his escape, and then, turning towards Slipslop, received such a cuff on his chops, that, his wrath kindling instantly, he offered to return the favour so stoutly, that had poor Slipslop received the fist, which in the dark passed by her, and fell on the pillow, she would most probably have given up the ghost. Adams, missing his blow, fell directly on Slipslop, who cuffed and scratched as well as she could; nor was he behindhand with her in his en-

deavours, but happily the darkness of the night befriended her. —
She then cried she was a woman; but Adams answered, she was
rather the devil, and if she was, he would grapple with him; and,
being again irritated by another stroke on his chops, he gave her
such a remembrance in the guts, that she began to roar loud
enough to be heard all over the house. Adams then, seizing her
by the hair (for her double-clout had fallen off in the scuffle),
pinned her head down to the bolster, and then both called for
lights together. The Lady Booby, who was as wakeful as any of
her guests, had been alarmed from the beginning; and, being a
woman of a bold spirit, she slipt on a nightgown, petticoat, and
slippers, and taking a candle, which always burnt in her chamber,
in her hand, she walked undauntedly to Slipslop's room; where
she entered just at the instant as Adams had discovered, by the
two mountains which Slipslop carried before her, that he was
concerned with a female. He then concluded her to be a witch,
and said he fancied those breasts gave suck to a legion of devils.
Slipslop, seeing Lady Booby enter the room, cried, "Help! or I
am ravished," with a most audible voice; and Adams, perceiving
the light, turned hastily, and saw the lady (as she did him) just
as she came to the feet of the bed; nor did her modesty, when
she found the naked condition of Adams, suffer her to approach
farther. — She then began to revile the parson as the wickedest
of all men, and particularly railed at his impudence in choosing
her house for the scene of his debaucheries, and her own woman
for the object of his bestiality. Poor Adams had before discovered
the countenance of his bedfellow, and, now first recollecting he
was naked, he was no less confounded than Lady Booby herself,
and immediately whipt under the bed-clothes, whence the chaste
Slipslop endeavoured in vain to shut him out. Then putting forth
his head, on which, by way of ornament, he wore a flannel night-
cap, he protested his innocence, and asked ten thousand pardons
of Mrs. Slipslop for the blows he had struck her, vowing he had
mistaken her for a witch. Lady Booby then, casting her eyes on
the ground, observed something sparkle with great lustre, which,
when she had taken it up, appeared to be a very fine pair of
diamond buttons for the sleeves. A little farther she saw lie the
sleeve itself of a shirt with laced ruffles. "Heyday!" says she,
"what is the meaning of this?" — "O, madam," says Slipslop, "I
don't know what hath happened, I have been so terrified. Here
may have been a dozen men in the room." "To whom belongs
this laced shirt and jewels?" says the lady. — "Undoubtedly,"

cries the parson, "to the young gentleman whom I mistook for
a woman on coming into the room, whence proceeded all the
subsequent mistakes; for if I had suspected him for a man, I
would have seized him, had he been another Hercules, though
indeed he seems rather to resemble Hylas." He then gave an
account of the reason of his rising from bed, and the rest, till the
lady came into the room; at which, and the figures of Slipslop and
her gallant, whose heads only were visible at the opposite corners
of the bed, she could not refrain from laughter; nor did Slipslop
persist in accusing the parson of any motions towards a rape.
The lady therefore desired him to return to his bed as soon as
she was departed, and then ordering Slipslop to rise and attend
her in her own room, she returned herself thither. When she was
gone, Adams renewed his petitions for pardon to Mrs. Slipslop,
who, with a most Christian temper, not only forgave, but began
to move with much courtesy towards him, which he taking as a
hint to be gone, immediately quitted the bed, and made the best
of his way towards his own; but unluckily, instead of turning
to the right, he turned to the left, and went to the apartment
where Fanny lay, who (as the reader may remember) had not
slept a wink the preceding night, and who was so hagged out
with what had happened to her in the day, that, notwithstanding
all thoughts of her Joseph, she was fallen into so profound a
sleep, that all the noise in the adjoining room had not been able
to disturb her. Adams groped out the bed, and, turning the
clothes down softly, a custom Mrs. Adams had long accustomed
him to, crept in, and deposited his carcase on the bed-post, a
place which that good woman had always assigned him.

As the cat or lap-dog of some lovely nymph, for whom ten
thousand lovers languish, lies quietly by the side of the charming
maid, and, ignorant of the scene of delight on which they repose,
meditates the future capture of a mouse, or surprisal of a plate
of bread and butter: so Adams lay by the side of Fanny, ignorant
of the paradise to which he was so near; nor could the emanation
of sweets which flowed from her breath overpower the fumes of
tobacco which played in the parson's nostrils. And now sleep
had not overtaken the good man, when Joseph, who had secretly
appointed Fanny to come to her at the break of day, rapped
softly at the chamber-door, which when he had repeated twice,
Adams cried, "Come in, whoever you are." Joseph thought he
had mistaken the door, though she had given him the most

exact directions; however, knowing his friend's voice, he opened
it, and saw some female vestments lying on a chair. Fanny
waking at the same instant, and stretching out her hand on
Adams's beard, she cried out, — "O heavens! where am I?"
"Bless me! where am I?" said the parson. Then Fanny screamed,
Adams leapt out of bed, and Joseph stood, as the tragedians
call it, like the "statue of Surprise." "How came she into my
room?" cried Adams. "How came you into hers?" cried Joseph,
in an astonishment. "I know nothing of the matter," answered
Adams, "but that she is a vestal for me. As I am a Christian, I
know not whether she is a man or woman. He is an infidel who
doth not believe in witchcraft. They as surely exist now as in the
days of Saul. My clothes are bewitched away too, and Fanny's
brought into their place." For he still insisted he was in his
own apartment; but Fanny denied it vehemently, and said his
attempting to persuade Joseph of such a falsehood convinced her
of his wicked designs. "How!" said Joseph in a rage, "hath he
offered any rudeness to you?" — She answered, she could not
accuse him of any more than villainously stealing to bed to her,
which she thought rudeness sufficient, and what no man would
do without a wicked intention.

Joseph's great opinion of Adams was not easily to be staggered,
and when he heard from Fanny that no harm had happened, he
grew a little cooler; yet still he was confounded, and, as he knew
the house, and that the women's apartments were on this side
Mrs. Slipslop's room, and the men's on the other, he was convinced that he was in Fanny's chamber. Assuring Adams therefore of this truth, he begged him to give some account how he
came there. Adams then, standing in his shirt, which did not
offend Fanny, as the curtains of the bed were drawn, related all
that had happened; and when he had ended, Joseph told him,
it was plain he had mistaken by turning to the right instead of
the left. "Odso!" cries Adams, "that's true: as sure as sixpence,
you have hit on the very thing." He then traversed the room,
rubbing his hands, and begged Fanny's pardon, assuring her he
did not know whether she was man or woman. That innocent
creature firmly believing all he said, told him she was no longer
angry, and begged Joseph to conduct him into his own apartment,
where he should stay himself till she had put her clothes on.
Joseph and Adams accordingly departed, and the latter soon was
convinced of the mistake he had committed; however, whilst he

was dressing himself, he often asserted he believed in the power of witchcraft notwithstanding, and did not see how a Christian could deny it.

CHAPTER XV.

The arrival of Gaffar and Gammar Andrews, with another person not much expected; and a perfect solution of the difficulties raised by the pedlar.

As soon as Fanny was drest, Joseph returned to her, and they had a long conversation together, the conclusion of which was, that, if they found themselves to be really brother and sister, they vowed a perpetual celibacy, and to live together all their days, and indulge a Platonic friendship for each other.

The company were all very merry at breakfast, and Joseph and Fanny rather more cheerful than the preceding night. The Lady Booby produced the diamond button, which the beau most readily owned, and alleged that he was very subject to walk in his sleep. Indeed, he was far from being ashamed of his amour, and rather endeavoured to insinuate that more than was really true had passed between him and the fair Slipslop.

Their tea was scarce over when news came of the arrival of old Mr. Andrews and his wife. They were immediately introduced, and kindly received by the Lady Booby, whose heart went now pit-a-pat, as did those of Joseph and Fanny. They felt perhaps little less anxiety in this interval than Œdipus himself, whilst his fate was revealing.

Mr. Booby first opened the cause by informing the old gentleman that he had a child in the company more than he knew of, and, taking Fanny by the hand, told him, this was that daughter of his who had been stolen away by gipsies in her infancy. Mr. Andrews, after expressing some astonishment, assured his honour that he had never lost a daughter by gipsies, nor ever had any other children than Joseph and Pamela. These words were a cordial to the two lovers; but had a different effect on Lady Booby. She ordered the pedlar to be called, who recounted his story as he had done before. — At the end of which, old Mrs. Andrews, running to Fanny, embraced her, crying out, "She is, she is my child!" The company were all amazed at this disagreement between the man and his wife; and the blood had now forsaken the cheeks of the lovers, when the old woman, turning to her husband, who was more surprised than all the rest, and having a little recovered her own spirits, delivered herself as follows: "You may remember, my dear, when you went a serjeant to Gibraltar, you left me big with child; you stayed abroad, you know, upwards of three years. In your absence I was brought to bed, I verily believe, of this daughter, whom I am sure I have reason to remember, for I suckled her at this very breast till the day she was stolen from me. One afternoon, when the child was about a year, or a year and a half old, or thereabouts, two gipsy women came to the door, and offered to tell my fortune. One of them had a child in her lap. I showed them my hand, and desired to know if you was ever to come home again, which I remember as well as if it was but yesterday: they faithfully promised me you should. — I left the girl in the cradle, and went to draw them a cup of liquor, the best I had; when I returned with the pot (I am sure I was not absent longer than whilst I am telling it to you) the women were gone. I was afraid they had stolen something, and looked and looked, but to no purpose, and Heaven knows I had very little for them to steal. At last, hearing the child cry in the cradle, I went to take it up — but, *O the living!* how was I surprised to find, instead of my own girl that I had put into the cradle, who was as fine a fat thriving child as you shall see in a summer's day, a poor sickly boy, that did not seem to have an hour to live. I ran out, pulling my hair off, and crying like any mad after the women, but never could hear a word of them from that day to this. When I came back, the poor infant (which is our Joseph there, as stout as he now stands) lifted up its eyes upon me so piteously, that, to be sure, notwithstanding my passion, I could not find in my heart to do it any mischief. A neighbour of mine, happening to come in at the same time, and hearing the case, advised me to take care of this poor child, and God would perhaps one day restore me my own. Upon which I took the child up, and suckled it, to be sure, all the world as if it had been born of my own natural body. And as true as I am alive, in a little time I loved the boy all to nothing as if it had been my own girl. — Well, as I was saying, times growing very hard, I having two children, and nothing but my own work, which was little enough, God knows, to maintain them, was obliged to ask relief of the parish; but, instead of giving it me, they removed me, by justices' warrants, fifteen miles to the place where I now live, where I had not been long settled before you came home. Joseph (for that was the name I gave him myself — the Lord knows whether he was baptized or no, or by what name), Joseph, I say, seemed to me to be about five years old when you returned; for I believe he is two or three years older than our daughter here (for I am thoroughly convinced she is the same); and when you saw him, you said he was a chopping boy, without ever minding his age; and so I, seeing you did not suspect anything of the matter, thought I might e'en as well keep it to myself, for fear you should not love him as well as I did. And all this is veritably true, and I will take my oath of it before any justice in the kingdom."

The pedlar, who had been summoned by the order of Lady Booby, listened with the utmost attention to Gammar Andrews's story, and, when she had finished, asked her if the supposititious child had no mark on its breast? To which she answered, "Yes, he had as fine a strawberry as ever grew in a garden." This Joseph acknowledged, and, unbuttoning his coat, at the intercession of the company, showed to them. "Well," says Gaffar Andrews, who was a comical sly old fellow, and very likely desired to have no more children than he could keep, "you have proved, I think, very plainly, that this boy doth not belong to us; but how are you certain that the girl is ours?" The parson then brought the pedlar forward, and desired him to repeat the story which he had communicated to him the preceding day at the ale-house; which he complied with, and related what the reader, as well as Mr. Adams, hath seen before. He then confirmed, from his wife's report, all the circumstances of the exchange, and of the strawberry on Joseph's breast. At the repetition of the word *strawberry*, Adams, who had seen it without any emotion, started and cried, "Bless me! something comes into my head." But before he had time to bring anything out, a servant called him forth. When he was gone, the pedlar assured Joseph that his parents were persons of much greater circumstances than those he had hitherto mistaken for such; for that he had been stolen from a gentleman's house by those whom they call gipsies, and had been kept by them during a whole year, when, looking on him as in a dying condition, they had exchanged him for the other healthier child, in the manner before related. He said, as to the name of his father, his wife had either never known or forgot it; but that she had acquainted him he lived about forty miles from the place where the exchange had been made, and which way, promising to spare no pains in endeavouring with him to discover the place.

But Fortune, which seldom doth good or ill, or makes men happy or miserable, by halves, resolved to spare him this labour. The reader may please to recollect that Mr. Wilson had intended a journey to the west, in which he was to pass through Mr. Adams's parish, and had promised to call on him. He was now arrived at the Lady Booby's gates for that purpose, being directed thither from the parson's house, and had sent in the servant whom we have above seen call Mr. Adams forth. This had no sooner mentioned the discovery of a stolen child, and had uttered the word *strawberry*, than Mr. Wilson, with wildness in his looks, and the utmost eagerness in his words, begged to be showed into the room, where he entered without the least regard to any of the company but Joseph, and, embracing him with a complexion all pale and trembling, desired to see the mark on his breast; the parson followed him capering, rubbing his hands, and crying out, "*Hic est quem quæris; inventus est, &c.*" Joseph complied with the request of Mr. Wilson, who no sooner saw the mark than, abandoning himself to the most extravagant rapture of passion, he embraced Joseph with inexpressible ecstasy, and cried out in tears of joy, "I have discovered my son, I have him again in my arms!" Joseph was not sufficiently apprised yet to taste the same delight with his father (for so in reality he was); however, he returned some warmth to his embraces; but he no sooner perceived, from his father's account, the agreement of every circumstance, of person, time, and place, than he threw himself at his feet, and, embracing his knees, with tears begged his blessing, which was given with much affection, and received with such respect, mixed with such tenderness on both sides, that it affected all present: but none so much as Lady Booby, who left the room in an agony, which was but too much perceived, and not very charitably accounted for by some of the company.

CHAPTER XVI.

Being the last. In which this true history is brought to a happy conclusion.

FANNY was very little behind her Joseph in the duty she exprest towards her parents, and the joy she evidenced in discovering

them. Gammar Andrews kissed her, and said she was heartily
glad to see her; but for her part, she could never love anyone
better than Joseph. Gaffar Andrews testified no remarkable
emotion: he blessed and kissed her, but complained bitterly
that he wanted his pipe, not having had a whiff that morning.

Mr. Booby, who knew nothing of his aunt's fondness, imputed
her abrupt departure to her pride, and disdain of the family
into which he was married; he was therefore desirous to be
gone with the utmost celerity; and now, having congratulated
Mr. Wilson and Joseph on the discovery, he saluted Fanny,
called her sister, and introduced her as such to Pamela, who
behaved with great decency on the occasion.

He now sent a message to his aunt, who returned that she
wished him a good journey, but was too disordered to see any
company: he therefore prepared to set out, having invited Mr.
Wilson to his house; and Pamela and Joseph both so insisted
on his complying, that he at last consented, having first obtained
a messenger from Mr. Booby to acquaint his wife with the
news; which, as he knew it would render her completely happy,
he could not prevail on himself to delay a moment in acquaint-
ing her with.

The company were ranged in this manner: the two old people,
with their two daughters, rode in the coach; the squire, Mr.
Wilson, Joseph, Parson Adams, and the pedlar, proceeded on
horseback.

In their way Joseph informed his father of his intended
match with Fanny; to which, though he expressed some reluctance at first, on the eagerness of his son's instances he consented; saying, if she was so good a creature as she appeared,
and he described her, he thought the disadvantages of birth and
fortune might be compensated. He however insisted on the
match being deferred till he had seen his mother; in which
Joseph, perceiving him positive, with great duty obeyed him,
to the great delight of Parson Adams, who by these means saw
an opportunity of fulfilling the Church forms, and marrying
his parishioners without a licence.

Mr. Adams, greatly exulting on this occasion (for such ceremonies were matters of no small moment with him), accidentally
gave spurs to his horse, which the generous beast disdaining —
for he was high of mettle, and had been used to more expert
riders than the gentleman who at present bestrode him, for
whose horsemanship he had perhaps some contempt — imme-

diately ran away full speed, and played so many antic tricks that he tumbled the parson from his back; which Joseph perceiving, came to his relief. This accident afforded infinite merriment to the servants, and no less frighted poor Fanny, who beheld him as he passed by the coach; but the mirth of the one and terror of the other were soon determined, when the parson declared he had received no damage.

The horse having freed himself from his unworthy rider, as he probably thought him, proceeded to make the best of his way; but was stopped by a gentleman and his servants, who were travelling the opposite way, and were now at a little distance from the coach. They soon met; and as one of the servants delivered Adams his horse, his master hailed him, and Adams, looking up, presently recollected he was the justice of peace before whom he and Fanny had made their appearance. The parson presently saluted him very kindly; and the justice informed him that he had found the fellow who attempted to swear against him and the young woman the very next day, and had committed him to Salisbury gaol, where he was charged with many robberies.

Many compliments having passed between the parson and the justice, the latter proceeded on his journey; and the former, having with some disdain refused Joseph's offer of changing horses, and declared he was as able a horseman as any in the kingdom, remounted his beast; and now the company again proceeded, and happily arrived at their journey's end, Mr. Adams, by good luck, rather than by good riding, escaping a second fall.

The company, arriving at Mr. Booby's house, were all received by him in the most courteous, and entertained in the most splendid, manner, after the custom of the old English hospitality, which is still preserved in some very few families in the remote parts of England. They all passed that day with the utmost satisfaction; it being perhaps impossible to find any set of people more solidly and sincerely happy. Joseph and Fanny found means to be alone upwards of two hours, which were the shortest, but the sweetest imaginable.

In the morning, Mr. Wilson proposed to his son to make a visit with him to his mother; which, notwithstanding his dutiful inclinations, and a longing desire he had to see her, a little concerned him, as he must be obliged to leave his Fanny: but the goodness of Mr. Booby relieved him; for he proposed to send his own coach and six for Mrs. Wilson, whom Pamela so very earnestly invited, that Mr. Wilson at length agreed with the entreaties of Mr. Booby and Joseph, and suffered the coach to go empty for his wife.

On Saturday night the coach returned with Mrs. Wilson, who added one more to this happy assembly. The reader may imagine much better and quicker too than I can describe, the many embraces and tears of joy which succeeded her arrival. It is sufficient to say she was easily prevailed with to follow her husband's example in consenting to the match.

On Sunday Mr. Adams performed the service at the squire's parish church, the curate of which very kindly exchanged duty, and rode twenty miles to the Lady Booby's parish so to do; being particularly charged not to omit publishing the banns, being the third and last time.

At length the happy day arrived which was to put Joseph in the possession of all his wishes. He arose and drest himself in a neat, but plain suit of Mr. Booby's, which exactly fitted him; for he refused all finery; as did Fanny likewise, who could be prevailed on by Pamela to attire herself in nothing richer than a white dimity nightgown. Her shift, indeed, which Pamela presented her, was of the finest kind, and had an edging of lace round the bosom; she likewise equipped her with a pair of fine white thread stockings, which were all she would accept; for she wore one of her own short round-eared caps, and over it a little straw hat, lined with cherry-coloured silk, and tied with a cherry-coloured ribbon. In this dress she came forth from her chamber, blushing and breathing sweets; and was by Joseph, whose eyes sparkled fire, led to church, the whole family attending, where Mr. Adams performed the ceremony; at which nothing was so remarkable as the extraordinary and unaffected modesty of Fanny, unless the true Christian piety of Adams, who publicly rebuked Mr. Booby and Pamela for laughing in so sacred a place, and so solemn an occasion. Our parson would have done no less to the highest prince on earth: for, though he paid all submission and deference to his superiors in other matters, where the least spice of religion intervened, he immediately lost all respect of persons. It was his maxim, that he was a servant of the Highest, and could not, without departing from his duty, give up the least article of his honour, or of his cause, to the greatest earthly potentate. Indeed, he always asserted that Mr. Adams at church with his surplice on, and Mr. Adams without that ornament, in any other place, were two very different persons.

When the church rites were over, Joseph led his blooming bride back to Mr. Booby's (for the distance was so very little, they did not think proper to use a coach); the whole company attended them likewise on foot; and now a most magnificent entertainment was provided, at which Parson Adams demonstrated an appetite surprising, as well as surpassing, everyone present. Indeed the only persons who betrayed any deficiency on this occasion were those on whose account the feast was provided. They pampered their imaginations with the much more exquisite repast which the approach of night promised them; the thoughts of which filled both their minds, though with different sensations; the one all desire, while the other had her wishes tempered with fears.

At length, after a day passed with the utmost merriment, corrected by the strictest decency — in which, however, Parson Adams, being well filled with ale and pudding, had given a loose to more facetiousness than was usual to him — the happy, the blest moment arrived when Fanny retired with her mother, her mother-in-law, and her sister. She was soon undrest; for she had no jewels to deposit in their caskets, nor fine laces to fold with the nicest exactness. Undressing to her was properly discovering, not putting off, ornaments: for, as all her charms were the gifts of nature, she could divest herself of none. How, reader, shall I give thee an adequate idea of this lovely young creature! the bloom of roses and lilies might a little illustrate her complexion, or their smell her sweetness; but to comprehend her entirely, conceive youth, health, bloom, beauty, neatness, and innocence in her bridal bed; conceive all these in their utmost perfection, and you may place the charming Fanny's picture before your eyes.

Joseph no sooner heard she was in bed than he fled with the utmost eagerness to her. A minute carried him into her arms, where we shall leave this happy couple to enjoy the private rewards of their constancy; rewards so great and sweet, that I apprehend Joseph neither envied the noblest duke, nor Fanny the finest duchess, that night.

The third day, Mr. Wilson and his wife, with their son and daughter, returned home; where they now live together in a state of bliss scarce ever equalled. Mr. Booby hath, with unprecedented generosity, given Fanny a fortune of two thousand pound, which Joseph hath laid out in a little estate in the same parish with his father, which he now occupies (his father having stocked it for him); and Fanny presides with most excellent management in his dairy; where, however, she is not at present very able to bustle much, being, as Mr. Wilson informs me in his last letter, extremely big with her first child.

Mr. Booby hath presented Mr. Adams with a living of one hundred and thirty pounds a year. He at first refused it, resolving not to quit his parishioners, with whom he hath lived so long: but, on recollecting he might keep a curate at this living, he hath been lately inducted into it.

The pedlar, besides several handsome presents both from Mr. Wilson and Mr. Booby, is, by the latter's interest, made an exciseman; a trust which he discharges with such justice, that he is greatly beloved in his neighbourhood.

As for the Lady Booby, she returned to London in a few days, where a young captain of dragoons, together with eternal parties at cards, soon obliterated the memory of Joseph.

Joseph remains blest with his Fanny, whom he doats on with the utmost tenderness, which is all returned on her side. The happiness of this couple is a perpetual fountain of pleasure to their fond parents; and, what is particularly remarkable, he declares he will imitate them in their retirement; nor will be prevailed on by any booksellers, or their authors, to make his appearance in "high-life."

AN
APOLOGY
FOR THE
LIFE
OF
Mrs. SHAMELA ANDREWS.

In which, the many notorious FALSHOODS and MISREPRSENTATIONS of a Book called

PAMELA,

Are exposed and refuted; and all the matchless ARTS of that young Politician, set in a true and just Light.

Together with

A full Account of all that passed between her and Parson *Arthur Williams*; whose Character is represented in a manner something different from that which he bears in *PAMELA*. The whole being exact Copies of authentick Papers delivered to the Editor.

Necessary to be had in all FAMILIES.

By Mr. *CONNY KEYBER*.

LONDON:
Printed for A. DODD, at the *Peacock*, without *Temple-bar*.
M. DCC. XLI.

[Title page of the second edition, 1741]

TO MISS FANNY, &c.

MADAM,

IT will be naturally expected, that when I write the life of Shamela, I should dedicate it to some young lady, whose wit and beauty might be the proper subject of a comparison with the heroine of my piece. This, those, who see I have done it in prefixing your name to my work, will much more confirmedly expect me to do; and, indeed, your character would enable me to run some length into a parallel, though you, nor anyone else, are at all like the matchless Shamela.

You see, Madam, I have some value for your good nature, when in a Dedication, which is properly a panegyric, I speak against, not for you; but I remember it is a life which I am presenting you, and why should I expose my veracity to any hazard in the front of the work, considering what I have done in the body. Indeed, I wish it was possible to write a Dedication, and get anything by it, without one word of flattery; but since it is not, come on, and I hope to show my delicacy at least in the compliments I intend to pay you.

First, then, Madam, I must tell the world, that you have tickled up and brightened many strokes in this work by your pencil.

Secondly, You have intimately conversed with me, one of the greatest wits and scholars of my age.

Thirdly, You keep very good hours, and frequently spend an useful day before others begin to enjoy it. This I will take my oath on; for I am admitted to your presence in a morning before other people's servants are up; when I have constantly found you reading in good books; and if ever I have drawn you upon me, I have always felt you very heavy.

Fourthly, You have a virtue which enables you to rise early and study hard, and that is, forbearing to over-eat yourself, and this in spite of all the luscious temptations of puddings and custards, exciting the brute (as Dr. Woodward calls it) to rebel. This is a virtue which I can greatly admire, though I much question whether I could imitate it.

Fifthly, A circumstance greatly to your honour, that by means of your extraordinary merit and beauty, you was carried into the ball-room at the Bath, by the discerning Mr. Nash, before the age

301

that other young ladies generally arrived at that honour, and while your mamma herself existed in her perfect bloom. Here you was observed in dancing to balance your body exactly, and to weigh every motion with the exact and equal measure of time and tune; and though you sometimes made a false step, by leaning too much to one side, yet everybody said you would one time or other, dance perfectly well, and uprightly.

Sixthly, I cannot forbear mentioning those pretty little sonnets, and sprightly compositions, which though they came from you with so much ease, might be mentioned to the praise of a great or grave character.

And now, Madam, I have done with you; it only remains to pay my acknowledgments to an author, whose style I have exactly followed in this life, it being the properest for biography. The reader, I believe, easily guesses I mean Euclid's *Elements;* it was Euclid who taught me to write. It is you, Madam, who pay me for writing. Therefore I am to both,

A most obedient, and
obliged humble Servant,

CONNY KEYBER.

LETTERS TO THE EDITOR.

The Editor to Himself.

Dear Sir,

However you came by the excellent *Shamela*, out with it, without fear or favour, Dedication and all; believe me, it will go through many editions, be translated into all languages, read in all nations and ages, and to say a bold word, it will do more good than the *C——y* have done harm in the world.

I am, Sir,
Sincerely your Well-wisher,

Yourself.

John Puff, *Esq; to the* Editor.

Sir,

I have read your *Shamela* through and through, and a most inimitable performance it is. Who is he, what is he, that could write so excellent a book? he must be doubtless most agreeable to the age, and to *his Honour* himself; for he is able to draw everything to perfection but virtue. Whoever the author be, he hath one of the worst and most fashionable hearts in the world, and I would recommend to him, in his next performance, to undertake the life of *his Honour.* For he who drew the character of Parson Williams, is equal to the task; nay, he seems to have little more to do than to pull off the parson's gown, and *that* which makes him so agreeable to Shamela, and the cap will fit.

I am, Sir,
Your humble Servant,

John Puff.

Note, Reader, several other commendatory letters and copies of verses will be prepared against the next edition.

AN
APOLOGY
for the LIFE of
MRS. SHAMELA ANDREWS.

Parson TICKLETEXT *to Parson* OLIVER.

Rev. SIR,

HEREWITH I transmit you a copy of sweet, dear, pretty *Pamela*,
a little book which this winter hath produced; of which, I make
no doubt, you have already heard mention from some of your
neighbouring clergy; for we have made it our common business
here, not only to cry it up, but to preach it up likewise: the
pulpit, as well as the coffee-house, hath resounded with its praise,
and it is expected shortly, that his L————p will recommend it
in a ———— Letter to our whole body.

And this example, I am confident, will be imitated by all our
cloth in the country: for besides speaking well of a brother, in
the character of the Reverend Mr. Williams, the useful and truly
religious doctrine of *grace* is everywhere inculcated.

This book is the "soul of *religion*, good-breeding, discretion,
good-nature, wit, fancy, fine thought, and morality. There is an
ease, a natural air, a dignified simplicity, and MEASURED FULLNESS
in it, that RESEMBLING LIFE, OUT-GLOWS IT. The author hath
reconciled the *pleasing* to the *proper;* the thought is everywhere
exactly clothed by the expression; and becomes its dress as
roundly and as close as Pamela her country habit; or *as she doth
her no habit,* when modest beauty seeks to hide itself, by casting off the pride of ornament, and displays itself without any
covering"; which it frequently doth in this admirable work, and
presents images to the reader, which the coldest zealot cannot
read without emotion.

For my own part (and, I believe, I may say the same of all
the clergy of my acquaintance) "I have done nothing but read
it to others, and hear others again read it to me, ever since it
came into my hands; and I find I am like to do nothing else, for

I know not how long yet to come: because if I lay the book down *it comes after me*. When it has dwelt all day long upon the ear, it takes possession all night of the fancy. It hath witchcraft in every page of it." —— Oh! I feel an emotion even while I am relating this: methinks I see Pamela at this instant, with all the pride of ornament cast off.

"Little book, charming *Pamela*, get thee gone; face the world, in which thou wilt find nothing like thyself." Happy would it be for mankind, if all other books were burnt, that we might do nothing but read thee all day, and dream of thee all night. Thou alone art sufficient to teach us as much morality as we want. Dost thou not teach us to pray, to sing psalms, and to honour the clergy? Are not these the whole duty of man? Forgive me, O author of *Pamela*, mentioning the name of a book so unequal to thine: but, now I think of it, who is the author, where is he, what is he, that hath hitherto been able to hide such an encircling, all-mastering spirit? "he possesses every quality that art could have charmed by: yet hath lent it to and concealed it in Nature. The comprehensiveness of his imagination must be truly prodigious! It has stretched out this diminutive mere grain of mustard-seed (a poor girl's little, &c.) into a resemblance of that Heaven, which the best of good books has compared it to."

To be short, this book will live to the age of the patriarchs, and like them will carry on the good work many hundreds of years hence, among our posterity, who will not HESITATE their esteem with restraint. If the Romans granted exemptions to men who begat a *few* children for the Republic, what distinction (if policy and we should ever be reconciled) should we find to reward this father of millions, which are to owe formation to the future effect of his influence. —— I feel another emotion.

As soon as you have read this yourself five or six times over (which may possibly happen within a week) I desire you would give it to my little god-daughter, as a present from me. This being the only education we intend henceforth to give our daughters. And pray let your servant-maids read it over, or read it to them. Both yourself and the neighbouring clergy will supply yourselves for the pulpit from the booksellers, as soon as the fourth edition is published. I am,

Sir,
          Your most humble Servant,

                    THO. TICKLETEXT.

Parson OLIVER *to Parson* TICKLETEXT.

Rev. SIR,

I RECEIVED the favour of yours with the inclosed book, and really must own myself sorry to see the report I have heard of an epidemical phrenzy now raging in town, confirmed in the person of my friend.

If I had not known your hand, I should, from the sentiments and style of the letter, have imagined it to have come from the author of the famous Apology, which was sent me last summer; and on my reading the remarkable paragraph of "measured fullness, that resembling life, out-glows it," to a young baronet, he cried out, C——ly C——b—r by G——. But I have since observed, that this, as well as many other expressions in your letter, was borrowed from those remarkable epistles, which the author, or the editor, hath prefixed to the second edition, which you send me, of his book.

Is it possible that you or any of your function can be in earnest, or think the cause of religion, or morality, can want such slender support? God forbid they should. As for honour to the clergy, I am sorry to see them so solicitous about it; for if worldly honour be meant, it is what their predecessors in the pure and primitive age never had or sought. Indeed the secure satisfaction of a good conscience, the approbation of the wise and good (which never were or will be the generality of mankind), and the ecstatic pleasure of contemplating that their ways are acceptable to the Great Creator of the universe, will always attend those who really deserve these blessings: but for worldly honours, they are often the purchase of force and fraud; we sometimes see them in an eminent degree possessed by men who are notorious for luxury, pride, cruelty, treachery, and the most abandoned prostitution; wretches who are ready to invent and maintain schemes repugnant to the interest, the liberty, and the happiness of mankind, not to supply their necessities, or even conveniencies, but to pamper their avarice and ambition. And if this be the road to worldly honours, God forbid the clergy should be even suspected of walking in it.

The history of *Pamela* I was acquainted with long before I received it from you, from my neighbourhood to the scene of action. Indeed I was in hopes that young woman would have contented herself with the good fortune she hath attained; and rather suffered her little arts to have been forgotten than have revived their remembrance, and endeavoured by perverting and misrepresenting facts to be thought to deserve what she now enjoys: for though we do not imagine her the author of the narrative itself, yet we must suppose the instructions were given by her, as well as the reward, to the composer. Who that is, though you so earnestly require of me, I shall leave you to guess from that *Ciceronian* eloquence, with which the work abounds; and that excellent knack of making every character amiable, which he lays his hands on.

But before I send you some papers relating to this matter, which will set Pamela and some others in a very different light than that in which they appear in the printed book, I must beg leave to make some few remarks on the book itself, and its tendency (admitting it to be a true relation), towards improving morality, or doing any good, either to the present age, or posterity: which when I have done, I shall, I flatter myself, stand excused from delivering it, either into the hands of my daughter, or my servant-maid.

The instruction which it conveys to servant-maids is, I think, very plainly this, To look out for their masters as sharp as they can. The consequences of which will be, besides neglect of their business, and the using all manner of means to come at ornaments of their persons, that if the master is not a fool, they will be debauched by him; and if he is a fool, they will marry him. Neither of which, I apprehend, my good friend, we desire should be the case of our sons.

And notwithstanding our author's professions of modesty, which in my youth I have heard at the beginning of an epilogue, I cannot agree that my daughter should entertain herself with some of his pictures; which I do not expect to be contemplated without emotion, unless by one of my age and temper, who can see the girl lie on her back, with one arm round Mrs. Jewkes and the other round the squire, naked in bed, with his hand on her breasts, &c., with as much indifference as I read any other page in the whole novel. But surely this, and some other descriptions, will not be put into the hands of his daughter by any wise man, though I believe it will be difficult for him to keep them from her; especially if the clergy in town have cried and preached it up as you say.

But, my friend, the whole narrative is such a misrepresentation of facts, such a perversion of truth, as you will, I am persuaded, agree, as soon as you have perused the papers I now inclose to you, that I hope you, or some other well-disposed person, will communicate these papers to the public, that this little jade may not impose on the world, as she hath on her master.

The true name of this wench was SHAMELA, and not Pamela, as she styles herself. Her father had in his youth the misfortune to appear in no good light at the Old-Bailey; he afterwards served in the capacity of a drummer in one of the Scotch regiments in the Dutch service; where being drummed out, he came over to England, and turned informer against several persons on the late Gin-Act; and becoming acquainted with an hostler at an inn, where a Scotch gentleman's horses stood, he hath at last by his interest obtained a pretty snug place in the custom-house. Her mother sold oranges in the play-house; and whether she was married to her father or no, I never could learn.

After this short introduction, the rest of her history will appear in the following letters, which I assure you are authentic.

LETTER I.

SHAMELA ANDREWS *to Mrs.* HENRIETTA MARIA HONORA ANDREWS *at her lodgings at the* Fan *and* Pepper-Box *in Drury-Lane.*

Dear Mamma,

THIS comes to acquaint you, that I shall set out in the wagon on Monday, desiring you to commodate me with a ludgin, as near you as possible, in Coulstin's-Court, or Wild-Street, or somewhere thereabouts; pray let it be handsome, and not above two stories high: for Parson Williams hath promised to visit me when he comes to town, and I have got a good many fine clothes of the old put my mistress's, who died a wil ago; and I beleve Mrs. Jervis will come along with me, for she says she would like to keep a house somewhere about Short's-Gardens, or towards

Queen-Street; and if there was convenience for a *bannio*, she should like it the better; but that she will settle herself when she comes to town. —— *O! How I long to be in the balconey at the Old House!* —— so no more at present from

Your affectionate Daughter,

SHAMELA.

LETTER II.

SHAMELA ANDREWS *to* HENRIETTA MARIA HONORA ANDREWS.

Dear Mamma,

O WHAT news, since I writ my last! the young squire hath been here, and as sure as a gun he hath taken a fancy to me; Pamela, says he, (for so I am called here) you was a great favourite of your late mistress's; yes, an't please your Honour, says I; and I believe you deserved it, says he; thank your Honour for your good opinion, says I; and then he took me by the hand, and I pretended to be shy: Laud, says I, sir, I hope you don't intend to be rude; no, says he, my dear, and then he kissed me, 'till he took away my breath —— and I pretended to be angry, and to get away, and then he kissed me again, and breathed very short, and looked very silly; and by ill-luck Mrs. Jervis came in, and had like to have spoiled sport. — *How troublesome is such interruption!* You shall hear now soon, for I shall not come away yet; so I rest,

Your affectionate Daughter,

SHAMELA.

LETTER III.

Henrietta Maria Honora Andrews *to* Shamela Andrews.

Dear Sham,

Your last letter hath put me into a great hurry of spirits, for you have a very difficult part to act. I hope you will remember your slip with Parson Williams, and not be guilty of any more such folly. Truly, a girl who hath once known what is what, is in the highest degree inexcusable if she respects her *digressions;* but a hint of this is sufficient. When Mrs. Jervis thinks of coming to town, I believe I can procure her a good house, and fit for the business; so I am,

Your affectionate Mother,

Henrietta Maria Honora Andrews.

LETTER IV.

Shamela Andrews *to* Henrietta Maria Honora Andrews.

Marry come up, good madam, the mother had never looked into the oven for her daughter, if she had not been there herself. I shall never have done if you upbraid me with having had a small one by Arthur Williams, when you yourself — but I say no more. *O! What fine times when the kettle calls the pot!* Let me do what I will, I say my prayers as often as another, and I read in good books, as often as I have leisure; and Parson Williams says, that will make amends. — So no more, but I rest

Your afflicted Daughter,

S——.

LETTER V.

HENRIETTA MARIA HONORA ANDREWS *to* SHAMELA ANDREWS.

Dear Child,

WHY will you give such way to your passion? How could you imagine I should be such a simpleton, as to upbraid thee with being thy mother's own daughter! When I advised you not to be guilty of folly, I meant no more than that you should take care to be well paid before-hand, and not trust to promises, which a man seldom keeps, after he hath had his wicked will. And seeing you have a rich fool to deal with, your not making a good market will be the more inexcusable; indeed, with such gentlemen as Parson Williams, there is more to be said; for they have nothing to give, and are commonly otherwise the best sort of men. I am glad to hear you read good books, pray continue so to do. I have inclosed you one of Mr. Whitefield's sermons, and also the dealings with him, and am

Your affectionate Mother,

HENRIETTA MARIA, &c.

LETTER VI.

SHAMELA ANDREWS *to* HENRIETTA MARIA HONORA ANDREWS.

O MADAM, I have strange things to tell you! As I was reading in that charming book about the dealings, in comes my master — to be sure he is a precious one. Pamela, says he, what book is that? I warrant you Rochester's poems. — No, forsooth, says I, as pertly as I could; why how now saucy chops, boldface, says he — Mighty pretty words, says I, pert again. — Yes (says he) you are a d—d, impudent, stinking, cursed, confounded jade, and I have a great mind to kick your a—. You, kiss — says I.

A-gad, says he, and so I will; with that he caught me in his
arms, and kissed me till he made my face all over fire. Now
this served purely, you know, to put upon the fool for anger.
O! What precious fools men are! And so I flung from him in a
mighty rage, and pretended as how I would go out at the door;
but when I came to the end of the room, I stood still, and my
master cried out, hussy, slut, saucebox, boldface, come hither —
Yes, to be sure, says I; why don't you come, says he; what should
I come for, says I; if you don't come to me, I'll come to you,
says he; I shan't come to you, I assure you, says I. Upon which
he run up, caught me in his arms, and flung me upon a chair, and
began to offer to touch my under-petticoat. Sir, says I, you had
better not offer to be rude; well, says he, no more I won't then;
and away he went out of the room. I was so mad to be sure
I could have cried.

*O what a prodigious vexation it is to a woman to be made
a fool of!*

Mrs. Jervis, who had been without, harkening, now came to
me. She burst into a violent laugh the moment she came in.
Well, says she, as soon as she could speak, I have reason to bless
myself that I am an old woman. Ah child! if you had known
the jolly blades of my age, you would not have been left in the
lurch in this manner. Dear Mrs. Jervis, says I, don't laugh at
one; and to be sure I was a little angry with her. — Come, says
she, my dear honeysuckle, I have one game to play for you; he
shall see you in bed; he shall, my little rosebud, he shall see
those pretty, little, white, round, panting — and offered to pull
off my handkerchief. — Fie, Mrs. Jervis, says I, you make me
blush, and upon my fackins, I believe she did. She went on thus:
I know the squire likes you, and notwithstanding the awkward-
ness of his proceeding, I am convinced hath some hot blood in
his veins, which will not let him rest, 'till he hath communicated
some of his warmth to thee, my little angel; I heard him last
night at our door, trying if it was open; now tonight I will take
care it shall be so; I warrant that he makes the second trial;
which if he doth, he shall find us ready to receive him. I will
at first counterfeit sleep, and after a swoon; so that he will have
you naked in his possession: and then if you are disappointed, a
plague of all young squires, say I. — And so, Mrs. Jervis, says
I, you would have me yield myself to him, would you; you
would have me be a second time a fool for nothing. Thank you
for that, Mrs. Jervis. For nothing! marry forbid, says she, you

know he hath large sums of money, besides abundance of fine
things; and do you think, when you have inflamed him, by
giving his hand a liberty with that charming person; and that you
know he may easily think he obtains against your will, he will
not give anything to come at all? — This will not do, Mrs. Jervis,
answered I. I have heard my mamma say (and so you know,
Madam, I have) that in her youth, fellows have often taken
away in the morning what they gave over night. No, Mrs.
Jervis, nothing under a regular taking into keeping, a settled
settlement, for me, and all my heirs, all my whole lifetime, shall
do the business — or else crosslegged is the word, faith, with
Sham; and then I snapt my fingers.

Thursday Night, Twelve o'Clock.

Mrs. Jervis and I are just in bed, and the door unlocked; if
my master should come — Odsbobs! I hear him just coming in
at the door. You see I write in the present tense, as Parson
Williams says. Well, he is in bed between us, we both shamming a sleep; he steals his hand into my bosom, which I, as if in
my sleep, press close to me with mine, and then pretend to
awake. — I no sooner see him, but I scream out to Mrs. Jervis,
she feigns likewise but just to come to herself; we both begin,
she to becall, and I to bescratch very liberally. After having
made a pretty free use of my fingers, without any great regard
to the parts I attacked, I counterfeit a swoon. Mrs. Jervis then
cries out, O sir, what have you done! you have murthered poor
Pamela: she is gone, she is gone.——

*O what a difficulty it is to keep one's countenance, when a
violent laugh desires to burst forth!*

The poor Booby, frightened out of his wits, jumped out of
bed, and, in his shirt, sat down by my bed-side, pale and trembling, for the moon shone, and I kept my eyes wide open, and
pretended to fix them in my head. Mrs. Jervis applied lavender
water, and hartshorn, and this for a full half hour; when thinking I had carried it on long enough, and being likewise unable
to continue the sport any longer, I began by degrees to come
to myself.

The squire, who had sat all this while speechless, and was
almost really in that condition which I feigned, the moment he
saw me give symptoms of recovering my senses, fell down on
his knees; and O Pamela, cried he, can you forgive me, my
injured maid? by heaven. I know not whether you are a man or

a woman, unless by your swelling breasts. Will you promise to forgive me? I forgive you! D—n you, says I; and d—n you, says he, if you come to that. I wish I had never seen your bold face, saucy sow — and so went out of the room.

O what a silly fellow is a bashful young lover!

He was no sooner out of hearing, as we thought, than we both burst into a violent laugh. Well, says Mrs. Jervis, I never saw anything better acted than your part: but I wish you may not have discouraged him from any future attempt; especially since his passions are so cool, that you could prevent his hands going further than your bosom. Hang him, answered I, he is not quite so cold as that, I assure you; our hands, on neither side, were idle in the scuffle, nor have left us any doubt of each other as to that matter.

Friday Morning.

My master sent for Mrs. Jervis, as soon as he was up, and bid her give an account of the plate and linen in her care; and told her, he was resolved that both she and the little gipsy (I'll assure him) should set out together. Mrs. Jervis made him a saucy answer — which any servant of spirit, you know, would, tho' it should be one's ruin — and came immediately in tears to me, crying, she had lost her place on my account, and that she should be forced to take to a house, as I mentioned before; and that she hoped I would, at least, make her all the amends in my power, for her loss on my account, and come to her house whenever I was sent for. Never fear, says I, I'll warrant we are not so near being turned away as you imagine; and, i'cod, now it comes into my head, I have a fetch for him, and you shall assist me in it. But it being now late, and my letter pretty long, no more at present from

Your Dutiful Daughter,

SHAMELA.

LETTER VII.

Mrs. LUCRETIA JERVIS *to* HENRIETTA
MARIA HONORA ANDREWS.

Madam,

MISS Sham being set out in a hurry for my master's house in Lincolnshire, desired me to acquaint you with the success of her stratagem, which was to dress herself in the plain neatness of a farmer's daughter, for she before wore the clothes of my late mistress, and to be introduced by me as a stranger to her master. To say the truth, she became the dress extremely, and if I was to keep a house a thousand years, I would never desire a prettier wench in it.

As soon as my master saw her, he immediately threw his arms round her neck, and smothered her with kisses (for indeed he hath but very little to say for himself to a woman). He swore that Pamela was an ugly slut (pardon, dear Madam, the coarseness of the expression) compared to such divine excellence. He added, he would turn Pamela away immediately, and take this new girl, whom he thought to be one of his tenant's daughters, in her room.

Miss Sham smiled at these words, and so did your humble servant, which he perceiving, looked very earnestly at your fair daughter, and discovered the cheat.

How, Pamela, says he, is it you? I thought, sir, said Miss, after what had happened, you would have known me in any dress. No, hussy, says he, but after what hath happened, I should know thee out of any dress from all thy sex. He then was what we women call rude, when done in the presence of others; but it seems it is not the first time, and Miss defended herself with great strength and spirit.

The squire, who thinks her a pure virgin, and who knows nothing of my character, resolved to send her into Lincolnshire, on pretence of conveying her home; where our old friend Nanny Jewkes is housekeeper, and where Miss had her small one by Parson Williams about a year ago. This is a piece of news communicated to us by Robin Coachman, who is entrusted by his master to carry on this affair privately for him: but we hang together, I believe, as well as any family of servants in the nation.

You will, I believe, Madam, wonder that the squire, who doth not want generosity, should never have mentioned a settlement all this while; I believe it slips his memory: but it will not be long first, no doubt: for, as I am convinced the young lady will do nothing unbecoming your daughter, nor ever admit him to taste her charms, without something sure and handsome beforehand; so, I am certain, the squire will never rest till they have danced Adam and Eve's kissing dance together. Your daughter set out yesterday morning, and told me, as soon as she arrived, you might depend on hearing from her.

Be pleased to make my compliments acceptable to Mrs. Davis and Mrs. Silvester, and Mrs. Jolly, and all friends, and permit me the honour, Madam, to be with the utmost sincerity,

> *Your most obedient,*
> *Humble Servant,*
>
> LUCRETIA JERVIS.

If the squire should continue his displeasure against me, so as to insist on the warning he hath given me, you will see me soon, and I will lodge in the same house with you, if you have room, till I can provide for myself to my liking.

LETTER VIII.

HENRIETTA MARIA HONORA ANDREWS *to* LUCRETIA JERVIS.

Madam,

I RECEIVED the favour of your letter, and I find you have not forgot your usual politeness, which you learned when you was in keeping with a lord.

I am very much obliged to you for your care of my daughter, am glad to hear she hath taken such good resolutions, and hope she will have sufficient grace to maintain them.

All friends are well, and remember to you. You will excuse the shortness of this scroll; for I have sprained my right hand, with boxing three new made officers. — Tho' to my comfort, I beat them all. I rest,

Your Friend and Servant,

HENRIETTA, &c.

LETTER IX.

SHAMELA ANDREWS *to* HENRIETTA MARIA HONORA ANDREWS.

Dear Mamma,

I SUPPOSE Mrs. Jervis acquainted you with what passed 'till I left Bedfordshire; whence I am after a very pleasant journey arrived in Lincolnshire, with your old acquaintance Mrs. Jewkes, who formerly helped Parson Williams to me; and now designs, I see, to sell me to my master; thank her for that; she will find two words go to that bargain.

The day after my arrival here, I received a letter from Mr. Williams, and as you have often desired to see one from him, I have inclosed it to you; it is, I think, the finest I ever received from that charming man, and full of a great deal of learning.

O! What a brave thing it is to be a scholard, and to be able to talk Latin!

Parson WILLIAMS *to* PAMELA ANDREWS.

Mrs. Pamela,

HAVING learnt by means of my clerk, who yesternight visited the Revd. Mr. Peters with my commands, that you are returned into this county, I purposed to have saluted your fair hands this day towards even: but am obliged to sojourn this night at a neighbouring clergyman's; where we are to pierce a virgin barrel of ale, in a cup of which I shall not be unmindful to celebrate your health.

I hope you have remembered your promise, to bring me a leaden canister of tobacco (the saffron cut), for in troth, this country at present affords nothing worthy the replenishing a tube with. — Some I tasted the other day at an alehouse, gave me the heart-burn, tho' I filled no oftener than five times.

I was greatly concerned to learn, that your late lady left you nothing, tho' I cannot say the tidings much surprised me: for I am too intimately acquainted with the family (myself, father, and grandfather having been successive incumbents on the same cure, which you know is in their gift); I say, I am too well acquainted with them to expect much from their generosity. They are in verity, as worthless a family as any other whatever. The young gentleman, I am informed, is a perfect reprobate; that he hath an *ingenium versatile* to every species of vice, which, indeed, no one can much wonder at, who animadverts on that want of respect to the clergy, which was observable in him when a child. I remember when he was at the age of eleven only, he met my father without either pulling off his hat, or riding out of the way. Indeed, a contempt of the clergy is the fashionable vice of the times; but let such wretches know, they cannot hate, detest, and despise us, half so much as we do them.

However, I have prevailed on myself to write a civil letter to your master, as there is a probability of his being shortly in a capacity of rendering me a piece of service; my good friend and neighbour, the Revd. Mr. Squeeze-Tithe, being, as I am informed by one whom I have employed to attend for that purpose, very near his dissolution.

You see, sweet Mrs. Pamela, the confidence with which I dictate these things to you; whom, after those endearments which have passed between us, I must in some respects estimate as my wife: for tho' the omission of the service was a sin; yet, as I have told you, it was a venial one, of which I have truly repented, as I hope you have; and also that you have continued the wholesome office of reading good books, and are improved in your psalmody, of which I shall have a speedy trial: for I purpose to give you a sermon next Sunday, and shall spend the evening with you in pleasures, which, tho' not strictly innocent, are however to be purged away by frequent and sincere repentance. I am,

> *Sweet Mrs. Pamela,*
> *Your faithful Servant,*
>
> ARTHUR WILLIAMS.

You find, Mamma, what a charming way he hath of writing, and yet I assure you, that is not the most charming thing belonging to him: for, tho' he doth not put any dears, and sweets, and loves into his letters, yet he says a thousand of them: for he can be as fond of a woman as any man living.

Sure women are great fools, when they prefer a laced coat to the clergy, whom it is our duty to honour and respect.

Well, on Sunday Parson Williams came, according to his promise, and an excellent sermon he preached; his text was, *Be not righteous over-much;* and, indeed, he handled it in a very fine way: he showed us that the Bible doth not require too much goodness of us, and that people very often call things goodness that are not so. That to go to church, and to pray, and to sing psalms, and to honour the clergy, and to repent, is true religion; and 'tis not doing good to one another, for that is one of the greatest sins we can commit, when we don't do it for the sake of religion. That those people who talk of vartue and morality, are the wickedest of all persons. That 'tis not what we do, but what we believe, that must save us, and a great many other good things; I wish I could remember them all.

As soon as church was over, he came to the squire's house, and drank tea with Mrs. Jewkes and me; after which Mrs. Jewkes went out and left us together for an hour and half — Oh! he is a charming man.

After supper he went home, and then Mrs. Jewkes began to catechize me, about my familiarity with him. I see she wants him herself. Then she proceeded to tell me what an honour my master did me in liking me, and that it was both an inexcusable folly and pride in me, to pretend to refuse him any favour. Pray, madam, says I, consider I am a poor girl, and have nothing but my modesty to trust to. If I part with that, what will become of me? Methinks, says she, you are not so mighty modest when you are with Parson Williams; I have observed you gloat at one another in a manner that hath made me blush. I assure you, I shall let the squire know what sort of man he is; you may do your will, says I, as long as he hath a vote for pallamant-men, the squire dares do nothing to offend him; and you will only show that you are jealous of him, and that's all. How now, minx, says she. Minx! No more minx than yourself, says I; with that she hit me a slap on the shoulder, and I flew at her and scratched her face, i'cod, 'till she went crying out of the room; so no more at present, from

Your Dutiful Daughter,

SHAMELA.

LETTER X.

SHAMELA ANDREWS *to* HENRIETTA MARIA HONORA ANDREWS.

O MAMMA! Rare news! As soon as I was up this morning, a letter was brought me from the squire, of which I send you a copy.

Squire BOOBY *to* PAMELA.

Dear Creature,

I HOPE you are not angry with me for the deceit put upon you, in conveying you to Lincolnshire, when you imagined yourself going to London. Indeed, my dear Pamela, I cannot live without you; and will very shortly come down and convince you, that my designs are better than you imagine, and such as you may with honour comply with. I am,

> *My Dear Creature,*
> *Your doating Lover,*
>
> BOOBY.

Now, Mamma, what think you? — For my own part, I am convinced he will marry me, and faith so he shall. O! Bless me! I shall be Mrs. Booby, and be mistress of a great estate, and have a dozen coaches and six, and a fine house at London, and another at Bath, and servants, and jewels, and plate, and go to plays, and operas, and court; and do what I will, and spend what I will. But, poor Parson Williams! Well; and can't I see Parson Williams as well after marriage as before: for I shall never care a farthing for my husband. No, I hate and despise him of all things.

Well, as soon as I had read my letter, in came Mrs. Jewkes. You see, madam, says she, I carry the marks of your passion about me; but I have received order from my master to be civil to you, and I must obey him: for he is the best man in the world, notwithstanding your treatment of him. My treatment of him, madam, says I? Yes, says she, your insensibility to the honour he intends you, of making you his mistress. I would have you to know, madam, I would not be mistress to the greatest king, no, nor lord, in the universe. I value my vartue more than I do anything my master can give me; and so we talked a full hour and a half, about my vartue; and I was afraid at first, she had heard something about the bantling, but I find she hath not; tho' she is as jealous, and suspicious, as old Scratch.

In the afternoon, I stole into the garden to meet Mr. Williams; I found him at the place of his appointment, and we stayed in a kind of arbour, till it was quite dark. He was very angry when I told him what Mrs. Jewkes had threatened — Let him refuse me the living, says he, if he dares, I will vote for the other party; and not only so, but will expose him all over the country. I owe him 150*l.* indeed, but I don't care for that; by that time the election is past, I shall be able to plead the *Statue of Lamentations.*

I could have stayed with the dear man for ever, but when it grew dark, he told me, he was to meet the neighbouring clergy, to finish the barrel of ale they had tapped the other day, and believed they should not part till three or four in the morning — So he left me, and I promised to be penitent, and go on with my reading in good books.

As soon as he was gone, I bethought myself what excuse I should make to Mrs. Jewkes, and it came into my head to pretend as how I intended to drown myself; so I stript off one of my petticoats, and threw it into the canal; and then I went and hid myself in the coal-hole, where I lay all night; and comforted myself with repeating over some psalms, and other good things, which I had got by heart.

In the morning Mrs. Jewkes and all the servants were frighted out of their wits, thinking I had run away; and not devising how they should answer it to their master. They searched all the likeliest places they could think of for me, and at last saw my petticoat floating in the pond. Then they got a drag-net, imagining I was drowned, and intending to drag me out; but at last Moll Cook coming for some coals, discovered me lying all along in no very good pickle. Bless me! Mrs. Pamela, says she, what can be the meaning of this? I don't know, says I, help me up, and I will go in to breakfast, for indeed I am very hungry. Mrs. Jewkes came in immediately, and was so rejoiced to find me alive, that she asked with great good-humour, where I had been? and how my petticoat came into the pond. I answered, I believed the devil had put it into my head to drown myself; but it was a fib; for I never saw the devil in my life, nor I don't believe he hath anything to do with me.

So much for this matter. As soon as I had breakfasted, a coach and six came to the door, and who should be in it but my master.

I immediately run up into my room, and stript, and washed, and drest myself as well as I could, and put on my prettiest round-ear'd cap, and pulled down my stays, to show as much as I could of my bosom (for Parson Williams says, that is the most beautiful part of a woman), and then I practised over all my airs before the glass, and then I sat down and read a chapter in *The Whole Duty of Man*.

Then Mrs. Jewkes came to me and told me, my master wanted me below, and says she, Don't behave like a fool; No, thinks I to myself, I believe I shall find wit enough for my master and you too.

So down goes I into the parlour to him. Pamela, says he, the moment I came in, you see I cannot stay long from you, which I think is a sufficient proof of the violence of my passion. Yes, sir, says I, I see your Honour intends to ruin me, that nothing but the destruction of my vartue will content you.

O what a charming word that is, rest his soul who first invented it!

How can you say I would ruin you, answered the squire, when you shall not ask anything which I will not grant you. If that be true, says I, good your Honour, let me go home to my poor but honest parents; that is all I have to ask, and do not ruin a poor maiden, who is resolved to carry her vartue to the grave with her.

Hussy, says he, don't provoke me, don't provoke me, I say. You are absolutely in my power, and if you won't let me lie with you by fair means, I will by force. O la, sir, says I, I don't understand your paw words. — Very pretty treatment indeed, says he, to say I use paw words; hussy, gipsy, hypocrite, saucebox, boldface, get out of my sight, or I will lend you such a kick in the — I don't care to repeat the word, but he meant my hinder part. I was offering to go away, for I was half afraid, when he called me back, and took me round the neck and kissed me, and then bid me go about my business.

I went directly into my room, where Mrs. Jewkes came to me afterwards. So, madam, says she, you have left my master below in a fine pet, he hath threshed two or three of his men already:

it is mighty pretty that all his servants are to be punished for
your impertinence.

Harkee, madam, says I, don't you affront me, for if you do,
d—n me (I am sure I have repented for using such a word) if
I am not revenged.

How sweet is revenge: Sure the sermon book is in the right, in
calling it the sweetest morsel the devil ever dropped into the
mouth of a sinner.

Mrs. Jewkes remembered the smart of my nails too well to go
farther, and so we sat down and talked about my vartue till
dinner-time, and then I was sent for to wait on my master. I
took care to be often caught looking at him, and then I always
turned away my eyes, and pretended to be ashamed. As soon
as the cloth was removed, he put a bumper of champagne into
my hand, and bid me drink — O la, I can't remember the health.
Parson Williams may well say he is a wicked man.

Mrs. Jewkes took a glass and drank the dear *monysyllable;* I
don't understand that word, but I believe it is bawdy. I then
drank towards his Honour's good pleasure. Ay, hussy, says he,
you can give me pleasure if you will; Sir, says I, I shall be always
glad to do what is in my power, and so I pretended not to know
what he meant. Then he took me into his lap. — O Mamma, I
could tell you something if I would — and he kissed me — and
I said, I won't be slobbered about so, so I won't; and he bid me
get out of the room for a saucy baggage, and said he had a good
mind to spit in my face.

Sure no man ever took such a method to gain a woman's heart.

I had not been long in my chamber before Mrs. Jewkes came
to me, and told me, my master would not see me any more that
evening, that is, if he can help it; for, added she, I easily perceive
the great ascendant you have over him; and to confess the truth,
I don't doubt but you will shortly be my mistress.

What, says I, dear Mrs. Jewkes, what do you say? Don't flatter
a poor girl; it is impossible his Honour can have any honourable
design upon me. And so we talked of honourable designs till
supper-time. And Mrs. Jewkes and I supped together upon a hot
buttered apple-pie; and about ten o'clock we went to bed.

We had not been a-bed half an hour, when my master came
pit-a-pat into the room in his shirt as before; I pretended not to
hear him, and Mrs. Jewkes laid hold of one arm, and he pulled
down the bed-clothes and came into bed on the other side, and
took my other arm and laid it under him, and fell a-kissing one

of my breasts as if he would have devoured it; I was then forced
to awake, and began to struggle with him; Mrs. Jewkes crying
Why don't you do it? I have one arm secure, if you can't deal
with the rest I am sorry for you. He was as rude as possible to
me; but I remembered, Mamma, the instructions you gave me to
avoid being ravished, and followed them, which soon brought
him to terms, and he promised me, on quitting my hold, that he
would leave the bed.

*O Parson Williams, how little are all the men in the world
compared to thee!*

My master was as good as his word; upon which Mrs. Jewkes
said, O sir, I see you know very little of our *sect*, by parting so
easily from the blessing when you was so near it. No, Mrs.
Jewkes, answered he, I am very glad no more hath happened;
I would not have injured Pamela for the world. And to-morrow
morning perhaps she may hear of something to her advantage.
This she may be certain of, that I will never take her by force;
and then he left the room.

What think you now, Mrs. Pamela? says Mrs. Jewkes; are you
not yet persuaded my master hath honourable designs? I think
he hath given no great proof of them to-night, said I. Your experience I find is not great, says she, but I am convinced you
will shortly be my mistress, and then what will become of poor
me?

With such sort of discourse we both fell asleep. Next morning
early my master sent for me, and after kissing me, gave a paper
into my hand which he bid me read; I did so, and found it to be
a proposal for settling 250*l.* a year on me, besides several other
advantageous offers, as presents of money and other things. Well,
Pamela, said he, what answer do you make me to this? Sir, said
I, I value my vartue more than all the world, and I had rather
be the poorest man's wife, than the richest man's whore. You
are a simpleton, said he; that may be, and yet I may have as
much wit as some folks, cried I; meaning me, I suppose, said he;
every man knows himself best, says I. Hussy, says he, get out of
the room, and let me see your saucy face no more, for I find I
am in more danger than you are, and therefore it shall be my
business to avoid you as much as I can; and it shall be mine,
thinks I, at every turn to throw myself in your way. So I went
out, and as I parted, I heard him sigh and say he was bewitched.

Mrs. Jewkes hath been with me since, and she assures me she
is convinced I shall shortly be mistress of the family, and she

really behaves to me as if she already thought me so. I am
resolved now to aim at it. I thought once of making a little
fortune by my person. I now intend to make a great one by my
vartue. So asking pardon for this long scroll, I am,

Your dutiful Daughter,

Shamela.

LETTER XI.

Henrietta Maria Honora Andrews *to* Shamela Andrews.

Dear Sham,

I received your last letter with infinite pleasure, and am convinced it will be your own fault if you are not married to your
master, and I would advise you now to take no less terms. But,
my dear child, I am afraid of one rock only: that Parson Williams,
I wish he was out of the way. A woman never commits folly but
with such sort of men, as by many hints in the letters I collect
him to be: but, consider, my dear child, you will hereafter have
opportunities sufficient to indulge yourself with Parson Williams,
or any other you like. My advice therefore to you is, that you
would avoid seeing him any more till the knot is tied. Remember
the first lesson I taught you, that a married woman injures only
her husband, but a single woman herself. I am, in hopes of seeing
you a great lady,

Your affectionate Mother,

Henrietta Maria, &c.

The following letter seems to have been written before Shamela
received the last from her mother.

LETTER XII.

Shamela Andrews *to* Henrietta Maria Honora Andrews.

Dear Mamma,

I LITTLE feared when I sent away my last, that all my hopes
would be so soon frustrated; but I am certain you will blame
Fortune and not me. To proceed then. About two hours after I
had left the squire, he sent for me into the parlour. Pamela, said
he, and takes me gently by the hand, will you walk with me in
the garden; yes, sir, says I, and pretended to tremble; but I hope
your Honour will not be rude. Indeed, says he, you have nothing
to fear from me, and I have something to tell you, which if it
doth not please you, cannot offend. We walked out together, and
he began thus: Pamela, will you tell me truth? Doth the resistance
you make to my attempts proceed from vartue only, or have I
not some rival in thy dear bosom who might be more successful?
Sir, says I, I do assure you I never had a thought of any man
in the world. How, says he, not of Parson Williams! Parson Williams, says I, is the last man upon earth; and if I was a duchess,
and your Honour was to make your addresses to me, you would
have no reason to be jealous of any rival, especially such a fellow
as Parson Williams. If ever I had a liking, I am sure — but I am
not worthy of you one way, and no riches should ever bribe me
the other. My dear, says he, you are worthy of everything, and
suppose I should lay aside all considerations of fortune, and disregard the censure of the world, and marry you. O sir, says I,
I am sure you can have no such thoughts; you cannot demean
yourself so low. Upon my soul, I am in earnest, says he, —— O
pardon me, sir, says I, you can't persuade me of this. How
mistress, says he, in a violent rage, do you give me the lie?
Hussy, I have a great mind to box your saucy ears, but I am
resolved I will never put it in your power to affront me again,
and therefore I desire you to prepare yourself for your journey this instant. You deserve no better vehicle than a cart; however, for once you shall have a chariot, and it shall be ready
for you within this half hour; and so he flung from me in a
fury.

*What a foolish thing it is for a woman to dally too long with
her lover's desires; how many have owed their being old maids
to their holding out too long.*

Mrs. Jewkes came to me presently, and told me, I must make
ready with all the expedition imaginable, for that my master had
ordered the chariot, and that if I was not prepared to go in it,
I should be turned out of doors, and left to find my way home on
foot. This startled me a little, yet I resolved, whether in the
right or wrong, not to submit nor ask pardon: for that, you know,
Mamma, you never could yourself bring me to from my childhood: besides, I thought he would be no more able to master his
passion for me now, than he had been hitherto; and if he sent
two horses away with me, I concluded he would send four to
fetch me back. So, truly, I resolved to brazen it out, and with
all the spirit I could muster up, I told Mrs. Jewkes I was vastly
pleased with the news she brought me; that no one ever went
more readily than I should, from a place where my vartue had
been in continual danger. That as for my master, he might easily
get those who were fit for his purpose; but, for my part, I preferred my vartue to all rakes whatever —— And for his promises,
and his offers to me, I don't value them of a fig — not of a fig,
Mrs. Jewkes; and then I snapt my fingers.

Mrs. Jewkes went in with me, and helped me to pack up my
little all, which was soon done; being no more than two day-
caps, two night-caps, five shifts, one sham, a hoop, a quilted-
petticoat, two flannel-petticoats, two pair of stockings, one odd
one, a pair of lac'd shoes, a short flowered apron, a lac'd neck-
handkerchief, one clog, and almost another, and some few books:
as, *A full Answer to a plain and true Account*, &c. *The Whole
Duty of Man*, with only the duty to one's neighbour torn out.
The third volume of the *Atalantis. Venus in the Cloyster: Or, the
Nun in her Smock. God's Dealings with Mr. Whitefield. Orfus
and Eurydice.* Some sermon-books; and two or three plays, with
their titles, and part of the first act torn off.

So as soon as we had put all this into a bundle, the chariot
was ready, and I took leave of all the servants, and particularly
Mrs. Jewkes, who pretended, I believe, to be more sorry to part
with me than she was; and then crying out with an air of indifference, My service to my master, when he condescends to inquire after me, I flung myself into the chariot, and bid Robin
drive on.

We had not gone far before a man on horseback, riding full

speed, overtook us, and coming up to the side of the chariot,
threw a letter into the window, and then departed without uttering a single syllable.

I immediately knew the hand of my dear Williams, and was
somewhat surprised, tho' I did not apprehend the contents to
be so terrible, as by the following exact copy you will find them.

Parson WILLIAMS *to* PAMELA.

Dear Mrs. Pamela,

THAT disrespect for the clergy, which I have formerly noted to
you in that villain your master, hath now broke forth in a mani-
fest fact. I was proceeding to my neighbour Spruce's church,
where I purposed to preach a funeral sermon, on the death of
Mr. John Gage, the exciseman; when I was met by two persons
who are, it seems, sheriff's officers, and arrested for the 150*l.* which
your master had lent me; and unless I can find bail within these
few days, of which I see no likelihood, I shall be carried to gaol.
This accounts for my not having visited you these two days; which
you might assure yourself, I should not have failed, if the
potestas had not been wanting. If you can by any means prevail
on your master to release me, I beseech you so to do, not
scrupling anything for righteousness sake. I hear he is just
arrived in this country; I have herewith sent him a letter, of
which I transmit you a copy. So with prayers for your success,
I subscribe myself

Your affectionate Friend,

ARTHUR WILLIAMS.

Parson WILLIAMS *to Squire* BOOBY.

Honoured Sir,

I AM justly surprised to feel so heavy a weight of your displeasure, without being conscious of the least demerit towards
so good and generous a patron, as I have ever found you: for my
own part, I can truly say,

Nil conscire sibi nullæ pallescere culpæ.

And therefore, as this proceeding is so contrary to your usual goodness, which I have often experienced, and more especially in the loan of this money for which I am now arrested; I cannot avoid thinking some malicious persons have insinuated false suggestions against me; intending thereby, to eradicate those seeds of affection which I have hardly travailed to sow in your heart, and which promised to produce such excellent fruit. If I have any ways offended you, sir, be graciously pleased to let me know it, and likewise to point out to me the means whereby I may reinstate myself in your favour: for next to him whom the great themselves must bow down before, I know none to whom I shall bend with more lowliness than your Honour. Permit me to subscribe myself,

> *Honoured Sir,*
>> *Your most obedient, and most obliged,*
>> *And most dutiful humble Servant,*
>>> ARTHUR WILLIAMS.

The fate of poor Mr. Williams shocked me more than my own: for, as the *Beggar's Opera* says, "Nothing moves one so much as a great man in distress." And to see a man of his learning forced to submit so low, to one whom I have often heard him say, he despises, is, I think, a most affecting circumstance. I write all this to you, dear Mamma, at the inn where I lie this first night, and as I shall send it immediately, by the post, it will be in town a little before me. —— Don't let my coming away vex you: for, as my master will be in town in a few days, I shall have an opportunity of seeing him; and let the worst come to the worst, I shall be sure of my settlement at last. Which is all, from

> *Your dutiful Daughter,*
>> SHAMELA.

P.S. Just as I was going to send this away a letter is come from my master, desiring me to return, with a large number of promises. — I have him now as sure as a gun, as you will perceive by the letter itself, which I have inclosed to you.

This letter is unhappily lost, as well as the next which Shamela wrote, and which contained an account of all the pro-

ceedings previous to her marriage. The only remaining one which
I could preserve, seems to have been written about a week after
the ceremony was performed, and is as follows:

SHAMELA BOOBY *to* HENRIETTA MARIA HONORA ANDREWS.

Madam,

IN my last I left off at our sitting down to supper on our wedding night,* where I behaved with as much bashfulness as the
purest virgin in the world could have done. The most difficult
task for me was to blush; however, by holding my breath, and
squeezing my cheeks with my handkerchief, I did pretty well.
My husband was extremely eager and impatient to have supper
removed, after which he gave me leave to retire into my closet
for a quarter of an hour, which was very agreeable to me; for
I employed that time in writing to Mr. Williams, who, as I informed you in my last, is released, and presented to the living,
upon the death of the last parson. Well, at last I went to bed, and
my husband soon leapt in after me; where I shall only assure
you, I acted my part in such a manner, that no bridegroom was
ever better satisfied with his bride's virginity. And to confess
the truth, I might have been well enough satisfied too, if I had
never been acquainted with Parson Williams.

*O what regard men who marry widows should have to the
qualifications of their former husbands!*

We did not rise the next morning till eleven, and then we sat
down to breakfast; I eat two slices of bread and butter, and drank
three dishes of tea, with a good deal of sugar, and we both looked
very silly. After breakfast we drest ourselves, he in a blue
camblet coat, very richly laced, and breeches of the same; with
a paduasoy waistcoat, laced with silver; and I, in one of my
mistress's gowns. I will have finer when I come to town. We
then took a walk in the garden, and he kissed me several times,
and made me a present of 100 guineas, which I gave away before
night to the servants, twenty to one, and ten to another, and
so on.

* This was the letter which is lost. — Oliver's note.

We eat a very hearty dinner, and about eight in the evening went to bed again. He is prodigiously fond of me; but I don't like him half so well as my dear Williams. The next morning we rose earlier, and I asked him for another hundred guineas, and he gave them me. I sent fifty to Parson Williams, and the rest I gave away, two guineas to a beggar, and three to a man riding along the road, and the rest to other people. I long to be in London that I may have an opportunity of laying some out, as well as giving away. I believe I shall buy everything I see. What signifies having money if one doth not spend it.

The next day, as soon as I was up, I asked him for another hundred. Why, my dear, says he, I don't grudge you anything, but how was it possible for you to lay out the other two hundred here. Lal Sir, says I, I hope I am not obliged to give you an account of every shilling; troth, that will be being your servant still. I assure you, I married you with no such view; besides, did not you tell me I should be mistress of your estate? And I will be too. For tho' I brought no fortune, I am as much your wife as if I had brought a million — Yes, but, my dear, says he, if you had brought a million, you would spend it all at this rate; besides, what will your expenses be in London, if they are so great here. Truly, says I, sir, I shall live like other ladies of my fashion; and if you think, because I was a servant, that I shall be contented to be governed as you please, I will show you you are mistaken. If you had not cared to marry me, you might have let it alone. I did not ask you, nor I did not court you. Madam, says he, I don't value a hundred guineas to oblige you; but this is a spirit which I did not expect in you, nor did I ever see any symptoms of it before. O but times are altered now, I am your lady, sir; yes, to my sorrow, says he, I am afraid — and I am afraid to my sorrow too: for if you begin to use me in this manner already, I reckon you will beat me before a month's at an end. I am sure if you did, it would injure me less than this barbarous treatment; upon which I burst into tears, and pretended to fall into a fit. This frighted him out of his wits, and he called up the servants. Mrs. Jewkes immediately came in, and she and another of the maids fell heartily to rubbing my temples, and holding smelling-bottles to my nose. Mrs. Jewkes told him she feared I should never recover, upon which he began to beat his breasts, and cried out, O my dearest angel! curse on my passionate temper, I have destroyed her, I have destroyed her! — would she had spent my whole estate rather than this had happened. Speak to me, my love, I will melt myself into gold for thy pleasure. At last having pretty well tired myself with counterfeiting, and imagining I had continued long enough for my purpose in the sham fit, I began to move my eyes, to loosen my teeth, and to open my hands, which Mr. Booby no sooner perceived than he embraced and kissed me with the eagerest ecstasy, asked my pardon on his knees for what I had suffered through his folly and perverseness, and without more questions fetched me the money. I fancy I have effectually prevented any further refusals or inquiry into my expenses. It would be hard indeed, that a woman who marries a man only for his money, should be debarred from spending it.

Well, after all things were quiet, we sat down to breakfast, yet I resolved not to smile once, nor to say one good-natured, or good-humoured word on any account.

Nothing can be more prudent in a wife, than a sullen backwardness to reconciliation; it makes a husband fearful of offending by the length of his punishment.

When we were drest, the coach was by my desire ordered for an airing, which we took in it. A long silence prevailed on both sides, tho' he constantly squeezed my hand, and kissed me, and used other familiarities, which I peevishly permitted. At last, I opened my mouth first. — And so, says I, you are sorry you are married? — Pray, my dear, says he, forget what I said in a passion. Passion, says I, is apter to discover our thoughts than to teach us to counterfeit. Well, says he, whether you will believe me or no, I solemnly vow, I would not change thee for the richest woman in the universe. No, I warrant you, says I; and yet you could refuse me a nasty hundred pound. At these very words, I saw Mr. Williams riding as fast as he could across a field; and I looked out, and saw a lease of greyhounds coursing a hare, which they presently killed, and I saw him alight, and take it from them.

My husband ordered Robin to drive towards him, and looked horribly out of humour, which I presently imputed to jealousy. So I began with him first; for that is the wisest way. La, sir, says I; what makes you look so angry and grim? Doth the sight of Mr. Williams give you all this uneasiness? I am sure I would never have married a woman of whom I had so bad an opinion, that I must be uneasy at every fellow she looks at. My dear, answered he, you injure me extremely; you was not in my thoughts, nor, indeed, could be, while they were covered by so morose a countenance; I am justly angry with that parson, whose family hath been raised from the dunghill by ours; and who hath received from me twenty kindnesses, and yet is not contented to destroy the game in all other places, which I freely give him leave to do; but hath the impudence to pursue a few hares, which I am desirous to preserve, round about this little coppice. Look, my dear, pray look, says he; I believe he is going to turn higler. To confess the truth, he had no less than three tied up behind his horse, and a fourth he held in his hand.

Pshaw, says I, I wish all the hares in the country were d——d (the parson himself chid me afterwards for using the word, tho' it was in his service). Here's a fuss, indeed, about a nasty little pitiful creature, that is not half so useful as a cat. You shall not persuade me, that a man of your understanding would quarrel with a clergyman for such a trifle. No, no, I am the hare, for whom poor Parson Williams is persecuted; and jealousy is the motive. If you had married one of your quality ladies, she would have had lovers by dozens, she would so; but because you have taken a servant-maid, forsooth! You are jealous if she but looks (and then I began to water) at a poor p——a——a——rson in his pu——u——u——lpit, and then out burst a flood of tears.

My dear, said he, for heaven's sake dry your eyes, and don't let him be a witness of your tears, which I should be sorry to think might be imputed to my unkindness; I have already given you some proofs that I am not jealous of this parson; I will now give you a very strong one: for I will mount my horse, and you shall take Williams into the coach. You may be sure, this motion pleased me, yet I pretended to make as light of it as possible, and told him, I was sorry his behaviour had made some such glaring instance necessary to the perfect clearing my character.

He soon came up to Mr. Williams, who had attempted to ride off, but was prevented by one of our horsemen, whom my husband sent to stop him. When we met, my husband asked him how he did with a very good-humoured air, and told him he perceived he had found good sport that morning. He answered, pretty moderate, sir; for that he had found the three hares tied on to the saddle dead in a ditch (winking on me at the same time) and added he was sorry there was such a rot among them.

Well, says Mr. Booby, if you please, Mr. Williams, you shall come in and ride with my wife. For my own part, I will mount on horseback; for it is fine weather, and besides, it doth not become me to loll in a chariot, whilst a clergyman rides on horseback.

At which words, Mr. Booby leapt out, and Mr. Williams leapt in, in an instant, telling my husband as he mounted, he was glad to see such a reformation, and that if he continued his respect to the clergy, he might assure himself of blessings from above.

It was now that the airing began to grow pleasant to me. Mr. Williams, who never had but one fault, *viz.* that he generally smells of tobacco, was now perfectly sweet; for he had for two days together enjoined himself as a penance, not to smoke till he had kissed my lips. I will loosen you from that obligation, says I, and observing my husband looking another way, I gave him a charming kiss, and then he asked me questions concerning my wedding-night; this actually made me blush: I vow I did not think it had been in him.

As he went along, he began to discourse very learnedly, and told me the Flesh and the Spirit were two distinct matters, which had not the least relation to each other. That all immaterial substances (those were his very words) such as love, desire, and so forth, were guided by the Spirit: but fine houses, large estates, coaches, and dainty entertainments were the product of the Flesh. Therefore, says he, my dear, you have two husbands, one the object of your love, and to satisfy your desire; the other the object of your necessity, and to furnish you with those other conveniencies. (I am sure I remember every word, for he repeated it three times; O he is very good whenever I desire him to repeat a thing to me three times he always doth it!) As then the Spirit is preferable to the Flesh, so am I preferable to your other husband, to whom I am antecedent in time likewise. I say these things, my dear, (said he) to satisfy your conscience. A fig for my conscience, said I; when shall I meet you again in the garden?

My husband now rode up to the chariot, and asked us how we did — I hate the sight of him. Mr. Williams answered, very well, at your service. They then talked of the weather, and other things; I wished him gone again, every minute; but all in vain, I had no more opportunity of conversing with Mr. Williams.

Well; at dinner Mr. Booby was very civil to Mr. Williams, and told him he was sorry for what had happened, and would make him sufficient amends, if in his power, and desired him to accept of a note for fifty pounds; which he was so *good* to receive, notwithstanding all that had passed; and told Mr. Booby, he hoped he would be forgiven, and that he would pray for him.

We make a charming fool of him, i'fackins; times are finely altered; I have entirely got the better of him, and am resolved never to give him his humour.

O how foolish it is in a woman, who hath once got the reins into her own hand, ever to quit them again!

After dinner Mr. Williams drank the Church *et cetera;* and smiled on me; when my husband's turn came, he drank *et cetera* and the Church; for which he was very severely rebuked by Mr. Williams; it being a high crime, it seems, to name anything before the Church. I do not know what *Et cetera* is, but I believe it is something concerning choosing pallament men; for I asked if it was not a health to Mr. Booby's borough, and Mr. Williams with a hearty laugh answered, Yes, yes, it is his borough we mean.

I slipt out as soon as I could, hoping Mr. Williams would finish the squire, as I have heard him say he could easily do, and come to me; but it happened quite otherwise, for in about half an hour, Booby came to me, and told me he had left Mr. Williams, the mayor of his borough, and two or three aldermen heartily at it, and asked me if I would go hear Williams sing a catch, which, added he, he doth to a miracle.

Every opportunity of seeing my dear Williams was agreeable to me, which indeed I scarce had at this time; for when we returned, the whole corporation were got together, and the room was in a cloud of tobacco; Parson Williams was at the upper end of the table, and he hath pure round cherry cheeks, and his face looked all the world to nothing like the sun in a fog. If the sun had a pipe in his mouth, there would be no difference.

I began now to grow uneasy, apprehending I should have no more of Mr. Williams's company that evening, and not at all caring for my husband, I advised him to sit down and drink for his country with the rest of the company; but he refused, and desired me to give him some tea; swearing nothing made him so sick as to hear a parcel of scoundrels roaring forth the principles of honest men over their cups, when, says he, I know most of them are such empty blockheads, that they don't know their right hand from their left; and that fellow there, who hath talked so much of *shipping*, at the left side of the parson, in whom they all place a confidence, if I don't take care, will sell them to my adversary.

I don't know why I mention this stuff to you; for I am sure I know nothing about *pollitricks*, more than Parson Williams tells me, who says that the court-side are in the right on't, and that every Christian ought to be on the same with the bishops.

When we had finished our tea, we walked in the garden till it was dark, and then my husband proposed, instead of returning to the company (which I desired, that I might see Parson Williams again), to sup in another room by ourselves, which, for fear of making him jealous, and considering, too, that Parson Williams would be pretty far gone, I was obliged to consent to.

O! what a devilish thing it is, for a woman to be obliged to go to bed to a spindle-shanked young squire she doth not like, when there is a jolly parson in the same house she is fond of!

In the morning I grew very peevish, and in the dumps, notwithstanding all he could say or do to please me. I exclaimed against the privilege of husbands, and vowed I would not be pulled and tumbled about. At last he hit on the only method which could have brought me into humour, and proposed to me a journey to London, within a few days. This you may easily guess pleased me; for besides the desire which I have of showing myself forth, of buying fine clothes, jewels, coaches, houses, and ten thousand other fine things, Parson Williams is, it seems, going thither too, to be *instuted*.

O! what a charming journey I shall have; for I hope to keep the dear man in the chariot with me all the way; and that foolish Booby (for that is the name Mr. Williams hath set him) will ride on horseback.

So as I shall have an opportunity of seeing you so shortly, I think I will mention no more matters to you now. O I had like to have forgot one very material thing; which is that it will look horribly, for a lady of my quality and fashion, to own such a woman as you for my mother. Therefore we must meet in private only, and if you will never claim me, nor mention me to anyone, I will always allow you what is very handsome. Parson Williams hath greatly advised me in this, and says, he thinks I should do very well to lay out twenty pounds, and set you up in a little chandler's shop: but you must remember all my favours to you will depend on your secrecy; for I am positively resolved, I will not be known to be your daughter; and if you tell anyone so, I shall deny it with all my might, which Parson Williams says, I may do with a safe conscience, being now a married woman. So I rest

Your humble Servant,

SHAMELA.

P. S. The strangest fancy hath entered into my Booby's head that can be imagined. He is resolved to have a book made about him and me; he proposed it to Mr. Williams, and offered him a reward for his pains; but he says he never writ anything of that kind, but will recommend my husband, when he comes to town, to a parson *who does that sort of business for folks,* one who can make my husband, and me, and Parson Williams, to be all great people; for he *can make black white,* it seems. Well, but they say my name is to be altered; Mr. Williams says the first syllabub hath too comical a sound, so it is to be changed into Pamela; I own I can't imagine what can be said; for to be sure I shan't confess any of my secrets to them, and so I whispered Parson Williams about that, who answered me, I need not give myself any trouble: for the gentleman *who writes lives,* never asked more than a few names of his customers, and that he made all the rest out of his own head; you mistake, child, said he, if you apprehend any truths are to be delivered. So far on the contrary, if you had not been acquainted with the name, you would not have known it to be your own history. I have seen a *piece of his performance,* where the person, whose life was written, could he have risen from the dead again, would not have even suspected he had been aimed at, unless by the title of the book, which was superscribed with his name. Well, all these matters are strange to me, yet I can't help laughing, to think I shall see myself in a printed book.

So much for Mrs. Shamela, or Pamela, which I have taken pains to transcribe from the originals, sent down by her mother in a rage, at the proposal in her last letter. The originals themselves are in my hands, and shall be communicated to you, if you think proper to make them public; and certainly they will have their use. The character of Shamela will make young gentlemen wary how they take the most fatal step both to themselves and families, by youthful, hasty and improper matches; indeed, they may assure themselves, that all such prospects of happiness are vain and delusive, and that they sacrifice all the solid comforts of their lives, to a very transient satisfaction of a passion, which how hot so ever it be, will be soon cooled; and when cooled, will afford them nothing but repentance.

Can anything be more miserable, than to be despised by the

whole world, and that must certainly be the consequence; to be
despised by the person obliged, which it is more than probable
will be the consequence, and of which we see an instance in
Shamela; and lastly to despise one's self, which must be the
result of any reflection on so weak and unworthy a choice.

As to the character of Parson Williams, I am sorry it is a true
one. Indeed those who do not know him, will hardly believe it so;
but what scandal doth it throw on the order to have one bad
member, unless they endeavour to screen and protect him? In
him you see a picture of almost every vice exposed in nauseous
and odious colours; and if a clergyman would ask me by what
pattern he should form himself, I would say, Be the reverse of
Williams: So far therefore he may be of use to the clergy themselves, and though God forbid there should be many Williamses
amongst them, you and I are too honest to pretend, that the body
wants no reformation.

To say the truth, I think no greater instance of the contrary
can be given than that which appears in your letter. The con-
federating to cry up a nonsensical ridiculous book (I believe the
most extensively so of any ever yet published), and to be so weak
and so wicked as to pretend to make it a matter of religion;
whereas so far from having any moral tendency, the book is by
no means innocent: For,

First, There are many lascivious images in it, very improper to
be laid before the youth of either sex.

2dly, Young gentlemen are here taught, that to marry their
mother's chambermaids, and to indulge the passion of lust, at the
expense of reason and common sense, is an act of religion, virtue,
and honour; and, indeed, the surest road to happiness.

3dly, All chambermaids are strictly enjoined to look out after
their masters; they are taught to use little arts to that purpose:
and lastly, are countenanced in impertinence to their superiors,
and in betraying the secrets of families.

4thly, In the character of Mrs. Jewkes vice is rewarded; whence
every housekeeper may learn the usefulness of pimping and
bawding for her master.

5thly, In Parson Williams, who is represented as a faultless
character, we see a busy fellow, intermeddling with the private
affairs of his patron, whom he is very ungratefully forward to
expose and condemn on every occasion.

Many more objections might, if I had time or inclination, be
made to this book; but I apprehend, what hath been said is suf-

ficient to persuade you of the use which may arise from publishing an antidote to this poison. I have therefore sent you the
copies of these papers, and if you have leisure to communicate
them to the press, I will transmit you the originals, though I
assure you, the copies are exact.

I shall only add, that there is not the least foundation for
anything which is said of Lady Davers, or any of the other
ladies; all that is merely to be imputed to the invention of the
biographer. I have particularly inquired about Lady Davers,
and don't hear Mr. Booby hath such a relation, or that there is
indeed any such person existing. I am,

Dear Sir,

Most faithfully and respectfully,

Your humble Servant,

J. OLIVER.

Parson TICKLETEXT *to Parson* OLIVER.

Dear SIR,

I HAVE read over the history of *Shamela*, as it appears in those
authentic copies you favoured me with, and am very much
ashamed of the character, which I was hastily prevailed on to
give that book. I am equally angry with the pert jade herself,
and with the author of her life: for I scarce know yet to whom
I chiefly owe an imposition, which hath been so general, that
if numbers could defend me from shame, I should have no
reason to apprehend it.

As I have your implied leave to publish what you so kindly
sent me, I shall not wait for the originals, as you assure me the
copies are exact, and as I am really impatient to do what I think
a serviceable act of justice to the world.

Finding by the end of her last letter, that the little hussy was
in town, I made it pretty much my business to inquire after her,
but with no effect hitherto: as soon as I succeed in this inquiry,
you shall hear what discoveries I can learn. You will pardon the
shortness of this letter, as you shall be troubled with a much
longer very soon: and believe me,

Dear Sir,

Your most faithful Servant,

THO. TICKLETEXT.

P. S. Since I writ, I have a certain account, that Mr. Booby hath caught his wife in bed with Williams; hath turned her off, and is prosecuting him in the spiritual court.

NOTES

Joseph Andrews (1742)

THE TEXT. Of the five editions of *Joseph Andrews* published during Fielding's lifetime, the first four show clear signs of authorial revision, the most extensive "alterations and additions" occurring in the second edition, which was through the presses by 31 May 1742. The present text is based largely on that of the fourth edition, published 29 October 1748, since that version incorporates all the earlier revisions as well as some significant changes of its own. One or two readings from previous editions and from the fifth edition have been admitted. Though care has been taken to preserve the substance of the text as Fielding wrote it, spelling, capitalization, punctuation, and italics (except where they affect the sense or emphasis of a given passage) have been normalized in the interest of the modern reader.

7. 2 (page 7, line 2)   "these little volumes": *Joseph Andrews* was originally published in two volumes.

7. 9–10   "HOMER . . . gave us a pattern of both these": Fielding refers to the *Margites,* a satirical epic having a fool, or *margos,* for its hero. Both Aristotle and Zeno accepted the work as Homer's.

7. 11   "Aristotle tells us": In the *Poetics,* IV, 10–12.

7. 19   "the critic": Aristotle in the *Poetics.*

7. 26   "the *Telemachus* of the Archbishop of Cambray": *Les Aventures de Télémaque* (1699), a didactic, allegorical prose epic by François de Salignac de la Mothe-Fénelon (1651–1715), a French theologian who was appointed Archbishop of Cambrai in 1695.

7. 32   "*Clelia . . .* the *Grand Cyrus*": The anglicized titles of voluminous French romances, all of which were translated into English during the seventeenth century and enjoyed a great vogue: *Astrée,* the several parts of which were issued 1607–28, is by Honoré d'Urfé (1567–1625); *Cassandre* (1644–50) in 10 vols. and *Cléopâtre* (1647–56) in 12 vols. are by Gauthier de Costes de la Calprenède (1614–63); *Clélie* (1654–60) and *Artamène, ou le Grand Cyrus* (1649–53), both in 10 vols., are by Mlle. Madeleine de Scudéry (1607–1701).

8. 1   "fable": One of the most elusive of the terms of epic criticism: it can refer either to the underlying moral of the work, or to the entire story, including the episodes.

8. 6   "sentiments": A term referring to the thoughts and manners of the characters, which in the serious epic must be dignified and decorous.

9. 1–2 "my Lord Shaftesbury's opinion of mere burlesque": Anthony Ashley Cooper, Third Earl of Shaftesbury (1671–1713), an influential moral philosopher of Deistical inclinations. The passage to which Fielding refers is from *Sensus Communis: An Essay on the Freedom of Wit and Humour* (1709), Pt. I, sec. 5.

9. 5 "some little success on the stage this way": See the Introduction, page viii.

9. 36–37 "the ingenious Hogarth": The painter William Hogarth (1697–1764), best known for his series of "moral fables" satiric of various aspects of contemporary society: *e.g.*, *A Harlot's Progress* (1732), *A Rake's Progress* (1735), *Marriage à la Mode* (1743–45). Fielding, who was a personal friend of Hogarth, greatly admired his work, to the extent that he more than once alludes to his paintings to clarify the description of characters in his novels.

10. 12–13 *"the Comedy of Nero, with the merry Incident of ripping up his Mother's Belly"*: The emperor Nero (A.D. 37–68) ordered the assassination of his mother, Agrippina, who, in a gesture of repudiation of her son, proffered her womb to the sword and was stabbed to death.

10. 17–20 "Aristotle . . . tells us . . . villainy is not its object": *Poetics*, V, 1–2.

10. 21–22 "the Abbé Bellegarde, who hath writ a treatise on this subject": *Reflexions sur le ridicule, et sur les moyens de l'eviter* (1696) by Jean Baptiste Morvan de Bellegarde (1648–1734).

11. 14 "our Ben Jonson": The English dramatist (1572–1637), best known for his satiric "humors" comedies: *e.g.*, *Every Man in his Humour* (1598), *Volpone* (1606), *The Alchemist* (1610).

11. 23–24 "bolt from his chair with his hat under his arm": An allusion to the sedan chair and to the fashionable way of carrying the three-cornered hat.

11. 38 "the poet": William Congreve (1670–1729). The verses are from his poem, "Of Pleasing; An Epistle to Sir Richard Temple," lines 63–64.

13. 20 "Plutarch, Nepos": Plutarch (c. A.D. 46–after 120), author of the well-known *Lives* of Greek and Roman statesmen; Cornelius Nepos (c. 99–24 B.C.), Roman biographer whose greatest work is his lives *Of Illustrious Men*.

13. 24–30 "the history of John the Great . . . the Champions of Christendom": Fielding facetiously refers to some popular penny romances that were hawked about by chapmen: *The History of Jack and the Giants*, *The History of Guy, Earl of Warwick*, *The Unfortunate Lovers: The History of Argalus and Parthenia*, and *The Most Famous History of the Seven Champions of Christendom: Saint George of England, Saint Denis of France, Saint James of Spain, Saint Anthony*

of Italy, Saint Andrew of Scotland, Saint Patrick of Ireland, and Saint
David of Wales, the first written version of which was done in 1596 by
Richard Johnson.

14. 8 "authentic papers and records": Richardson posed as the
editor, not the author, of Pamela's private correspondence, and in his
Preface used the ruse to praise his own work.

14. 9–10 "the lives of Mr. Colley Cibber": Colley Cibber (1671–
1757), actor, playwright, and poet-laureate. Though once on friendly
terms, Cibber and Fielding had been at odds for some time, Fielding
having satirized the comedian in *The Author's Farce* and *The Historical
Register*. In his autobiography, *An Apology for the Life of Mr. Colley
Cibber, Comedian* (1740), Cibber had called Fielding "a broken wit"
and had charged him with debasing the stage with such slanderous
and abusive works that he made necessary the Licensing Act of 1737.
Fielding retaliated in *The Champion, Shamela,* and in his first novel.
Specifically, the passage here alludes to Cibber's statement early in
Chapter III of the *Apology:* "I am now come to that crisis of my life,
when Fortune seem'd to be at a loss what she should do with me.
Had she favour'd my father's first designation of me, he might then,
perhaps, have had as sanguine hopes of my being a bishop, as I afterwards conceived of my being a general, when I first took arms, at the
Revolution. Nay, after that, I had a third chance too, equally as good,
of becoming an under-propper of the State." Fielding also hits, in
general, at the fulsome tone of Cibber's addresses to his superiors and
at his prodigious vanity — a trait to which the comedian, with justice,
is constantly confessing.

14. 19–20 "the excellent essays or letters prefixed to the second
and subsequent editions": In the first edition of *Pamela* Richardson had
allowed two commendatory letters to be prefixed to his work; in the
second edition he inserted twenty-four additional pages of these "puffs,"
including a poem.

14. 28–31 "male chastity . . . the only virtue which the great
Apologist hath not given himself": Though Cibber was something of a
fop and a gambler, he seems not to have been especially notorious as
a philanderer. Fielding may remember Pope's line in the *Epistle to
Arbuthnot:* "And has not Colley still his lord and whore?"

15. 20 "Merry Andrews": Clowns.

15. 37–38 "bound an apprentice, according to the statute": 5 Elizabeth, cap. 4, known as "the Statute of Apprentices."

16. 1–2 "the god Priapus": In Greek mythology, the grotesque god
of fertility, whose special care was gardens, where his statue was placed
as a kind of scarecrow guardian.

16. 2 "Jack o' Lent": Usually a human effigy to be thrown at, but
here apparently a scarecrow.

16. 6 " 'whipper-in' ": A huntsman's assistant who keeps the hounds from straying from the main pack.

16. 23 "to play booty": To throw the race deliberately for profit.

17. 12–14 "no more than Mr. Colley Cibber, apprehend . . . malice and envy to exist": In the *Apology,* Chapter I, Cibber writes: "My ignorance, and want of jealousy of mankind has been so strong, that it is with reluctance I even yet believe any person, I am acquainted with, can be capable of envy, malice, or ingratitude. . . ."

18. 6 "churchwarden": A lay officer of a parish church, elected by the parishioners to assist the clergyman with administrative duties.

18. 10 "the *Whole Duty of Man*": A favorite devotional work published in 1658, and probably written by Richard Allestree (1619–81), chaplain to the King and provost of Eton.

18. 10–11 "Thomas à Kempis": Thomas à Kempis (1380–1471), Augustinian monk and author of the widely read *Imitation of Christ,* a pious work tracing the soul's progress to spiritual perfection.

18. 18 "Baker's *Chronicle*": *A Chronicle of the Kings of England, from the time of the Romans Government unto the Death of King James* (1643) by Sir Richard Baker (1568–1645). The passages to which Joseph Andrews refers, somewhat inaccurately, may be found in the *Chronicle* under the headings, "Casualties happening in [the] time" of Henry IV and Queen Elizabeth.

18. 28 " 'to improve his talent' ": Cf. the parable of the talents, Matthew 25:14–30.

19. 2 "a modus": A modus substituted a fixed money payment for the tithe of the produce that parishioners were expected to pay the Church. Over the years the value of the produce tended to increase, but the amount of the modus remained as originally fixed, thus, in effect, gradually diminishing the real income of the clergyman.

22. 10–11 "whom . . . we shall hereafter call JOSEPH": An allusion to the chastity of the biblical Joseph, who resisted the solicitations of Potiphar's wife. (Genesis 39:7–20.)

24. 21 "discover": reveal, disclose.

24. 32 "clerk": The parish clerk was a layman who assisted the clergyman by looking after the church precincts, leading the congregation in responses, assisting at baptisms and marriages, and "setting psalms," *i.e.,* singing the first line of a hymn so that the congregation could follow.

25. 35 "ratifia": A liqueur made from the stones of peaches or apricots.

26. 14 " 'green-sickness' ": A kind of anemia that sometimes affects young girls at puberty, giving a greenish tinge to the complexion.

27. title *"the sublime style"*: The term used to describe the grand and lofty language appropriate to the epic or heroic modes in literature.

29. 20 "the great Rich": John Rich (1682?–1761), theatrical manager who was largely responsible for the enormous contemporary vogue of "entertainments" and pantomimes, in which he took the role of Harlequin and astonished audiences with spectacular tricks and stage effects. He was satirized by writers like Fielding and Pope for debasing and vulgarizing the theaters.

29. 33 "juggler": A sleight-of-hand artist, a magician.

30. 1 "Hesperus": The evening star.

30. 4 "Thetis": A Nereid of the sea, where the sun in classical literature rose and set.

30. 6 "Phoebus": Apollo, god of the sun.

32. 19–20 "poets talk of the 'statue of Surprise' ": Cf. Ovid, *Metamorphoses*, III, 418–19, where Narcissus gazes at his image in stupefaction and remains motionless like a statue carved from marble; or Shakespeare's *Richard III*, III, vii, which in Cibber's version reads: ". . . each like statues fix'd,/ Speechless and pale, star'd in his fellow's face. . . ."

32. 21–22 "Surprise made one of the sons of Crœsus speak, though he was dumb": Crœsus, king of Lydia (c. 560–546 B.C.), had two sons: one was accidentally killed; the other was mute. During the capture of Crœsus' citadel by the army of Cyrus, a Persian soldier approached Crœsus to kill him. Seeing his intention, Crœsus' son was shocked by fear into uttering his first words: "Fellow, slay not Crœsus." (Herodotus, I, 85.)

32. 24 "Mr. Bridgewater, Mr. William Mills": Actors who performed in Fielding's plays. Fielding was especially fond of "honest Billy Mills," a good man, if no very good actor; he died 17 April 1750.

32. 27 "Phidias, or Praxiteles": Athenian sculptors of the 5th and 4th centuries B.C., respectively.

32. 28 "my friend Hogarth": See note to p. 9, lines 36–37.

34. 18–19 " 'mophrodites . . . singing in an opera' ": Mrs. Slipslop means hermaphrodites, of course, and refers to the *castrati* who sang in the Italian opera, which was very popular in London and the target of much criticism from those who thought it was contributing to the decline of the legitimate theater.

36. 35 "the hall of Westminster": A court of justice in London.

36. 35 "Serjeant": A lawyer's title.

39. 20 "Sir John's family": Fielding's error for Sir Thomas's.

40. 9 "the closest Cornish hug": The wrestlers of Cornwall were famous.

40. 33 "Timotheus . . . called plain Tim": Probably the inn-keeper, "Mr. Timothy Harris," whom Fielding compliments in *Tom Jones*, VIII, 8.

43. 3–4 " 'to prevent the jury's finding *that they fled for it*' ":

Fleeing the scene of a capital crime was an offence for which the fugitive, even if innocent, was liable to forfeit all his goods.

44. 4 "transported for robbing a hen-roost": In order to supply the plantations with servants, it had been the practice since the seventeenth century to transport beggars and felons to the colonies.

44. 22 "Nantes": Brandy, from Nantes, France.

44. 24 "Hungary-water": A distilled water made of rosemary flowers and spirit of wine.

45. 1–6 " '*conveyance . . . ejectment*' ": The bawdy double-entendres in this passage depend on the jargon of real property law. Some of the less obvious terms are as follows: a *conveyance* is the transference of property from one person to another; an *incumbrance* is a burden on property, such as a mortgage; an *heir in tail* is a person who succeeds to an estate by virtue of a deed of entail, whereby the estate is settled on a number of specific persons in succession; an *ejectment* is the process of expelling a person from his holding.

45. 33 "odes . . . sweeter than those of our *laureat*": Cibber succeeded Laurence Eusden as poet-laureate in 1730; his wretched odes, composed annually on the occasions of the New Year and the King's birthday, were a standing jest.

46. 12 " 'The law makes us provide for too many' ": Since barracks were scarce in England, soldiers were quartered in the villages. Innkeepers were compelled to lodge them and to supply them with food and beer on an allowance of only four pence a day for each man.

47. 15–16 "the malign concoction of his humours": Medicine in the eighteenth century was still very much under the influence of the humoral pathology of Hippocrates. According to this doctrine, the health of the body depends upon the perfect mingling of the four basic humors: blood, phlegm, yellow bile, and black bile. When one of these elements predominates or is defective, sickness results.

47. 16 "suscitation": An excitation or quickening.

48. 4 "sneaker:" A small bowl of punch.

51. 34 " 'Galen and Hippocrates' ": "The divine Hippocrates" (c. 460–355 B.C.), as Fielding's contemporary, Robert James, called him, "to whom we are obliged for most things in medicine." Hippocrates was a famous Greek physician and medical theorist of the Age of Pericles. Galen (c. A.D. 138–201) was his equally celebrated disciple, who studied in Alexandria and Rome. The authority of these men was undisputed until the time of Vesalius in the sixteenth century, and it was still very influential in Fielding's day. They were voluminous writers; it is more than doubtful that the pockets of Fielding's surgeon could contain their works.

52. 10 " '*Veniente accurrite morbo*' ": The surgeon's misquotation of Persius, *Satires*, III, 64: "*venienti occurrite morbo*" ("Oppose the disease at its first approach").

52. 13 " *'Ton dapomibominos poluflosboio thalasses'* ": Two un-related Greek phrases from the *Iliad:* *"Ton dapomibominos"* ("answer-ing him") and *"poluflosboio thalasses"* ("of the loud sounding sea").

52. 15 " 'the gentleman has caught a *traitor'* ": Considering the context and the reaction of the company, *traitor* makes little sense and is probably a printer's error for *Tartar.* The slang phrase, "to catch a Tartar," was applied to one who finds himself caught in a trap he has laid for another.

52. 25 " *'occiput'* ": The back of the skull.

52. 25 " *'divellicated'* ": Torn apart.

52. 26 " *'pericranium'* ": The membrane enveloping the skull.

52. 27 " *'pneumatic'* ": Affecting respiration.

53. 36–37 *"bona waviata,* and belonged to the lord of the manor": *Bona waviata* are goods that are stolen and waived, or left behind, by the thief in his flight. As a punishment to the owner of the goods for not making pursuit, they were forfeited either to the king or to the lord of the manor.

55. 31–32 "three volumes of sermons": Fielding overlooked this slip in revision. In Chapter 16 and thereafter, they are nine volumes.

55. 32–33 "an advertisement . . . by a society of booksellers": Thomas Osborne, a friend of Richardson's, was the founder of "the Society of Booksellers for promoting of learning, by purchasing of manuscripts, copies, &c. design'd for the press." The advertisement which tempted Adams toward London appeared in the newspapers, including Fielding's *Champion,* from March 4th to August 8th, 1741.

57. 3–5 "the *Attorney's Pocket-Companion* . . . Mr. Jacob's *Law-Tables* . . . Wood's *Institutes"*: Three legal handbooks of the period — *The Attorney's Pocket Companion; or A Guide to the Practisers of the Law* by John Mallory of the Inner Temple; *The Statute-Law Com-mon-plac'd: or, A General Table to the Statutes* by Giles Jacob (1686–1744); and *An Institute of the Laws of England* by Thomas Wood (1661–1722).

57. 8 "the maid's oath would convict the prisoner": The testimony of one witness was sufficient evidence, except in cases of treason, where two were required.

57. 9 *"è contra, totis viribus":* "Mightily of the opposite opinion."

59. 31–34 "liable to be indicted for the thief's escape": Since the thief was lawfully held in his house, Mr. Tow-wouse could be legally considered as jailer and his house a prison. For allowing a prisoner to escape, the jailer would be charged with a misdemeanor (if he was merely negligent) or with a felony (if he acted voluntarily). The punishment for negligence was a fine; for voluntary complicity, the jailer was judged guilty of the crime for which the prisoner was being detained. Negligence could not be charged, however, for failing to pursue a criminal at night.

60. 3 " 'deal board' ": A thin pine board.

60. 8 "cider-and": A hot drink made of brandy, cider, spices, and sugar.

60. 42 " 'he was to make up a sum' ": He owed a sum of money due on a certain date.

63. 19–20 " 'one Tillotson's sermons' ": John Tillotson (1630–94), Archbishop of Canterbury and a leader of the latitudinarians. He was famous for his lucid sermons and his "natural, easy" manner of preaching.

65. 22 "bookseller": In the eighteenth century, virtually synonymous with "publisher."

66. 12 " 'Whitefield or Wesley' ": George Whitefield (1714–70) and John Wesley (1703–91) were the zealous and indefatigable evangelists who about 1738, in an effort to reform the apathy and worldliness within the Church of England, began the movement known as Methodism. Whitefield's strong Calvinistic bias eventually caused him to break with Wesley; it was also the cause of Fielding's repeated attacks on him. (See the Introduction, pp. xiv-xv and xxviii.)

66. 14–15 " '30th of January' ": The anniversary of the execution of Charles I in 1649. Sermons preached on this date, therefore, were usually political.

66. 33 " 'licensing act' ": The Theatrical Licensing Act was passed 21 June 1737. See Introduction, p. ix.

67. 14–15 " 'Toland, Woolston, and all the free-thinkers' ": In the early years of the eighteenth century, John Toland (1670–1722) and Thomas Woolston (1670–1733) were among the most notorious of the freethinkers, a term virtually synonymous with Deists, who disputed the orthodox doctrine of the Church and the authenticity of a religion based on claims of a special revelation as distinct from the evidence of the natural creation. Toland's *Christianity Not Mysterious* (1696) inaugurated a heated dispute between orthodoxy and Deism that lasted a generation. As a result of his equally controversial *Discourses on the Miracles of our Saviour* (1727–29), Woolston was found guilty of blasphemy, fined, and imprisoned for a year.

67. 26 " 'enthusiasm' ": Excessive zeal or emotionalism in religion; a false sense of the divine presence.

68. 14–15 " 'A Plain Account of the Nature and End of the Sacrament' ": This work, a rational, mystery-dispelling account of the eucharist, was published in 1735 by the latitudinarian Bishop of Winchester, Benjamin Hoadly (1676–1761), whom Fielding greatly admired. Hoadly argued that the Lord's Supper is a simple memorial of Christ's death and sacrifice and an occasion to remind Christians of their moral duty to their fellow men. The book was attacked by a host of writers, among them William Law.

68. 27–28 " 'the Alcoran, the *Leviathan*, or Woolston' ": The Koran, of course, is the sacred book of Mohammedism. *The Leviathan: or the Matter, Form, and Power of a Commonwealth, Ecclesiastical and Civil* (1651) was the work of the philosopher Thomas Hobbes (1588–1679): it defined man as a rapacious, basically immoral creature motivated by self-interest and pride, and it subordinated Church to State. For these reasons, the book and its author were repeatedly attacked by the divines. For a sketch of Woolston, see note to p. 67, lines 14–15.

69. 30–31 "caught . . . with the manner": "To be *Taken with the manner*, is where a thief having stolen any thing, is taken with the same about him, as it were in his *hands*; which is called *flagrante delicto*." (Jacob, *New Law-Dictionary*, 4th ed., 1739.)

70. 20 "the western circuit": One of the eight districts in England and Wales through which judges and barristers traveled twice a year to hold court.

73. 12–13 "the sum total, commonly found at the bottom of our first page": The price of a book or pamphlet was often printed at the foot of the title-page.

74. 9–10 "Montaigne, who promises you one thing and gives you another": The *Essais* of Michel Eyquem de Montaigne (1533–92) were first published in 1580. Montaigne frequently digresses, in a kind of conversational manner, from the subject indicated in his titles (*e.g.*, "Of Coaches," "Of the Resemblance of Children to Their Parents," or "Of Lame People"), a practice that was much discussed by perplexed critics.

74. 22–26 "Homer . . . hawked them all separately": An allusion to a controversial story, found in Aelian and reported by Rapin, that Homer's epics originally existed as independent episodes or "rhapsodies" which were first assembled into their present form at the direction of Pisistratus. In his "Essay on the Life, Writings, and Learning of Homer" prefixed to Pope's *Iliad* (1715), Thomas Parnell observes that Pisistratus divided each epic "into twenty four books, to which were afterwards prefix'd the twenty four letters" of the Greek alphabet.

74. 27 "by subscription": A method of guaranteeing publishers from financial loss: prospective patrons were solicited to commit themselves to purchase a copy or copies of a projected work.

74. 28–34 "publishing by numbers. . . .": Instead of, or in addition to, publishing a work entire, booksellers would occasionally release it in a series of weekly or monthly parts. Several dictionaries were issued in this way, among them Bayle's and the fourth edition of Ephraim Chambers' *Cyclopedia*. But Fielding probably had in mind the first publication of the Society of Booksellers for Promoting Learning (see note to p. 55, lines 32–33), Robert James' *Medicinal Dictionary*, announced in June 1741, though it did not begin to appear until

the following January. Thomas Osborne was the bookseller in question, who, while posing as a "benefactor to the public," released the work by numbers at an unusually high price.

74. 35 "Virgil . . . his poem": The *Aeneid*.

74. 38 "Milton went originally no farther than ten": *Paradise Lost* (1667) originally contained ten books only; not until the second edition in 1674 did it appear in its final form of twelve books.

75. 1–2 "what books are proper for embellishment, and what require simplicity": According to a precept of Aristotle (*Poetics* XXII, XXIV, 11), the diction of an epic poem should be varied, admitting embellishment in descriptive passages where action lags, but maintaining simplicity at other times. According to another principle, this time found in Horace, the opening or exordium should be couched in modest, unadorned language.

76. 7 " '*ut ita dicam*' ": "So to speak."

76. 12 "a verse out of Theocritus": In Theocritus, *Idyll* IV, 41–43, Corydon consoles Battus for the loss of his love: "Soft you, good Battus; be comforted. Good luck comes with another morn; while there's life there's hope; rain one day, shine the next." (J. M. Edmonds, trans.)

77. 4 "an easy pad": An easy-paced road horse.

78. 11 "Æschylus": Æschylus (c. 525–456 B.C.) was the first of the great Greek tragic poets. His works, permeated with a religious spirit that Adams must have found congenial, include *The Suppliants, Seven Against Thebes*, the *Oresteia*, and *Prometheus Bound*.

82. 20 " 'squinny-gut' ": Very thin, "skinny."

82. 37 "the thimble and button": The ancestor of the shell game. A professional sharper called a "thimblerigger" would place a small object, in this case a button, under one of three thimbles, quickly change their positions, and then challenge the bystanders to guess under which thimble the button would be found.

88. note "This letter was written by a young lady": Probably by Fielding's sister Sarah (1710–68), who turned novelist herself in 1744 with *The Adventures of David Simple*, to which her brother contributed a Preface.

89. 37 "smarts": Beaus.

91. 9 "ridottos": A favorite social occasion of the time, consisting of music and dancing.

91. 14 "rich as . . . an Attalus": the wealth of the Attalids, kings of the Hellenistic city of Pergamon (269–133 B.C.), was proverbial. In particular, the "Testament of Attalus [III]" (c. 170–133 B.C.), bequeathing his kingdom to Rome, was celebrated by the poets as the type of lucrative good fortune.

91. 28 "to smoke him": To make him out, to understand him.

92. 40 " 'sneaking' ": Penny-pinching and generally contemptible.

93. 23 " 'the Country Interest' ": Another name for the Country
Party or the Patriots, who opposed Walpole's administration and
claimed to be champions of the best interests of the country as a whole
rather than of any special factions. By making Bellarmine a member
of the turn-coat Opposition — a stroke added to the revised second
edition of the novel — Fielding sharpened the satire of his former
party.

93. 38 " 'Corinthian assurance . . . more than Lais herself' ": The
luxury and profligacy of Corinth was notorious. Lais, who was stoned
to death about 340 B.C. by a mob of apprehensive wives, was a celebrated courtesan of that city.

100. 41–42 "he looked like the ghost of Othello. . . .": The traveler
exposes his ignorance by quoting Macbeth's words to the ghost of the
murdered Banquo: "Thou canst not say I did it. Never shake/Thy
gory locks at me" (III.iv.50–51).

102. 20 " 'Boniface' ": After the jovial character in Farquhar's
Beaux' Stratagem (1707), the name given to an innkeeper.

104. 35 " '*Myhummetman*' ": Slipslop's version of "Mohammedan."

106. 41 " 'a Smithfield match' ": A marriage for money.

107. 4–5 "the saying of Solomon. . . .": Cf. Proverbs 13: 24.

108. 33 " '*Our-asho*' ": Slipslop means "Horatio."

110. 28–29 " 'that affair of Carthagena' ": In the spring of 1741
the British attacked the Spanish stronghold of Carthagena in the West
Indies, but the assault was entrusted to raw, undisciplined troops, and
it was badly mismanaged by General Wentworth. What should have
been a victory was turned into a disaster for the English.

110. 35 "trained-bands": A trained company of citizen soldiers.

111. 17 " 'alderman of a corporation' ": Corporation is the name
for the civic authorities of a borough or incorporated town, including
the mayor, aldermen, and councillors.

111. 33 " 'Church was in danger' ": "The Church in danger" was
a cry raised repeatedly by the clergy during the early years of the
eighteenth century. For the most part, it was used by High Churchmen, such as Sacheverell, who feared and resented the incursions of
nonconformists and dissenters; but the latitudinarians raised it, too,
against the influence of Jacobitism and "popery."

112. 6 " '*Ne verbum quidem, ut ita dicam*' ": "Not so much as a
word, so to speak."

112. 40 " '*Non omnia possumus omnes*' ": "All things are not in
the power of all" (Virgil, *Eclogues*, viii, 63).

114. 17 " 'Paris fights, and Hector runs away' ": In the *Iliad*, XI,
Paris, the abductor of Helen and not much of a fighter, wounds Diomedes and others of the Greeks; in XXII, Hector, the Trojan champion,

turns and flees as Achilles approaches the gates of Troy.

114. 19–23   " 'the great Pompey . . . left the battle of Pharsalia' ":
The decisive battle that determined the leadership of Rome was fought
at Pharsalia in 48 B.C. When Pompey's cavalry broke before Cæsar's
charge, he retired to his tent in a fit of grief and shame.

114. 21–22   " 'Cicero and Paterculus, have formed such elogiums' ":
For the "eulogies" of Pompey to which Adams refers, see Cicero, *Orations*, "On the Manilian Law," and Paterculus, *Roman History*, II,
xxix.

118. 13–15   "used her as some very honest men have used their
country . . . to rifle her himself": This passage, added to the second
edition, squints at the treachery of Fielding's former party, the so-
called Patriots, who began scrambling for places in the government as
soon as Walpole fell from power in February 1742.

118. 26   " 'Heus tu' ": "Ho there!"

119. 5–6   "Kensington, Islington, Hackney, or the Borough": These
places — to the west, north, and south of the City, or central part of
London — were much frequented: the Gardens in Kensington were
a fashionable place of resort; Islington, with its spa and tea-gardens,
was popular for a Sunday outing; Hackney was a fashionable suburb;
through the Borough of Southwark, on the south side of the Thames,
ran the chief thoroughfare from London to the southern counties, and
here, too, were prisons, brothels, and the Southwark Fair.

120. 21–22   "£80 for apprehending the robbers": By law, the reward for capturing a highwayman and prosecuting him to conviction
was £40, together with his horse, arms, money, and any other goods
taken with him.

121. 9   "the art of a Shepherd": Jack Sheppard (1702–24), robber,
highwayman, and escape-artist extraordinary. In the space of some
five months before he was hanged in 1724, he broke prison four times.

123. 12–13   " 'If she had not provided herself a great belly' ": Preg-
nant women condemned to death could plead their condition in hopes
that the sentence would be mitigated or deferred.

123. 14   " 'Turpin' ": Dick Turpin (1705–39), notorious highwayman, hanged in 1739.

123. 16   " 'Turpis' ": Latin for "shameful," "disgraceful."

123. 22   " 'benefit of the clergy' ": Originally, clergymen were
exempt from trial by a secular court; since very few other people
were literate, the ability to read was a convenient test of a clergyman,
who could thereby gain his exemption. Later, on his first conviction,
anyone who could read was granted "benefit of clergy" and exempted
from the sentence. But by the eighteenth century the privilege was
being withdrawn from more and more offences, one of which was
highway robbery.

123. 26–27 "to 'cap' verses": A contest in which each participant tries to cap the quotation of his opponent with another beginning with the last letter of the verse his rival has used.

123. 28 "*Molle meum levibus cord est vilebile telis*": The wit's misquotation of Ovid, *Heroides*, XV, 79: "*molle meum levibusque cor est violabile telis*" ("My heart is tender and easily pierced by the light shaft").

123. 34 " '*Si licet, ut fulvum spectatur in ignibus haurum*' ": The wit's garbled version of Ovid, *Tristia*, I, v, 25: "*scilicet ut fulvum spectatur in ignibus aurum,/ tempore sic duro est inspicienda fides*" ("Truly, as yellow gold is tested in fire,/ So loyalty must be proved in time of stress").

124. 4 " '*Mars, Bacchus, Apollo, virorum*' ": Adams is more familiar with the Eton Latin grammar than his antagonist. In that textbook, the chapter on the gender of nouns opens as follows: "Propria *proper* names quæ *which* tribuuntur *are assigned* maribus *to the male kind* dicas *you may call* mascula *masculines;* ut *as,* sunt *are* Divorum *the names of the heathen Gods;* Mars *the God of war,* Bacchus *the God of wine,* Apollo *the God of wisdom;* Virorum *the names of men. . . .*"

124. 23 "the *mittimus*": A writ from a justice of the peace to a jailer, directing him to take an offender into custody.

124. 28 " '*ignoramus*' ": This term, meaning "we are ignorant," was used by the grand jury when they judged the evidence against a person insufficient to bring him to trial.

125. 26 " '*Pollaki toi*' ": "Often." The parson apparently misconstrues the opening words of Æschylus' *Seven Against Thebes*, 227.

128. 17 "the fate of Pygmalion": The story of Pygmalion, the legendary king of Cyprus who fashioned an ivory statue of a perfect woman and fell in love with it, is told in Ovid, *Metamorphoses*, X, 243–97.

128. 19 "as helpless a condition as Narcissus": For rejecting the nymph Echo, Narcissus was made to fall hopelessly in love with his own reflection in a pool of water. See Ovid, *Metamorphoses*, III, 339–510.

128. 20 "*Quod petis est nusquam*": "What you seek is nowhere" (Ovid, *Metamorphoses*, III, 433).

128. 23 "*Cœlum ipsum petimus stultitia*": "In our folly we seek the very heavens" (Horace, *Odes*, I, iii, 38).

129. 27 "Lethe": The river of oblivion in Hades.

130. 1 "counterfeit": A portrait.

132. 32 "his Majesty's Bear-Garden": The Bear-Garden in Hockley-in-the-Hole, Clerkenwell, was the scene of rough and violent sports — the baiting of bears and bulls, wrestling, cudgel-playing, and the like.

132. 33 "hops": Informal dancing parties.

133. 21 "levee": A morning reception of visitors by a person of distinction.

135. 10–12 "a look . . . not unlike that which Cleopatra gives Octavia in the play": Dryden's *All for Love,* III.

135. 28 "as many tongues as Homer desired": Homer wished for ten tongues and ten mouths. (*Iliad,* II, 489.)

135. 42 " 'he had no licence. . . .' ": To be married within the Church, it was necessary either to procure a licence from the bishop or, more properly, to publish the banns three times. But before the Marriage Act of 1753 any contract made before witnesses was deemed legally valid.

136. 35 " '*Heureka*' ": "I've found it!" — Archimedes' cry when he discovered the principle of specific gravity.

137. 4–5 "might more properly be called a farmer": As Fielding pointed out in *The Champion,* in order that they might better attend to their spiritual offices, the clergy were forbidden by law to take lands to farm or to buy and sell in markets.

137. 23 "night-gown": A dressing gown.

138. 18 " '*Nihil habeo cum porcis*' ": "I have nothing to do with swine."

139. 26–27 "worshipped her husband, as Sarah did Abraham": Cf. I Peter 3:6.

140. 3 " 'warm' ": Rich.

140. 21 "a led captain": A sycophant or parasite.

141. 11 " 'the tithing-man' ": The parish constable.

141. 26 " 'the poor's rate' ": By an Act of 1597, officers in each parish were empowered to levy a tax to support the poor.

144. 7–8 "*Turne . . . attulit ultro*": "Turnus, what none of the gods would have dared to promise you as you wished, lo! rolling time has brought unasked" (*Aeneid,* IX, 6–7).

145. 31 "the parish of St. James's": Near the royal palace, St. James's Square was the most fashionable square in London, and on St. James's Street clubs and eating houses abounded.

150. 23 " 'Seneca' ": Lucius Annæus Seneca (c. 5 B.C.–A.D. 65), Roman moralist and philosopher of the Stoic school.

150. 27 " 'vails' ": Tips.

152. 7–8 " 'Holland shirts' ": Shirts made of a fine linen from the province of Holland in the Netherlands.

153. 2 " 'Covent Garden' ": A district in London notorious for its brothels.

153. 8–9 " 'those cursed *guarda-costas* . . . before the beginning of the war' ": By treaty English ships were forbidden all traffic in Spanish waters except for the trade in slaves. Extensive smuggling began in the West Indies, and Spanish coast-guard vessels, regarding the English as privateers, harassed and boarded British merchantmen.

It was the captain of a *guarda-costa* who cut off the ear of Captain Richard Jenkins in 1731, an incident that later came to public notice and gave its name to the war with Spain that was formally declared on 19 October 1739.

153. 11 " 'between wind and water' ": That part of a ship that is sometimes above water and sometimes submerged.

153. 11 " 'forced to strike' ": To lower the ship's sail or flag as a sign of surrender.

154. 20 " '*Cœlum non animum mutant qui trans mare currunt*' ": "Those who cross the sea change climate, but not their state of mind" (Horace, *Epistles*, I, xi, 27).

154. 22–33 " 'seen the Pillars of Hercules . . . and called at Colchis, to see if there is ever another golden fleece' ": In this passage Adams uses the classical names for places that the innkeeper would otherwise have recognized. The Pillars of Hercules are the Rock of Gibraltar and Mt. Abyla, on opposite sides of the Straits of Gibraltar; according to the legend, they were originally one mountain, torn asunder by Hercules. Carthage was a city on the Gulf of Tunis in North Africa, destroyed by the Romans in 146 B.C. Scylla and Charybdis, the monsters that hindered Odysseus' passage homeward, were thought to be a treacherous rock and whirlpool in the Straits of Messina. It was actually Icarus, Dædalus' son, who fell into that part of the Aegean Sea which bears his name. (For the story, see Ovid, *Metamorphoses*, VIII, 183–235.) The Cyclades are islands that circle the sacred island of Delos in the Aegean Sea. The Euxine Sea, the Greek name for the Black Sea, was crossed by the Argonauts on their voyage eastward to recover the golden fleece at Colchis.

154. 24–25 " 'where Archimedes was found' ": When the Romans under Marcellus captured Syracuse in 212 B.C., a soldier came upon Archimedes, the famous mathematician, and killed him as he was engaged in solving a problem, so abstracted that he was unaware of the sack of the city.

154. 27–28 " 'Helle . . . described by Apollonius Rhodius' ": Fleeing Thebes with her brother Phrixus on the back of a flying ram of golden fleece, Helle became dizzy and plunged into the straits now called the Dardanelles, but known to antiquity as the Hellespont. It was to recover the golden fleece of the ram that the Argonauts sailed for Colchis, a story recounted in the *Argonautica* of Apollonius Rhodius, who, however, devotes only two brief lines to the fate of Helle (I, 256–57).

154. 37 " 'the Levant' ": The eastern part of the Mediterranean. Adams understands the root of the word (from *lever*, to rise; hence the East in reference to the sun), but he goes too far and mistakes the location.

155. 7–8 " 'the story of Socrates' ": Cicero, *Tusculan Disputations*,

IV, xxxvii, 80, is the principal source of the story; he gives the name
of the physiognomist as Zopyrus.

155. 30–31 " 'Trade . . . as Aristotle proves. . . .' ": *Politics*, I,
esp. iii, 23, and iv, 5.

155. 34 " 'the *Gazetteers'* ": Since June 1735 *The Daily Gazetteer*,
printed by Samuel Richardson and subsidized by Walpole, had been
the government's main organ for purposes of propaganda. Walpole
bought up quantities of the newspaper and had them distributed gratis
throughout the country. Among the "parsons" that contributed to the
paper were Henry Bland, Dean of Durham, and Francis Hare, Bishop
of Chichester.

157. 15–16 "my Lord Clarendon . . . and Rapin": The works and
authors Fielding refers to are as follows: *The True Historical Narrative
of the Rebellion and Civil Wars in England* (1702–04) by Edward
Hyde, Earl of Clarendon (1609–74); *Memorials of the English Affairs*
(1682) by Bulstrode Whitelocke (1605–75); *The History of England*
(1707–18) by Laurence Echard (1670?–1730); and *Histoire d'Angle-
terre* (1723–25) by Paul de Rapin de Thoyras (1661–1725). Fielding,
of course, is ridiculing the way in which some historians allow a
favorite bias to distort the facts. For this purpose, the histories of
Clarendon, a Royalist, and Whitelocke, a Puritan, were well suited.

158. 6–7 "the true history of Gil Blas": *Gil Blas de Santillane*
(1715–35), a great picaresque novel by Alain-René Le Sage (1668–
1747).

158. 16 "Scarron": *Le Roman comique* (1651–57), a lively anti-
romance by Paul Scarron (1610–60).

158. 16–17 "the history of Marianne and *Le Paisan Parvenu*": *La
Vie de Marianne* (1731–41) and *Le Paysan parvenu* (1735–36), novels
by Pierre Carlet de Chamblain de Marivaux (1688–1763).

158. 21 "modern novel and Atalantis writers": An allusion, especially, to the scandalous *roman à clef, Secret Memoirs and Manners of
Several Persons of Quality of Both Sexes. From the New Atalantis*
(1709), by Mrs. Mary de la Rivière Manley (1663–1724).

158.29 "what Balzac says of Aristotle. . . .": Fielding refers to the
second of *Deux discours envoyez à Rome, à Monseigneur le Cardinal
Bentivoglio* (1627) by Jean-Louis Guez de Balzac (1594–1654).
Averroës had praised Aristotle as the perfection of Nature; a later
philosopher, Balzac remarks, extended the hyperbole, calling him,
"UNE SECONDE NATURE."

158.33–34 " 'those stilts,' which the excellent Voltaire tells us,
in his Letters. . . .": *Letters Concerning the English Nation* (1733),
Letter 18. "Stilts" is Voltaire's metaphor for the figurative style that
he thinks characteristic of the English tragic drama.

158.37 "Beyond the realm of Chaos and old Night": Fielding's
misremembrance of Milton's *Paradise Lost*, I, 542–43: "A shout that

tore Hell's concave, and beyond/ Frighted the reign of Chaos and old Night."

159. 1 "Mariana's": *Historia general de España* (1601) by Juan de Mariana (1536–1623).

160. 24–30 "I could name a peer": Probably Philip Dormer Stanhope, Fourth Earl of Chesterfield (1694–1773), patron of letters and, at the time *Joseph Andrews* was being written, a leader of the Opposition against Walpole's ministry.

160. 30–37 "I could name a commoner": Ralph Allen (1694–1764), philanthropist and patron of letters. Fielding's long and friendly association with Allen, who was to become the model for Squire Allworthy of *Tom Jones*, stems from about this period. Allen made a fortune devising a system of cross-posts for England and Wales and then purchased the valuable stone quarries near Bath. Of this stone he built the magnificent Palladian mansion which Fielding here calls a "palace."

161. 30 "according to Milton, darkness visible": *Paradise Lost*, I, 63.

162. 35–36 *"Est hic . . . honorem"*: "Here is a spirit that scorns the light [life], and believes that honor which you pursue to be well bought with a life" (Virgil, *Aeneid*, IX, 205–206).

163. 33 *"petit-maîtres"*: Fops.

165. 41–166. 4 " 'Mr. Pope . . . his Homer' ": Alexander Pope's magnificent, if free, translation of the *Iliad* in heroic couplets was published in six volumes, 1715–20. In 1725–26, a version of the *Odyssey* followed in which Pope was assisted by William Broome and Elijah Fenton.

166. 16–18 " 'what Cicero says of a complete orator . . .' ": *De Oratore*, I, 6.

166. 19–20 " 'the philosopher' ": Aristotle, who refers to Homer as "the poet" in *Poetics*, XXII, 9.

166. 22–23 " 'his *Margites*' ": See notes to p. 7, lines 9–10 and 11.

166. 31–32 " 'praised . . . for not choosing the whole war' ": *Poetics*, XXIII, 5.

166. 36 " '*Trojani Belli Scriptorem*' ": "Writer of the Trojan War" (Horace, *Epistles*, I, ii, 1).

166. 37 " '*Pragmaton Systasis*' ": "Arrangement of the incidents" (*Poetics*, VI, 12).

167. 2–4 " 'his manners, which Aristotle places second . . .' ": *Poetics*, VI, 19. Adams refers to Aristotle's discussion of "character."

167. 14–15 " 'Aristotle in his 24th chapter' ": *Poetics*, XXIV, 14.

167. 21–23 " 'the two episodes where Andromache is introduced' ": *Iliad*, VI, 407–39, and XXIV, 723–45.

167. 25–27 " 'Sophocles falls short' ": In the *Ajax*, 485–524.

167. 33–34 " 'as to the [diction], Aristotle . . . is very diffuse' ":
Poetics, XIX, 7–XXII, 19.

167. 35–36 " 'that great critic . . . calls *Opsis*' ": *Poetics*, VI, 28.

169. 8 "jealousy": Suspicion.

169. note "the observation which M. Dacier makes": In the Preface
to *Le Plutus et les Nuées d'Aristophane* (1684).

169. note "Mr. Congreve . . . in his *Love for Love*": *Love for Love*
(1695), II, ii.

170. 41–42 "the great horse": A war horse.

171. 28 " '*Write letters to yourself!*' ": By underscoring Adams'
astonished outburst and Wilson's reply, Fielding seems to be calling
attention to a private joke, cracked, good-naturedly, at the expense of
his friend, the Reverend William Young — the forgetful and very
learned curate who was the flesh-and-blood original of Parson Adams.
Stories of Young's absent-mindedness were widely current. Among
them is this, recorded by a contemporary: shortly before the publication of *Joseph Andrews*, Parson Young "endeavoured by a feigned
letter to himself to get leave of his patron to spend a fortnight in the
country; but this letter, containing the pretended invitation, he put
into his patron's hand sealed and unopened, which piece of absence
discovered the scheme, so little was he able to act this little piece of
disingenuity."

171. 34 " 'H——d's' ": Mother Haywood was the proprietress of
a house of ill-fame in Covent Garden.

172. 21 "Lincoln's Inn Fields": The site of another playhouse.

172. 36 "St. James's coffee-house": Situated on the southwest
corner of St. James's Street, this was a favorite meeting place for
Whigs and officers of the palace guards.

173. 19 "the Temple": The Inner and the Middle Temple are two
of the Inns of Court, legal societies where prospective lawyers study
for admission to the bar.

174. 8 "a City apprentice": The City is that part of London
situated within the ancient boundaries; it is the center of financial and
commercial activity.

174. 19 "all the campaigns under the Duke of Marlborough":
John Churchill, First Duke of Marlborough (1650–1722), victorious
commander of the British forces against France, 1702–11.

176. 11–13 "railed at the beautiful creatures . . . as Juvenal
himself": An allusion to Juvenal's *Sixth Satire*, a diatribe against
women.

177. 22 "whisk": Another name for whist.

177. 23 "revoke": To renege in the game of whist.

177. 28 "*eclaircissement*": A mutual understanding, especially between lovers.

177. 42 *"ignis fatuus"*: A will-o'-the-wisp.

178. 38 "sp — wing": *I.e.*, spewing, vomiting.

181. 26 "civility-money": A "tip" given to a jailer to secure his good will.

182. 3–4 "Thus Prior, Rowe, Pope . . . received large sums": Nicholas Rowe (1674–1718) was the chief tragic dramatist of Queen Anne's reign; his *Tragedy of Jane Shore* was published by subscription in 1714. Matthew Prior (1664–1721) made some 4000 guineas from the subscription publication of his *Poems on Several Occasions* in 1719, and Pope's Homer, issued in the same manner, earned its author about £9000.

183. 12–13 "Plato himself did not hold poets in greater abhorrence": In discussing the education of the Guardians in *The Republic*, Plato advised the strict censorship of poetry, which lied about the nature of the gods and appealed to the emotions rather than to the intellect.

183. 14 "on Sundays only": By statute, all Sunday arrests were unlawful.

190. 4–5 " 'the late famous King Theodore' ": Theodore Stephen, Baron von Neuhof (1686–1756), a German adventurer, crowned as Theodore I of Corsica in 1736, but expelled by the Genoese in 1738. He fled to England, where he was imprisoned for debt but eventually released and supported by benefactors for the rest of his life.

194. 21 " 'King's Scholars' ": Scholars on the foundation at Westminster, a distinguished "public" school, who attend either Christ Church, Oxford, or Trinity College, Cambridge. The university to which Adams refers is probably Oxford, since that was the school of his original, the Reverend William Young. (See note to p. 171, line 28.)

195. 6 " '*gloriari non est meum*' ": "It is not for me to boast."

195. 18 " '*Hinc illæ lachrymæ*' ": "Hence proceed all those tears" (Horace, *Epistles*, I, xix, 41).

195. 20–23 " 'that fine passage in the play of Cato' ": Adams slightly alters Juba's reply to Syphax in Addison's *Cato*, II, v: "If knowledge of the world makes man perfidious,/ May Juba ever live in ignorance!"

196. 5 "Chiron's time": Chiron, the wise old centaur, was the legendary mentor of heroes, among them Achilles, Jason, Hercules, and Aeneas.

196. 12–13 " '*Nemo mortalium omnibus horis sapit*' ": "No man is wise all the time" (Pliny, *Natural History*, VII, xl, 131).

198. 13 " 'Ammyconni, Paul Varnish, Hannibal Scratchi, or Hogarthi' ": Joseph's garbled versions of the names of celebrated painters, the first three Italian: Jacopo Amigoni (1675–1752), Paolo

Veronese (1528–88), and Annibale Carracci (1560–1609). Amigoni lived in England from 1730–39 and, among other works, painted the Queen's portrait. The last name in the series is, of course, another compliment to Hogarth.

198. 38–39 "'a man that lived at a place called Ross'": Pope celebrates the benevolence of "the man of Ross," John Kyrle (1634?–1724), in his *Epistle to Bathurst*, 250–90.

198. 39 "'another at the Bath, one Al — Al —'": Ralph Allen again (see note to p. 160, lines 30–37), whom Pope compliments for his charity in *Epilogue to the Satires*, Dialogue I, 135–36.

199. 14 "Henley himself": John "Orator" Henley (1692–1756), an eccentric preacher and "zany," as Pope called him, who left the Church to set up his "tub," or pulpit, in Newport market.

201. 12 "Turnus": The champion of Latium in Virgil's *Aeneid;* he flees from Aeneas during the final battle, Book XII.

201. 41 "Mallet": David Mallet (1705–65), Scotch poet and dramatist, whose tragedy of *Mustapha* (1739) was applauded by the Opposition for its allusive attack on Walpole. Here, however, Fielding praises Mallet's prose style in *The Life of Francis Bacon*, published by Andrew Millar in 1740.

201. 41–202. 1 "that Dedication and Preface . . . of the Life of Cicero": *The History of the Life of Marcus Tullius Cicero*, by the Cambridge theologian and librarian, Conyers Middleton (1683–1750), was published in February 1741. Fielding was irritated both by Middleton's fulsome dedication of his work to John Lord Hervey, a contemptible courtier and a favorite agent of Walpole, and by Middleton's condescending disparagement, in his Preface, of *Observations on the Life of Cicero*, a work by Fielding's friend and patron, George Lyttelton, the man to whom he later dedicated *Tom Jones*. In *Shamela* Fielding had parodied Middleton's Dedication, and later in *Joseph Andrews* he roughly (in every sense of the word!) paraphrased a passage from it in describing the unscrupulous politics of Beau Didapper, for whom Lord Hervey was the original. (See note to p. 269, lines 18–24.)

202. 11 ff. "grasped his cudgel. . . .": In mock-heroic style, the history of Joseph Andrews' cudgel imitates the account of Achilles' shield in the *Iliad*, 478–613.

202. 12–13 "a mighty strong man of Kent": William Joy (d. 1734), called "Samson, the strong man of Kent," performed remarkable feats of strength in the early part of the century.

202. 15 "Mr. Deard's best workmen": William Deard (d. 1761) was a London jeweler, toymaker, and pawnbroker.

202. 17 "the Park": The Mall in St. James's Park, near the royal palace, was the fashionable public walk of the day.

202. 22 "a certain long English baronet": An ironic reference to "Long" Sir Thomas Robinson (1700?–77), commissioner of the excise under Walpole and appointed Governor of Barbados in 1741. He was very tall, very dull, and very extravagant, managing to ruin himself by the lavish balls he gave for the *beau monde*.

202. 24 "the first night of Captain B——'s play": Charles Bodens (d. 1753), officer in the Coldstream Footguards and Gentleman Usher to the King. His play, *The Modish Couple*, seems not to have been his at all, but rather the work of Lord Hervey and the Prince of Wales, who wished to conceal their authorship and so persuaded Bodens, who was also the court pimp, to stand in their stead. But knowledge of the ruse apparently leaked to the public, and when the play opened on 10 January 1732, it was roundly damned.

202. 28 "Mr. Cock": Christopher Cock, a well-known London auctioneer of the time.

203. 18–19 "no 'babler,' no 'overrunner' ": A "babler," or "babbler," is a hound that barks too much; an "overrunner" is one who runs past the scent, thus losing the trail of the hare or fox.

203. 23 "Mr. John Temple": Probably the Hon. John Temple, Esq. (1680–1752), younger brother of Henry Temple, First Viscount Palmerston. Through his marriage with his cousin Elizabeth, granddaughter of the distinguished statesman, Sir William Temple, he acquired the estate at Moor Park, Surrey — approximately fifty miles from the scene of Adams' "roasting."

204. 26 "preponderate": To consider beforehand.

211. 11 " 'taw' ": A game of marbles.

211. 18–19 " 'Scipio, Lælius . . . in amusements of the most trifling kind' ": Scipio Africanus Minor (c. 185–129 B.C.), Roman orator and general of great distinction; Caius Lælius, "the Wise" (b. c. 186 B.C.), also an eminent orator and soldier, renowned for his learning and wisdom. The friendship of these two men was well-known. Parson Adams remembers Cicero's story that, for relaxation, Scipio and Lælius would go on excursions into the country and take pleasure in such boyish amusements as gathering mussels and shells. (*De Oratore*, II, 6.)

213. 26 "commons": Victuals.

214. 20–21 "a priest of the Church of Rome . . . who understand our laws": The lot of the Roman Catholics in England was very severe. By law, their priests were liable to a fine of £200 and could be charged with high treason for saying Mass. And laymen, if they refused to deny even the spiritual authority of the Pope, were subject to the penalties of recusancy — fined £20 a month for not attending church, forbidden to hold any government office, to prosecute suits at law, or even to travel over five miles without a special licence.

362 Joseph Andrews

214. 24–27 " 'easier for a cable-rope . . .' ": Adams' emendation of Matthew 19:24 had been proposed by other biblical scholars, but it is not generally approved.

216. 8 " 'Rabbit' ": Drat.

218. 30 "hanger": A short sword hung from the belt.

218. 37–38 *"with a lumpish noise, and his halfpence rattled in his pocket"*: Fielding's brilliant mock-heroic adaptation of a line that recurs in the *Iliad:* «δουπησεν δὲ πεσών, ἀράβησε θὲ τεύχέ ἐπ αυτψ» ("He fell with a thud, and his armor clanged upon him").

219. 7–8 "where . . . the natural and artificial noses are conjoined": The venereal disease often attacked and destroyed the nose.

221. 1 " 'Booth' ": Barton Booth (1681–1733), a famous tragedian.

221. 2 " 'Otway' ": Thomas Otway (1652–85), poet and playwright, best remembered for his blank-verse tragedies, *The Orphan* (1680) and *Venice Preserved* (1682).

221. 10 " 'Bettertons and Sandfords' ": Thomas Betterton (1635–1710), the most celebrated tragedian of his time; and Samuel Sandford (fl. 1661–1700), who excelled as a stage villain.

221. 42–222. 1 " 'Fenton's *Mariamne,* Frowd's *Philotas,* or Mallet's *Eurydice'* ": Tragedies performed, respectively, in 1723, 1731, and 1731; the authors are Elijah Fenton (1683–1730), Philip Frowde (d. 1738), and David Mallet (see note to p. 201, line 41.) The plays by Fenton and Mallet were quite successful, but Frowde's lugubrious performance died after six nights.

222. 3 " 'your Dillo or Lillo' ": George Lillo (1693–1739), author of *The London Merchant* (1731) and *Fatal Curiosity* (1736), and a man whom Fielding admired both as a person and as a dramatist.

222. 5 " 'Quin' ": James Quin (1693–1766), the leading actor between the retirement of Booth and the emergence of Garrick.

222. 5 " 'Delane' ": Dennis Delane (d. 1750), a popular tragedian.

222. 6 " 'young Cibber' ": Colley Cibber's disreputable son, Theophilus (1703–58), was, like his father, a successful comedian.

222. 6 " 'Macklin' ": Charles Macklin (1697–1797) acted in several of Fielding's comedies, but was best known for his portrayal of Shylock.

222. 7 " 'Mrs. Clive' ": Catherine "Kitty" Clive (1711–85) was a favorite comic actress, much admired for her fine singing voice. Fielding dedicated his *Intriguing Chambermaid* to her in 1734.

222. 8 " 'Lees' ": Nathaniel Lee (1653?–92), a writer of heroic tragedies whose most successful plays were *The Rival Queens* (1677) and *Theodosius* (1680).

222. 10–21 " '—— No more; for I disdain . . . and sleep till morn' ": From Lee's *Theodosius,* II, i, where Varanes protests his love for Athenais.

222. 22–23 " 'this disdain of Otway' ": The line from Otway's

The Orphan, I, i, reads: "Who'd be that sordid foolish thing call'd man . . . ?"

226. 3 "the *Consolation*": *The Consolation of Philosophy* by Boethius (c. A.D. 480–524).

226. 17–21 "the following soliloquy": Joseph's quotation is a rough version of *Macbeth,* IV. iii. 258–62, where Macduff laments the murder of his wife and children.

226. 26–27 " '*Cato* and the *Conscious Lovers*' ": Addison's *Cato* (1713) and Sir Richard Steele's *The Conscious Lovers* (1722) were among the most popular plays of the century. *Cato* is a tragedy in the classic manner, with a philosopher and orator for its hero; *The Conscious Lovers* is a sentimental comedy that moralizes against duelling and improper relationships between the sexes. Parson Adams was bound to approve!

229. 16 "no greater security than a bond and judgment": A certificate binding a person to pay a certain sum of money and assigning his chattels as security for the debt.

230. 32 " 'come to the parish' ": To seek relief of the parish, which, under the Poor Law, was obliged to provide for its poor.

231. 24 "put": Duffer.

232. 25–27 "the language of a late Apologist": At the close of Chapter IV of his *Apology,* Cibber refers to "those several vehicles [*i.e.,* the actors], which you will find waiting in the next chapter, to carry you thro' the rest of the journey, at your leisure."

233. 31 " 'the Gymnosophists' ": A sect of ascetic Hindu philosophers who wore little clothing and ate no meat.

241. 41–42 " 'never been able to pay for a licence' ": Unless a curate was formally licensed and admitted to his cure by the bishop of the diocese, he could be removed at pleasure by either the bishop or the incumbent.

243. 20 " 'drab' ": A slut.

244. 13 " 'Bridewell' ": In London, a house of correction for minor offences.

247. 19 "*verbatim & literatim*": "Word for word and letter for letter."

253. 29 " 'puisny' ": Puny.

255. 16 " '*Common Garden*' ": The colloquial name for Covent Garden, a disreputable district.

257. 5 "second climacteric": The "climacteric" was thought to be a critical stage in life, when a person's health, character, and fortune were especially subject to change. These times were usually said to occur every seven years.

264. 33–34 " 'Matthew the 5th, and part of the 28th verse' ": Fielding is having some fun here at Adams' expense. The latter part

of Matthew 5:28, which the parson omits as "foreign" to his purpose, reveals the inappropriateness of the text to the subject of sexual love *in marriage:* "But I say unto you, That whosoever looketh on a woman to lust after her hath committed adultery with her already in his heart."

265. 15–17 "'Had Abraham so loved his son Isaac'": Genesis 22:1–18.

266. 2–3 "'his first lesson in *Quæ Genus'*": In the Eton Latin grammar, the section treating the gender and declension of heteroclite or irregular nouns begins, "*Quæ genus aut flexum variant. . . .*"

266. 8 "'My poor Jacky'": Fielding's slip: Adams later calls his son Dicky.

266. 31–32 "younger brother wishes his elder": According to the right of primogeniture, the title and property of a family descends to the eldest son and his heirs.

268. 31–32 "'Non mea renidet in domo lacunar'": From Horace, *Odes,* II, xviii, 1–2: *Non ebur neque aureum/ mea renidet in domo lacunar*" ("No ivory or golden cornice glitters in my home").

269. 18–24 "'Though he was born to an immense fortune . . . so very large a share'": The original of Beau Didapper was John Lord Hervey (1696–1743), the little, foppish, effeminate courtier whose services as Sir Robert Walpole's favorite agent had been rewarded in 1740, when "the great man" made him Lord Privy-Seal. Fielding, taking his cue from Pope, had already ridiculed Hervey as Miss Fanny in Conny Keyber's Dedication to *Shamela,* which parodies the fulsome Dedication to Hervey that Conyers Middleton prefixed to his *Life of Cicero.* (See note to p. 201, lines 41 ff.) The first of the quoted passages in the account of Didapper is Fielding's own condensed and inverted version of two paragraphs in which Middleton celebrates his patron's patriotism. (Dedication to *The Life of Cicero* [1741], I, ix–xi.)

269. 25–27 "'As he was entirely well satisfied with his own person and parts. . . .'": In some bad verses, Lord Hervey cruelly ridiculed not only Pope's poetry and morals, but his birth and crooked body. Pope replied in *A Letter to a Noble Lord* (1733), satirizing Hervey under the name of Fannius, an enemy of Horace: "This *Fannius* was, it seems, extremely fond both of his *poetry* and his *person*. . . ."

270. 31 "'Propria quæ Maribus'": See note to p. 124, line 4.

278. 39–40 "quoted many texts of Scripture": In particular, Ephesians 5:22–23.

283. 14 "'a-jinketting'": A Slipslopism for "junketting."

288. 5 "'Hylas'": Hylas, of whom Hercules was fond, was a young man so beautiful that he was drowned by nymphs, who fell in love with him and pulled him into their spring.

288. 21 "hagged out": Worn out.

289. 12–13 " 'in the days of Saul' ": The encounter between Saul and the Witch of Endor is told in I Samuel 28:7–25.

291. 41 " 'removed me, by justices' warrants' ": In the event that his own parish should be unable to support him, a poor person could be removed to another parish by order of two justices of the peace.

292. 7 " 'chopping' ": Strapping, healthy.

293. 18 " '*Hic est quom quæris; inventus est*' ": "Here is the one whom you seek; he is found."

298. 9 "recollecting he might keep a curate at this living": The practice of pluralism — a clergyman's holding more than one benefice at the same time — was much abused in the eighteenth century, and Fielding disapproved of it. But he was even more concerned over the poverty of the inferior clergy: Adams' regular stipend of £23 a year, though not unusually small for a curate at this time, was hardly enough to provide for his family. Given this deplorable situation, Fielding seems to say, if Adams was not to abandon his parishioners, his only means of earning a living was to become a pluralist.

298. 23–24 "to make his appearance in 'high-life' ": A hit at Richardson's two-volume sequel to *Pamela* (December 1741), which traces the fortunes of its heroine "*in her Exalted Condition,*" in a series of letters "*between Her, and Persons of Figure and Quality, upon the most Important and Entertaining Subjects, in Genteel Life.*" By choosing to use the words, "high-life," however, Fielding may have wished to put an edge on the mischief here; for in May 1741 a spurious continuation of Richardson's book had appeared, bearing the title, *Pamela's Conduct in High Life.* This work caused Richardson's vanity no end of embarrassment and, in announcements in the journals, he was at pains to deny any connection with it.

Shamela (1741)

THE TEXT. The present text is based largely on that of the second edition of *Shamela*, which Fielding revised, briefly, before its publication on 3 November 1741. The "accidentals" of the text have been brought into closer agreement with modern usage.

Title-page "Necessary to be had in all Families": Here Fielding pokes fun at such statements as this from the prefatory "puffs" to *Pamela:* "it will be found worthy a place . . . in all families."

301. heading "To Miss Fanny": "Lord Fanny" was Pope's name for the effeminate John Hervey, Baron of Ickworth (1696–1743), courtier, occasional poet, and agent of Walpole. (See *First Satire of the Second Book of Horace*, line 6.) But here Fielding mocks, in close parody, Conyers Middleton's fulsome Dedication to Hervey in his *Life of Cicero*, published in February 1741. (See notes to JA, p. 201, lines 41 ff., and p. 269, lines 18–24.) To be fully appreciated, the two dedications should be read side by side, for Fielding's every paragraph is a ludicrous imitation of Middleton. In general, for Conny Keyber, read Conyers Middleton; for Miss Fanny, read Lord Hervey; for the *Life of Shamela*, read the *Life of Cicero*.

301. 31* "exciting the brute (as Dr. Woodward calls it) to rebel": John Woodward (1665–1728), physician, geologist, and Fellow of the Royal Society, whose eccentric theories made him a target for the wits. Though the phrase (used in reference to Hervey), "superior to every temptation, that can excite an appetite to rebel," is Middleton's, Fielding here alludes to Woodward's much-ridiculed treatise, *The State of Physic and of Diseases, with an Inquiry into the Causes of the late Increase of Them* (1718), wherein the good doctor traces all the evils of civilization — sickness, stupidity, poverty, faction, rebelliousness, atheism — to one cause: the rich pastries and seasoned meats and sauces of "the New Cookery." (See *State of Physic*, Section 47.)

301. 36 "Mr. Nash": Richard "Beau" Nash (1674–1762), the celebrated dandy of the age, who made Bath into a splendid resort for the world of fashion.

302. 6 "leaning too much to one side": An allusion to Hervey's politics.

303. 4–5 "do more good than the C——y have done harm in the world": Pope was reported as saying that *Pamela* "will do more good than many volumes of sermons." "C——y": *i.e.* "clergy."

---

* In the line-counts, the headings, salutations, and closings are omitted.

303. 9 *"his Honour"*: *I.e.*, Sir Robert Walpole (1676–1745), the Whig prime minister from 1721–42. For Fielding's relations with Walpole, see Introduction, pp. viii–ix, xvi–xvii.

303. 9–11 "he is able to draw . . . hearts in the world": An inversion of a compliment to Richardson found in the "puffs" to *Pamela*.

304. 2 "a little book which this winter hath produced": *Pamela* was published 6 November 1740.

304. 5–6 "the pulpit . . . hath resounded with its praise": Shortly after its publication, Dr. Benjamin Slocock had recommended *Pamela* to his congregation at St. Saviour's, Southwark.

304. 7–8 "his L——p will recommend it in a —— Letter": His Lordship is Edmund Gibson (1669–1748), a pious and conscientious divine who, after his appointment as Bishop of London in 1723, wrote frequent "pastoral" letters to the clergy of his diocese.

304. 13 ff. " 'soul of *religion*. . . .' ": The quoted passages in Parson Tickletext's letter are lifted almost verbatim from the letters to the editor prefixed to the second edition of *Pamela* — with, of course, the exception of strategic alterations by Fielding.

305. 21 " '(a poor girl's little, &c.)' ": The original reads, "(a poor girl's little, innocent, story)."

305. 23–30 "To be short, . . . the future effect of his influence": Though not in quotation marks, this paragraph is also a close parody of two passages found in the prefatory letters to *Pamela*. As an example of Fielding's technique here, compare the appropriate lines in *Shamela* with this from the original: "I was thinking, just now, as I return'd from a walk in the snow, on that old Roman policy, of exemptions in favour of men, who had given a few, bodily, children to the Republic. — What superior distinction ought *our* country to find (but that policy and we are at variance) for reward of this *father, of millions of* MINDS, which are to owe new formation to the future effect of his influence!" (p. xix).

305. 37–38 "as soon as the fourth edition is published": The second edition of *Pamela*, which Fielding apparently used, was published in February 1741, the third in March, and the fourth in May, a month after *Shamela* appeared.

306. 6–7 "the author of the famous Apology, which was sent me last summer": See notes to *JA*, p. 14, lines 9–10. Cibber's *Apology* was published in April 1740; a second edition appeared in May.

306. 10 *"C—ly C—b—r"*: *I.e.*, Colley Cibber.

308. 8 "the Old-Bailey": The central criminal court in London.

308. 9–10 "Scotch regiments in the Dutch service": In 1665, when war broke out between England and the Netherlands, the Dutch Republic compelled the British regiments that had been serving them to swear allegiance to Holland against their native land, or be cashiered. The English refused, but the Scotch complied and remained in the Dutch service for a century. The allusion here thus, in effect, makes Shamela's father a traitor to his country.

308. 11–12 "the late Gin-Act": The consumption of cheap gin was a prevalent, and often fatal, vice among the poor. In 1736 Parliament tried to correct the situation by passing Sir Joseph Jekyll's bill to impose a prohibitive duty on all spiritous liquors. The Act was very unpopular with the public and went virtually unenforced; if discovered by the mob, those who tried to inform against offenders were in danger of their lives.

308. 25 "put": Duffer.

309. 4 *"the Old House"*: The Drury Lane Playhouse.

311. 12–13 "Mr. Whitefield's sermons": See Introduction, pp. xiv–xv and xxviii, and notes to *JA*, p. 66, line 12.

311. 13 "the dealings with him": *A Short Account of God's Dealings with the Reverend Mr. George Whitefield* (1740), an autobiographical "confession," wherein Whitefield relates how he was rescued by the grace of God from a life of sin and depravity and directed into the priesthood.

311. 17 "Rochester's poems": John Wilmot, Second Earl of Rochester (1647–80), notorious libertine of the court of Charles II and a writer of obscene and pornographic love poetry.

318. 11 *"ingenium versatile"*: "Versatile genius." The phrase acquires additional ironic point if we recall the original context, Livy's praise of Cato: "his genius was so equally suited to all things that you would say that whatever he was doing was the one thing for which he was born" (Livy, XXXIX, xl, 5).

319. 7–8 "his text was, *Be not righteous over-much"*: Ecclesiastes 7:16. With a brilliant ironic twist, Fielding makes William preach on a text that had been first used by Dr. Joseph Trapp in a sermon against Whitefield and the Methodists delivered in April 1739. Trapp used the text to attack the enthusiasm of the Methodists and to reprove Whitefield for his slurs against the clergy. It was the occasion of a warm and lengthy controversy between the two divines.

321. 7 "old Scratch": A name for the devil.

321. 15–16 "the *Statue* of *Lamentations"*: *I.e.*, the "Statute of Limitations" of 1623 (21 Jac. I, cap. 16). By this Act, an action to recover a debt had to be brought within six years. Williams is something less than prompt in meeting his obligations.

322. 33 "paw": Naughty, obscene.

323. 6–8 *"the sermon book"*: Shamela's version of a passage from Robert South (1633–1716), a divine whom Fielding greatly admired. South's original wording: "Revenge is certainly the most luscious morsel that the devil can put into the sinner's mouth."

323. 17 "the dear *monysyllable*": See under "monosyllable" in Eric Partridge, A *Dictionary of Slang and Unconventional English*.

327. 25 "one sham": A "dicky."

327. 28 "one clog": A woman's wooden-soled shoe.

327. 29–33 "*A full Answer.* . . . *Orfus and Eurydice*": As one would suppose, the catalogue of Shamela's library reveals her to be without taste, morals, or sound religion. For *The Whole Duty of Man* and the *Atalantis,* see notes to *JA,* p. 18, line 10, and p. 158, line 21. *A full Answer to a plain and true Account, &c.* is one of the many works written in reply to *A Plain Account of the Nature and End of the Sacrament of the Lord's Supper* (1735) by the latitudinarian Bishop Benjamin Hoadly; Parson Adams praises Hoadly's tract in *Joseph Andrews* (see notes to *JA,* p. 68, lines 14–15). *Venus in the Cloyster: Or, the Nun in her Smock* was a notorious piece of pornography translated from the French in 1724 by one Robert Samber; it caused its unscrupulous publisher, Edmund Curll, to be hauled before the King's Bench. For *God's Dealings with Mr. Whitefield,* see note to p. 311, line 13. Lewis Theobald's opera-pantomime, *Orpheus and Eurydice,* with John Rich playing Harlequin in the comic interludes, was performed in February 1740 and ridiculed by Fielding in *The Champion* (February 21, May 24, 1740).

328. 27 "*Nil conscire sibi nullæ pallescere culpæ*": "To be conscious of no wrongdoing, to turn pale for no fault" (Horace, *Epistles,* I, i, 61).

329. 15–16 "as the *Beggar's Opera* says": John Gay's *Beggar's Opera* (1728), a popular "Newgate pastoral" about rogues and highwaymen. Shamela quotes Lucy Lockit's lament for the imprisoned Macheath (III, xv).

330. 26 "camblet": A fabric of wool and silk or goat hair.

330. 27 "paduasoy": A corded silk fabric.

332. 31 "lease": *I.e.,* leash.

333. 8 "higler": A hawker, often one who exchanges poultry and game for commodities of the town.

335. 21 "a catch": A round.

335. 24 "corporation": See notes to *JA,* p. 111, line 17.

336.21 "*instuted*": *I.e.,* instituted into his new benefice.

337. 6 ff. "a parson . . . *who writes lives*": The reference is obscure, but Professor Woods believes that the Reverend Thomas Birch (1705–66), a prolific biographer, is meant. (See *Philological Quarterly,* XXV [1946], 251–53.)

340. 3 "the spiritual court": A court having jurisdiction in religious and ecclesiastical matters; matrimonial causes came under its authority.